WALKING OUT

One Teacher's Reflections on Walking Out of the Classroom to Walk America

Amie Adamson

Thank you to Diedre, Marcia, Andrea, and Dain for reading the first iterations of this project. Thank you to the Quad for screaming in laughter along with me regarding the inspiration for much of this. Thank you to Chad, my "perfectest man," for believing in me and supporting all of the things that make me who I am. When's our next marathon?

WALKING OUT

Walking Out

In February of 2015, I left my job teaching high school English mid-year and embarked on a 2200-mile backpacking journey. I was burned out and emotionally exhausted. Never was I so ready to do anything than I was to leave public education in California and just walk with all of my basic needs on my person in a 52-liter backpack. I hiked from the Atlantic coast of Delaware to Larned, KS, in three stints, generally following a connection of established scenic trails and low-traffic backroads known as the American Discovery Trail.

Every evening after walking on average 14 to 22 miles per day, I recorded my thoughts and activities in an online blog. The point of blogging was to let my family and loved ones know how I was progressing and where I was, that I was safe and alive. But the writing soon became one of my favorite parts of hiking. No matter how tired or unsure I was about what lay down the road for me, or where I was going to sleep the next night, writing was a non-negotiable and joy-giving culmination to my walking day. When people ask me what I miss the most about hiking, I respond that I miss the freedom and what thru-hiking does to my body and spirit, but I probably miss writing about it the most.

Between hiking stints and after stopping my journey west on foot, I returned to public education in my home state of Kansas. I began writing about what it's like in the modern classroom. Like many teachers, I am greatly concerned, angered, enervated, and saddened about this brave new world of public education in which we find ourselves. I have taught English for eighteen years in public schools in two states, taught honors and remedial curriculum, in both large and tiny schools, and one year in an alternative school serving our community's least educable. I think I speak for a lot of teachers when I say that we no longer recognize our own profession.

My writing about teaching was to provide catharsis for myself and my close colleagues at the alternative school. It made me happy to make my teaching friends laugh. I longed for their feedback on whether I had captured the essence of how some students, the low expectations, the battle not to be undermined, and the overall public education malaise makes a teacher feel. I write because I crave dialogue and camaraderie in my professional life as well as in my backpacking life, and thus the words that follow came to life.

This book is a collection of my backpacking journal and essays about teaching. With the exception of some typos, punctuation, glaring redundancies, and parenthetical expressions, I left the blog entries pretty much as is. I left the fragments and truncated sentences because I wanted my hiking writing to maintain the authentic feel that I wrote the vast majority of it in a tent with my thumbs on an iPhone 4.

In the rereading and editing of all that follows, I can hear myself. My tone undulates as I read my thoughts from years ago. I hear primarily excitement, humility, gratitude, reflection, humor, calculation, surprise, and increasing confidence emanating from my hiking journal, imperfectly executed as it was. Alternately, I can hear myself wax passive, frustrated, exasperated, humorous, and at times sardonic in my teaching reflections. As I reread my own words, this emotional gamut stands.

I hope you enjoy reading about my journeys as a lone female hiker and simple English teacher as much as I enjoyed writing about them. As they say in recovery, take what you like, and leave the rest.

Cheers!

Amie

Crossing the Rubicon
Tuesday, February 03, 2015

Hello, all.

Crossed the Rubicon yesterday and gave thirty days' notice at work and at my condo leasing office. Three years of reading, thinking, plotting, abiding, saving, speculating, talking, reassuring, prepping my family and best friend, and--of course--hiking! are giving way to the reality that I am going to give something like this a shot.

I have been quite a studier on this journal site, specifically a studier of those who have gone before. I am firing up my own page here to get an idea of who else may be considering an east-west ADT attempt this March.

Amie

Wednesday, February 04, 2015

A splendid five mile hike after work this evening. The fog began rolling in around 4:30, no wind, an ideal conclusion to the day. Now that I have officially set forces in motion, I've been mentally honing down what few pieces of gear I still need to pick up over the next month. I also thought about the great pieces I have already been using almost daily over the past two years, one of which is my North Face Denali fleece. I love this jacket. It is pretty light, it has a cell phone stash pocket, a fleece-lined hood, a heavy-duty zipper that would survive atomic fallout, sturdy material where your pack straps rest, and--bonus--it seems to be wearable for long periods of time without stinking.

I purposely test how many times I can hike with this thing, even when I know the day will grow warm and I will eventually just tie it around my waist, and even after it gets the salt ring from so much sweat, before it screams for a wash. I even used it as a pillow once over a year ago when I took some camping gear out to test. It also has little clippies at the wrist to which you can attach gloves.

I also just saw on Facebook this evening that a hiker will be starting the first week of February on the east coast. I am looking forward to following his journal if he keeps one and soaking up even more insight from those who have gone before.

Amie

Friday, February 06, 2015

Picked up a few more small pieces of gear today. Pretty much down to needing a battery pack for charging my phone. Although it's on the heavy side, I think I will be starting off carrying my iPhone 4. I have a few weeks yet to acquire the battery pack.

Today I hiked 10 miles, and while mulling over gear needed, I thought of more gear greatness already in my repertoire. Notably, I will be bringing my Black Diamond tent that I have not used since July. Last summer, I followed the Lewis and Clark Trail, driving not hiking, and camped a lot along the way to save money and to test my tent. I think one of the greatest moments of contentment I have felt in the last year or so was while I was camping with it. I had driven into Fort Benton, Montana, recently named Montana's most iconic town by the way, and I spent a day touring the Upper Missouri River Interpretive Center and the Northern Plains Agriculture Museum. Wanting to stay overnight so that I could see Old Fort Benton and eat a meal at the Grand Union Hotel, I dropped anchor at a small campground just outside town. I set up the tent about 300 feet from the south bank of the Missouri River, and about dusk I heard a "swishing" noise in the river. I wondered, "Who the heck is swimming in the Missouri at 9:30 at night?"

I unzipped the tent door, and there was a deer walking through the shallow water near the bank. She paused for a minute or so, very still in the fading light. It was such a pretty sight, and she finally walked behind some tall grass. I was texting back and forth with my best friend, while continuing to watch for the deer to come back. He wondered why I was still awake, and I said I kept unzipping the flap to look for the deer. That was a beautiful evening, just one of several that I spent in my Black Diamond tent at spots along the L&C route in Nebraska, the Dakotas, Montana, Idaho, and Oregon. That one stands out though.

I know the tent will do great on this trip, too.

Amie

Saturday, February 07, 2015

It's been a bit since a steady, morning-long downpour has graced us here on Califorai's central coast, so I took full opportunity of today's rain to vet my Sierra Designs rain pant with a Patagonia capilene 3 pant underneath. I hiked in the rain pants once before, and of course they are clammy alone. The capilenes underneath help a lot. The Sierra Design pants also have a large stash pocket with a zipper on the right thigh. Another bonus.

I also want to remark on the shoe I plan to start with: Montrail Mountain Masochist with Outdry. These shoes are tanks for your feet. The Outdry has so far kept socks and feet dry in rain, and these Montrails also have kept out the trail dust. I really sloshed around in puddles today purposely, and water got in over the tops of them, so now I will see how long it takes them to dry.

I have another pair of these I have used a few times to break in, although I have noticed this great shoe requires almost no break-in period. However . . . cue sad tuba, I cannot find them anymore. I see the men's shoe and boot, and the women's Mountain Masochist sans Outdry, but not these. I hope Montrail brings them back. I ordered another Montrail shoe, a light-weight runner, that would suffice for summer. I will hike in those tomorrow if it does not rain.

On a different note, I breathed a sigh of relief this evening after speaking with my sister on the phone. I had texted her Monday night to let her know I would be in KS in a month to spend a week or so with everyone there (and hiking) before jaunting off to the east coast. She never replied the remainder of the week. I was growing quite sure that she was questioning my mental health, or staging an intervention for the moment I set foot back in Kansas.

Neither turned out to be the case. One of my nephews had played with her phone and somehow turned off the texting, and they are still trying to figure out how to fix it. When I talked to her tonight, she was excited and thinks this idea is cool, or at least okay. Wshew! The last thing I want to accomplish here is to call my sanity into question.

Amie

Sunday, February 08, 2015

The Montrail MM's were still drying, so I hiked ten in the Montrail Fluid Flex II. A less burly shoe, they will be fine for summer and for flat, unchallenging terrain. I also hiked with trekking poles today. My rationale for taking the poles is that a) even the tiniest amount of stress per step removed from my feet, knees, and hip joints is a net benefit, b) if a poisonous snake tries to get me, perhaps the snake will strike the pole first, c) they can double as a weapon, and d) sometimes when I am hiking uphill my arms pump up and down comically, and I laugh at myself thinking I must resemble a kid named Milton Milton from one of Bill Bryson's books about his Midwest upbringing in the fifties and sixties. Milton Milton always thought he was a piece of piston-operated machinery, milling around working his arms like pistons firing, thinking he was a steamshovel or the like. I fell into a rhythm with the poles after a few miles. I like them, and if I later decide I don't need them I can bounce them forward or send them back.

I was talking shop and gear with our chemistry teacher at school the other night, and I told him that trekking pole use is suggestive of the body mechanics of cross country skiing, or in KS, the next best thing: the Nordic Track we had in our living room for a few years when I was in high school. I remember Dad using the Nordic Track, and I did too between cross country and track seasons when it was too windy or cold to go out and run in the off season. However, as the weather warmed up, the poor Nordic Track slowly devolved into a 500 dollar coat and purse rack. I don't know when Mom and Dad sold it, but ten miles with the trekking poles made me laugh aloud again because I thought about the Nordic Track and all the unnatural uses to which it was put.

I know I am not the only one to lampoon this fine piece of exercise equipment. I asked Mr. C the other night about his opinion on trekking poles, and then asked him if he ever had a Nordic Track. It deteriorated into a 500 dollar coat and purse rack in his house, too.

Getting outside whenever possible and engaging in the real activity beats the simulated version on a machine every time. Unless it's thirty below outside.

Amie

Wednesday, February 11, 2015

In 2008 I read Elizabeth Gilbert's book *Eat, Pray, Love*. I liked the book, and the author reminded me so much of my friend Amanda, a fantastic Spanish teacher whom I met while teaching in southeast KS. In her book, Gilbert wrote about "calling out to the universe." Gilbert was told during her travels that if she needed or desired something to call out to the universe to provide it. I have been requisitioning the universe a bit lately, and a couple of my universe callouts were answered over the past two days.

In a previous post, I mentioned that I hoped Montrail would continue making the shoe I have been hiking with, and I checked their website to find yesterday that the company just came out with the Mountain Masochist III. I am relieved to see this shoe will still be available.

The universe delivered in yet another way this afternoon. About a year ago I met a lady named Andrea at Orcutt Trails, which is a public park and trails system where I hike a lot. Through conversations and trail/gear talk, this goal of mine eventually became one discussion point. There have been a few times over the past six months when random encouragement has come from people I don't know. People who have engaged me about hiking, or asked if I happened to be the lady who was training to walk across the country. Those fortuitous questions and atta-girls have come just when I was needing a boost. Pretty cool. These random encouragers knew me through Andrea.

So I had petitioned the universe to let me see Andrea and her friend at Orcutt Trails one more time before I left the area because I wanted to say thanks for the trail magic before I have even set foot on the trail. I indeed saw her this afternoon. Ask, and ye shall receive.

Amie

Saturday, February 14, 2015

Did nine miles this morning. For two weeks now I have had 30 lbs. in my pack. I will throw in five more lbs. next week, and then bump up to 40 soon. I figure I have about a month until start date. I have two weeks left at work before the jumping-off point.

My pack is a basic grey REI Flash 52. I bought this pack in June of 2013, and I have easily day-hiked 1200 miles with it. Probably closer to 1500. I really like it, and I know if something happens to it, REI has made its nephew: a slightly bigger Flash in a light blue color.

A friend and I went hiking today with our respective packs at Los Flores Ranch, a very nice trail park operated by the City of Santa Maria. CA. We were laughing so hard as we put on our packs because their contents are completely opposite. Here is my pack: a beach towel in the bottom, three gallons of water and other sundry items for ballast, iPhone and iPod cases dangling off the straps, side pockets stuffed with GPS, sunscreen, lip balm, water bottle, and pepper spray. My pack connotes hiking , or birdwatching, depending on what kind of hat I am wearing.

Here is Ken's pack: a heavy-duty day pack, replete with three entire changes of clothing, including insulated one-piece long johns; AA and AAA batteries; two hundred feet of quarter inch nylon rope; notebooks; pens and pencils; binoculars; a multitool; a rigging handbook; four carabiners rated to 25 kilo newtons; a Buck combination knife/hatchet pack; two pairs of gloves, one leather and one kevlar; a high-visibility hooded sweatshirt with the sleeves ripped out; and a helicopter radio flypack with buck knife and hardhat light.

I think we were prepared for anything this tame municipal trail could offer.

Cheers!

Amie

Sunday, February 15, 2015

An occurrence of note this past week is that people have begun to write nice messages in my Trail Journal guest book. I have received encouragement from NJ, KY, CA, WV, and from two people who plan to hike this trail at some point in the near future. Someone wrote who has also explored San Luis Obispo. I have even gotten a tip on where I can buy the Montrail shoes. Thank you so much.

Nearly everyone to whom I have mentioned this goal has been kind and encouraging. Funny how the universe works, in that the curiosity and good wishes have come just at the right moment. Our tech aficionado Mark came into my classroom this morning and wished me well. Other hikers at my favorite spots, Los Flores Ranch, Point Sal, Orcutt Trails, and Cuesta Ridge, have said to go for it.

Another teacher at work, Mr. Casillas, encapsulated this spirit of the challenge the another night when he said that someone many years ago told him he was the kind of person who could be in the middle of a room that was completely engulfed in flames, and he would fully expect someone to walk in and hand him an iced tea. Mr. C told them, "I do expect the iced tea, and guess what? Someone brings it!"

One week left before storing my household accoutrements. Trying to give my best to my students these last class periods before taking off, trying to hike and keep my feet tough and my body used to miles carrying thirty pounds. Fighting off the chest crud that everyone seems to have right now. Following on Facebook the hiker who started the ADT about a week ago.

Godspeed!

Amie

Sunday, February 22, 2015

I bid a fond farewell today to one of my favorite running/hiking spots in SLO County, Cuesta Ridge east. When cresting Cuesta Pass on the 101 FWY, look to the right or left. The cars parked in the turnouts belong to people bicycling, hiking, walking their dogs, or running either of these two trails. I prefer the east side, where a gravel road gradually rises for 4.5 miles, and from which one can view at various points the city of SLO, the nine volcanic plugs stretching inland from Morro Bay, the ocean, and hear the soft hiss of traffic on 101 that recedes the farther you get. This hike is cool, too, because the live oaks and grazing lands begin to give way to pine at around 2 miles up. At elevation 2400 feet or so, the Los Padres National forest announces itself, and cathedral silence descends upon you, broken only by birds, critters moving about in the trees, and hellos from other hikers or cyclists. The east trail branches off, and you can keep moving up or hike all the way to Lopez Lake, so I hear. It's a great place, and if you really want to challenge yourself, both east and west trails go on for miles and miles. One last challenging part, particular to the east side, comes when driving back south to SLO or north to Atascadero. The peak is now behind you, and merging with your car back onto the 101 can be hairy. People come barreling over the pass unaware there is a turnout from which crazy hikers will be wanting back into civilization. Boy, I really have to reverse uphill, give my old 4-banger car a running start, and step on it to get up to speed- yes, even going downhill. Every now and then an 18-wheeler has turned out, and then my runway is partially blocked, forcing me to "pole position" around the truck to get on the road. It's funny, now that I am safely down the grade once again, of course.

I hiked 14 today, 7 uphill paired by 7 downhill. This is the first time I have completed that 14 miles with the trekking poles and 30 lbs. in my pack, and my feet are much less trashed at the bottom with poles. Yay, poles! It also rained off and on throughout, and kudos to another solid performance by the Sierra Design rain shell pant, my poncho, and my new gloves I found on sale, Black Diamond Glissade glove with a waterproof liner. It's funny how I have never seen a mountain lion clear up there, nary a wild animal, not even a snake. The one place I have seen a mountain lion is the most tame hiking area, Orcutt Trails. Hopefully my luck holds, and the less docile segments of the animal kingdom continue to give me wide berth.

'Twas also a relief today and yesterday to feel I am putting this cough and chest crud behind me. Friday I went to work anyway, as preparing even passable sub plans with my schedule is tantamount to writing a physics equation. Friday's sojourn at Orcutt Trails was not really a hike, but more my stumbling around for 5 miles. Pretty sure I had a temperature at some point Friday, but I remained in denial and slogged through the day. Yesterday I hiked 10, and today's 14 rounds out the weekend. Body, heal thyself.

These Montrails are definitely going to be played out by the time I am ready to head east. Glad I have another new pair waiting in the wings.

I private Facebook messaged my family up north in Sacramento yesterday and let them in on my plans. I told them I just might be back to Sacramento in several months, but not in the normal way. I haven't heard back from Brian, Cathy, Terry, or Carly. Either they gave up Facebook for Lent... or they are staging an intervention.

Cheers!

Amie

Friday, February 27, 2015

A thousand thank-yous to guestbook signers who have offered a meal or warm wishes. Recent commenters are from WA state, Illinois, and from Cynthia Welch, who is set to finish her cross country walk very soon. Way to go, Cynthia!

Packing commences this weekend, so I am culling gear clothing from "civilian" clothing. I will be starting, in addition to the capilene 3 top and bottom, with a long-sleeved 1/4 zip shirt with a high neck and thumbholes. I have been wearing this shirt in warm weather and as a layer since October. My Mountain Khakis Peaks flannel is also coming with me, a flannel that scored excellent backpacker reviews. Rounding out the tops category is the Sierra Designs hiking tank with wide shoulder straps and a built-in shelf bra. I wore this tank all last summer on my L and C trip and barely washed it, as it has an anti-stank treatment that lasts for a finite number of washings.

The final pant I have is the REI Sahara, a grey 3-way zip off pant. I have worn these as shorts for two years, and they are great. They're stretchy, and the zippers for the rest of the pant parts are color coded, so you don't have to guess which leg zips onto which side. I have a Buff convertible neck cowl/balaclava/beanie that is fleece on one side, a Black Diamond beanie, and a neon yellow Carhartt beanie that my uncle Terry bought me when my Sacramento family came to Lake Tahoe to watch me run a 5k. He bought it so they could spot me amidst the other runners, and I think it will work well as a high-vis piece since all my other gear and pack are muted colors.

All systems remain go, with the exception of weather alerts starting tonight, lasting through Sunday, that could sandbag my precise driving route through NM, the Texas and Oklahoma panhandles, and southwest KS. Crikey. I am planning to begin the drive to KS on Monday. Maybe the storm will have cleared out by then. Hmmmmmm. Will be keeping an eye on that situation. I don't really want to take the I-10 southerly route. Taking the 10 always reminds me of the movie *Easy Rider*. That, and the 10 would add too many miles; plus, I know well the 40 route in conjunction with HWY 54. We shall see.

Amie

Saturday, February 28, 2015

Well, it's official: I'm unemployed and off the grid, so to speak. I would be lying if I said there was no anxiety whatsoever associated with that status, even though going Galt is once again of my own volition. But I have turned this adventure over in my head so many hundreds of times the last 2 or 3 years, that its anticipation and reality have by now melded into one.

A great and busy last day at Pioneer Valley High School yesterday. Thank you to the Ruelas sisters for the Starbucks gift card and funny farewell message. I will definitely break that gift card out on the drive east next week, and it may even get put to strange double use as an ice-scraper. Thank you to my fifth period class who brought food and punch for a little farewell party. Thank you to Mr. C for buying my trekking poles.

I believe I now have established a budget for the journey. I am still waiting for the last portion of my paycheck to get kicked back to me. I suppose the school district office is waiting to receive my check-out sheet to make sure I returned everything before issuing the final remittance. I have met few teachers in my life who would seriously try to abscond with the district silverware, but I guess everyone has to be official.

It's kind of funny. My things have been slowly bifurcating into two categories: headed for a storage unit, or going with me. I have been organizing the pack gear, and somehow each piece is in a different stuff sack from how it arrived. I only spent money on one dry sack, a Sea to Summit dry sack, for my sleeping bag. The stuff sack the sleeping bag came in is carrying my tent. The tent's stuff sack is holding extra clothes, and I have my few toiletry items in a sack of mysterious origin. Plus I have some small Ziploc bags and a trash compactor bag on deck. I hope all this miscegenation of stuff sacks does not offend the trail gods.

And yes, if any past PV students ever read this, Ms. A is headed back toward the middle of the country, so it's now no longer a bag; it's a sack.

Amie

Sunday, March 01, 2015

Tomorrow after putting the last load in storage, I'll head to Mom and Dad's, driving part one of what is a two-day drive to Derby, KS. My car will be laden with my pack, wine gifts from various beautiful Santa Barbara and San Luis Obispo County wineries, and a few non-hiking clothing items, shoes, and personal paperwork I will need for getting myself UN-unemployed in a few months.

The drive from Cal to KS is a trek I've covered many times, but this time I am not too sure whether the ol' girl (my '02 Infiniti) has another 1400-mile trip in her. I remember listening to NPR's *Car Talk* a while back, and Click and Clack took a caller who was preparing to drive his old heap all the way cross country. Tom, Ray, and the caller began placing bets on whether the car would make it, and in which state the thing would break down. It was great fun at the expense of the caller, and Tom and Ray invited the listeners to join them in a virtual "laying on of hands" to consecrate the car prior to the drive. I will perform my own rites tomorrow, and I can hear Tom and Ray's infectious laughter in the background.

Any talk of cars in my family ultimately wanders to the topic of an old Buick we used to have as well as a term in our family's lexicon for big, old, nasty cars: a chizzler. A chizzler is any American-made car from the '70s or early '80s that predated fuel injection; had only two huge doors that weighed 300 lbs. each; was not one of the iconic muscle cars; probably had an 8-track player; was likely a shade of brown or chartreuse; contained within its name the word Delta, Brougham, or Classic; may not have featured power steering; had a trunk that could haul a small couch; was actually built of metal; and in the summers smelled vaguely of vomit. Chizzlers never zipped around town. They lumbered. And starting one, especially in Midwest winters, may have required 4 or 5 pumps of the gas pedal when turning the key.

I once asked Mom and Dad the precise etymology of the word chizzler. They said they didn't know, that chizzler is just what they called those behemoth cars, especially when the cars aged and began deteriorating. If anyone in southeast Iowa by chance ever happens to read this, did anyone else use this word besides our family? We would love to be enlightened whether chizzler is a familiar *nom de guerre*, or if only we bandy this word about.

My car is Japanese and its most defunct and laughable feature is a cassette deck, so it has not quite attained chizzler status. Nevertheless, I am only 90% sure it can pull this drive off. Boston and Cubby, successful ADT hikers, wisely reiterated in their journal that "hope is not a strategy." I certainly hope it makes it there, but my strategy is that if it quits or starts smoking, I will call AAA and get a tow to the nearest metropolis with both a junkyard and a car-rental agency. The car will be my tithe to the universe, whereupon I will rent a car for the rest of the drive to KS.

If anyone on the slight chance happens to be reading this who lives along I-40 or HWY 54, check back intermittently in the next 72 hours. You may be offered a free Infiniti, "as is" of course.

Here's to road trips that set great adventures in motion, reliable Japanese cars, and chizzlers.

Cheers!

Amie

Slurpee Size Matters

One student whom I had the pleasure of facilitating at the Kansas alternative school in which I served was named Barney. Barney was classified as a sophomore. I was never sure of his chronological age. His birthday came and went one day. I had spied the birthday alert in our online gradebook, and when I happily brought it up at the beginning of class, he acted put off that someone mentioned his birthday. He did not elaborate on how old he was, plans for activities or gifts, nothing of the sort. He didn't seem complimented that I remembered his birthday, as if his birthday were a cold place in his soul he did not want another human finger to touch. Barney's physical appearance suggested eighteen to twenty shopworn years while his mental capacity suggested about age twelve. His social aptitude denoted either a mental patient in the vicissitudes of impending dementia or one whose level of fucks he aspired to give regarding personal care and decorum hovered near zero on a typical day.

Barney came to my class during term four. He was enrolled in the first semester of ninth grade English. I never learned what happened to his first attempt at ninth grade English. Maybe he slept through his freshman year. Maybe he was out over the country's highways and byways with his truck-driving uncle. Maybe his parents treated his education in a similar fashion to how they treated his birthday. I did not ask.

As with many of the alternative school students, Barney took the requisite three or so weeks to complete one eleven-sentence academic paragraph. He wrote about self-driving cars. Barney and I were able to relate on this topic. I helped him come up with one of his three points for his paragraph. He and I agreed that many folks would eschew automated vehicles. Like many drivers, we both love the freedom of being in control of our own cars out on the open road, the subtlety of the mind relaxing and frolicking in thought while remaining just alert enough to keep our vessel between the lines and on course. Outside our shared love for driving, I reached to find any other commonalities with Barney.

Barney was one of the most disgusting human beings I have ever encountered of any age. I do not say this out of smugness or condescension. He just was. The stale, baked-in body odor combined with cigarette smoke and days of unwashed sweat pervaded his person and belongings. The smell was just the beginning. Barney was a larger student and could manspread with the heavyweights. My colleagues and I often described students in our Acellus oline recovery classes sitting in their chairs like mushrooms, i. e. bent over with head down, asleep, clothing creeping down or up in such a way that midsection flesh in various dimensions often presented itself from both a side and rear view. Barney would mushroom in his chair if I let him, and in his efforts to appear awake, he would manspread with zeal.

Barney would also lean back in his chair and raise an arm to rest over his head or to comb through his somewhat long hair. The effect achieved here was that armpit aroma would increase in both intensity and radius permeated. Leaned back, he would rest his head against my cabinet and fall asleep with his right arm draped over his head. I would wake him up primarily so that he would perhaps move the arm back down and quarantine the armpit stench. His clothing would rarely provide a barrier to the smell, as he often removed his hoodie that spring semester to reveal a muscle shirt or tee with sleeves cut out. The class would then gain a view of his pasty armpit and his underarm hair fanned out from their flesh creases as if gasping for air.

Regardless of arm position, Barney would also spread his knees and thighs wide. His slightly slumped position in the chair afforded him the perfect amount of space to spread his lower appendages because if he slumped down far enough under the table on which the student laptops were locked down, he would rest his knees against the outer classroom wall. There he could recline easily while the wall prevented him from sliding the rest of the way out of his chair. The manspreading I could ignore; the free and open way he would dig at his balls while spread out in his seat I could not. I would watch his right hand travel from the mousepad of his laptop, through his oily hair, and down to his crotch, where he proceeded to execute a maneuver on his testicles that was an amalgam of digging, pulling, scratching, rearranging, and pinching while casing both inner thighs all the way down to what is referred to as the 'taint. I once wondered if he were giving himself a proctology exam. Then the right hand would travel directly back to the laptop, where it would resume its tapping and clicking.

Barney made zero effort to hide his activities. He dug at his balls openly during class as well as while walking down the hall. And while in my class Barney enthusiastically manipulated his sack from the outer regions of his jeans, this was not always the case in every class. A colleague one afternoon reported that Barney had reached his hand down his pants and pulled at his balls during her class. I asked if his hand pervaded all garments. She said she did not make a case study of his sack-itching session closely enough to discern.

In addition to ripped out sleeves, Barney's tees and muscle shirts would at times feature cartoon characters or slogans. One day Barney strode down the hall toward my room, and I noticed he was wearing a ripped, neon green tee shirt featuring *Star Wars'* Yoda wielding a light saber. As he got closer I realized the caption read "Matters Size Does." Once he got into class, I asked him to put his hoodie back on, as his shirt was out of dress code. He did not laugh or appear at all embarrassed or titillated at my calling him out on the subtle insinuations of Yoda's transposed prurience. He seemed unaware that the shirt was unsuitable in any way and got on with zipping up his hoodie without protest.

At the end of class, a fellow classmate commented that he had seen worse implications on student tees in his time, and that the Yoda shirt really wasn't that bad. The classmate had a friend who had donned a Nike shirt emblazoned with the slogan "I'm skilled in every position" to sports practice nearly every day one year. I concurred that Barney's Yoda outerwear was funny, but my mirth had limits. Boundaries especially applied in the alternative school where most students' emotional maturity was severely stunted, and a few of my juniors and seniors still found underwear hilarious.

Barney came ambling down the hall later that day for class in a neighboring room with, once again, Yoda's aphorism on size in full exhibition. I called him over and privately reminded him the shirt was dress code noncompliant. It needed to be covered up. He did as I asked and went to class. I was not exposed to the Yoda tee again that term.

In-class nut sack quarrying and an inappropriate Yoda shirt were not Barney's only social inadequacies. He would walk down the hall during passing period with both hands on his face trying to pop a zit. He would stare straight ahead, squeezing with all his might with students walking and mingling next to him. He would bust zits in class as well, not caring if anyone saw. His hands always went directly back to the student laptops after probing his face for any new pustules that had arisen. He saw no need to wash his hands or to partake of the sanitizer I kept in my room for student use. The patina of hand filth he and a couple other students displayed made my colleagues and I conjecture one day whether they ever washed their hands following a restroom visit.

One's first instinct after spending several weeks with students who wear the same dirty jeans, fouled hoodies, and who never seem to wash themselves may be to feel sorry for them. They must not be able to afford laundry detergent. Maybe no one was able to make it to the laundromat this week to wash the child's bedding, towels, and clothes, I think. Particularly during the winter, maybe the hot water heater in the student's home is not working. The household finds it too cold to take a shower. Maybe the parents are absentee or lack enough care for their own hygiene, and so the neglect trickles down to the children's cleanliness as well. But then I see that these same students have a smartphone. And their zombie-like scrolling as they trudge down the hallway suggests someone pays for a monthly data plan. Fellow teachers saw Barney with Bluetooth headphones, another household pecuniary output, the cost rivalling months' worth of store brand laundry detergent. Teachers also remained vigilant in looking for Barney's smartwatch, another expensive gadget.

Barney was not unique. The students with terrible hygiene, who claim poverty at every turn, who protest most loudly about paying two dollars for a new set of earbuds when they've lost or torn up their free pair always have a smart phone. These mobile devices and their associated expenses are typically pricey. The bodily odors in many students' clothes mix with cigarette smoke. Cigarettes are not free. The argument that these families are unable to shoulder the cost of doing laundry is a hard sell. Counselors, administrators, and school nurses privately chat with these students about their hygiene to no avail. Office staff give them deodorant, donated and laundered clothes. Our brand new alternative high school facility had showers the students could have used. Wallowing in one's own filth is ultimately a choice.

Another student we could never reach, keep awake, or get to school often enough to finish our appallingly low graduation requirements was a young man named Larry. Larry was another student whose age was not commensurate with his grade level according to credits completed. Like Barney, Larry was never cheeky or defiant. In fact, Larry was exceedingly polite and gracious. Even when I would wake him up for the fourth time in one morning, his response was never bitter. When I caught him in violation of our Acellus-only policy, using the Internet to search what appeared to be translated Middle English quatrains of prayers or chants, he was contrite. Larry just wanted to talk. And talk. And talk. Larry's purported areas of expertise on which he would expound without end knew no limits: mythology, any pagan religion, the history of Third Reich, Dungeons and Dragons, the symbolism behind every birthstone, sword fighting, any metropolitan-area Renaissance festival, the merits and deficiencies of e-cigarettes, The *Clan of the Cave Bear* book series, or any other book or author brought up in class, numerology, esoteric philosophers going back decades, river dancing, a previously undiscovered purpose of Stonehenge at its genesis, you name it. My attempts to find other students' interests in a hobby, movie, or music genre —even boring attempts at rustling up some small talk about the weather— would draw Larry like a tractor beam into the conversation.

Larry dressed himself about the same every day. All winter he wore a heavy black coat that covered a hoodie which eventually gave way to a shirt that I called his Dirk Diggler. The fabric of this long-sleeved shirt was slightly shiny and looked slick. The background was white, and the shirt had what appeared to be bright goldfish, turquoise figures in the apex of their golf swing, and palm trees patterned all over it. Its large collar hearkened unto seventies disco. Nothing in the year of our Lord 2019 wardrobe would have matched the shirt except bell-bottomed jeans, but given Larry's short and very stocky legs, a pair of baggy, navy blue sweatpants completed the ensemble.

School started at 7:40. Larry observed our official starting time maybe once or twice before he finally dropped out in March. The middle of first period tended to be Larry's preferred arrival time—if he came to school at all. After the initial phase of tardy and truancy write ups, I asked Larry why he was late every day. He claimed a battery of excuses. His alarm didn't sound. His mom's car would not start. His brother took forever getting ready. And his most frequent account for why he was tardy became my favorite: bicycle failure. Larry's bike must have been the worst bicycle on the globe. The bicycle one morning would not keep air in its tires. The chain fell off its sprocket the next. Another flat the next morning. The handle bars came loose and lost steering capacity as the week waned. A pedal broke, and his foot recurrently slipping off the plastic remains of the pedal, causing him to have to walk the bike the rest of the way to school, hence the tardy.

Larry's sad bicycle tales of woe knew even fewer limits than his stories and supposed realms of knowledge. I had begun doubting the veracity of much of Larry's musings early in the year. The ceaseless and varied bicycle malfunction reports fortified my suspicions. I believed less and less of what Larry said in class on most topics. The boy just needed positive attention from normal, mentally healthy adults. His endless hijacking of others' conversations with meandering yarns of quasi-truths were a means to that end.

One week before Christmas, Larry reported to class tardy and during passing period, informed the teachers as he was following us down our hall that he had recently taken up Irish dance lessons at one of the local churches. We received this account with a grain of salt. A colleague and I later took it upon ourselves to Google the church Larry said had been offering the lessons. The church existed, but we did not see a slate of Lord of the Dance classes outlined in the online church bulletin. Enough truth emerged from Larry's story, combined with our church-stalking, that we visualized Larry's short, stubby legs in baggy sweatpants jigging away at his evening river dancing lessons.

Another day Larry publicized that he was also receiving fencing instruction. I told him that he could demonstrate what he had been learning the last five minutes of class, not during class, as he had again arrived tardy and burnt up precious work time while I kept shutting down his expostulating on which paleolithic eras produced which forms of amber, which Gary Paulson books were in the *Hatchet* series, why the Acellus world history teacher was wrong about Egyptian embalming, etc. The hour drew to a close. In the open area next to my desk, he went through a series of motions that, in his mind, he probably thought resembled Arya Stark besting Brienne of Tarth with her dagger in the Winterfell courtyard. But in reality, his movements bore greater likeness to a corpulent ballerina in a '70s porn star shirt and navy sweats with knees bent and toes perpendicular, trying to stick a screwdriver in a light socket and quickly pull it out without getting shocked. Larry would perform an invisible sword movement, then adjust his foot placement ever so slightly while uttering "Wait a sec." Only to thrust the imaginary weapon at his invisible foe again, place his index finger in the air and "Oops, just a sec." Left toes slightly out, bend at the knees again, lunge, adjust. Bend, stab, adjust. A formidable pantomime took place in my room, one that I reenacted later for my colleagues.

As winter plodded on, I heard the dulcet tones of his smoker's cough-burdened, 45-minutes-tardy "Good morning" less and less. The administration eventually suspended Larry for a few weeks for his incorrigible truancy. My hall mates and I began commenting on how Larry's incessant Greek chorus of mundane classroom chitchat had deafed our ears not a speck in the preceding weeks. I'd be lying if I said that his suspension was not partly a relief. We wondered if he would return to school when he had completed his sentence.

A few mornings later a colleague entered my room in a fit of laughter bursting with an account of a Larry spotting. The previous afternoon on her way home, she had seen Larry riding his fabled bicycle, now fully operational in the middle of the day, of course. The bicycle had appeared to be a child's bicycle. Either that or its seat and handlebars were adjusted to accommodate a person with a vastly different torso-to-leg length ratio, for as Larry peddled the bicycle, his knees were coming up nearly to his underarms. In his right hand, he was holding a giant Slurpee aloft like a torch. Any drop of the Slurpee arm would send the right knee crashing up into his arm from underneath. And depending on the speed and wattage generated by his pedal stroke, the collision would send the Slurpee careening down onto the sidewalk or splattering his sweat-panted sartorial splendor.

Aside from Larry having breathed enough life into his bicycle to ride up to the quick mart for the extra large Slurpee, we did not hear much more about Larry that year than what we already knew. He had a brother in a mental health care facility, an ill grandmother on her death bed. What Larry will do with the rest of his life is anyone's guess.

In my mind's eye, I see myself at a future Shakespeare living history exhibit or Renaissance fair. I hear a gravelly but jolly voice call out my name from the leotarded and rapier-wielding masses. It's Larry. He is dressed in medieval friar's vestments clutching a horn of mead in his chubby, smoke-stained fingers. A fleshy wench with equally dirty fingernails on his arm, he raises his ale to me in a raspy wassail. I raise my giant Slurpee in acknowledgement of his toast, duck my head in laughter, and proceed on.

Coming in Hot at One A. M.
Wednesday, March 04, 2015

Clouds part. Cue celestial voices. The car made it.

Under normal circumstances when driving halfway across the country, I start heading east out of California day one at about 4 in the morning. It gets me out of the desert by mid-day, and I can pass the halfway point and then arrive in Derby on day two at a decent hour and before dark. Due to moving festivities on Monday, I had only made it to Kingman, AZ, which is essentially the CA/AZ state line. Therefore, yesterday, I was just tootling along through the rest of AZ and NM, not pushing the car, and enjoying Sirius/XM's Outlaw Country and Bluegrass Junction, which sounds like a non-stop episode of *Hee-Haw*. I fully expected that I would leisurely stay over near Tucumcari and finish out the drive this morning.

My sister then called me with the updated Weather Service tidings of sleet, snow, and wintry mix starting in the OK panhandle and proceeding east to the Wichita area around midnight.

Tootling then gave rise to "pin your ears back and go." I'm sure I aroused suspicion near Guymon, OK, as the white car with out of state plates careened into the gas station with a sense of urgency unseen in those parts for a while, driven by the strange lady in pigtails who pranced to and from the gas pump wearing pink shoes.

Bollucks to babying the car. I outran the snow front. Although I am a bit tired, today has been delightful. Dad had made strong percolator coffee this morning, and the fireplace is going. I went out around 10 to hike, and it felt so good to have my pack back on and to unkink my legs after two days of driving-induced entropy. I really wanted to test my clothing in true cold, as it ranged from 20 to 27 degrees during my 9.5 miles, Kansas wind out of the north. I wore the capilenes under the Sahara pant, the capilene top under the Mountain Khakis flannel, with the North Face jacket. I wore my neck cowl, both beanies, and one pair or Smartwool socks. I was warm, but the fronts of my thighs and fingers got a little cold in the face of the north wind. Good to know I still have one more layer that could be put on with the rain shell pant and the quarter zip long sleeve.

I took the sleep pad roll off the outside of the pack and made sure there was nothing dangling from it that could suggest vagrancy as I walk around here. I don't want anyone to phone in a complaint about a possible transient on my first day.

I rummaged around Mom and Dad's kitchen for some ballast, and I could not find any gallons of water, so I weighted it down today with a filled plastic jug and a relatively heavy glass blender. I need to pick up some water gallons this afternoon; otherwise I will begin hauling around Mom's decorative crocks. I carried maybe 20 pounds today, which is satisfactory for post 800-mile drive and 5 hours of sleep. Going to see my sister and nephews this evening. So good to be here, and getting here without incident is a huge hurdle cleared (celestial voices).

Long drive: conquered. Two bullets: dodged. My butt: saved!

Amie

Saturday, March 07, 2015

Walked 12, 14, and 13.5 miles the last three days, respectively. Yesterday the morning started at 19 degrees, but the wind had shifted out of the south, so the day warmed nicely. I have yet to pile on all my layers, so I feel hopeful that what I plan to carry can withstand the cold okay. Today was very nice with the early afternoon at 70 degrees. Just a few small traces of old plowed snow remained on the sides of the dirt roads and around curbs.

Received my little battery pack in the mail, so I charged it up and tried it out. It is the Lithium 4400 made by PowerPractical. PowerP also makes a cook pot that charges mobile devices while it is cooking, but I went with the little charger because I already have a stove, the Pocket Rocket. The stove boils water in my small cookpot quickly. I used it last summer on my L and C trip. I have to fess up that the main reason I am carrying the little stove, pot, and fuel canister is that I am hopelessly addicted to my morning coffee. Not too sure I am ready to give that up quite yet.

Anyway, yesterday while I was walking the battery pack charged my iPhone over the course of about 5 miles while I was listening to music. Today it charged the phone in around 3 miles, no music. I know these are not standard units of measurement, but it's a good reference for me. And the battery pack, my phone, and both charging cables stuffed in a Ziploc bag fit into my fleece jacket pocket. Oh, and the battery pack doubles as a flashlight. I also have a Black Diamond headlamp, but I will take both lights to begin.

The flat dirt road east of town is nice, but remembering that much of the trail in Delaware is road/pavement walking, I backtracked into town today and made myself walk on pavement for 4 or so of the miles. I have broken in the new pair of Mountain Masochists, so I will wear the Fluid Flex shoe for any more pavement walking. I hate to put the MM on pavement already because of the way I walk. Many people pronate when they walk or run, which is when the foot strikes on the inside. My footstrike is the opposite. I supinate. It's frustrating because the outside edges on my shoes wear down very quickly. The uppers of my shoes after about 400 miles can still look brand new, but the outer heel can be ground down to nothing. I destroy shoes, and I have to be careful to avoid shoes that are motion controlled. Motion control shoes have extra support on the inside. I accidentally bought a pair one time. I kept tripping as my ankles would turn out, as if I were constantly spraining them on nothing or stepping off invisible curbs. A stury yet flat hiking shoe or trail runner with no gimmicks is best.

Talk of shoes always reminds me of the book *Born to Run*. I met a guy in Orcutt named Luis Escobar who went to a remote location in Mexico, where he and some other runners found a tribe of Indians who were phenomenally good distance runners. This trip and the searching out of this tribe of runners was the topic of *Born to Run*. The tribe ran in what amounted to a flat, homemade sandal held onto the foot with a strap. The Americans convinced some of those Indians to come to the US, where they annihilated our runners outfitted in expensive modern shoes and gear. Not saying I plan to hike in an old tire connected to my feet with a string, but the physiology of healthy running and the counterproductive results of constantly tinkering with our modern footwear is an interesting topic broached in *Born to Run*.

I always know when it's time for new shoes because the outside of my right knee will ache a bit. Sure enough, I look at the shoe and the outer heel is toast.

Still great to be here. The Wichita State Shockers lost today, so our Shocker game party we had has been changed to a board game and hanging out party. I don't have to have my hike finished at a certain time tomorrow, but I will probably go out early because my nephews are coming over. I must challenge Kaden to a rematch of Monopoly because he beat me last summer.

Amie

Tuesday, March 10, 2015

I have chosen a start date of March 19. I was considering starting on the Ides of March to be English-teachery, but even if I scoffed at "beware the Ides of March," starting on the 15th would have me driving on Friday the 13th. I am not really superstitious, but I chose not to shake my fist at both Shakespeare's Soothsayer and Friday the 13th. Plus, March 19 is my nephew Dain's birthday. I will start on his birthday to honor him. A tertiary reason for waiting another week is that I am not quite ready to leave here yet.

Yesterday's walk was 15 miles, mostly on pavement, and today's distance was close to 15 although I walked for time, five hours, rather than measuring exact distance with my GPS. The GPS uses up batteries like mad, but I have gleaned that my average moving pace over the last couple of years is between 2.7 and 2.9 mph.

Today while walking I received a few waves from folks driving down the dirt roads. A friend and I had a reflective conversation a couple years ago about the Midwest wave and its varietals. This is the wave that one gives and receives when passing someone coming from the opposite direction on a two-lane highway or a dirt road. And you don't have to be a farmer in your old truck to display either of these waves. The first is the Two Finger Steering Wheel Wave. With one hand on the wheel at the twelve-o'clock position, lift only the index and middle fingers into the air at the oncoming car. And the fingers shall lift a bit diagonally, not straight up. Then place the two fingers back onto the wheel. Viola! You have just acknowledged your neighbor or the stranger who is also negotiating the same backroad that may not feature a center line.

The second style of wave is the Index Finger Wag. This wave lets the driver remove only one finger from the wheel. Depending which hand is on the wheel, and still at the twelve-o'clock position, lift only the index finger this time and flick it quickly to the right or left. This action will also countenance the other driver, but perhaps in a more curmudgeonly fashion, or maybe the driver is feeling lazier that day and one finger will do. Today I received an amalgam of both of these waves. The driver, who did happen to be in his old truck, lifted the index, middle, and ring fingers from the wheel and offered a kind smile. I lifted my trekking pole in reply. It' s been a long time since anyone has proffered these waves on a dirt road. Or blown dust in my face after passing me going sort of fast. How refreshing!

Speaking of refreshing, something else I had forgotten about this part of the country is that there is definitely more of a sense of personal space. When you approach an intersection in town and you have the right-of-

way at a crosswalk, the cars stop about ten to fifteen back from the intersection, letting the pedestrian cross before they approach. There is a lot of
open space here, and people are happy to give everyone their space and take
as much as they want. There is a lot of wide open space in Santa Barbara
County too, which is why I liked it so much.

Now onto other random observations regarding sights and sounds I
have missed or never noticed until I left. At the grocery store the other
night, I saw a guy wearing old Wranglers, not too tight, thank heavens, a
pair of beat-up boots, and a black Don't Tread on Me T-shirt. I stopped in my
tracks in the cheese section and gawked at him for a minute as if he were
a rare museum piece. Everyone on the radio and in person sounds twangy
like me, and the checkout lady asked me if I wanted my gallons of water in a
sack instead of a bag. Why, yes, I believe I would.

Cheers!

Amie

Sunday, March 15, 2015

Made a Cabela's run yesterday and added Platypus hydration bladders, 1 and 2 liters. I've found that a regular 1.5 liter plastic bottle fits perfectly into the side mesh pocket of my pack, and the collapsible containers will add to water-carrying capabilities.

Wednesday through Friday's walks were just under six hours, each on a mix of dirt roads and pavement around town. Yesterday I walked for four hours. The afternoon temps have been mild, climbing into the seventies. I've been wearing, the latter part of this week, my Outdoor Research sun-runner cap with the removable neck bib, neck bib deployed. I discovered a secondary duty this cap performs. In addition to keeping your neck and ears from getting scorched, the bib really keeps the wind out of your ears. The neck bib has a drawstring that the wearer can adjust, and the bib can enclose much of your face if you wish. I like it, but I was joking yesterday that the whole cap-bib ensemble makes me feel as if I am wearing a khaki-colored Darth Vader mask.

Been sleeping wonderfully in my Nemo Stratoloft 25 bag the past 2 weeks. The Nemo is a rectangular bag, which I know adds bulk and ounces, but I cannot abide those mummy-style bags. I tried a nice Kelty bag once a couple years ago. It was a great product and kept me toasty at 36 degrees that night, but I was traumatized the next day from being confined to its narrow footbox and shoulder region. It gives me the heebeejeebees thinking about mummy bags even now. I love my Nemo bag.

My possessions are diverging once again into two categories: what comes with me in the pack and the rental car on Tuesday when I begin the drive to Delaware, and what stays here in Mom and Dad's guest room closet. I've made a list of my few financial obligations that will need to be addressed when I am gone. I have also made a "warning" list of all the things that are wrong with my car when others drive it in my absence, or sell it if the neighbors complain that it is blighting the neighborhood. It is an odd feeling to see one's life laid out in its totality on three pieces of notebook paper and some documents locked in a fireproof safe. But I have grown accustomed to maintaining a rather minimalist lifestyle the past 7 years or so.

I've been quasi-homeless before, flitting off somewhere to try something new and experience a new place, new job, new geography and attractions to explore. It's kind of funny to think that most of what I have is in a storage unit on the west coast, a bit of furniture and boxes are here in my sister's closet and basement in the middle of the country, and in a few days, barring a disaster, I will be plopped down on the opposite coast with everything to sustain me in a backpack. What's wrong with me? Actually, at this precise moment in time, not a thing!

Thank you, Mom and Dad, for writing a few checks for me while I am gone. Thank you, Andrea and Gary for babysitting my stuff the past 6 years. I'll get my crap out of your house eventually, I promise.

I am now going to dress and walk early this morning because everyone is coming over for grilled steak this afternoon, and upon beating Kaden at Scrabble last night, but losing at Wits and Wagers, Aunt Amie is on a 3-1 run in the board game department. I must work on my winning streak this evening.

Amie

The Passive-Aggressive Paragraph: A New Genre

One of the brighter students I had at the alternative school was named Colton. Colton was a junior. Tall and thin, Colton wore jeans and Chuck Taylors to school every day. He paired with these either an army green jacket, a grey hoodie, or, in the words of Jack Black from the film *High Fidelity*, a Cosby sweater. Colton allowed his bangs to cover his eyes, which prevented me from seeing whether he was asleep at his computer. When Colton wanted to ask a serious question, he would turn around in his chair, tip his head back, and speak with eye contact barely achievable from beneath the bangs. His head and neck position during sincere questions reminded me of a small child wearing a too-large baseball cap, tipping the cap backward to peer from under its bill. Conversely, when Colton wished to use sarcasm or complain, he would speak with his eyes curtained. One day upon getting summoned to the office for discipline, Colton exited class anticipating the behavior referral upon which he had yet to lay eyes with the eloquent, "This school is about to fuck me yet again." The bangs remained in place for this blistering exodus.

Colton presented himself as rather dour, yet in class discussions of *Lord of the Flies* or *Of Mice and Men*, his insights into the deeper meanings within those books were always incisive. His contributions about the reading aligned with the deep questions the authors had hoped their audiences would explore. Colton's literary acumen elevated the class discourse in a modern English course landscape where literature teachers are too often peppered with sparkling repartee such as Why does there have to be so much description? These chapters suck. Why is Curley such a tool? or my favorite, Why can't we just watch the movie?

Among Colton's other positive qualities lay a love of nineties music. Colton and I could talk grunge bands, rock bands, and alternative music hailing from the nineties and early 2000s. One day I had the Weezer ditty "Sweater Song" in my head. I had woken up early that morning singing it, and during Colton's class period, I began its famous line, "If you want to destroy my sweater ... " Colton knew to complete the line with " ... just hold this thread while I walk away."

Moreover, during Term 4, I set my Turnitin.com teacher key to reference another rock band. Turnitin.com is a website through which students submit their essays. The website checks for plagiarism, including whether the student has plagiarized himself by trying to turn in to other teachers work they have submitted for a prior class, also having used Turnitin.com. I set my Term 4 teacher key to 100011. This number combination forms lyrics in a song by the band Clutch. When I gave Colton the login key, I asked of which 2000s song my key reminded him. He didn't know at first, but then popped his head in my door a few minutes later and said, "It's that Clutch song!" I enjoyed sharing a love of this music genre with Colton.

Another one of Colton's bright spots was that he liked to read. When he was supposed to be working on his online English 11 curriculum in my class, I would often find him reading his library book rather than paying attention to the Acellus instructional videos. He would tuck his book between his arms, long shaggy bangs covering his eyes to disguise further that his attention was not riveted on the material. One term in my class, Colton was reading an Alice in Chains biography chronicling the rise and fall of the nineties grunge band in which we both shared an interest. I was often conflicted about letting Colton read during his Acellus lessons. His attention needed to be on the instruction, but I have always felt squeamish about getting after a student for reading a book. I would sometimes gently remind Colton that Alice in Chains was not part of the English 11 content standards. He would sheepishly close the book and place it aside, only to resume the chapter in another class or the next day in English when I was not looking.

During the final term of that year, Colton had stated that he wanted to vagabond around Europe after graduation. I, of course, brightened and encouraged his interest in travel. Colton probably gravitated toward backpacking Europe not so much by his burgeoning propensity for seeing the world outside southern Kansas, but for another reason. Colton was one of those young people who insist upon taking up the worn-out cause of *sticking it to The Man*.

Colton was quiet most of the time, but he would be the first to speak up to eviscerate any school rule he found fascist or that oppressed his perceived rights in any way. Colton operated under the misconception that our principal held fast to certain rules simply because he "said so," and per Colton, our building's lead was abusing his authority as principal. Colton loved to quibble over minutiae within the student handbook. Dress codes and cell phone policies? Pure despotism! Our no-hood rule? Quashing the right to self-expression! Teachers' instilling decorous workplace attitudes and behaviors within juniors and seniors? A totalitarian regime! Staff's expecting students to bend their will to established rules based on research and best practices for developing brains? Bowing to The Man! On and on, ad nauseam. I surmised that, to Colton, a stint backpacking would sidestep parental and societal post-graduation expectations and, by proxy, foil The Man.

Three particular instances in just my class come to mind when Colton resisted the Establishment. Each time the Establishment won. Colton's first counteroffensive could best be described as Battle of the Hawg Dollars. Hawg Dollars are small coupons schools print which feature the school name, maybe its mascot, and usually the latest school slogan, acronym, or mission statement. Our mascot was the hedgehog, thus Hawg. Another school where I served used PRIDE on its coupons: Preparation, Respect, Integrity, Doing the right thing, Excellence. Another school created Viking Vouchers highlighting the school's non-negotiable behaviors. Pick a positive word that starts with any letter of the alphabet, and it emblazons a school's version of the Hawg Dollar somewhere across the country.

Beyond reminding students to toe the PRIDE (or insert acronym here) line, the coupon's purpose is twofold. Teachers are to catch students—even high school students—doing something good or going above and beyond in some way in academics or display of good character. The teacher is then to give the voucher to the student while making the student aware of what he or she did to earn it. The coupons can typically be used to purchase food items, school gear, or other tokens in the student store.

This is all well and good. But again, the idea is to encourage students to display outstanding behaviors and rise above the tide of mediocrity. Like academic expectations, the bar for dispensing Hawg Dollars eventually sagged. Under pressure from admin to implement Positive Behavioral Intervent Strategies, and continually build relationships with students, teachers find themselves rewarding Hawg Dollars for things kids should do anyway. One teacher was rewarding Hawg Dollars when a student finished an Acellus class. To me, finishing a class with a passing grade is its own reward. But I too have been guilty of rewarding Hawg Dollars for mere trifles. One morning, a lone student arrived to class on time. Everyone else was absent or tardy. I awarded the only punctual attendee two Hawg Dollars, then a few minutes later chided myself for having rewarded a senior for doing something he is supposed to do anyway.

Later in the spring semester at the alternative school, the administration were apprised that teachers had apparently been giving out too many Hawg Dollars. In accordance with basic economic principles, there was currency inflation and the student store snacks had dwindled. The Hawg Dollar program was quickly becoming unsustainable. We were asked to be a bit more modest with our distribution of Dollars. My intuition was momentarily reaffirmed. I didn't hand out many Hawg Dollars and glistened with self-satisfaction that I had not contributed much to the downward spiral of Hawg Dollar value. My Hawg Dollar hubris deflated quickly when we learned that a new system of Dollars was soon to commence. Each teacher would be given a set number of Dollars. Like marked drug money, they would also feature a numbering system identifying the teacher who gave out the Dollar. The stakes rose. I was once again feeling pressure to search out something stellar a student did to merit the Dollars. I felt as if my fidelity to PBIS were going to be judged now partially on how many of my Dollars circulated through the admin office's central bank.

In our school's case, Hawg Dollars held value for an additional reason. Students could choose to forego the cornucopia of junk fare the Dollars could buy and save them instead to buy their way out of detention. I did not elect to accept Hawg Dollars for my piddly 20-minute teacher detentions, which I assigned charily as teachers are also under increasing pressure to reduce the number of referrals we write, another tentacle of PBIS.

Nonetheless, our detention room supervisor would accept ten Dollars in exchange for an hour of student detention time. This detention time had to be office-assigned, however. Colton found himself during Term 3 owing me a 20-minute detention for three tardies to my first hour. The accumulated time he was tardy to my class far exceeded the 20-minutes I was forcing him to serve, so I declined his ten Dollars and insisted that detention was supposed to suck. Get up 20 minutes earlier and get here to serve in the morning, avoid the office referral for a detention no-show, and be on time to first period, all in one pass of the sword.

Colton elected to fall on his sword. He lost the Battle of the Hawg Dollars because he opted to refuse to serve my detention, take the office referral along with its fellow traveler: discipline points that accumulated toward expulsion. He then bribed the detention overseer with ten Hawg Dollars to get out of the hour of owed time now on his plate. Colton initially felt he had stuck it to Adamson, I'm sure.

However, later in Term 4 I saw Colton was marked absent by reason of suspension for refusing to stay for afternoon Seminar one Friday. Apparently Colton had miscalculated how many discipline points he had already accrued from ditching my detention. He also failed to consider that Hawg Dollars were bogus currency for bargaining one's way out of a days-long suspension.

Colton's second counteroffensive I dubbed Battle of the Planner. Teachers everywhere can empathize with the futility of student planners. A planner, or agenda, or whatever highfalutin-sounding name one's local school district has misappropriated upon these small, spiral bound, organizational tools carries a full retail value of about five dollars. Each school's planner typically contains that year's school calendar, policies contained in the student handbook, specifically tailored slots for each school day of the week where students can write down assignments and due dates for each class period, important deadlines for senior graduation requirements, as well as some fun facts or inspirational quotes meant for the student's edification. I postulate that in the race for district accreditation, many school improvement committee chairpersons decided in some district office smoke-filled back room that a great way for schools to teach students responsibility, one of many districts' school improvement pillars, was to purchase a planner for every single student in the building and expect them to use it. In no teacher world anywhere have more than a handful of students during the last five minutes of class dutifully copied the evening's homework assignment or upcoming due date of his or her own accord. Planners are discarded into the garbage, lost, relegated to the back of student lockers only to be found again in May upon locker cleanout. Students who do use them, at least at the high school level, casually scrawl imprecise tasks into the assignment calendar to placate teachers who require a planner be filled out as part of the class grade.

When I facilitated—not taught!—four sections of Multi-Tiered Sysytems of Support classes for a year in a prior district, one of the students' grade components for the hour was that every day they filled out their planner. The idea was that MTSS students especially learned to pay attention to assignments and deadlines. The goal being of course to promote self-efficacy and the organizational skills they lacked. The first few weeks I meticulously checked planners on Fridays and gave a grade based on specificity of assignment, correct due dates, and so on. I came to learn that the MTSS paras also received lesson plans and due dates from the regular classroom teachers and constructed a detailed grid in the Tier support classrooms of when everything was due. It became clear that we were doing for the student what the student should be doing for himself, another robust current feeding the undertow in the education system.

However, I refused to give up requiring a planner, as the planner grade was on the scoring rubric we decided to use for all MTSS students. But because all the planner footwork had been done by the paras, students were overall uninvested in filling out planners. On Friday before I checked planners, all they really had to do was copy the previous week's work from the classrooms' white boards. Still, this did not prevent me from grading even the most indolent and laconic of planner entries. *Period One: study. Period Two: read some stuff. Period Three: work. Period Four: some math problems. Period Five: work. Period Six: free day.* I continued to ask for planners all year out of protest. Unfortunately, I also continued to enable students who were often profoundly unaware of any coursework requirements beyond what we MTSS teachers and the paras wrote on the board. I dug overdue, crumpled work out of their binders. I ran in circles to obtain second and third copies of lost handouts and placed them right in front of kids. I walked completed assignments to the classroom teachers. Administration, counselors, and special education nomenklatura expected us to do as much for the student as we could possibly contrive, including think, plan, and organize in his stead. The planner served no real purpose. Each unintelligible scrawl in the assignment boxes was window dressing. We thought ahead for them.

One year at a tiny high school in southeast Kansas, another institution of matriculation where planners were bought but rarely used, high crimes and misdemeanors were perpetrated against a student planner. A perpetually bullied freshman boy had come to me privately to report that a nasty fellow freshman had pushed him around in the boys' restroom and flushed his planner down the toilet. This restroom incident occurred years before anti-bullying became every school district's sacred cow. However, I reported the incident to our building principal anyway. He did nothing about it to my knowledge. The picked-on student's mother came up to the school one morning visibly upset that her son was being bullied. Understandably, she was more upset that the bully had acted with impunity. I was sympathetic about the planner flushing incident. I relayed that I had reported it to my higher ups, apparently to no avail, and she would have to express her concerns over serial bullying to someone above me. Not only did the malfeasance of flushing a planner down the toilet go unpunished, but I was also never aware that the bullied child was issued another planner. Should not the administration, in all its desire to hew to the hallowed school improvement plan, have caught wind that this boy was one of the few outliers who used the planner and salved his suffering with another one? Funny, that.

The planners at the alternative school, though, took on a slightly different purpose. These student planners still featured entries for daily logs of progress and due dates. Our planners also took on the role of communication tool for weekly progress reports. An extra section contained a weekly grid for each Acellus class and its progress. The idea was that every Thursday, each teacher delineated in the planner the student's precise grade and progress for his or her course. The student was to take the planner home and have Mom or Dad sign it. If the student was passing all courses to all teachers' satisfaction, he then earned early release from school on the following Friday. Moreover, the parent remained abreast of the child's performance every week. Our use of planners at the alternative was the most pragmatic of any planner diktat at any school in my experience. Granted, the students were not the ones filling in the grades on Thursdays, as it was the teacher's responsibility to calculate an accurate percentage of the child's progress through the Acellus program every week. But our use of the planner forced each pupil at least to stare at any abysmal grades in broad daylight, and the students had a stake in getting the planner correctly filled out and signed because getting out of school on a Friday afternoon is a big deal.

Regardless, water quickly ran downhill with regard to planners. Our students absorbed forthwith that if they had a failing grade in any class, they would not be earning early release that Friday. The M. O. then became that the failing students would refuse to produce a planner to be signed by any teacher at all. In classic fixed mindset persona, the student would grumble, "I have to stay Friday anyway; it's dumb to even get my planner signed." Or the more passive-aggressive students would make a show of ransacking the backpack in a huff, pull out the tired, wrinkled planner opened to the colossally wrong school week, and slam it on the table for the instructor to sign. Even if planner-slamming produced a buckshot of teacher signatures by the end of the day, the students who had any F's at all would then decline to take the planner home to show the parent, decrying the school-home communicative errand "a waste of time" or "dumb as hell." Students blustered under their breath about planners. Yet their protestations were frequently loud enough for me to hear because, having replaced the Acellus headset swiftly in a show that I or the "fucking retarded" planner was not worth the student's time of day, the noise of the Acellus instructor obscured the student's audible comment to his own ear while assailing my own.

During late fall and early winter staff meetings, the topic of planners would sporadically arise. Some teachers proposed to do away with planners since so few students were using them. Other teachers, including myself, chose not to fight the planner battle and kindly signed planners for the few students who were passing everything and found it important to leave early on Fridays lawfully rather than cut Seminar. Other teachers remained clueless how to implement the planner even months into the year, assigning a student the privilege of early release with a current period grade of 13%.

Nevertheless, the subject of chucking the planner altogether was repeatedly tabled until Term 4. After spring break, our principal decided that we as a staff would go forth for the remainder of the year as a united front and demand that every student cough up a planner every single week, regardless of his potential for Friday early release. We were to inform the students on Monday that they had four days to find their planner, dig it up, get it out from under the bed, buy a new one, or conjure one with a séance. If the student did not have a planner on Thursday morning, we were to send him to the front office, at which point he would be given a brand-new planner. His student fee account would be charged the five dollars, payable in full along with any other outstanding student fees before the student would be allowed to walk at graduation.

Tapping into my prescience from nearly two decades of teaching high school and nearly five months basking in Colton's sedition, I predicted that Colton would be one of our conscientious dissenters and planner holdouts. Colton had long since stopped unearthing his planner in my class before Christmas. Even when students refused to allow me to sign their planner with the failing grade, I would verbally relay their individual progress and recap for them the lessons and projects they needed to complete, only to get an intense "Okay" or "Yeah, I know" in return. Colton would either retort with the heated "Okay" or nod his head under his unkempt bangs that obscured whether he had even lain eyes on his scintillating three percent in my class, a grade that I had written in his planner in red ink.

I had Colton second hour each day, and I began prepping him on Monday of Planner Ground Zero Week. With fidelity to PBIS, I kindly reminded him that he would be required to show his planner that coming Thursday. I did so using non-threating body language and relationship-preserving proximity techniques.

Planner day arrived. I saw him coming down the hall en route to his first hour class. I became willing to lift from a colleague's shoulders the burden of pulling up the drawbridge to class and dispatching Colton to the office to secure a new planner if he arrived empty handed. I asked Colton about his planner, and he indeed had one. I don't know if he triangulated his original planner or acquiesced to buying a new one. His muffled reply was something about having "bowed to The Man," and the planner began making its regular appearance on the table next to his laptop.

So when Colton expressed interest in dabbling in the off-grid life, I asked him if he had read Jon Krakauer's *Into the Wild*. Colton had heard about it, and of course he was familiar with the soundtrack, much of which was sung by Eddie Vedder, another nineties music mogul. I immediately loaned Colton my copy of *Into the Wild*, realizing that I was probably shooting myself in the foot with regards to him completing assigned work for my second hour class because I had just handed him something else to read furtively instead of finishing English. I dangled the carrot and told him I would love to talk backpacking and gear, but first he needed to finish English 11B, the same class on which he had been spinning his wheels since before the Battle of the Hawg Dollars. The first step of which was writing an eleven-sentence C. S. E. paragraph. I knew I was drawing the combat line at that point, the first shot fired in the Battle of the C. S. E. Paragraph. The paragraph was Colton's third and final resistance against The Man. This time The Man wore the mantle of the English department politburo. The Establishment won this time as well, but not before both Colton and I unnecessarily squandered inordinate amounts of class time, emotional energy, serenity, and patience to elicit from a thoughtful and literate 17-year-old a simple, cogent, eleven-sentence piece of writing over an acceptable topic.

The eleven-sentence C. S. E. (Claim, Support, Explain) paragraph was the only piece of writing the alternative program's English courses demanded of students. In the traditional schools, a teacher in the mainstream classroom may assign during one semester of English one to three full essays. Perhaps more, in the honors and AP tracks. The junior and senior English courses may ask that students write more lengthy and complex essays, essays that require students to implement several sources and address opposing viewpoints.

In the alternative program, however, to pass one semester of English 9, 10, and 11, the student turns in and reaches a 70% threshold, according to an administrator-approved rubric . . . one paragraph. One. This procedure would take the average fifth grader about three class periods. Not in our program. Here was the process for getting one eleven-sentence work across the finish line.

The student first logs onto the SIRS research database. He chooses a topic and reads articles that address a contemporary issue. The SIRS database does a terrific job of assessing both sides of current issues, lest the student always on the hunt for an out attempt to accuse SIRS, the school, or the English teacher of being prejudiced and attempting to pigeonhole him into writing about a subject that goes against his nascent and often contradictory beliefs to produce what will surely be a pedestrian screed at best.

Once the student locates a published article from a reputable source dealing with the subject of his choosing, with a few caveats of course, the student is to print the chosen source. Then he has to read it. The articles are typically written at about the third to fifth-grade level, as most mainstream newspapers are. The authors' points are never buried in layers of irony, scholarly jargon, or obfuscating passages containing methodology or statistics; the article's intent is always clear. The student is then to take a position on the issue that his article presents.

Once the student forms a stance on the issue and has advanced beyond the base compulsion merely to retell the article, he must then form a topic sentence. Unfortunately, the teacher finds it obligatory to talk most students through writing a topic sentence. Despite years of previous high and middle school writing instruction, the student must still be coached away from starting every topic sentence with *How . . . Like when . . .* or *Why we should . . .*

Once a complete thought is set down at the top of the color-coded, fill-in-the-blank outline prepared ahead of time by the teachers and already containing transitions and sentence starters, the student is to come up with three points that support the topic sentence. Points being the student's own thoughts, not cribbed directly out of the source. At this point in the procedure, I usually have to take away the printed article and hide it from the student to get him to word three points without scouring someone else's prose to tell him "what to think."

With the skeleton of the outline not already done for the student filled in, the task is now to search for text evidence that supports what the student wishes to illuminate for the reader and plug evidence into the remaining colored slots in the outline. While the cognitive demand elevates at this juncture just a tic, it puzzles me beyond comprehension what an immense time sinkhole this segment becomes. Even in the mainstream classroom, students will spend hours staring at articles. They go online and stare at screens for geological ages, even when research deadlines are clear from the outset. Students lose themselves down many Internet rabbit holes, perpetually claiming they "need another article," or they "can't really find anything." If allowed, the student will spend weeks of class time looking at articles. Even just using one approved database such as SIRS, the students' staring at screens becomes a time and effort black hole.

And while the student is "looking for better evidence," the teacher must keep the student awake, off the cell phone, away from irrelevant websites or YouTube rap videos in the background. There are basically two ways to avoid the class time sinkhole that is "looking for a better article": the teacher provides bona fide articles and evidence ahead of time from which students are required to choose, or the teacher reads the student's sources for him and suggests passages that would weave nicely into the paragraph's fabric. In short, teachers, out of exasperation and concern for making judicious use of limited class time, increasingly capitulate and do the thinking for the student. I have been guilty on both counts.

Once the textual support is plugged in and actually supports the points the student wants to prove, the student must then complete the final open portions of the outline, also color-coded, which require that the student elaborate on their evidence. Elaborating on the evidence requires the student to connect the evidence to the point made, and perhaps discuss further implications their point suggests. What is not acceptable is simply rewording what they have already said. Common are single paragraphs that belabor the same statement nine times.

Also not acceptable is plagiarizing more material from the article in place of hearing the student's original voice to round out the point he wants to make. All English teachers have read what is supposed to be an argumentative paragraph or essay that simply retells the article or book. Or the more indolent student may submit a thinly disguised rehash of the article's abstract, sandwiched between inscrutable sentence fragments that purport to serve as topic and concluding sentences.

Once the C. S. E. eleven-sentence outline reflects halfway lucid development of the topic sentence, the student is now ready to type the paragraph. Also placed into the student's lap are MLA formatting instructions along with a sample paragraph showing what their finished product should look like. The final frontier of exertion at this point becomes threefold. Avoid reliance on the spelling and grammar check to seek and destroy all errors, complete the Works Cited page containing one entry, and pass the online plagiarism checker that not only scans for writing ripped from the Internet, but also for students attempting to resubmit essays they have used for teachers in the past. Once the paragraph passes the plagiarism check, it then must earn a score of 70 percent, as determined by a rubric that is also color-coded to match each of the arguments.

Often a C. S. E. paragraph does not pass muster *vis-a-vis* the rubric. Or the student has, in the words of one student who I caught twice inventing evidence, "paraphrased too much." Delivering the verdict that the paragraph needs corrections to reach 70% will occasion a wide variety of rejoinders from those students whose opus magnum still has not produced eleven sentences that go together and make sense.

Of course, the teacher's desired reaction is that the student gleefully skips back to the computer after receiving instructor's written comments and puts a little more thought into the problematic parts. Make the mechanics adjustments, fix the formatting, whatever it takes. Don't forget: we're talking eleven sentences.

More common student responses to a failed paragraph include, first, the silent retreat. This is where the student says nothing, but returns to his or her seat in a huff to stare at more screens. Within the layers of silent retreat lie avoidance, playing with one's hand for an hour straight, disassembling his mechanical pencil, or turning on Acellus and working on another class besides English, purportedly to show the teacher that more important classes exist on the student's docket than fixing that "sorry-ass paragraph." Also within the silent retreat, the student may play the anxiety card and ask to go to the Quiet Room. Or, like many students who learn the magic public-school incantations and buzz phrases for getting them out of work, the student may claim, "I'm having a bad day. Can I go work in Teacher X's Room?" Teacher X being either the gentler, more permissive teacher with the PBIS-approved bedside manner who may allow the student to sit and color; or another teacher who has no clue what caricature of a secondary-level writing piece crossed the desk of the teacher from whom the student has just absconded, and will let the student work on something constructive and investigate later.

Another common response to a failed C. S. E. paragraph is what my colleague next to me calls toddlers sitting in high chairs banging their spoons. This reaction begins with a loud exhale exaggerated in both length and force. The exhale will be accompanied by the student casting low-volume aspersions upon the school, the English course, the assignment itself, and the instructor. These calumnies may or may not be entirely audible or in complete sentences, as the student does not wish to earn a discipline referral for outwardly blaspheming a teacher. The spoon-banging response may also comprise statements indicative of self-sabotaging and self-fulfilling prophesies. *I'm just gonna go get my GED, Fuck this shit, My dad said this school blows dick anyway*, or *It doesn't matter; I'm moving back to (enter name of whatever school the student quit and subsequently cursed two months ago) anyway*, and other slight variations on these themes.

The final response to a sub-par C. S. E. paragraph is the door slammer. The door slammer is the functionally illiterate yet angry and entitled student who has spent his public education career feeding on grievance kibble. This student becomes an exploding supernova as he thrashes about packing up his backpack, indiscriminately fat-fingers the laptop keyboard to close Google Docs or shut down Acellus, grabs his cell phone out of the cell caddy in a fashion that rivals Scylla snatching Odysseus' soldiers from the ship, and as a parting gesture slams the classroom door behind him loud enough to rattle the doors of neighboring classrooms and alert an entire wing of the building that a fellow student has once again grandstanded on his way down to the Quiet Room. At this point in the day, given the student's performance, the Quiet Room has just taken on its other name, its real name. This is a designation all teachers everywhere know. It is non-PBIS compliant. But after experiencing vicariously a colleague's classroom door nearly ripped from its hinges, real educators don't care. This room is known in Teacher Mother Tongue as ISS.

After hours or months have pssed, and the student acquiesces to making the corrections and reaches 70%, a day later or the following school year, the student has harvested one eleven-sentence academic C. S. E. paragraph. Colton's paragraph voyage began some time in February. He burnt a few days staring at screens. He then approached my desk timidly one morning with his color-coded handout containing the paragraph instructions, broken down into minute, easily accomplished steps. One of those baby steps required that the teacher approve the student's topic and initial his handout. The timidity with which Colton approached me suggested he planned to attempt another *coup* and write about one of our school's four forbidden topics. Like George Carlin's Seven Dirty Words, our school had identified four subjects on which students could not write essays or academic paragraphs. While the four illegal topics would not infect students' souls, curve their spines, or keep the country from winning the war, the verboten topics would probably cause classroom mayhem, hurt feelings, and a thread of semi-literate commentary on the local community Facebook "chatter" page regarding how the alternative school is run by a bunch of conservative reactionaries, weirdo liberal transsexualism proponents, hillbilly xenophobes, or closeted pot-smoking instructors who just don't want to do their jobs and teach young people how to engage in healthy, civil debate and conflict-resolution. All in the same thread.

The four verboten writing topics were abortion, gay marriage, illegal immigration, and legalizing marijuana. I will go on record by stating that I agreed with the ban on these subjects. After nearly two decades of teaching high school writing and speech, I had read countless, nearly identical legalizing marijuana essays that flog the same tired arguments. But more importantly, at the alternative school especially, most of the students possessed the emotional maturity and self-regulating ability of elementary students. Talking over one another, hurt feelings, further entrenchment of existing student guilt and shame regarding these issues or others, shouting down classmates, name-calling, and an uptick in behavior referrals on "gay marriage debate day" all seemed imminent to me had these subjects been allowed. Or had the wrong student caught wind that her neighbor happened to believe that gays who marry should be burnt at the stake.

Colton's first topic choice was the United States' war on drugs. I kindly reminded him that legalizing marijuana was one of the outlawed topics, and he would need to choose something else. He returned to his computer station where he spent the next few class periods staring at more screens. He approached a second time wanting to write about building the wall on our southern border. Again I nudged him away from this issue, as illegal immigration was also a prohibited topic. This time he spoke back, claiming that outlawing certain topics was "weak," and we had a brief but healthy class discussion on why the administration and teachers felt that all students' feelings and the overall culture of the school were better served by not allowing students to delve into these sensitive issues. I told Colton that if he wanted to protest further, he could torch one of his limited hall passes from my class and go argue with the principal. If the principal signed off on allowing Colton to pen eleven sentences plus a Works Cited over building the wall, then the border wall was fair game.

Colton went to the office but was a fugitive from class only for a few minutes. He stalked back into the room wordlessly, bangs in place, and returned to his computer where he recommenced staring at screens. A classmate asked Colton if the principal shot him down. Colton replied in the affirmative, at which point another class debate ensued over why students have to write essays for English class. This time I shut the dispute down by directing Colton to the city of Topeka, where he could stick it to The Man by arguing with the Kansas State Board of Education.

Another eighty-minute class period or two went by before Colton put a finger in the air and submitted a third topic request: birth control. Assuming the role of the smiling bureaucrat yet again, I recapped for the Colton the illegal subjects and asked that if he wrote his paragraph on birth control, he needed to avoid discussion of the morning-after pill, as it is an abortifacient, and abortion as a writing topic was also not permitted. After a transitory pout, Colton returned to the soft glow of his screen, his withdrawal a hybrid of the silent retreat and the spoon-banging toddler.

Shortly I heard my classroom printer fire up. Colton had apparently decided not to test the gay marriage waters by concocting a fourth tangential topic request. He approached for the fourth time with a SIRS article over teaching cursive writing in the public schools. This time I was able to serve cordials instead of corrosions. But before knighting his topic choice by initialing his handout, I asked what position or side of the argument he planned to take over teaching cursive writing. He sullenly replied from behind his bangs, "I don't know . . . that it's good?" I clapped, fist-pumped the air, and signed off on cursive writing forthwith. Colton did not share my animation in his grossly delayed fulfillment of step one in writing a C. S. E. paragraph: choosing a topic. He returned to his work area to begin reading and highlighting his article for evidence that supported his thesis.

The above all transpired before spring break. After spring break, I would walk by Colton's work area day after day to check on his progress. I would find the printed article next to his open laptop and the still-blank color-coded outline under his folded hands. His SIRS articles were open, and I was not sure if he was still staring at screens "looking for better evidence," sleeping, or reading my *Into the Wild* book while my back was turned. His bangs still covered his eyes, so I would have had to crouch down extremely low right next to him to the point of creepiness to see where his eyes were focused. Therefore, I offered my help almost daily, then generally left him alone. I refused to do his assignment for him. As March turned to April, the one-page outline slowly began to take shape with Colton's hand-written points, evidence, and elaboration. He seemed particularly stuck one day. Given that he had made some headway himself, I asked what he was thinking for a third and final point on why public schools should continue teaching cursive writing. He said, "I don't know. The only other thing this article talks about is kids being able to read a letter from Grandma and communication between the generations. That's so dumb." I said I didn't think it was a dumb point. I suggested that he go ahead and use the letter from Grandma point just to tie up the assignment, and that maybe it was all right just this once to suck it up and write three or four sentences about something he found "dumb" in order to pass English 11B. He reiterated, "This is dumb," but continued poking along on the outline.

In early April, he did put a hand in the air to request my assistance with his Works Cited page. I thought to myself, Finally . . . he has decided to stop procrastinating by sitting there in his seat formulating ways to subvert this simple assignment. A few days later, Colton printed his cursive writing paragraph. I wanted to take a quick look at it before sending him to the trouble of submitting what he believed to be his final copy via Turnitin.com. Students typically have corrections to make, and it often provokes less of a baby fit from them if I show them what still needs correcting before they think they've submitted it and washed their hands of it.

Colton handed me his printed draft and I braced myself. In PBIS-compliant tones, I asked Colton to show me his parenthetical documentation, required in writing of this sort. He shrugged and said he didn't put any in. I said it was no problem. That was an easy fix. I then asked him to point to where his article's first piece of evidence ended and his own original elaboration began. He said the whole paragraph was pretty much the article talking. I asked if he just sort of retold the article, to which he disclosed that he didn't have anything to say about cursive writing so yeah, the whole paragraph was lifted from the article. He sat back down and stared at the screen for a couple more days.

It was at this point that Colton was suspended for cutting Seminar. I assume he did quite a bit of reading during his time off, for he returned my copy of *Into the Wild* the same day he returned to class, indicating he had finished it. There were sixteen days left in the term. The only change to Colton was that his bangs were now another half-inch longer. He spent his first day back in my second hour staring at screens with his hands folded and working on an Acellus class other than English. He did not work on the paragraph. At the end of class, I told Colton that I had missed him while he was gone, as I had no one else with whom to discuss my rock band musical odyssey during my Saturday long runs. Colton and I wrapped up class lauding much of the Puddle of Mudd catalogue, lambasting Nickelback.

On the last day April, Colton submitted an acceptable paragraph. I was able to overlook that he titled his paragraph "Cursive Writing Paragraph." I also expediently ignored that he had appeared to tap the space bar an undetermined number of times to center his title haphazardly rather than taking the Google Docs' shortcut of clicking align center. His writing voice was flat, unengaged. He repeated himself a couple of times. I did not have the mental bandwidth left to grade it objectively for a few days after he turned it in. It was the best I would get without my verbally dynamiting our school's PBIS edifice with my scorching tone and, in turn, inciting Colton to bang his spoon or effect the silent retreat all the way to the end of the school year. Therefore, in my mind only, during that following Saturday's long run as my feet crunched methodically on the gravel road, I denounced Colton. I upbraided my career and what it has become in a cathartic litany worthy of the door-slamming exploding supernova.

Colton, this has been the most profoundly draining months-long campaign to get a single paragraph out of you. We have simplified this process for you to the point of asininity. We have set you up to complete this assignment without committing galactically stupid errors such as hitting the space bar to center a title or using the wrong form of "there." Fix the absurdities you should have learned to avoid in the fifth grade before you lay these pages at my or any teacher's feet again. Why is this simple writing task a race to the back nearly every time? Why is teaching high school feeling uncannily like teaching third-grade language arts? This is increasingly the most absurd enterprise upon which I have ever embarked. I did not sign up for this.

After I disontinued my cross-country hike in 2018, I replied to an email from a blog reader who had asked why I stopped my backpacking journey. In my reply, I discussed my only regrets regarding stopping. One, I regretted that I did not go to Spain and hike the Camino de Santiago. I will someday. The Camino is not going anywhere. Two, I missed the writing at the end of every day. I truly love writing. I love the reflection. I love the flow that one finds as a writer when the words just come. I missed doing the backpacking blog every evening, chronicling what happened that day, how I felt, what I thought about. I tried in each entry to capture that precious day of freedom and its observations in a way that was engaging to me as well as readers, for my journal is the only tangible record I have that any of my 2200-mile walk even exists. I loved the challenge of writing about what may have been a foreign place or experience to many readers while fetching their interest and making them feel as closely as possible what I felt. I had forgotten the joy that writing held for me until I took it up while hiking along the American Discovery Trail. In class, I can try to convey my love for this craft to students and show them many examples of writing that are beautiful, funny, clever, and erudite. However, all that energy and delight I exude for writing increasingly seems to fall flat in the modern classroom. It is a great irony, I suppose, that the primary impetuses behind my decision to teach English, my great love for reading and writing, find less and less fertile ground to germinate in public education. I enjoy writing the most when I am nowhere near the classroom.

A few days later, I graded Colton's paragraph, turned on his Acellus online curriculum, opened my bottom cabinet drawer, and placed his cursive writing piece away in the marginal student work boneyard. I signed his planner for that week on a photocopied counterfeit student planner. He had forgotten his planner again. The counselors had caved, giving him a photocopy of that week's assignment grid instead of making him buy a new one, as we had agreed at staff meeting. He retreated behind his bangs and my copy of *The Scarlet Letter* I loaned him.

Here I Go
Thursday, March 19, 2015

Destination: Milton, DE
Today's Miles: 16
Start Location: Cape Henlopen State Park
Trip Miles: 16

I arrived in Rehoboth Beach safe and sound yesterday afternoon after a two-day drive. And the rental car industry exacted some sweet revenge on me. My adventuring the past few years has been aided and abetted by my renting cars for my travels, and I have driven a lot of "unlimited miles." I imagine that Hertz, Avis, and Enterprise have been keeping a dossier on my activities, and when my name pinged in someone's computer that I was needing a small car to get from Kansas to Delaware, some bigwig pressed his or her fingertips together and hissed, "Eeeeeeexxxxxxccelllllllent. We shall give her a Hyundai with no cruise controlllllll."

When I picked up the car, I was busy checking the tires and making sure my nephew could legally ride up front with me for the short drive back to Derby. I did not think to check for cruise control until early Tuesday morning, by which time I was already on the Kansas Turnpike, and it was too late to turn around and request a new car. *Mea culpa*, I am punished.

No matter, day one was a great drive. Southern Indiana and northern Kentucky are gorgeous. I saw many tidy farms and pristine properties. I can only imagine what that country looks like when the trees are green. Day two's drive was getting rough, but the trail coordinator picked me up in front of the small K-Mart-Avis combination upon my arrival, and she whisked me off to give me a preview of the first 15 miles of the route. Then her family hosted me last night.

I made it official and got started this morning around 8:45. I walked up to the beach and just got my toes close enough to the water to snap a photo. Then I exited the beach pavilion area and got going. The trail wound through the state park, mostly on a bike path, very peaceful. I was very good to myself today, taking it slow and easy, getting used to the format of the Turn-by-Turns. It felt good to stretch my legs back out and unkink everything. I did not pressure myself today whatsoever. The weather was cool, almost no wind until early afternoon. I quickly took off a beanie and then the gloves. The trail passed many neighborhoods, and I found grass or a soft shoulder most of the time. I actually made it to Milton earlier than I thought, about 3:15. I left a couple of items at the Connors' house today, subtracting a few pounds from the pack to ease me into day one. I will add those back to my pack for tomorrow's trek. I am very pleased with my mileage today.

The Connors are hosting me again tonight, and then I will see what tomorrow brings. Day one in the books.

Cheers!

Amie

Friday, March 20, 2015

Destination: Just shy of Bridgeville, DE
Today's Miles: 15
Start Location: Milton, DE
Trip Miles: 31

Started this morning around 9 from the quaint downtown area of Milton. The weather could not decide whether to rain on me, snow, or grace me with a wintry mix of tiny ice pellets, so it indulged itself and did all three. The temperature hovered just above freezing, so the road was never slick. I was warm all day, with two layers on bottom, three on top, switching out the fleece for the rain jacket. I wore both beanies and my poncho. The pack and the poncho do double duty as wind breaks, but there was not too much wind today. I walked through the Redden State Forest area and more rural routes. A steady drizzle all day kept me from getting my phone out whatsoever, but I did have to take the TBTs from my Marmot jacket pocket, where they stayed dry, to look at them, and they got wet today and are becoming shabby due to handling them so much. One positive aspect of the frequent turns in the directions is that I can discard a page quickly and do not have to rely on it for weeks. It is not supposed to rain tomorrow.

I passed by an old white farmhouse surrounded by bare trees. This farmhouse could have been the one from the original black and white *Night of the Living Dead*. I also passed a cabin that looked like my mental picture of the Noonans' lake house named Sarah Laughs, from Stephen King's novel *Bag of Bones*.

My plan was to make it to Bridgeville, where, according to the TBTs, there was a bed and breakfast. However, about 2 miles outside of town the intensity of the rain foiled my plot. I felt strong and could have walked several more miles, and was hoping simply to make it to town without having to remove my glove and expose the directions to the elements again.

To the rescue this afternoon were Jerome and Gisela, an older couple going into Bridgeville to pick up Gisela's medication. They stopped and asked if I wanted a ride home. I declined at first, explaining what I was doing and that I just had a couple miles to go, and then asked about the bed and breakfast. They said they would give me a ride despite my pack getting the backseat wet, and what began as a short jaunt into town evolved into their taking me out for dinner at Sal's, where my offer to pay was refused, and a drop off at a different motel near Sal's. I think we hit it off when Jerome asked where I was from. He liked my answer because he is from

Michigan, and when Gisela turned around and looked at me, she immediately knew I am of German descent. She is German and still speaks with a heavy, beautiful accent. Over dinner we talked about people and traveling and current issues.

Hot soup and grilled chicken salad for dinner, an extremely hot shower, and my shoes lying on top of the heater, I am content. A good, good day despite getting a wee bit wet through the right side of my poncho where it snaps. My gloves got soaked, and I am not as impressed with them after today, but I know now that when it rains I will have to forego using the trekking poles as much and keep hands inside poncho. It took a long time for the water to penetrate, but still, Grrrrrrrrrrrrr. Or I could just place plastic (bags? sacks? Back to a coastal region, not sure) over my hands when it rains and still use the poles.

All other rain gear got an A for the day, the gloves a C+. Jerome and Gisela an A+ and some extra credit, the motel an A, the weather a D-.

Thank you for those who have continued to email through this Trail Journal site. I read them all. Back to the drop off point in the morning, and take it from there.

Amie

Saturday, March 21, 2015

Destination: Starr, MD
Today's Miles: 14.80
Start Location: Denton, Maryland
Trip Miles: 45.80

There is a discrepancy between yesterday's stopping point and today's starting point. Let me explain how this happened. Jerome and Gisela insisted when they dropped me at Days Inn last night that they would pick me up this morning and drive me back to Bridgeville, to the trail. I agreed. So when they arrived, it was just the sweetest thing. In the car was their big Atlas book, just like the one I take when road tripping. Jerome wanted me to point out the towns in KS where I was raised. He then wanted to show me the little town in Michigan where he was raised. They asked me, "What is that little Swedish or Norwegian town in your part of California?" It turns out they knew of Solvang. We then looked at the TBTs, and Jerome was having fun driving around the backroads. He pointed out landmarks, the neighbors' properties, and was excited when he knew he was approaching and could spot the Denton, MD, water tower from a different direction. He said, "Wow, you have provided Gisela and me (both in their seventies and retired) with so much mental stimulation! We are going to drive these roads again and check out those directions going the other way." He then wanted to get me at least to the Maryland state line, and then across HWY 404 safely. So I allowed them to drop me in the town of Denton. Gisela had said, "We had better do right by her; she is German." So I skipped the last 17 miles or so of the Delaware portion and began where I did.

Now, that may seem like cheating, but I consider the fun that Jerome and Gisela had--driving new roads, talking about the Midwest, and doing something new--as my returning the favor for last night's Italian dinner and a car ride. I will make up those missed miles at some point, going off trail to get to services, or backtracking, something. No worries. Plus, skipping the rest of Delaware solved the problem of the decomposing directions.

A few miles into the day, I knew I would be needing to take off my pack to get out another page of TBTs. The last entry on the page in my hand was at Stevensville road. I kept looking for something clean on which to set my pack prior to Stevensville Road. The trail soon provided. At the exact corner of Stevensville there was a nice property, and the owners had placed a perfectly good washer and dryer set on the corner with a plywood sign that said, "FREE. Not sure if working." I hesitated at first, but the washer was waist height, perfect for placing my pack on it for a minute. I retrieved the page, reloaded my pack onto my back, and then set off again laughing, wondering if the "FREE. Not sure if working" was also a statement about my status at this moment in time. The trail does indeed provide, and at times with a wickedly subtle sense of humor.

At the village of Starr, no services, a man named Eli called to me from his yard interested if I was hiking the trail. I said yes, and he asked if I needed anything, water, etc. I said I was good on supplies, but I would just be looking for a place to camp tonight, yard or property of someone with permission. He offered his field adjacent to their house, a portion of which is on higher ground and dry after yesterday's rain. It was only 4:00, but continuing the trend of being good to my feet and legs, I accepted, and here I am. Eli and his wife and three-year-old are my hosts for tonight, from a couple hundred yards away. Thanks!

I've been issued a fun challenge by Kaden, one of my nephews. Andrea and Kaden looked up hiking scavenger hunts, and they made me a list enumerating the things I am to find and check off the list. I have been keeping my phone put away, yesterday due to rain, and other times due to navigation and paying attention to my footing, but as the miles stretch out, I will get with the program and note some items on this list.

And while this walk is a challenge to myself, I have been told by both sisters that my nephews have been talking about me at their schools, so now that settles it. The pressure is truly on.

Amie

Sunday, March 22, 2015

Destination: Kent Narrows, MD
Today's Miles: 16
Start Location: Starr, MD
Trip Miles: 61.80

Today's walking was harder. I camped last night and slept okay. I have a couple of things to tweak regarding the sleep pad setup. I was repacked and off by 7 or so. It was early and cold. The wind today was one of those seemingly multidirectional winds that are in your face regardless of which direction you walk. My energy was lower today despite my righteous camp stove coffee. I think the adrenaline was starting to wear off, and while the temperature improved as the day progressed, the trail surface worsened. The roads were not heavily travelled, but the shoulder was grass and slanted steeply most of the way. On some passes, when a car came, I stepped off into the ditch and supported most of my weight and the pack weight with one foot. I was delighted to walk 16 miles, though, and again I took it very slow and easy. I stopped three or four times today to rest a minute. Then I came to Kent Narrows, where an inn right along the road was weaving its siren song. If I were Cliff Claven from *Cheers*, I would say, "Uh, hey, Normy. You know where the Narrows part of the appellation Kent Narrows comes from, don't ya? It is named after the narrow and general precipitous nature of the ditches and shoulders that surround the roads on the outskirts of that fair city." However, the trail did provide today even though I had to work for it. There was a dollar bill floating in a rivulet. The water was none too clear, so I fished it out with my trekking pole and let it dry in the wind. I now have laundry money for the last two days' worth of clothing.

Then this afternoon while checking in at the motel, I asked the lady if they offered a AAA discount, as the rate here near the Chesapeake is understandably high. She said yes, and I dislodged my AAA card that I had cut in half before leaving, so the card has only my name and the numbers. It did the trick. I could tell I was feeling punchy because I thought about that scene in *Planes, Trains, and Automobiles* where John Candy presents the twisted and burnt-to-a-crisp credit cards in an attempt to pay for their room after the car they're driving catches fire. My AAA card isn't that bad, but it probably looked suspect.

I snapped a pic of an old courthouse in Queen Annes County. It complies with Kaden's list because look at the date. 1708! It is old, for the U.S. anyway. Okay, Kaden, check one off. You will have to help Aunt Amie keep track of what items are left as time progresses. Apparently I also walked a bit of a Civil War Trail today too. There was a plaque commemorating a battleground site at one point.

There are two grocery stores about 2 miles down the road for a resupply pit stop in the morning. I am craving soy milk. I am still being gentle on myself and getting used to the daily rigors and privations gradually. I am tired today but not depleted. The point here is to explore and have fun.

And while I have the giggles from feeling tired, I thought I would mention that a reader signed my guestbook who has also had concerns about snakes. He looked up the facts regarding how many people are killed annually by snakes, and apparently many more people were killed by toasters than snakes in 2012. Good thing I am not carrying a camp toaster in my pack.

Cheers!

Amie

Monday, March 23, 2015

Destination: Annapolis, MD
Today's Miles: 13.20
Start Location: Kent Narrows, MD
Trip Miles: 75

Today was a mish-mash of scenery, activities, and hiking pace. I started early this morning, a bit before 8:00, crossing the Kent Narrows Bridge and wending my way along the Cross Island Trail, one of the many trails concurrent with the American Discovery Trail. The couple of miles on the CIT were very beautiful, with trees on both sides and a few people walking their dogs or jogging. The temperature was cold again this morning, starting off around 30. But the sun came out quickly, and my layers kept me warm.

I did not get as many miles today because I had a few tasks to accomplish. The first was to get across the Chesapeake Bay Bridge. Pedestrians are not allowed to walk across it. Now on the official trail TBTs, there is a phone number to call to arrange a pedestrian crossing for the cost of thirty dollars. But many other hikers ahead of me, right now and from years past, have simply stuck their thumbs out while approaching the bridge, and someone has picked them up. I did not want to do either.

About a mile from the Chesapeake Bridge and while I was still on the CIT, the trail grooming guy stopped his orange Kubota tractor to talk with me about the walk. He had seen Ryan W recently, from his description of his cart, and he had just seen the other Ryan or Steve, not sure which, who are also hiking right now and at various points ahead of me. We chatted briefly about the ADT and where it actually ends. He then mentioned that I needed a ride across the bridge. I said I did not want to put my thumb out, and he offered his business card with phone number and offered to drive me over if nothing else materialized. I took the card and went on.

A mile or so later, an elderly gentleman using an oxygen tank pulled over and asked what I was doing. I explained, and then, not figuring him for an ax murderer, asked if he was crossing the bridge by chance. He said he would drive me over. He did so, I offered to pay the 6-dollar toll for his return drive, he refused, and then dropped me at St. Margaret's Road and said he was glad to have met me. First obstacle of the day cleared.

St. Margaret's passed through some beautiful neighborhoods, and the trail soon approached the nearly mile-long bridge that overlooks the United States Naval Academy. It was a great view of the Academy. I followed the trail through a small neighborhood with a few homes that made me think of a Norman Rockwell scene. I had been on mostly sidewalk today (ouch!) so I slowed the pace down again and eventually came to Tawes Natural Resources Center. The center has lots of exhibits, entry is free, and most importantly they have a cafeteria. Today was the first day that I actually sat down to a lunch. I ate a meatball sub and some pasta salad. I felt out of place. The cafeteria served the workers it seemed, and I was the only one in there not in work or dress clothes, not to mention the huge pack. But it was nice to eat leisurely. I studied the TBTs, knowing today would either be a short day, or I could crank it up and make 14 more miles after lunch to the next point of services shown in the data book. I decided to split the difference and use my MapQuest app to bring up other hotels and grocery stores and get a respectable distance in for the day. The town of Parole would have me stopping too soon. Besides, I peeked down the street that would lead me to Parole's services, and one business that stood out was a huge Easy-Pawn shop. Nope. It looked more like On Parole. I proceeded on.

Task two on today's docket was to resupply. I ate the last of my pack food last night, so a grocery store was definitely in order. MapQuest showed a motel with Safeway right across the street. Bingo. By this time I was walking very quickly, still on sidewalk (ouch!) not feeling that camping anywhere near Annapolis tonight OR hiking 9 more miles by dark were sane options for me. I had been in contact with Steve off and on all day, and he has been just a few hours ahead of me for a few days. Very cool. We will likely meet soon. My mini AAA card scored me another 10% discount for tonight. The Safeway has been thoroughly raided by moi, and I got my half gallon of soymilk. I have consumed half of it already. I will likely finish it off walking down the road tomorrow. All is right with the world.

Another word about the three hikers ahead of me. They have helped me in small ways twice without their even knowing it. I told Steve, who is walking barefoot, that when I was in Delaware's Redden Forest I saw a bare footprint in the muddy shoulder once, a print that I assumed was his, so I knew I was on the right path. Today the Kubota-driving trail caretaker talked to me on account of having seen them first. This in turn morphed into an offer to shuttle me across the Chesapeake. Thanks, guys!

So today was not a fun day, but it was a necessary day, and I am restocked for a bit. The pack will be heavier again tomorrow too, but maybe today's paltry mileage will give rise to even greater strength and endurance tomorrow. Thanks again for the guestbook comments. I love reading them.

Amie

Tuesday, March 24, 2015

Destination: Old Bowie, MD
Today's Miles: 19.20
Start Location: Annapolis, MD
Trip Miles: 94.20

Now that's more like it. While yesterday felt like a great expenditure of energy for a 13 mile yield, today was the opposite: less energy yielded 19 miles. The trail surface was better today, with some wider shoulders, more grass, not much sidewalk. And I had no extraneous tasks to accomplish. All energy could be applied to walking.

The ADT ran concurrent with the WB&A Trail for a bit today, and I crossed a neat old iron bridge over a highway. One lady asked me about my trek today. She had seen me earlier and then this afternoon in a park that sits next to the WB&A. She was encouraging. Other than that, I really didn't talk to anyone today. A couple hellos. One man out in his yard blowing leaves must have seen Steve walk into Old Bowie just ahead of me because when I passed he shouted over the leaf blower, "Keep going! He's a couple hours ahead of ya that way!" He pointed down the road, and the leaf blower didn't miss a beat. It was funny.

Stealth camping in a corner nook behind a church tonight. I went up to the church and to the pastor's office to ask, but all doors were locked and lights were off. Not much else to report for today, just a goodly distance for being my first week.

Amie

Wednesday, March 25, 2015

Destination: Greenbelt, MD
Today's Miles: 13.50
Start Location: Old Bowie, MD
Trip Miles: 107.70

Stealth camping was a success. I packed and set off early. An hour or so into my day, a car pulled into a turnout just ahead of me, and a lady stepped out and asked if I was Amie. I replied in the affirmative, and she explained that her name was Becky and she had just seen Steve a few minutes ahead of me. That little turkey! We have been within a couple hours of each other for several days. She is a follower of Trail Journals and was a successful Appalachian Trail hiker in 1992. We spoke for a few minutes, shook hands, and she went on to work.

The trail surface was nice for a bit after that, following a rather lightly travelled road and passing by an ag research center. It was around that point that I caught sight of Steve's green poncho. I figured he was out of calling distance, and I didn't want to yell or brandish my poles in the air and call a bunch of attention to myself. He turned a corner and disappeared. I am sure we'll meet up eventually.

Also along that stretch of road were several rumble strips in the pavement every few hundred feet or so. As the cards passed, I decided that, depending on each vehicle's speed, tires' circumference, and frequency of cars hitting the rumble strips in succession, the sound created was of a band of beginning tuba players blowing into their tubas two notes at a time. The "tuba notes" varied in pitch and duration as different types of cars and trucks passed. A small car zipping by created a high note. A slow truck created a low wubbering sound, similar to the noise likely created by Ralph and Piggy when they first tried blowing into the conch in Golding's *Lord of the Flies*. As Golding said of Ralph and Piggy's conch blowing, and as my nephew Dain would have stated regarding the larger cars, the larger vehicles created a farting sound. Ah, hiking humor.

Around noon I entered the city of Greenbelt and lost the trail at a lake trail that was supposed to go toward Greenbelt Road and the park. I retraced my steps looking for where I erred. Finally I gave up and MapQuested the American Legion just near the park and got there that way.

Greenbelt Park is a federally managed site, and I wandered in unafraid of being accosted because along with my AAA card, I also brought my federal lands pass I bought last summer, which covers entry fees and camping fees at any site managed by NFS, BLM, and so forth. I felt like Beavis and Butt-head in the episode when they wander the halls of Highland High and when approached, they say, "We have a pass. Yeah."

Greenbelt Park was great, although I took extra steps again when I saw orange cones with a sign indicating AUTHORIZED VEHICLES ONLY as I headed toward the south entrance, per the TBTs. I took that to mean authorized people only, and went a different way only to get near the north entrance again. I asked a ranger finally, and was granted permission to proceed toward the south entrance and Goodluck Road.

Goodluck Road. How fortuitous. Becky had emailed and invited me to dinner with her and some of her friends, and she offered to host me and the use of their washer and dryer.

I was treated to a divine meal at a Mexican restaurant and a good night's sleep. A thousand thank-yous, Becky and Nan, for dinner and taking in a stray for the night.

Here's to fellow hikers, both past and twenty minutes ahead of me, hilarious rumble strip farting noises, and always having a pass.

Cheers!

Amie

Seeing Red

In public education, no idea is so bad that it will lack enthusiasts. The modern school is a petri dish of experiments. Few of these ideas have to do with rigorous curriculum that prepares students for the university. Even fewer address vocational skills to segue our young men who are not university bound into a trade or apprenticeship that will immediately benefit them when they leave the K-12 conveyor belt. Rather, school illuminati devise strategies to accommodate the needs of our society's broken students.

Broken students are angry, often without the vocabulary or maturity to articulate why. Broken students are from fatherless homes, or homes that have been a revolving door of stepdads, shack-ups, and other fly-by-night parenting situations that leave the child with attachment issues and a mistrust of adults. Broken students are the girls who hate their bodies and their appearance. These girls self-harm and self-medicate. Broken teenage girls today express similar levels of anxiety as the average mental patient did in the 1950s. Broken students are intellectually stunted. Due to excessive absences, poor nutrition, frequent moves and school changes, broken students have severe gaps in their learning. Many high school math students do not know their multiplication tables. Many cannot read. Many cannot construct a complete sentence.

What does a school do with an illiterate 17-year-old? The answer from on high is to modify. As an assistant principal told me one year when two perpetually off-task students, one angry, one illiterate, held steady 58 percents in my Tier English class, which was already a modified curriculum, "modify, modify, modify." *Modify what?* The low-lexile books that I already read aloud to them? The eighth-grade level vocabulary study? The simple, two-sentence daily language activity to which I give them the answers? Teachers feel pressure, in Teacher Mother Tongue, to dumb down not only their curriculum, but also broken students' behavior, social, and attendance expectations.

Ideas for what to do with broken students become the focus of books that teachers are assigned to read during the school year. Students are released from school periodically for teacher inservice days that speak to mental health and suicide prevention. When I was going through the teacher prep courses in college, we learned that schools legally act *in loco parentis*, in place of parents. Fast forward twenty years later: schools are the parents. Myriad experts who have never taught in the public classroom, administrators who wanted out of the classroom, and authors who used to be in the classroom tell teachers that our job is so much more than teaching content.

That has always been partially true; however, now the art of teaching young people how to act, how not to hate themselves, how to stop leaning heavily on the crutch of trauma sustained in years past subsumes the teaching of reading, science, music, and deep math competency. Broken students will not learn, teachers are told, until they have been emotionally regulated and nursed back to mental health. It is, according to the prevailing winds, now the schools' mission to lick children's psychological wounds during the school day as well. While this may be a worthy mission, it is one for which I am unqualified.

The alternative school served many shattered students. Our counselor's and assistant principal's yeoman's efforts to calm and guide students and to connect them to services far beyond our reach were yokes I was not equipped to bear. Emotional powwows in the office were not enough of a cure for what ailed our students, so of course students dragged the anxieties and drama into our classrooms on a regular basis. Accordingly, teachers sometimes had to break the glass in case of fire and employ school strategies that put out the flames of physical infirmity and mental conflagrations.

One tool at the alternative school that left simple core content teachers like me drawn and haggard was known as the red pass. The red pass was a quarter sheet of paper, red of course, that was stapled into the back of the student's planner. Students who legitimately needed to leave the classroom more than the allotted ten times during a term for valid medical reasons were given a red pass by the health office or the administration. Pregnant girls, students with diabetes, or generally any student with a bona fide, documented, and pressing health need that theoretically could not wait until passing period or lunch was given a red pass.

When the student needed to leave class, he flashed the red pass at the attending classroom facilitator—not teacher!—and dallied directly off to what was supposed to be a destination germane to his medical need. Administrators believed the red pass was invoked in a very controlled way. Students were delivered a stern warning that they were not to abuse the red pass. Each nodded in dogged earnestness. But far too many special pleaders and red-pass recipients then crossed the Rubicon into a vast exile of hall wandering, enabled by the slip of paper now bearing the scathing misnomer Special Medical Pass.

The majority of students who possessed the red pass, in the teachers' minds, fell into one of several categories: they didn't need it, they abused it heavily, or we were really not sure why they came to school at all. One student was Javier. Tall and very thin, Javier sported an early nineties Kid-and-Play haircut. Javier had diabetes, and so was given a red pass. Javier was in my first hour for Term 4, and he came to school maybe once a week. He was by age a senior, but was still plodding his way through English 10A and 10B for the duration of the year. He would choose a topic for his academic paragraph, I would give him the needed materials, and then I would not see him for another week. Sometimes he would be absent so long that by the time he returned, I had forgotten what he was writing about, and he had lost the materials anyway.

Essentially each time he came back to school, he was starting over on the English 10B recovery curriculum. About ten minutes into first hour, he would flash his red pass and ask to go to the nurse to check his blood sugar, I presume. He would then come back and request to use the restroom 30 minutes later. Not a savant on how often a diabetic really needed to use the bathroom, I always let him go for fear of a reprimand or lawsuit for not taking a knee to the red pass.

The same story held for other teachers' classes. Javier made so little progress in any classes that we truly did not know why he was enrolled at the alternative school. He didn't do any work at home. I hypothesized that he came to us once every ten days to receive free health services and to use our restrooms.

A student several years ago in my traditional high school MTSS class had something tantamount to the red pass. Lyla suffered from the entire alphabet soup list of mental ailments, and she likely suffered some self-image issues as well. Lyla was very large, unhealthily so. She was to be allowed to go to the health office whenever she felt as if she were going to pass out, an episode the school nurse assured me she made herself do as an attention-seeking technique. In Tier Support, Lyla was doing an independent book study through our Fuel Ed online courses, and like most Tier students, she would never stay awake and focused long enough to read *A Raisin in the Sun* if I did not read it aloud to her. Lyla would fall asleep as I read. I would make her read a page aloud to me in the effort to keep her alert, but her portion was so choppy and mispronounced that I am sure she never comprehended the parts she read—and probably not mine given the number of times I looked over to see her sleeping. When she got sleepy enough after lunch or pressured enough to perform a little work for my class or others, she would invoke her right to go to the nurse due to feeling a faint coming on. I would walk her to the nurse's room, and a couple of times she did make herself pass out. There was no way I could hold her up. The best I could do was grab onto her clothing to stop her fall as best I could. I would run and grab the nurse, who would pat her shoulder and coo over her to get her to wake up. Lyla would lie down for a bit, then proceed on to her next class having escaped *A Raisin in the Sun*, World History Google classroom activities, or English literature terms on Quizlet for yet another 45 minutes.

Another student at the alternative school who stumbled upon the red pass and the giant fairytale land beyond the doors of the magical wardrobe was named Arden. Prior to his inauguration into the red pass club, here was Arden's pattern in my second hour social studies class. Arden came to class with his earbuds in, loudly rapping to whatever was blasting through his earbuds, earbuds which magically never worked five minutes later when they were to be used to work on his Acellus lessons. Arden was usually hyper and dancing around as well, likely in the throes of a Monster or Red Bull or sugary fare inhaled in the locker bay during passing period. When the bell rang, he did not sit down, but continued punching the air, circling the classroom, freestyle dancing, talking to everyone around him using profanities or whatever rap mogul parlance was popular at the moment. When I would attempt to begin class with Good Things, another PBIS bell-ringer activity, he would interrupt whoever was trying to share and carry on rude side conversations that bore me aloft to the land of too much information, a land from whose borne no traveler returns. I could never unhear Arden's plans for his next piercing, whose legal troubles he saw on whose social media story, or what latest plights a classmate's probable baby daddy was embroiled in as a result of engaging in sexual congress with a fourteen-year-old.

Once I settled everyone and work time began, Arden would quickly fall asleep. No common-sense strategies worked to keep him awake. He would move to the standup desk with the fidget bar only to pull a stool to the standup desk, put his head down, and fall asleep. I made him sit right by me for several weeks so that I could tap his elbow or nudge him out of slumber once I saw the head tilting forward. If I did perk him up momentarily, he would use the opportunity to socialize and get others off track so that I would have to quell the drama that Arden rustled up like a west Texas dust devil.

We teachers penalized students in their daily participation grade for sleeping in class. And after some consecutive weeks of F's for classroom participation as well as an F in social studies for unsatisfactory progress, Ardern's mother sent me a hand-written note asking me to exercise patience and understanding with her son's fatigue. His medication regime was in a state of flux, and he was seeing a new doctor. I struggled to understand the tone and import of her note. Was she annoyed that Arden earned F's every day for sleeping? Was I to let him sleep? What was the precise number of times I was to wake him up in class before throwing my hands in the air? Three? Ten?

Arden apologized for sleeping. Lo, though he confessed he repented not, for he continued to breakdance into class, disturb the peace for fifteen minutes a day, then crash heavily, Roman Empire Acellus lecture notwithstanding. A few days later, I received a typed physician's note. This letter also thanked me for my patience with Arden's sleepiness. I put the note on my clipboard and retreated in this battle. After all, class was so much more peaceful with him in his post-Monster and junk food coma.

One day soon after I began letting Arden sleep, the principal did a walk through. He noticed Arden leaned over his table and laptop sleeping, breathing deeply and steadily, blissfully unaware that school was taking place about his person. I immediately felt guilty for being caught doing nothing about a sleeping student. I explained to the principal that I could not keep Arden awake, and then I made the tragic error of showing our building lead the physician's note. A day or two later, an email in all of Arden's teachers' inboxes proclaimed that Arden was being put on a red medical pass for one purpose only: when Arden felt tired, he was to get up out of his seat, leave the classroom, and take a very brisk walk up and down the hall to revive himself. He was then immediately to return to class, as refreshed as if he had just taken the Nestea Plunge, and resume work.

Here is what really happened. Arden began flashing his red pass like one flashing his credentials in an old Soviet airport customs. He would freely roam the campus, go to the bathroom, or go to the front office to use his cell phone on some "emergency" errand. He was mysteriously wide awake while undertaking all these commissions. His time out of class began to equal and then surpass his time in front of the social studies curriculum.

One morning I overhead another student who had run out of hall passes ask Arden how come he got to leave the room all the time. Arden replied, "Dude, get something wrong with you, and you get a red pass." Arden was not in my class once the fall semester ended. My hall mates reported that Arden flashed his red pass regularly that spring to report social media drama to our school resource officer, hang out in the office on his phone, and generally be out of class.

Another student named Reyanne played her red pass like that old 1980s video arcade game Frogger. In Frogger, the player is a frog icon that has to jump across a road of moving vehicles going in both directions without getting squashed. Reyanne used her red pass to jump from classroom to bathroom to nurse to counselor's office with her final destination being anywhere but in school. Reyanne came to us later in the school year. A ward of the state, she was also hopping from home to home like Frogger jumping from car to van to dune buggy. What kept Reyanne moving was likely her advanced age and its associated baggage (she was a senior), coupled with the fact that she reportedly told her latest adoptive family that she had "felt like she wanted to hurt them." Reyanne did not emote much at all. Her face was usually devoid of expression to the point of creepiness. Every now and then I encounter a student with cold, dead fish eyes. Reyanne was one of them. She hardly ever smiled. Whatever medical problem warranted her red pass, she flashed it from day one that she entered my class. She too needed to go to the nurse or restroom every 45 minutes, for what reasons I did not care to know.

For those unfamiliar with the ecosystem of public schools, the restrooms are where the weirdness happens. Many schools are festooned with cameras recording students' every move, campus security on duty, and a general lack of privacy on campus for very good reasons. Everything students do not do at home, they want to do at school, e. g. sleep, wander around unaccounted for with boyfriends and associates with grim life prospects, gorge on junk food and soda, and so forth.

Male students reportedly ate in the bathroom. Our male custodian, who did restroom checks every 30 minutes, and our male admin would walk in to find a small horde of boys shoveling in Hot Cheetos or their ilk. Finally, one afternoon our assistant principal said to a frequent flier and bathroom snacking connoisseur, "Uh, you guys know people poop in here, right?"

Conversely, everything we do not allow students to do in the classroom, they want to do in the bathroom: eat, talk about untoward subjects, pee and wipe feces on the seats, vandalize, be on cell phones, smoke, vape, fight, and sleep (yes, that is correct). At the alternative school, there was really nowhere to hide except in the restroom stalls. There was so much hiding and hanging out in the bathroom stalls, that I began noticing a phenomenon as I made frequent use of the student bathroom, which was closer to my room than the staff restroom. I dubbed this bizarre phenomenon Shoes That Don't Make Restroom Noises.

Shoes That Don't Make Restroom Noises are those that the teacher can see beneath the stall door. The shoes are still, but no typical noises indicative of using the restroom ever peal forth from the stall. These shoes are silent. And depending on the hour of the day, the enigmatic, no-restroom-noise shoes were the same one or two pair every time. The student to whom the magic shoes belonged just wanted to hide out in the bathroom stall on the phone for a bit. Reyanne was a frequent wearer of Shoes That Never Made Restroom Noises. It got so bad that our female counselor during Term 3 began popping into the restroom at the start of every class, and sure enough, Reyanne was in there, her tell-tale silent shoes and army green backpack making no noise yet answering like role call.

Reyanne's jig and abuse of the red pass was eventually up, first because the nurse finally put her foot down and would no longer allow Reyanne into the health office due to false reports of bullying she attempted to stir up in the health office. The nurse told us teachers that even if Reyanne were getting ready to throw up (read: make herself throw up) we were to pull over the trash can and wish her the best. Reyanne also abused her red pass by making her way to the counselor's office to report that she was going to kill herself. I do not think suicide is a joke, and threats have to be taken seriously, yes. But by this time, Reyanne had learned that threatening to kill herself was a way out of school for a while. It was a successful avoidance technique as well as a way to get attention. The school had no choice but to report Reyanne's statement to child protective services. Reyanne and her red pass would disappear from school for a while, and then she would reappear a few days later to resume her Frogger game with the red pass.

Although as the year was drawing to a close, there were fewer safe lily pads for her to summon her pass to reach. The nurse had banished her, the counselor was tired of dialing 911, I had asked that she be removed from my class for epic stretches of game-playing and refusal to work. She spent a few weeks hopping like Frogger from restroom to office to class, not accomplishing much. Eventually an out-of-state family elected to take her. In her time at our school, she learned a speck of Algebra, maybe a spot of English, and that falsely threatening to kill oneself is a golden (red?) ticket out of responsibility.

As Tolkien wrote, all who wander are not lost. Another student who wandered with his red pass but who was definitely lost was Camden. Camden's red pass came to be stapled into his planner due to what the administration called his "anger issues." At no conference, awards night, or even his expulsion hearing did I see a father. The source of his anger may or may not have stemmed from the lack of a father. Through other teachers and information revealed at his expulsion hearing, the focus of which was his threatening to "hit me in the face" if I didn't get away from him, I learned that the mother had been trying to get his medication switched; he had suffered pancreatitis as a child; he had a mother and grandmother who were willing to accuse me, the counselor, our resource officer, and anyone under the sun of provoking Camden. We were at fault for not allowing him to switch classes and teachers every time he took a notion to or was told "no," and forcing Camden to use a restroom which had pee and feces on the toilet seat. We were told that he was apparently "very good with his baby sister," likely because the baby never told him what to do or corrected his hateful behavior. I don't enjoy saying this about people, but Camden was just an ugly young man, inside and out. He walked down the halls with a perpetual smirk on his face. He was startingly white with flaming red hair, yet he spoke in a gangster rapper-like dialect when he was arguing, telling teachers what he was not going to do, or issuing parting remarks as he stormed out of the classroom and attempted to slam the door back into its latch. Other students grew weary of Camden's tantrums. His ugly behavior began provoking laughter and eye-rolling because our classroom doors, in a hilarious and anticlimactic denouement, bounced back with a slight, bass-laden "boinging" sound due to their rebounding off of the lockdown magnet in place over the latches' inserts.

Therefore, after a few rounds of door slamming, cursing teachers, storming out of classes, and attempts at circumventing every policy in the student handbook, administrators gave Camden—you guessed it— a red pass! The concept behind giving this particular student a red pass was that if Camden felt himself becoming angry, he was to show the teacher the red pass. Without questioning Camden or inquiring as to his intended destination, the teacher was to allow Camden to leave class, whereupon he was to proceed directly to the front office where he could take a few minutes to cool down. The idea was that Camden would learn to regulate himself and avoid more blowups.

Here is what really happened. Camden used his red pass to get out of class when he wanted to avoid following a rule or simple teacher request. I hypothesize that Mom or Grandma or Camden also played the pity card over childhood health issues because as the weeks progressed, Camden was then allowed to leave class whenever he wanted on his red pass due to health issues and the need for unfettered access to the bathroom. Camden also made frequent appearances in the office with his cell phone, claiming he needed to make the proverbial emergency parent text or call. Another student told a colleague that Camden used his red pass to go sit in the restroom and watch *Family Guy* on his phone.

A slight but equally maddening variation on the red pass was the *de facto* red pass. In contrast to the red pass *de jure*, this new invisible pass belonged to a student who had red pass status without an actual red pass stapled into his planner. Like the Supreme Court justices who have cited "emanations and penumbras," nonexistent rights, and other effluvia within the Constitution, a student named Arturo claimed he would leave class whenever he wanted without flashing any red pass credentials at all. Arturo signed himself out whenever he pleased, ignoring that he had surpassed his maximum number of restroom passes, ignoring the associated detentions for going AWOL from class about 20 minutes per day, and challenging the teachers to "go ahead and write me up; see what the principal has to say about it." Indeed, the principal took a few teachers to task, myself included, over attempting to "punish" Arturo when he had a documented medical reason for needing constant access to the restroom. Never mind that he never showed anyone his Special Medical Pass, and the exact medical reason for his unlimited entrée to the restroom remained murky the entire school year.

Arturo would use his red pass to be tardy to class. It was only after I wrote him up and noted on his referral in fine print rivalling legalese that his referral was for tardies that Arturo came to class on time. He would "show the teachers" by immediately getting up to go to the restroom after the bell rang. When he did return, he entertained the class by making bird noises, gliding to his duffel bag repeatedly to put on lotion or spritz some dreadful cologne, or trying to get a rise out of other students or female teachers.

One afternoon when Arturo was supposed to watching his instructional videos for English 10A, I watched him tear up several sheets of notebook paper. He then wadded up part of the debris to resemble the innards of a blunt, and used the rest to roll two fake joints. He left them at his computer at the end of class. I kept them as exhibits in case he was in danger of not graduating—a rare occurrence in public education; if you show up and breathe, you graduate—and once again found myself powerless to stop him from doing whatever he wanted during my class with his *de facto* red pass and bizarre patronage from the principal, the rhyme or reason behind which remained a conundrum.

Other students here and there had red passes. Many viewed the office, quiet room, restroom, health office, and classrooms as revolving doors through which they could continue turning without remaining anywhere solid for the class's prescribed tenure of 80 minutes. We teachers began wondering if we too could get a red pass so that we could sit in the lounge and grade. A colleague had discovered that Arturo had a job at one of the local Pizza Huts. She asked Arturo how his red pass worked at Pizza Hut; was he allowed off the cookline or away from his customers at every whim? Joking aside, we probed the legal implications of red pass use as well. When red pass holders flashed their goods and dallied off to unknown and evolving destinations, what was the protocol if we went into lockdown? I never truly knew where my red pass club members were at any given time. What liability issues faced us if a student just left campus? Got hurt or pregnant during class time? Committed suicide in a restroom? Teachers were not to call into question where students were or be concerned with the length of time out of class, was the tacit message. What protections besides video surveillance were in place?

When the ubiquity of red passes and their barefaced misuse finally threatened to turn my colleagues and me into clock tower snipers, someone finally brought the red passes up in a Friday afternoon staff meeting. The administrators listened. We were then apprized in an email that students who came up to the office during class time were given three strict choices.

Choice one, they could turn in their cell phone and use the quiet room for classwork. Choice two, they could go in the airlock and have five minutes to cool down or get their anxiety under control and then immediately return to class. Choice three, they could see the principal or counselor, both of whom maintained an open-door policy for emotionally needy students, for better or for worse when it came to campus organization and management. Teachers were informed that students would not be allowed to sit in the office on their phones, eavesdropping on office business, chatting up the secretaries, and generally loitering to avoid industry or teachers they did not like that day.

Content with these new guidelines for our red VIP backstage pass holders, we teachers continued to nod in weary assent and genuflect to the red pass when a student displayed the crimson slip of paper dangling from the back page of his planner. Trips through the front office on our prep periods still bore witness to a conga line of students lounging on the office couch on phones, standing at the secretary's station buying a snack, working at a corner office table on offline assignments that did not appear to match any of our Acellus course curricula. My hall mates and I felt helpless yet culpable with regard to our high school inculcating this special-pass ethos into students. When I taught at a large high school on California's central coast, I remember our English department chairs telling the English teachers that they had just left a meeting with the local community college's guidance counselors. The guidance counselors had kindly impressed upon us high school staff that in addition to teaching writing and reading skills that would propel students to a successful college English experience, we also needed to be focusing on soft skills. Accountability, good attendance, work ethic. One of the college counselors had expressed that she recently had a young lady in her office who had chosen to see the guidance faculty instead of going to her appointed class. Then when their meeting was over, the young college student had asked for a pass to the class she had chosen to skip.

What can I do to fight the indulgent culture and attendant decline in standards within this brave new world of public education? Drive myself crazy fighting administrators, their edicts, and the soft bigotry of low expectations? Spend more of my time explaining to parents the particulars behind their child's poor grades? Step onto the dais in front of panels of counselors and special education personnel to defend myself time and again in a Kafka-esque trial of who I am fundamentally as an English teacher?

I'll pass.

Thursday, March 26, 2015

Destination: Georgetown, D. C.
Today's Miles: 19.80
Start Location: Greenbelt, MD
Trip Miles: 127.50

Becky dropped me at the south entrance of Greenbelt park, and I followed a network of trail systems and parkways through the D. C. area. Today was warmer, in the seventies, and many people were out there with me jogging and enjoying the sun, especially later in the afternoon. I crossed under some ornate bridges, one of which I believe was called Devil's Chair Bridge. There was an old cemetery high atop a hill above the trail that was very cool too. The tombstones were large and ornate. It reminded me of the graveyard from a picture in a children's book I had when I was little. It was a haunted mansion story, and the books had 45 records that played along with the story, supplemented with sound effects. That particular book's pictures were very scary, with high creepy windows in the mansion and a churchyard like the one I saw today, but with eyes everywhere.

I enjoyed the park and knew I was getting close to the Towpath, so I hurried myself to get out of the park and to Georgetown because I obviously could not camp in that park, even stealth camp. I have read and heard about historic Georgetown, but I had never been there until today. Very cool. I am definitely coming back here, and I will have to come back anyway because I did not take any of the detours to sightsee in D. C. Plus, Mom has been want-ing to go to the Northeast for a long time, and so we will come back when I look presentable and others can tour the city as well.

The Canal Inn is my home for the night, and I am ready for the C & O Towpath and softer terrain tomorrow.

Amie

Friday, March 27, 2015

Destination: Swain's Lock Campsite, C & O, MD
Today's Miles: 16.33
Start Location: Georgetown, D. C.
Trip Miles: 143.83

A light rain fell as the trail exited Georgetown. The sprinkles finally stopped and I spent the first few hours of walking studying the system of locks that assisted boats up this canal. I read a lot of the signs along the path that explained the history of the canal, the various lockhouses, and the great falls of the Potomac. This is really interesting, and I now have the second building older than 1860 for Kaden's list, if he approves.

At mile 8, the directions indicated an opportunity for a food stop, and I took advantage of it. MapQuest indicated that the closest grocery store was a co-op right off the trail. As I got closer I saw the sign on the store, and it was a natural food market. I knew this would be pricey, but every step off the trail works against your day, so I went in.

Here is where it got funny. I didn't see any shopping baskets outside the store, so I grabbed a cart, one of those tiny carts that fancy grocery stores have. I walked inside and realized my pack was going to be a problem. The aisles were narrow, and near the front was a rack of ceramic plates and mugs with suns or something on them, and they were probably unnaturally expensive. There were also wine bottle displays stacked along the aisles. I knew that one wrong turn with my pack could send wine and dishes crashing to the floor, so I took off my pack. The cart was so small that only my pack would fit in there along with the poles, leaving no room for groceries.

So I found where the baskets were stacked and balanced the shopping basket on top of my pack and began pushing this ensemble around the small aisles. One of the workers looked at me , and I said hello and grabbed some baby carrots. I ended up buying the carrots, some Kashi bars, water, and some granola. I would have picked up a few more things, but even with the pack off I kept hearing wine bottles tinkling, and I was sure I was on the verge of purchasing a case of broken wine. Or if I left the cart and pack in an aisle while I ventured down another aisle, the worker and another customer kept having to squeeze by it to get through.

I approached the checkout guy and gave my standard greeting that I have been using at hotels: "Hello. I'm not homeless or anything. I'm hiking this trail that goes along here. I know how this looks." I paid and left the store, deciding that it would be a safe move to go ahead and put the poncho on again. I was having trouble getting the left side of the poncho over my pack, and the checkout guys came out and helped me drape the pack correctly. He was either being nice or was trying to hurry me along and away from the front of the store.

Back to the towpath. At mile 14 was a visitor's center for the great falls tavern, an old building that began as a small lockhouse. I sat for a few minutes to spell my feet and watch the video about the Potomac River Gorge. Found a spot on high ground at this site. There are actually two other people camping here. I am surprised. I don't think they are doing the ADT. I am still waiting to meet Steve.

Amie

Saturday, March 28, 2015

Destination: White's Ferry, MD
Today's Miles: 19.10
Start Location: Swain's Lock Campsite
Trip Miles: 162.93

A cold day of relentless wind in my face, but, wow, I found a rhythm today. Packed up camp and got started about 8:30. My fingers and toes were cold for about two miles. Toes finally warmed, but for about an hour I had to cross my arms while holding the trekking poles at a strange angle to keep my hands hidden under my arms and out of the wind. I started off walking quickly and then kept it up even after I warmed a bit. Twelve miles went by very quickly. I saw a few joggers and cyclists this morning, but barely anyone else as the day progressed. I finished off the baby carrots for breakfast and then destroyed the rest of the cranberry granola in a moving lunch because I felt so great that I did not want to sit down and jinx anything.

Last night it got down to 28, and I slept in the capilene bottoms and two shirts. I keep a pair of Wigwam sock liners in my clean clothes compartment, and I wear those at the end of the day because they are light, loose, clean, and yet they are still a layer to wear in the sleeping bag on cold nights. I also bring into the sleeping bag my fleece jacket and another shirt layer. I do this to have an extra layer warm for the cold morning, and I also use them as a "Deedee." Let me explain.

My niece Addison, like many kids, has a blankie. Like a Woobie from the *Mr. Mom* movie. My sister Ashley called her blanket her Bankie. My cousin Jason called his blankie his Guy. Addie calls hers a Deedee. I don't know why. Addie has had several Deedees, and they are usually pink or have pink on them somewhere. Addie and I had a serious intellectual conversation over Christmas about how all Deedees are blankets, but not all blankets are Deedees. Addie loves her Deedees, and the rest of us have taken to calling blankies Deedees from time to time as well. Dain, Addie's brother, does not like to wear clothes when he is at home, and he is usually wrapped in a blanket. But he loudly protests that he does not have a Deedee. I use my fleece jacket as a Deedee. I snuggle up with it at night, and I will claim it proudly. It is warm and ready to go for packing up the bag, pad, and tent in the cold. By the way, Addie, Aunt Amie is in the state of Maryland right now. Have Mom help you look it up.

I saw a raccoon today hanging out on the side of the path. He just stared at me as I passed by. I saw some more neat lockhouses, but other than that I was just mentally free to walk and think, being that the path is long and straight, and the sights and roads entering and exiting the path are miles apart.

Around 2:45 I began reconsidering my campsite plans for the night. I had totally planned to camp at the 18.5 mile mark for the day, and I was there fairly early in the day, lots of light left. But the wind was just bitter and relentless, and I checked the weather app again and the low for tonight is supposed to be 21. It seemed that the farther west I walked, the lower the low was becoming. My bag is rated to 25 degrees. I was fine last night at 28, but the wind was not blowing last night to put an edge on the cold temp. I did not want to chance it. I decided to bypass the campground and head over the Potomac to Leesburg, Virginia. That would also give me an extra trail mile on the day. At White's Ferry, I got in line with the cars to board the ferry. Those on foot are charged one dollar to cross. I was waiting when a sweet lady named Luisa rolled down her window and asked if I wanted to get in and wait. We talked for a sec, and she was headed to Leesburg as well and she said she would drop me at the first motel we came to. Deal. Thank you, Luisa! I hope you had a nice time shopping and a good dinner.

Leesburg has a stylish downtown area that is charming to say the least. Love it. She dropped me at a B and B, but after hearing the price, I made a phone call and decided it was worth another half mile of walking, wind at my back, to save 25 bucks. So motel it is. I spent an hour or so doing trail chores, which consist of laundry, washing and drying my cookpot, rinsing the mud off the bottom cuffs of my rain pants, rinsing out the trash compactor bag I place my dirty shoes in when I bring them into the tent for the night, spreading out my sleeping bag to dry out any of last night's condensation, and eating. All is well. I think I have this room at about 85 degrees right now. I will turn it down before sleeping, but it is nice to be warm. Tomorrow the high is supposed to reach 50, perfect. Today I don't believe it got much above 32.

I was very happy with my energy level and stamina today. Tomorrow it is back to the towpath with a warmer day and all Deedees freshly laundered.

Cheers!

Amie

Sunday, March 29, 2015

Destination: Calico Rocks Campsite, MD
Today's Miles: 12.20
Start Location: White's Ferry, MD
Trip Miles: 175.13

Today's trail mile count is short because I walked back to the towpath from the motel. And that's okay because I got to walk through the cute downtown area of Leesburg on a quiet Sunday morning with few people out and about. I figure it was about 4.5 miles back to White's Ferry and then onto the path, so overall I did a fair amount of walking.

I only count unidirectional, on-trail miles in my daily mileage. I don't count miles I spend backtracking (only happened a couple times so far), miles riding in a car, or off-trail miles to get groceries or what have you.

Today was warmer and sunny. The towpath passed a couple more lock-houses, an aqueduct, several entry points for cars, and people were walking and bicycling today at most points along the path. A few people asked how far I was going and then wished me good luck when I told them about the ADT. One lady talked about her friend who is hiking the Appalachian Trail in small sections. Her friend is still working on little bits at a time, and she is now in her seventies. Great! I read an article in *Running Times* a few years back about a man in his nineties who still runs road races. There was a picture of him running, slowly of course these days, but he looked fit as could be. I had that picture on the refrigerator for a long time.

So how far am I going on this trail? Well, as I have been telling everyone in person, I will keep going until

a) I reach the end in CA.

b) I am consistently no longer having fun.

c) I spend my budget, and will need to stop and look for a new job.

d) Find myself going too slowly and unable to cross the mountain ranges at pivotal times in the year.

If c) occurs, I know that working on the trail in segments over the course of a few years is an option. Work, save, work on the trail some more.

If d) begins to occur, I have also considered bicycling to the end. I have been wanting to buy a nice bicycle ever since I moved to CA, and this may be my excuse. Right now I am only thinking about two days into the future. Do I have food? Supplies? Water? Are my batteries charged, literally and figuratively? Am I dry? Rested? Safe? These are the questions that concern me right now, and I will get as far as I can get.

The wind has completely stopped. It is supposed to be 36 tonight, much improved over 20, and in the 60s this week.

Amie

Monday, March 30, 2015

Destination: Huckleberry Hill Campsite, MD
Today's Miles: 15
Start Location: Calico Rocks Campsite, MD
Trip Miles: 190.13

I slept so hard last night that I did not hear the other camper come in. The other camper was the elusive Steve. We finally meet! He was packed up and ready to walk before I was, so he went ahead and took off after we shook hands and made introductions. An hour or so into my morning, I met up with a couple walking their two dogs, and the three of us ran into Steve. The dog walkers turned back east, and Steve and I continued west and chatted for about ten miles today. It was very pleasant, and it seemed we were keeping about the same pace comfortably.

I needed to make a town stop in Brunswick for groceries, and he chose to come into town also to get lunch. On our way into Brunswick an older man came out of his house and asked if we were hiking the AT. We said no, the ADT, and explained that it followed the towpath right outside of town. The man talked for a bit and then told us to wait, that he had something he wanted to give us. He came back outside with a paperback book about the C & O. Steve took it, and we thanked him and continued on. He flipped through the book and turned it over, and saw the sticker that read, "Property of Public Library." We chose to believe that the man had the book checked out for so long that he bought it and then gifted it to us. That, or he bought it at the library's inventory reduction sale.

We made a Subway stop where I ate a double chicken salad with spinach. The salad was just what I needed. We then made a grocery run at the CVS Pharmacy because one of the locals said the actual grocery store had closed down. But CVS sufficed. I was able to find coffee, good granola, and some dried fruit. Steve ripped out the parts of the C & O book that discussed the miles we had already covered and regifted those pages to the trashcan. We proceeded to roam the premises with contraband, e. g. the rest of the library book, now defaced.

The lunch/grocery run complete, we headed back to the towpath. This added about 2.5 off-trail miles to my day, but it was necessary. We proceeded west, and we crossed the point where the north/south Appalachian Trail crosses the ADT. We saw one hiker who looked pretty serious. Shortly we came to the footbridge that leads to Harper's Ferry. Steve turned south at that point, wanting to find an outfitter for some resupply, and he wanted to stay in the youth hostel there. A hostel did not sound appealing to me, and I have walked too many off-trail steps the last couple days, so I continued on to the next campsite. We parted ways. It was nice to have a hiking buddy for one day.

I chose a tent spot that is next to a pile of cut and stacked wood. It serves as a nice windbreak. Also, last night's campsite was right next to the B & O Railroad line. Many trains passed during the night. It didn't bother me too much, but I don't think the rail line is as close to this site. And I didn't know the B & O was real. I thought it was just a railroad in the Monopoly game. I had also seen an old rail car marked Reading Railroad back in the eastern-most part of Maryland. I didn't know the Reading was real either. I learned something new. I guess the B & O Railroad waking me up last night was my delayed punishment for cheating my sisters at Monopoly years ago.

And speaking of punishment, if anyone from the Brunswick Public Library is looking for their missing C & O book, it went south to Harper's Ferry.

Amie

Tuesday, March 31, 2015

Destination: Big Woods Campsite, MD
Today's Miles: 19.80
Start Location: Huckleberry Hill Campsite, MD
Trip Miles: 209.93

Woke up, peeked around the woodpile, determined there were no public library bounty hunters with torches and pitchforks, packed up, and proceeded on. Last night was my best night of camping sleep so far, and I made a good distance today. Today's walk was a little less physically challenging and more psychologically challenging. This part of the towpath feels a little more remote. There were still a few entry and exit points to and from the towpath in case of emergency, and I saw a few people, but not as many as on previous days. In addition, I knew I would be camping one more night before a town night, so I stayed off my phone. No looking at email, text, no checking my global position or playing on MapQuest to see what was around me. I knew my PowerPractical had at least one more full iPhone charge, but I wanted to make sure I had power to get through tomorrow and to pinpoint services. Also, today was strictly trail. No wandering into civilization to groceries or water. The scenery does not change too much on the towpath, so mental discipline was key today. I believe that one trait necessary for long hikes, whether one is thru-hiking a trail or just going for a long day hike, is the ability entertain oneself mentally without an outside aid or gadget.

Today was also the first time I took my water from the Potomac. Here is how I did it. I wanted to wait until there was an easy access point to the river. The canal to my right is always an option too, but the canal water usually isn't moving too quickly, if at all. So mid-morning there was a footpath leading to where a small, clear, and fairly fast-moving stream was emptying into the river. I took both Platypus bladders and my small cookpot to the edge of the little stream. I used the cookpot as a scoop, and then poured water gradually into the small mouths of the containers. It was also an opportunity to rinse some of the coffee residue from the cookpot. I placed the pot back into its ziploc bag, and then treated both containers of water with the Aqua Mira. Aqua Mira is a chlorine-based system that has the user mix 7 drops each from 2 small bottles. These drops sit for a few minutes to activate, and then the mixture is poured into one liter of water. In 15 to 30 minutes, the water is ready to drink. The mixture itself has a stale chlorine smell, but once it has treated the water for the appropriate amount of time, there is no odor at all. So I had 3 liters of clean water for the rest of today and for coffee the next.

Made it to Big Woods campsite, which reminds me of the Laura Ingalls Wilder books, especially *Little House in the Big Woods*. I am happy with today's progress.

Amie

Wednesday, April 01, 2015

Destination: Williamsport, MD
Today's Miles: 16.82
Start Location: Big Woods Campsite, MD
Trip Miles: 226.75

Civilization and motel night. I need it after three consecutive nights camping, and last night I did not sleep well. There were birds near the campsite that, when they chirped, sounded just like the sharp chirping noise that a household smoke detector makes when its battery is low. And although it was warmer yesterday, last night it got cold. I got up to find a thin layer of ice coating the tent poles and covering the trekking poles and poncho that I leave outside the tent. The cold pushed my sleeping bag's comfort threshold. As Joey Lawrence used to say, "Whoa!"

So today's walk was a push-through to get to town for a motel night, shower, and groceries in the morning. The towpath was remote again for 12 or so miles, wound under Interstate 81 and then directly to Williamsport, where motel, McDonald's and a few convenience stores are about a mile from the trail. I was pretty wiped out today, and my sixteen miles reminded me of that scene from *Lonesome Dove* when Gus and Call are pushing the cattle herd through the Badlands. Deets, their tracker and scout, comes back to the herd and reports how much farther to the next source of water: "Eighty miles, Captain." Everyone is dehydrated, the herd stumbles along, and then when the cattle know they're near the water, they rush to it. I sat down a couple times today to rest for a minute when the miles crept by. There are signposts every mile of the towpath that tell how far you have gone. They are nice when I am energetic, but the mile markers taunt me on days like today. My energy perked up when I picked up two chicken wraps and a salad at McD's before checking into the room, where I am now clean, fed, and content. Thank you, McD's, for offering foods other than just fries and cheeseburgers.

It is weird to check my appearance too after three and a half days of not looking at myself at all. I give today's appearance three very startled Joey Lawrence "Whoa!"s.

I want to give a shout out to Aunt Donna, Aunt Norma, and Uncle Rod. I know you guys have been thinking about me, and I have received your TJ guestbook messages. Thank you! If you get bored and feel like walking for a day, I'll let you know my exact location, and you can come walk with me for a bit. And we can time it so that you would not be walking with me after three or four consecutive, no-shower camping days.

    Amie

Thursday, April 02, 2015

Destination: Licking Creek Campsite, MD
Today's Miles: 17.20
Start Location: Williamsport, MD
Trip Miles: 243.95

After getting settled in the motel last night, I had some pain in my left heel. There was a tiny bit of discoloration. A few ibuprofen did the trick, and I believe I know the culprit. There was about a 3-mile section of the trail yesterday that had been reworked and completely paved over with sidewalk (cue primordial scream), and while it looked quite nice along the river, it wreaked havoc on my left heel. Plus, I remember hustling along during that section, ironically, so I could get off the sidewalk and back onto the lovely soft dirt towpath my feet and legs know so well. Therefore, I slowed way down today, remembering to be nice to myself. This is not a race.

The weather was warm today and there was no wind. In fact, I saw and heard several boats on the river. I had my jacket tied around my waist all day and nearly took the flannel off as well. The low tonight is supposed to be high forties, which will make for much more pleasant and leisurely camp coffee and packing up in the morning.

More irony, those mile markers went by quickly today even though I made it a point to walk carefully. The first 6 or 7 I glanced at and thought, "Oh, another mile again? Already? Rad." I ate a snack that was a first and that I loved: Clif bars, the white chocolate macadamia ones. Yum! I picked up a couple this morning on the way out of Williamsport just to try. I usually find Clif bars to be too much like candy when I am not exercising literally all day. I will be partaking of those more often on the trail. I wish macadamia nuts weren't so expensive. They are so yummy and good for you also.

I wore my sunrunner cap today (the Darth Vader hat) instead of beanies, which also felt great. It shields more of my face and my nose from the sun and just felt lighter. The beanies are very warm, but I don't always like to have the neon yellow one showing and, as students would say, "putting me on blast." So I cover most of it with the purple one. This adds warmth and makes me less conspicuous, but two beanies on top of each other makes me look sort of like a conehead. Oh well, this isn't a fashion show, although I do find my Mountain Khakis flannel to be pretty stylish. Khaki Darth Vader or conehead, take your pick. All I need to add to my eyebrow-raising trail fashion choices would be a pair of cowboy boots worn with sweatpants. Family inside joke.

Want to give a shout out today to my cousins Jordan, Jessica, Joel, and Suzie. Thank you for the nice notes the past couple of days. If I don't always reply, or if there is a 2 or 3 day turnaround time in text or emails, I am not ignoring. I am just triaging battery life for days between towns. I need to save power for an emergency and locating services by day four. Another shout out to Mom again for taking care of my checkbook.

On another positive note, I noticed at three campsites, including this one, that the National Park Service has installed at least some of the pump handles on the pumps that bring up clean water for the towpath's hikers and bikers. I will try out the pump in the morning, as I still have about a liter left right now. Easy access to water without getting it from the river or traipsing into town is good news.

Here's to fashion faux pas on the trail, great weather, a good number of trail miles on the day, and simple pleasures like pump handles.

Cheers!

Amie

Friday, April 03, 2015

Destination: Hancock, MD
Today's Miles: 8.08
Start Location: Licking Creek Campsite, MD
Trip Miles: 252.03

Last night was my best night of camp sleeping yet. I hope I can keep saying that. I think what helped was that it was warm enough to where I did not have to keep the sleeping bag totally closed over my face and head. I could "snuggle" with the top of the bag like a Deedee and just breathe normally without losing heat through my face and head during the night. When it gets down into the thirties, I have to keep pulling the bag's hood over my head, totally burying my face.

I got up at 6 and quickly rustled up some coffee. The weather app showed a 100 percent chance of rain by 8, and I did not want to be packing every-thing up in a big, sloppy mess. I made use of the bright flashlight feature on my PowerPractical while packing because it was not light enough yet. It had rained some overnight, so the outside of the tent was wet, and a bit inside from condensation. This soaked my tent stuff sack, which in turn mois-tened the pack where I connect the tent bag to the outside. I have another trash compactor bag with me, and I will definitely be tweaking how I pack the wet tent from now on. I have an idea I will try the next time I pack a wet tent.

So I stopped at the pump before I began hiking to fill the one-liter Platy-pus. I knew Hancock was only 8 miles away, so I just topped off the one bottle. I counted, and it took exactly 58 arm pumps to bring up the water, aim my bottle properly, and get it filled. I adjusted my technique about halfway through by leaning on the handle a bit near the end of a pump so that I could focus on aiming the mouth of the bottle. The water's precise exit point kept moving as the water left the pump. It reminded me of the film version of Homer's *Odyssey* when Odysseus tries to fill his bag of water, and Aeolus, god of wind, plays with Odysseus by moving the waterfall so that he cannot get the bag under the falling water. Odysseus keeps mov-ing his water bag, perplexed, and finally Aeolus explains why he is teasing Odysseus. I did not think any gods were toying with me, and I think 58 arm pumps are a square deal for treated water at one's fingertips every few miles.

I got in 8 miles today, and it's funny how an 8-mile day feels like a zero day. The weather indicated storms this afternoon and through the night. Plus, I need to do laundry. I did not do laundry two nights ago because they did not sell detergent at the motel. I had no more clean clothes. So I got a room in Hancock, not too far off trail, where it has been trail chores this afternoon and staying off my feet to heal my heel, and avoid possible thunderstorms during the midnight hours.

There was a Subway right next to the motel, where I indulged in a double chicken salad again. Two thumbs up to Subway for selling salads. There was also a small grocery next door, and I satisfied my craving for calcium and protein with more soymilk and some plain yogurt. I will have to hit up the store again in the morning. It's on the way back to the towpath, where I don't believe there is an opportunity for lodging for several days, and I speculate that food opportunities will be confined to convenience store nuts and such for the next couple of days.

One chore this afternoon was to trim my bangs. They are getting long. I am tempted to just let them grow, or "Let 'er buck," but there are two problems with letting my bangs go. One is that they fall in my eyes when I try to sleep. Very annoying. The other is that I have to wear bangs because I have a massively huge forehead, so they'll need to be cut anyway eventually. One of my uncles used to say he didn't have a forehead; he had a fivehead. I do too. Best I keep it covered up. I used the little scissors on my Swiss army knife to trim them. I don't look as shaggy now.

Speaking of Homer's epic poetry, one phrase among many that the bard repeats is "the gift of sleep." Based on which translation one uses, the reader encounters passages such as, "And Odysseus lay down and received the gift of sleep," or "Athena granted Telemachus the gift of sleep." Sleep truly is a gift. Homer was right. An undertaking like this is not possible without plentiful sleep. Read many hikers' trail journals, and one common subtext is where and how they slept.

And hiking all day every day is a gift too. I'm glad I get to do it for a while.

Amie

Saturday, April 04, 2015

Destination: Devil's Alley Campsite, MD
Today's Miles: 20
Start Location: Hancock, MD
Trip Miles: 272.03

First legit twenty-mile trail day. Stopped at the grocery store and re-stocked before walking back to the towpath. I am learning to stuff food in every nook and available airspace anywhere in my pack. Every zipper pouch, the tent stuff sack, and then a couple days later it feels like Christmas when I find some oatmeal or energy bar I forgot I purchased lurking among clothes or other nonedible items. It's as if I hid it from myself. Always a joyous occasion to find those sneaky food items on the trail.

And for those doing this trail any time in the future, Hancock, MD, is a great rest and resupply town. Everything is within about a half mile of the path, and there are no crazy shoulderless roads to negotiate if you stay at the Super 8. Just my two cents.

So I spoke just a teensy bit too soon regarding the treated water pumps. They all do now have handles, but some are very stiff, and I could not even get any water out of one of them even though I stopped counting at around 90 pumps of the handle. Someone stronger than I am needs to rastle with a few of them and get things moving. Other pumps quickly fill my water containers with minimal effort on my part. I keep thinking that it is good I am almost off the towpath; otherwise, I am going to be nursing a shoulder injury in my advanced age. *Professional tennis injury, Amie? Softball? Torn rotator cuff?* Naw, it's an old Park Service water pump injury . . . But the water, something I take for granted that pours forth from the faucet, is a great service to the folks in this park. Weather was warm today, and it looks to be a nice Easter Sunday.

Amie

Sunday, April 05, 2015

Destination: Town Creek Campsite, MD
Today's Miles: 17.46
Start Location: Devil's Alley Campsite, MD
Trip Miles: 289.49

Happy Easter!

Another day of warm weather. Today I wore shorts for the first time. Beware the white legs headed west. Today was also the day I walked through the Paw Paw Tunnel. It was a great feat of engineering in its time and is over half a mile long. I used the PowerP for a flashlight because it is also very dark despite being able to see the exit point waaaaaaaay down at the other end. You can hear the dripping sounds and plopping noises of water droplets falling into the canal, but you cannot see the canal below you. You can see the path and tiny pinpricks of others' flashlights or bicycle lights as they come near. It was also cold in the middle of the tunnel. There is an outdoor trail that circumvents the tunnel if you do not want to go through it, but it is much longer to go around. I wanted to walk through the Paw Paw, and it is one of those experiences that reinforces great respect for the engineering of the nation's arteries and thoroughfares two centuries ago.

The towpath remains flat, the nearly imperceptible elevation changes only signaled by the locks every few miles. The surrounding countryside is slowly giving way to hills and "hollers." I am reminded that the next state will be hilly terrain and much more challenging. I hope my calf muscles remember those long uphills at Cuesta and Point Sal in California. I heard bluegrass music coming from a car with West Virginia plates yesterday. I love bluegrass, which is a genre I listen to on solo excursions. I am missing listening to music or talk radio when walking, but that is okay. It's funny the songs and thoughts that come into your head when your thoughts are unencumbered with daily cares. I think about not only some of the bands and songs on Kyle Cantril's show *Track by Track* on Bluegrass Junction, but also other weird random thoughts such as an outfit I wore eight years ago or a childhood toy or restaurant I haven't thought of in a long time. Long trips like this give the psyche time to reorganize its files and shuffle things about.

A new state is right around the corner. This is my last night camping on the towpath.

Amie

Monday, April 06, 2015

Destination: Just Shy of Fort Ashby, West Virginia
Today's Miles: 15.70
Start Location: Town Creek Campsite, MD
Trip Miles: 305.19

Another cold morning following on the heels of a warm evening. Although I don't think I had an audience, I really beclowned myself this morning and periodically throughout the day. Normally at night, I have been sleeping in the capilene bottoms. They sort of serve as long johns or long underwear. Then in the morning I throw on a second bottom layer. The capilenes are wicking and good at regulating temperature as one warms up. Well, it was so toasty in the tent last night that I went to sleep without the long johns. I brought them into the sleeping bag with the other layers, and in the middle of the night I woke up chilly and slipped them on. I had a disconcerting feeling that I slipped them on backward, with the shorter "front" side in the back, and they felt lacking in the hindquarters, but I ignored it and got warm.

When I woke up cold, I dressed and was speedy about packing up. My last stop before proceeding west on the towpath was another pump so I could have a few miles' worth of water. This particular pump handle misbehaved a bit and really required my leaning into it to get water flowing. I set the Platypus on the ground for a few seconds so I could use both arms. Meanwhile, my fleece jacket had ridden up above my pack's waistbelt as it is wont to do, and the still-backward long johns had fallen perilously low so that I was now mooning any fellow users of the towpath as I struggled to get water. I know there was crack exposure because I could feel the cold breeze back there.

I hitched up my pants and proceeded on. In a few miles it was hello, West Virginia! I think there's a John Denver song in there somewhere, but I could be mistaken. I needed to make a quick resupply stop, and I asked about services at the bridge that crosses into WV. The toll booth attendant was unsure of any services on the WV side, so I backtracked a bit to Old Town, MD, where the only cafe, inside an old schoolhouse, was closed on Mondays. I pulled up the still-backward long johns again and stopped into the post office to inquire about food. Old Town had nothing. However, the postal service worker gave me a granola bar and four bottles of water. Thank you, postal service.

It was back to rural roads and a little bit of traffic. The day warmed, and

94

I took off the rain pant, leaving only the long johns which were now constantly making me moon the traffic approaching from behind, but for the sleep pads on the bottom of my pack covering everything up back there. I didn't receive any honks or comments, so the sleep pads must have provided cover.

I was close to Fort Ashby when I spotted a church at my next turn. I decided to camp behind it before going into town. I approached to ask, but no one was there. I found a level spot and finally got rid of the offending pants and finished off the water, the granola bar, and a couple servings of oatmeal I had left. Overall a good day despite a mile or so of backtracking.

I will put my clothes on correctly in the morning prior to heading into civilization.

Amie

Tuesday, April 07, 2015

Destination: Keyser, WV
Today's Miles: 15.25
Start Location: Just Shy of Fort Ashby, West Virginia
Trip Miles: 320.44

Stealth camping successful. One car had pulled into the church parking lot around dusk, but I think it was just a turnaround, and not anyone checking on the tent behind the building. It rained a bit overnight, but the morning was clearing off and the camp pack-up was not too cold. I walked into Fort Ashby and ate a delicious breakfast BLT at Etta's Taste of the Town and had another cup of coffee.

The trail today was mostly on rural paved roads, and the scenery I would describe as pastoral, very nice homes and farms. Some of the farms had signs at the edge of the property noting who owned the farm or homestead and the names of the members of the family who live on the land. Very beautiful.

A few miles into the day, a man named Brian pulled onto the road on his tractor, turned it off, and asked how far I was going on the trail. He has seen many hikers come through the area. We talked a few minutes about past hikers, what towns contained what services, and where I was from. I mentioned Kansas, and he said many years ago he worked the wheat harvest one summer, and had cut wheat in Inman, KS. Yep. I know where that is. The next house up, his mother had come out to get her mail, and she asked if I needed anything. I said just some water. She invited me into the house to use the kitchen tap. She showed me the family photo, pointed out one of her daughters who is also a teacher, and said she was glad to have met me.

Freshly provisioned with water, I continued on. A few miles later, a man named Lawrence spoke to me and said he had received a call about a hiker headed his way. He and his wife Judith wanted to feed me lunch if I would accept, and it turns out they had just hosted Ryan C, fellow ADT pilgrim, a couple of weeks ago when it was cold. I went up to the house, and I must admit I cut a swath through their lunch offerings. I was hungry! I was decided that I would get in a few more miles on the day and call when I got near the school several more miles down the road.

Lawrence and Judith took me out for dinner and then offered the use of their guest house above the garage. The quarters were beautiful, with full kitchen, bedroom, laundry, just the greatest. The wood in most of the quarters is from trees on their property, and Lawrence and Judith said they had lived there for a bit when they were remodeling their home. We joked about remodeling, as constant house remodeling is a phenomenon I grew up with. I remembered the time our fridge was in the living room while our kitchen was out of order while being upgraded. We looked at some maps of the upcoming Dolly Sods region and some local roads. It gave me an idea of what was coming up for me the next few days.

A thousand thank-yous, Lawrence and Judith, for great accommodations. Another good, good day, and I was dressed properly the entire time.

Amie

Wednesday, April 08, 2015

Destination: Martin, WV
Today's Miles: 15.94
Start Location: Keyser, WV
Trip Miles: 336.38

Breakfast of cereal, banana, and coffee, and then Lawrence drove me back to the drop off point. Today was very still with a slight mist falling off and on. The trail continued to wind through farmland and mostly tidy homes with large lawns. Although the trees are still mostly bare, the lawns and vast pastures are green.

For some reason the past couple of times I have walked by cows grazing along their fence, the cows have followed me. I haven't even been eating when they follow me, either. Usually cows spook and run away, but these have walked right along the fence beside me until they reach the end of their pasture and then stare at me as I amble away.

The walking proceeded nicely although I was walking more slowly due to yesterday's resupply. Three bags of granola, some nuts, dried fruit, Clif bars, a Powerade, and water really weighted the pack down, but the small towns along the trail did not offer services. The next few coming up were map dots, not even a convenience store.

Later in the afternoon I met a man named Gary who has a son doing missionary work in Latvia. Yep. We know where that is. Mom, Dad, and my youngest sister lived in Estonia for several years, and I had a boss in college who was Latvian. He said that most people don't know where Latvia is. I laughed and said that most people have never heard of Estonia. What a small world it has seemed the last couple of days. We talked about the Baltic region, differences in lifestyles here in the states and over there, and the trails through and around the Dolly Sods area. I had a delicious dinner of chili and pound cake.

Gary said that a good breakfast for him a lot of mornings is coffee and a slice of pound cake. He was right. A fairly uneventful day, but a good day.

Amie

Friday, April 10, 2015

Destination: Petersburg, WV
Today's Miles: 35
Start Location: Martin, WV
Trip Miles: 371.38

I am going to roll the last two days into one entry because they felt like two halves of the same continuous effort. The mileage for two days is a guess. I am off trail momentarily, so I am basing the distance on time hiking and the effort it felt like I expended.

Yesterday I walked from Martin to Streby, knowing the Sods were coming up. I was expecting a long climb up to the Sods and the possibility of freezing temps. I was nervous about this stretch, but the outcome was different—and I guess a bit better.

Thursday I stealth camped after already having begun the climb up. I camped on a hillside with a flat spot big enough for the tent. My feet were pointed slightly downhill, so I had a bit of a funhouse effect a couple times during the night, but I slept surprisingly well. This morning I continued up. I treated the climb the same as I took the 7-mile climb up Cuesta back in CA: slow and easy. I took a couple of breaks to treat and drink water and to remove a layer, as it was actually fairly warm. I knew to continue into the boundary of the wilderness area on Fire Road 75, which I had been climbing, and the trail directions had me essentially cutting west through the middle of the Sods and then back onto WV roads and into another state park. Think of the Dolly Sods as an oval, my entering the oval at the top right, and the idea was to cut left through the center of the oval.

I stopped once for about five minutes and let my tent dry in the fierce wind at the top. The wind is notorious up there, and there is actually a wind farm being built. I continued on with the directions, which told me to cut across on the Blackbird Knob Trail. I found the trailhead fine and headed west. By this time it had begun to rain. Blackbird Knob Trail started out with a wooden footbridge as its surface, and I was delighted. Then the bridge ended and the trail was made of rocks and pine needles. And I will describe the trail as the rocks became fewer and it made its way west: goopy, sodden, boggy, muddy. Ridiculously slow and slippery, I could go on. I kept on it for a while, trying to eye the trail yet walk around it on the higher forest bed to keep my shoes from getting soaked through. Eventually the rocks ended, and I had to step into the muddy water. I felt like Principal Ed Rooney from *Ferris Bueller's Day Off* when he sneaks around Ferris's house to try to spy. He stomps in some mud next to a spigot, which sucks his shoe clean off of his foot. He then steps on the spigot, which turns the water on full blast, and sprays his sock, pants, and other foot, all the while Mr. Rooney is cursing under his breath.

Sigh

The trail eventually just ended in a confusion of trees and undergrowth, and I could not make heads or tails of where to go without crawling under some tree branches and risking getting so far off that I would be lost. I turned around and went back to the wide and clear Fire Road 75. It was still raining, and I slogged over to the Red Creek Campsite to hide in one of the two restroom buildings. I could hear voices in one, so I opened the door to the other, and there were two Boy Scout troop leaders, Gary and Theresa, in there hiding from the deluge, having had the same idea! Five Boy Scouts were making the small racket in the other restroom. They invited me in, haha, and next to the commode we made introductions, and they explained they had also camped last night but were concerned about the high wind and rain. They didn't want to risk staying up in the Sods in the weather and ruining these boys on camping forever. I asked if they would give me a ride down the hill if they decided to bail, and they agreed, twenty minutes later telling the boys they were bailing. I felt like less of a woos for wanting off the Sods if the Boy Scout leaders concurred that staying the night up there again would be royally un-fun.

We all walked the 5 or 6 miles back to their cars. I kept studying the map, hoping there was an alternate way to the west side of the Sods and onto WV 32. I didn't really want to go off trail, and the rain had stopped. But the western edge contained no Fire Road. Alas, I was ditching the ADT. But, to my credit, I actually hiked all the way through the Sods north to south, and covered as much of it as the book route would have sent me. The Sods did not completely defeat me. It did reroute me. I just did not want to risk those internal, mucky trails alone.

About a mile from the cars, we approached a scenic overlook. I took some pictures of the scouts and both leaders, and Gary wanted a picture of me and the boys. He said he would show the picture and tell everyone that the strange lady was their sherpa. That I had carried all their gear for them. I laughed and agreed to a photo, explaining that I had barely looked at my appearance for two days, so look out.

They dropped me at a very cute mom 'n pop motel here in Petersburg. I will look at the data book and maps and find a way to rejoin the actual trail as soon as possible. My shoes are drying quickly over the heater, I touched base with people who miss me, and all is well.

Here's to campground chemical toilet buildings for being a stellar location for meeting great people.

Cheers!

Amie

Saturday, April 11, 2015

Destination: Petersburg, WV
Today's Miles: 0
Start Location: Petersburg, WV
Trip Miles: 371.38

My first zero day. The hotel clerk had offered to drive me to Seneca Rocks, which would be closer to my data book directions, but she was off work at 8 this morning. I woke up at 7:15, which gave me 45 minutes to pack everything up that was strewn about the room, eat breakfast, and make a reroute plan. Not happenin'. Plus, this motel room is cozy and cheap. I decided to rest a day.

After eating fruit for breakfast, the morning consisted of chores. I cleaned out my pack, reorganized gear, washed my cookpot and spork in the sink, and drank tons of water. I am becoming quite the connoisseur of tap water from various regions. The spring water in this part of WV is very good.

The clerk found me in the breakfast room before she left and gave me a WV highway map. Thank you! I have a plan to get back on track. I used my phone to pinpoint the towns that have services, and hopefully they're still in business. I found that I am east of the Sods and Canaan Valley. Drat. Extra miles.

I really try on hotel nights not to make a huge mess in the rooms. I try not to get leaves all over the heater and floor when drying out my tent, or get dirt everywhere from my shoes. I don't want to feel like I am pulling a *Fear and Loathing in Las Vegas* on these motel rooms.

I caught up on reading the news and then found the *Godfather* marathon on AMC. How have I never watched these films in succession before? Really got into them while resting. I found it hard to stay off my feet and make myself be still today. I guess that is somewhat of a positive, as the Sods and hiking 6 or so miles after a long climb in wet shoes while keeping the pace of 16-year-old Boy Scouts at the end of the day didn't wreck me as much as I thought it might. That, or it's inertia and I am totally in denial. Anxious to get walking again in the morning. It is supposed to be clear and in the seventies the next few days.

Amie

Sunday, April 12, 2015

Destination: Seneca Rocks, WV
Today's Miles: 20.40
Start Location: Petersburg, WV
Trip Miles: 391.78

I set off fairly early from the Homestead Inn and headed southwest toward Seneca Rocks. My goal, after studying the highway map, was to return to the trail at Phillipi. I marked a route that would give me a town or two with services along the way, and I would also not backtrack east, which is why I decided against hooking back up at Parsons or Davis.

The weather was great, sunny and in the seventies. I quickly got into my shorts, and today was the first time I used my calf-high Goretex gaiters. I am so glad I brought these because they really protect my legs from weeds and pricklies on the shoulders of roads, and they keep the pebbles and dirt out of my shoes. The first 8 or 10 miles of road had a beautiful, wide grass shoulder. There were cabins every half mile or so for rent, and it made sense because I passed a town called Cabins. There were a few cars parked along the shoulder here and there, and people were fishing or, as in the case of two ladies I met, kayaking. One of the ladies grew up in Shawnee Mission, KS.

At around mile ten, I happened upon a great little country store. What a find! I stopped in, and there was a small eating area where I was able to set down my pack and walk around to pick up some snacks. And use the restroom in a dignified manner, very important and increasingly rare these last few weeks. The store was very cute, with WV merchandise and a mountaineer flavor. The bags of horehound and sassafras candy grabbed my interest, as well as the Bourbon in a Bag, which turned out to be taffy. I didn't want to spend money on junk calories, although the hard candy would be fun, so I settled on some peanut butter crackers and a pecan log. The pecan log turned out to have a vanilla nougat and sugary center and very few pecans. I kicked myself for not just grabbing the wild huckleberry chocolate bar instead.

As the day progressed, I saw some interesting sights. There was a junky cabin perched precariously at the edge of the river with a wooden platform extended out over the water. I don't know what was supporting it. On top at the edge was a seat that looked to have been removed from the back of someone's minivan. I guess the person will fish in comfort. I wouldn't sit on it for fear of plunging into the river, minivan seat, wood planks, all. I saw a few replicas of Boyd Crowder's truck from the show *Justified.*

I ended the day walking into Seneca Rocks. At my highways' intersection there was a nice campground. I strode onto the property, and a sign gave the prices for parking your RV, renting a teepee, or planting your tent for the night. I didn't want to rent a teepee, and I looked for a camp host to pay the eight bucks' fee for tent camping, but could find no person, cabin, or teepee that looked official. So I dropped anchor anyway and figured if anyone from the teepee rental office did a sweep to see if there were any squatters, I would just apologize and pay. It was very warm at the end of the day, and it was lovely not to have to jump right into my sleeping bag. Right around the corner is Yokum's Grocery for a bit more trail food and water in the morning.

A great day. I think this has been my favorite day so far.

Amie

Monday, April 13, 2015

Destination: Just outside Harman, WV
Today's Miles: 14
Start Location: Seneca Rocks, WV
Trip Miles: 405.78

Well, I inadvertently scammed the teepee place out of eight bucks. Didn't mean to, but there you have it. Stopped into the grocery and picked up a few things and a gallon of water. I filled both bladders and then forced myself to finish off the rest of the gallon as I walked the first couple of miles. I am glad I did because it heated up again today. I was still off trail at this point, which means that I didn't know the condition of these roads or what the shoulders were like. They are not interstates by any account, but you just don't know the technicalities or whether they have been deemed safe for walking. I fully expected to get the law called on me, which has not happened yet, but yesterday I did get my very first blister from stepping off onto the grass shoulder later in the day when it was warm. This put my left foot at a weird angle and gave me a dime-sized blister under the callous there. I left it alone and proceeded to walk on it today. It didn't give me too much trouble.

The first few miles climbed a bit but not too harshly. I walked by an old Mennonite community, and there was a church just beyond it whose pastor was named Dusty Twigg. Farms for a bit, and then the road began to climb. And climb. And hairpin curve. And climb some more. I felt as if I were climbing back into the Sods. Miles of climbing. I finally reached the top and saw the sign that read "Eastern Continental Divide." Well, no wonder! Sheesh. I felt a great sense of accomplishment, and I didn't even really feel tired. I was just worried about the blister and the possibility of forming new ones walking downhill for a long stretch.

At the top just past this sign was a group of three line trucks, the big bucket trucks for working on power lines. There was also a line crew of 5 or 6 guys standing around their trucks. I don't know if they were contemplating driving down that narrow road with all the curves or what. I approached them and they got quiet. There was a pregnant pause. I said hello, they returned the salutation, and one of the guys, probably the foreman, said to one of his guys, "You see, Walker, if she can walk up it, you can surely drive one of these trucks down it." I turned around and smiled.

I got to the bottom of the grade and could feel another blister on my toe coming on. I knew I had not gone far on the day, but the long climb slowed my pace down. I decided to pop into the public library in the small town of Harman to inquire about a motel or bed and breakfast. I wanted to keep walking, but I also smelled bad from sweat (80s today) and sunscreen. Plus, I wanted to check my feet. There were two ladies in the library who were helpful in describing the area and what was ahead as far as motel or camping. I almost rented a cabin from the librarian, but with no chance to do laundry there, I decided to proceed on and wait to spend money when guest laundry was available.

I continued west out of Harman and bought a Gatorade at the gas station. I made it another mile maybe when a blue car pulled over and honked. It was Jill from the library. She had called her husband and told him about me, and wanted to get his permission to bring me home. He is of the travelling bent, and he had said, "Yes, bring her on home."

Jill opened the trunk and said, "C'mon, get on in. Let's get you a bed for the night and a meal and a load of laundry." I was ushered into their home, an old Mennonite church built in 1906/7, and refurbished into a great two-story home with beautiful ceilings and my favorite: woodstoves. I told Jill and Mike that before I got too social I needed to brush my teeth, unbrushed since the previous night, and clean up, uncleaned since the motel night. Wowza.

I got a shower and started my load of profoundly unbiblical laundry. We sat out on the porch and talked a bit. Mike and Jill got their porch swing back into commission on my account and let me be the first to try it out for the summer season. Dinner was venison steaks, potatoes, cauliflower, and salad. The greatest. I got a tour of Mike's blacksmith shop and the evening's topics of conversation were many, mainly focusing on religion, the state of the union, travelling, and hiking.

I went to bed about 8 to the sounds of sheep baaa-ing. A day that started out pretty tough ended up perfect. And Jill had run my laundry through the washer a second time. A wise woman.

Amie

Back on the Map

Tuesday, April 14, 2015
Destination: Junction of CR 2/3 and 1/1
Today's Miles: 15.15
Start Location: Just outside Harman, WV
Trip Miles: 420.93

Breakfast was toast, grits, ham, and eggs. Jill drove me to Phillipi, the closest town that would put me back on the ADT TBTs. In other words, back on the actual trail. She stopped for gas at Kroger and I picked up a few groceries. We found Pike St. I put on my pack, she said a prayer over me, and I was off. Thank you, thank you, Jill and Mike, for meals, laundry, accommodations, and prayers for my spirit of discernment.

At breakfast I calculated the mileage had I stayed in the Sods and walked the data book route to Phillipi. I also calculated how far I have actually walked from Red Creek Campsite, which was up there in the Sods where I veered from the trail. As it stands right now, I owe the trail about 34 miles, counting the ride I got into Denton on my third day out. I figure I have walked maybe 12 miles of off-trail pursuits, so I am not doing too bad. I am close to even-steven on mileage to this point according to the data book. Besides, today the trail was twisting and turning around the Tygart River. At few points did I feel as if I were walking due west. Several times the TBTs had me heading northeast or southeast on a county road.

Moreover, the route was hard to pin down a couple times today. At one intersection, there were three possible roads. The county roads were not marked, there was no ADT blaze, and so I resorted to my old-school compass, GPS waypoints, and dead reckoning. I took the correct road, as validated a few miles later by a homeowner who verified the county road and gave me a bottle of water. In addition to the CR numbers, the roads have names, such as Rushing River Road or something, which is what people put on their mailboxes. The volunteer fire department uses some other numerical designation. The GPS only pulls up major state roads and interstates. So with no cell phone service in the valleys, one must depend on a basic compass and the "feel" for how far one has trekked since the last directional point. It's tiring. I never went off trail today, but I was slow in keeping on it. All in all, if this trail pointed west more, I would feel guilty about the 34 miles of cheating.

I had drained both blisters and given them Band-Aids. They did okay today. I favored them a bit on my left foot, which slowed me down too.

Early afternoon an SUV pulled up beside me, and I heard the driver say, "Hello, we're not psycho hillbillies or anything. We met Josh Seehorn (Outdoor Josh) last year when he came through and just wondered if you were hiking the trail." It sort of reminded me of my "I'm not homeless or anything" speech I give every few days. One of the passengers said, "Well, if ya got a set, ya got a set," a recurring theme of people I meet from time to time. I laughed. I don't know if this takes a set so much as lots of reading and all kinds of prep. I've never really thought of myself as having a set. I just become interested in things and want to go see, try, or experience them. Anyway, they gave best wishes and drove on.

The trail continued to wind along the Tygart River most of the day. I found a place to camp around 7. I had the peanut butter crackers for an evening meal. Where I camped was near a cemetery and small church. This did not scare me. The church was built in the 1830s, so I figure the souls resting there have been at peace for quite some time, and they would have no cause to bother with me.

Here's to one's internal compass, physical, emotional, and spiritual navigation, and having a set.

Cheers!

Amie

Wednesday, April 15, 2015

Destination: Grafton, WV
Today's Miles: 16.10
Start Location: Junction of CR 2/3 and 1/1
Trip Miles: 437.03

I was slow again today. Part of it was my treading lightly on the blisters. Another factor was that my head was a smidge lower than my feet at my campsite last night, so I had a little funhouse effect a couple times during the night. Didn't sleep the best, but not the worst, either. And I did not have my morning coffee today. I need to pick up another fuel canister, and it was chilly this morning; therefore, I did not want to have a cold coffee beverage, even with vanilla creamer. Plus, I just like walking slowly at times. This is not a race against anything.

The trail was confusing twice again today. The county roads at their junctions went unlabeled. Once around Hiram, I saw the brown post with the ADT blaze and the arrow lying in the ditch. The post was broken off near its base, perhaps by snowplows, a car wreck, or someone messed with it. I was able to use my phone a bit more today, which was great. MapQuest does bring up all the tiny county roads. Use of my phone helped greatly today.

The trail wound around Tygart Lake and Tygart State Park. I did feel like I was walking west more often today. Random observation, I saw a sign on one home that looked like the "Slow, Children Playing" sign, but instead the sign said "Slow, Adults Playing," and instead of a silhouette of a child running, there were silhouettes of a banjo, guitar, and maybe a mandolin.

Happy Tax Day as well, I know, grrrrrrrrrr. A funny story did come to mind while walking, being that it is tax day. I think it was Becky who hosted me in MD who told me about a guy who was hiking the Appalachian Trail, and he was doing his taxes while on trail. Hahahaha! I laughed aloud thinking of hikers dragging the forms along. I did my taxes back in February. So if I was spotted using my cell phone today, it was probably a peek at a maps app, not my last-minute taxes.

This was also day two in a row again of wearing the long johns (on correctly) being that it was cooler. Wearing the bottoms several days in a row reminds me of a character from one of the Craig Johnson Longmire mysteries, I think *Junkyard Dogs*. There was an old man in the book who lived in such squalid conditions and never bathed, that his leg hair had grown through his long johns. Even hiking laundry doesn't get that bad.

After walking through the state park, the trail entered the town of Grafton. On the outskirts of town, there were some neatly kept homes and some people out on their lawn tractors manicuring their large, lush lawns. But once I got into town, I hate to report, I walked a couple miles through a sad, run-down town. Nearly every home is weather faded with paint peeling, junk stacked everywhere. The town looks like an old coal mining town or some kind of manufacturing town now defunct. Or it reminds me of a rust-belt city, old brick buildings decaying. I wish I could report better. I am not trying to judge Grafton or measure WV by this standard at all. But this town really struck me. There doesn't look to be much opportunity for its people. I hope I'm wrong.

I wanted a motel tonight. I needed to dry out my tent, and it may be raining in the morning. There is only one gig in town, and my fears that this motel might be a microcosm of Grafton proved valid. The front part of the motel room looks like it may have been remodeled in the nineties, when burgundy and dark green were popular. The bathroom and sink area, however, still have the 1950s pink, I am sure all original tile, shower, and fixtures. There is seriously a plunger sitting next to the toilet, out in the open with no shame, as if a plugged toilet is enough of a recurring problem that they just said, "To hell with it," and left the plunger in the offending bathroom. It is really a doozie. This is the first time ever that I have placed a motel hand towel in the bottom of the shower for me to stand on while showering.

Ryan C, who is a couple weeks ahead of me, commented in one of his journal entries that one motel he stayed in could be complimented for driving away repeat customers. I wonder if this is the one. I feel no qualms about spreading my tent to dry in here. I will be sleeping in my sleeping bag for sure.

I have to spruce up today's gloomy municipal vista and hikinglodging report with some humor. My nephew Dain has been my frequent road tripping and travelling buddy. He likes to ride to Grandma's with me in the car from CA to KS. One time when Dain was about 6, we made the drive, and he had been asleep in the back seat. I drove into Tucumcari, NM, which is also pretty run down, with lots of old junk cars everywhere and closed gas stations and businesses. Dain, who is used to CA suburbia and everything looking fairly new, had woken up and popped his head up. He sleepily looked around at Tucumcari and the crumbs of the Route 66 era, kind of turned his nose up at it, and said, "Amie, this town looks old." It was so cute and funny. I said yes, that it was older than what he was used to seeing. On every long drive, Dain, Ashley, or I point out some crummy part of a town we drive through and wonder if Dain thinks it looks old.

If Dain were to walk into this room, he would go into the bathroom and say, "Amie, this motel looks old. Let's leave."

I agree with your astute observation, Dain.

Amie

Thursday, April 16, 2015

Destination: Bridgeport, WV
Today's Miles: 22.71
Start Location: Grafton, WV
Trip Miles: 459.74

I slept very well last night, and I feel like I was a tad harsh on the poor Grafton motel. I will give it one additional point for having complimentary coffee in the lobby that was actually not weak, but I take back half a point for no breakfast and no small personal coffee maker in the room. I also refund it half a point because the shower, which was clearly installed prior to all the do-gooder regulations on low-flow shower heads and energy star water heaters, was hot with good pressure. I will award it the other half point when it is clear I did not contract a previously eradicated strain of toe rot from walking on the floor.

The marginal motel reminds me of a bright student named Mikaela I had about eleven years ago. She and her family travelled all over the country showing horses, and for one assignment in my speech class, she wrote a hilarious speech about all the terrible hotels and motels she had visited during their travels. I still have that speech. I keep it in my folder of past student work that I use for class writing samples from time to time. Mikaela, I thought of you today as I left the questionable motor lodge, but in a good way!

The trail was much better today, easy to follow at most turns. It rained a bit off and on, but not enough to soak through my shoes. It really has to come down to permeate the shoes. My socks and feet stayed dry. I passed by some nice homes and properties as the trail neared Bridgeport. I received the one-finger steering wheel wave from a man driving a truck pulling a trailer loaded with 2 x 4's. I saw some ducklings waddling along. They were so cute. Alas, they scurried away before I could get a picture.

As the trail neared Bridgeport, I began looking for somewhere to camp. Nothing presented itself, and soon the trail left CR 1 and followed Highway 131. I found this 2-mile section entering Bridgeport to be very harrowing and dangerous. There was no shoulder, the ditch was filled with water, and I was stopping every 5 to 25 steps it seemed to lean into the hillside and plunge my left trekking pole into the earth to lean out of traffic. Not cool. And once you're in it, there's no sense in backing out and backtracking because you'll be on a narrow shoulder going the opposite direction, only to find yourself taking extra steps to reroute into Bridgeport. The adrenaline was flowing these two miles. I can't believe I did not get honked at once.

I then walked a few miles through Bridgeport, a nice town. I passed by their middle, high, and elementary schools. There were events going on at each one it seemed, as the parking lots were full. It had begun raining again a bit, and I knew I was already 20 miles into my day, so I was trying to find a camping spot. There was absolutely nothing that would be acceptable or that would hide me. I followed the trail on past the schools and up a hill that seemed to be leaving town, but only more neighborhoods presented themselves.

The CR wound back to the right again, nearing Interstate 79, and I checked the directions again to see just when I would be back in a rural area. The trail crossed under the interstate. Don't worry, no walking on I-79, and then next for points of interest was a mall. I spotted a Super 8 off to the right and made a judgment call. It was nearing 7, I didn't know how many more miles it would truly take to clear the town once and for all and find a safe camping spot, and it was still raining a bit. Two motel nights in a row is not good on the budget and was not in the day's plan, but safety comes first.

So here I am and all is dry, clean, cozy, and well. It is raining right now and looks as if f it may rain again in the morning. I may use the rainy morning for a load of laundry, coffee, and breakfast, and check out at the last possible second. That may be tough for me because I am an early morning person. I like to get the day and the hiking moving ASAP.

Strong mileage today. Tomorrow I will pass Clarksburg, and I believe I will be stepping onto a rail-to-trail path soon.

Amie

Crossing Highway 50

Friday, April 17, 2015
Destination: Wolf Summit, WV
Today's Miles: 19.54
Start Location: Bridgeport, WV
Trip Miles: 479.28

I woke around 6:30 fully expecting to do a quick load of laundry prior to hitting the road. I gathered my quarters and dollar bills, heading for guest laundry even before my first cup of java. Of course, the machine that dispenses single units of detergent was out of order. I went to the front desk to inquire politely whether they sold the small boxes from behind the desk, as many motels do, since their machine was broken. The answer was a terse "no." Hmpf. Just for that, I spirited away an extra apple from the breakfast area to eat later as a snack. Ha.

I packed and waited for the quick little rain shower to subside, then was off and walking at my usual time. The trail left Bridgeport and followed small county roads once again for a few miles. The town of Clarksburg was next on the agenda. I did not need to partake of any services in Clarksburg, so I scooted through it.

I was almost passing under Highway 50 to leave town when a grey truck slowed next to me. I glanced to my right swiftly and then looked straight ahead, probably giving them a "buzz-off" look in the process. The driver then honked once, a very timid staccato honk, and then a voice timidly asked, "Are you hiking . . . the ADT?" At this point I figured the truck's occupants were probably bona fide, so I gave them my attention. And who in the passenger seat did I spy? Ryan W, fellow hiker. Ryan is walking to raise awareness for war vets' PTSD and the tragedy of veteran suicide. The driver pulled over and we made introductions. Ryan has chosen alternate routes a bit to stay on paved roads with his cart and to remain in more populated areas to get the word out for his cause. But I caught up with him today in Clarksburg. That now makes two other 2015 hikers I have met in person. Happily met!

Ryan was actually getting ready to do a TV spot for I believe the local news, so I wished him luck. Before I proceeded on, they asked if I needed anything. I replied, just a bottle of water if you have any on ya. He stuffed three bottles of water and some Clif snacks into the side pockets of my pack, and his buddy gave me some cherry tomatoes. The chance meeting put a pep in my step.

112

I then followed the map out of town on a CR that crossed HWY 50. Again. This was a 4-mile jog west, and at its terminus, the map has the hiker walking on HWY 50 for 9/10s of a mile. Huh? Then the correct exit was to the north, meaning I had to cross 50 for the fourth time in one day.

I chilled at the junction for a second or two and psyched myself up for a mile of bedlam. There is a huge shoulder on HWY 50, but the traffic is moving swiftly and it's loud. I made it just fine. I was only honked at once, and it was by a trucker. It could have been an angry trucker, a lecherous trucker, or a concerned trucker. I'm not sure which.

Safely onto a CR once again, I began thinking of a childhood memory that involved HWY 50. When my sister Andrea and I were little, we lived in a house that was just a few hundred yards south of HWY 50. The general whisper of the traffic noise was a given, and it used to lull me to sleep at night when my bedroom windows were open. We were allowed to ride our bikes, tricycles, scooters, and roller skates around the neighborhood, but heading north toward HWY 50 was verboten.

One afternoon we got home from the store, I think, and Mom went into the house for about 1.7 seconds. In her absence, Andrea jumped onto a little 4-wheeled scooter of hers, I believe it was a plastic horse scooter, and made north for HWY 50 as fast as her little legs could push her. Mom came back out the front door to see Andrea vanishing on the horizon, heading north toward HWY 50. She ran after Andrea and snatched her off the scooter. Andrea received a few spankings on the way back to the house, and I don't remember the tractor beam pull of HWY 50 ever being a problem again. But don't feel bad, Andrea, for getting a spanking due to this road. Heck, I wanted to paddle myself for walking on it and crossing it repeatedly today.

After leaving HWY 50 with white knuckles, I pried the trekking poles from my grasp and saw that my terrain quickly changed for the better as I set foot on the North Bend Rail Trail. I walked on it a bit before deciding to call it a day. And this trail has mile markers too like the C & O. I checked the directions, and the mile markers are pretty close to counting down the miles to the Ohio border.

I also saw that I was approaching the first tunnel through which this trail passes. There are several, and while most of them are shorter than the Paw Paw Tunnel, one of these is reputed to be haunted. I have read about these tunnels, but I can never remember which tunnel is the one. Supposedly a ghostly lady in a white dress is still a presence in one of them.

Now, do I really believe that a ghost in a white dress is going to follow me through a silly old stone tunnel and get me? Psssht. No.

All the same, I shall leave possibly haunted tunnels for in the morning.

Amie

Saturday, April 18, 2015

Destination: West Union, WV
Today's Miles: 16.83
Start Location: Wolf Summit, WV
Trip Miles: 496.11

Woke up to a very foggy and still morning. The outside of the tent was soaked, inside also from condensation. I made my cold coffee concoction since I am still in need of stove fuel.

I continued along the NBRT today, and I walked through two tunnels. You can see the light at the opposite end, and it's visually tricky. You think at first you won't need a flashlight. Then you get a hundred feet or so into the tunnel, and it gets very dark. The flashlight quickly comes out so that you may watch your footing. The tunnels are also cold, even on an eighty degree day. You can feel the cold emanating from them before you enter.

I soon entered Salem and rejoiced in the greatest of days in hiking life: mail drop day! Thank you, Aunt Donna for the Subway card. Perfect. Thank you, Mom and Dad for the box of goodies, including a small green army bag. The bag was my grandpa Adamson's, and he carried it with him during his time in the military. I will now carry it along with me.

I rearranged my pack a bit while in the post office, and I sent back the Denali fleece, both beanies, the heavier pair of Smartwool socks, and the long johns. So, Mom, when this box arrives, it would be best to open it quickly over the washing machine, hold your nose, dump contents into machine, slam the lid, and exit the area for a bit.

I still have layers with me, the gloves, and Marmot jacket. I took a little rest around 2:00 to spread out the tent to dry in the sun. There was a paved area with a guardrail, perfect to lay out the tent. There was a slight breeze, and a couple times I picked it up and let it billow a bit. It dried fast, and I also checked for bugs. There was one small spider and an ant trying to ride along. I put a stop to that, and repacked it. I can tell the difference in weight between carrying a wet tent and a dry one.

I knew I was approaching West Union. The WV trail coordinators live near there, so I gave Sharon a call and we chose a pick-up spot. I finished out my hiking day, and I got to spend the evening with her and her husband. A load of laundry, a meal, a bed, overall a really nice day.

I now have Grandpa Adamson watching over me as well.

Amie

Next Item on Kaden's Scavenger Hunt

Sunday, April 19, 2015
Destination: Ellenboro, WV
Today's Miles: 17.92
Start Location: West Union, WV
Trip Miles: 514.03

All right, Kaden, here is another item to check off your list. I saw some pretty red flowers today. Aunt Amie thinks this will meet or exceed the qualifications for your nature hunt.

Breakfast with Sharon and Paul included French toast, bacon, fruit, avocado, hot coffee, and bananas for the road. The joke at breakfast was that Sharon sometimes stands at the bar to eat, while Paul sits. This makes her more apt to clear the meal's dishes quickly because she can pivot back and to the right to the sink in one efficient movement. Paul got his plate swept away fairly quickly upon finishing his breakfast, then mentioned that it was okay because when he was in the military, if you looked up from your plate, you must have been finished eating. I was the slow one at breakfast, but I got my fill.

They dropped me back at the trail before they headed to church. A nice evening, a fun morning, thank you, Sharon and Paul.

The rail trail went through two more tunnels today, and in the very first one of my morning, I had another couple Principal Ed Rooney mud moments. The entrance to it was pretty much water wall to wall. So much for having my favorite socks clean for a couple days' use. The two tunnels today were shorter, and I believe I will reach the, ahem, haunted tunnel tomorrow.

Yesterday just before West Union, two of the NBRT's maintenance personnel were waiting for me next to the old train depot as I walked by. One man follows Trail Journals, and he knew who I was as I approached. I am not used to people knowing who I am. They wanted to let me know that there was a washout in the trail a few miles up. They explained how to get around it, and they gave me a business card in case I got hung up around the downed portion. They also gave me the large, colorful brochure about the trail, campsites, history, and such. Thanks! So today I rerouted for just a couple miles along Old Highway 50 (that thing again!) and then regained the trail at Wright Road, just as they had dispatched to Sharon late last night. No problem.

As the old railroad trail passes through and near these tiny towns, I think of how many small towns sort of withered and blew away when the railroads stopped coming through. I saw an old, abandoned building with benches out front that could have been the old Whistle Stop Cafe from Fannie Flagg's book *Fried Green Tomatoes.* I crept up on the porch and peeked in the front door. The place was dark and looked to be full of bric-a-brac. I'll bet it was a happenin' little place at one time.

One former railroad town that is one of my favorites is Los Alamos, hidden just off the 101 in Santa Barbara County, CA. The main street in town, Bell St., sort of froze in time when the trains stopped coming through. It is still a teensy town, but it has become quite a foodie destination. My favorite was the 1880s Union Hotel when Bobby Ostini was head chef there. The impact of the nation's railroads on the rise and fall of little communities was significant.

A light rain fell off and on most of the afternoon, and as the day wore on, I was checking the weather for a break in the rain to do a quick tent set-up. I put up the tent while inside it for the first time this evening. I knew it could be done, but I have never had reason to try until today as I felt some sprinkles come down while I unpacked the tent. Mission successful, and it is sprinkling just a bit now. Tomorrow it is supposed to rain more, and I will be hitting the North Bend State Park, so maybe I will have a bit of a respite from the elements when I get there.

Except for my spectacularly vile shoes that are in need of replacing, all is well.

Amie

Monday, April 20, 2015

Destination: Just Shy of Walker, WV
Today's Miles: 21.90
Start Location: Ellenboro, WV
Trip Miles: 535.93

Around 2 a.m. a lil' squall blew through. There were a few flashes of lightning, a couple rumbles of thunder, and it rained very hard for about 30 minutes. A few minutes into the rain shower, I felt a few minuscule droplets begin hitting my face. I thought, "Oh no, the tent is leaking in this downpour. All is lost." But what was happening was quite a bit of pressure was created from the large raindrops, which were striking the tent, which then caused the small condensation droplets on the inside roof to release and fall bit by bit. Solution? I keep a PakTowl in my hip belt of my pack. The PakTowl packs down to about the size of a golfball, and it's easy to forget I have it. But I remembered it this morning and used it to wipe the condensation from the tent walls. I and the gear stayed dry, except for what touches the tent wall and gets damp from condensation. The rain passed, and I fell back asleep after an hour or so. The tent gets an A+. Last night's quality of sleep gets a C.

I rousted myself at daybreak and peeked out the door. The sun was coming out, and there were very few clouds. I put my wet shoes back on and cringed, and then cringed again when I saw a gentleman walking slowly in my camp's direction. *Oh no*, I thought, *busted for stealth camping!* I began mentally prepping my defense and closing arguments, including my I'm Not Homeless or Anything overture. I played it cool, and when he was near he drawled, "Now that's whatcha cowl a tany howse!" I replied in my best twangy flatlander dialect, "Yayah, and it keeps my dry." I wasn't trying to be rude or make the fun of the way he talked; I was just trying to build a sense of camaraderie before being questioned about the tent's placement. He lumbered on, not seeming to find my camp spot odd at all. Yessssssss. In the clear.

I knew from the previous night's research that there was at least a gas station just around the corner. A gas station would have some joe. I regained the trail and made the curve, only to spot a McDonald's also. A large, whole milk latte. *O, the Joy!* I got my latte as well as good wishes from a worker and a customer who noticed I was likely on the Rail to Trail.

Despite the negative expectations I had whipped up in my own mind in the middle of the night listening to the rain, the trail conditions turned out

117

to be nice. The slightly raised gravel rail bed was pretty dry, and there were few mud puddles to skirt. The sun stayed out most of the morning. I passed through the haunted tunnel unbothered. I didn't even know it was the one until a few hours later when I checked the trail brochure for mileage.

I stopped during one sunny spell to dry at least the inside of the tent. I repacked it and then put the PakTowl in my left hand and sort of wound it around my left trekking pole so it could flap in the breeze and dry as I walked. I felt a bit like Steven Tyler from Aerosmith, who always had some flamboyant scarf wrapped around his microphone stand when he sang. He would use the scarf to fling the mic stand around to punctuate his singing. I didn't fling my pole around with the PakTowl, but I thought of Aerosmith videos just the same.

I later met a fellow hiker, one of the few folks I've seen using the trail, and he was 63. He said his trail name was Firefly, and he was training himself for the AT. He looked and sounded much more experienced than I, and we chatted then went our opposite directions.

I went through the charming little town of Cairo. I stopped at the Trail-side Cafe and had a grilled chicken salad. I wanted to linger longer, but I knew I was going to get rained on again before the evening was through, and I needed to step it up and get as close to Parkersburg and a motel before calling it a day. I can only abide sticking my feet in wet, cold, swampy shoes so many mornings in a row. I am just not that hardcore.

Sure enough, it poured one more time, and it stopped just before I reached the last tunnel on the NBRT. I was hoping I could hide out in the tunnel and wait out the rain as I was watching the clouds gather. Shoes, soaked again. This motivated me even more to get a move on. One more night of possibly rainy camping tonight and wet shoes tomorrow were tolerable as long as the next day could be a town day. Good miles for today, and I didn't even get any Aerosmith songs stuck in my head while trying to fall asleep.

Amie

Tuesday, April 21, 2015

Destination: Parkersburg, WV
Today's Miles: 14.10
Start Location: Just Shy of Walker, WV
Trip Miles: 550.03

Today was one of those days that started off irritating and then ended divinely. I rose at my usual time with a get 'er done attitude. I wanted to get to Parkersburg in time enough to do an early motel check-in, giving me time to relax, enjoy the room, get things drying, and do some studying of the Ohio maps and plan for the next few days. Furthermore, at the top of my checklist was scoping out an upcoming post office and getting new shoes in the mail forthwith.

I got up and indulged myself in a string of negative thoughts that went something like this: *I'm tired of wet shoes in the morning. Why do I always seem to be camping on rainy nights? I'm tired of packing this wet tent. I don't feel like braiding my hair. I'll just let it be ratty, I don't care. I totally need a new toothbrush. This grass is too tall right here; it's gonna soak my shoes even more before I even make it three steps. I am still out of stove fuel. Why is this Thermarest mattress so hard to squish the air out of and roll up small? Why do those birds have to chirp all night, even when it's sprinkling? I'm tired of hauling this trash sack around. I hate sunscreen. Why are there, like, a million small towns along this rail trail, but none of them seem to have a gas station or cell phone service? This pack strap is hurting my left shoulder already. These trekking pole straps are soaked. I don't want to get my gloves back out. It's almost May; it shouldn't be all cold and stuff in the mornings anymore. Why do sticks keep getting caught in the strap of my gaiters and I have to break my stride and pick them out, like, once a day? Why can't these people clean the junk out of their yards? Why do these dogs keep barking at me when I am clearly out of their range of vision? Are they barking thinking about me? Do I smell that bad? How much longer to Parkersburg? Didn't I just pass mile marker 3? Cue Napoleon Dynamite: Gosh!*

Four or five miles into the pouting, walking, and kicking the air, and when my hands were warm, I made a cold coffee beverage. My attitude and pace vastly improved. I skittered into Parkersburg, and MapQuested lodging. Here I had to make another judgment call. Sort of close to the trail included a Travelodge and Knight's Inn. Right on the trail, one block over, was a hotel with a name for which I was unsure of the pronunciation, indicating it was probably expensive. I called to make sure the hotel was open and legit and I wanted a heads-up on the price before I walked there. It was a bit spendy. I hesitated, and then I remembered that Ryan C's sister told me that Ryan's awful motel experience was in Parkersburg, so I headed for the hills, stayed on trail, and chose the nice one.

There was a doorman who stared at me when it became clear I was bound for this establishment, and I spoke using a crisp, almost British accent when I explained to the desk clerk that I had just called and would like to take the queen room. I delivered my I'm Not Homeless or Anything speech with a sophisticated lilt and cadence I have not employed for a while, and I was in. And I saved $15 using AAA.

Aaaaaah, the complaints of the morning are now obscured in the dust of a hot bath, a robe in the closet, lots of water to drink, and a bed that does not need the mattress corners checked for evidence of bedbugs. My rain-exposed belongings are drying, and I have spent a couple hours looking at what Ohio has to offer. New shoes are en route to my next maildrop. Now if I could only get the current shoes a bit further away from the bed so I cannot smell them as I bask in this excellent room.

Plus, I look at this night's splurging as my present to myself because I will cross over into my fourth state in the morning.

Amie

Wednesday, April 22, 2015

Destination: Layman, Ohio
Today's Miles: 18.88
Start Location: Parkersburg, WV
Trip Miles: 568.91

Woke early and made steady use of the hotel room's Keurig machine . I checked the weather obsessively while making some final trail notes. It was supposed to stop raining around 11, which would give me plenty of time for checkout and a decent hiking day. I enjoyed some coffee while watching the rain come down and tried waiting it out. An hour later, I was growing antsy, and the weather forecast had changed anyway, suggesting rain until early afternoon. So I got on the road around 9:30, petitioning the universe to make the rain stop, or rain softly enough that my shoes would not get soaked again.

I crossed the Ohio River and entered my fourth state under a rain shower. I stopped into Kroger for a grocery run, crammed everything into my pack, and I was off. The scenery in Ohio today was similar to WV, but some of the farms and houses are starting to look like Iowa. I tackled a few hills this morning. One or two hills were pretty steep, and then the hiker was teased because it looked as if you had a short downhill, only to find the road flat or just a less strenuous uphill for a piece. One of those M. C. Escher drawings came to mind, in which the staircases look to be going down, but upon studying the drawing, one realizes they are also going up.

The rain indeed stopped today shortly, and I found myself not necessarily going slow, but just enjoying the feel and movement of walking. I let my mind wander, no goal destination, no weather to outrun, just put one foot in front of the other. A nice feeling.

I passed an auto repair shop with a trailer home next to it. A few customers said hello, and then when I passed the trailer, someone leaned out the window (no screen in the window) and said, "Hey, what trail is this again?" I yelled back the name, and they pulled their heads back inside the trailer after saying thanks. It was really funny. I hope they get some screens on their trailer windows before summer rolls around.

The temperature dropped this afternoon, and the wind picked up. Lower temperatures is an acceptable trade-off for a dry week, in my book, though. As I neared my stopping point for the day, a family who lives along the trail waved a hello and offered to fill up my water containers for me. Awesome!

Good mileage, clear trail directions, and a pack full of yummy food. I am content. So long and thank you, West Virginia. You were kind to me.

Amie

Thursday, April 23, 2015

Destination: Chesterhill, OH
Today's Miles: 15.06
Start Location: Layman, Ohio
Trip Miles: 583.97

So the campsite I chose last night was between a little church and an A-frame home of a couple named David and Nancy. The family who gave me water just around the corner suggested I ask permission to drop anchor there. They said Nancy painted beautiful ceramic and china dishes, as well as designs on earrings and sold her wares at craft fairs and such. David's hobby was Old West reenacting-style firing of rifles and pistols. They would sometimes see him out on his land performing target practice, firing the old cowboy guns Old West style: with the hammer. I figured, what could be safer? A quiet little church on one side, and a rugged character on the other who can fire a six shooter literally from the hip and hit what he's aimin' at. I slept soundly. It was my best night yet of tent sleep.

Before I went to sleep, however, Nancy came outdoors and introduced herself. She said that when I woke up, just come over and knock on the door and I was welcome to "use the facilities." I did so, and I was more than ecstatic to use the restroom in a dignified manner and have running water with which to brush my teeth. Then she invited me to sit down and have some coffee with her, and I was doing cartwheels. When she asked if she could fix me some eggs, I was practically breakdancing. Not only did I get eggs, but they also bake homemade bread every night, and she carved off six huge slices and got out a canning jar filled with a heart-healthy butter mixed with canola oil. I ate three slices and made liberal use of the delicious butter. Breakfast was magnificent.

We chatted for a bit, and I thanked her for the food and facility inspection opportunity. I proceeded on after packing a mostly dry tent. The wind had quit last night upon my request just after I snuggled down into my bag. I had placed my poncho around the footbed of the bag to keep condensation off that portion anyway and to keep my feet warm. It worked. I will try that trick more often, although sometimes the poncho is too dirty and I don't want it touching anything, so it has to sit in the corner. I am really picky about keeping the inside of the tent clean.

One noteworthy topic that came to mind after I left David and Nancy's was how, except for the instance in the Dolly Sods when I asked for a ride

123

down the mountain, all the help I have been given has been offered to me. Every ride, meal, bed, water top-off, the hand of grace has been extended in my direction. Now that I am just a bit down the trail, more offers from those who live along have been arriving, some because they know the trail, and others because they have helped the guys who are ahead of me, and they know I am coming around the bend soon. All the help is much appreciated.

One person who is a major-league trail angel and who had contacted me a couple days prior was a guy named Jamie. He does maintenance for the Buckeye Trail along with his brother, and he was an AT hiker a few years back. Today was day two in a row of okay temperatures but a fiercely cold wind that I have not felt since the towpath. Jamie offered to pick me up in Chesterhill, and I said, sounds good!

What happened next was not his fault. I arrived at the appointed pick- up spot in Chesterhill about 30 minutes before 4. Jamie was to have been there at 4, and given that I had stopped the constant movement, the wind was really starting to cut through my three top layers and two pairs of pants. I went around to the side of the public library and hid in the doorway there to avoid the wind. The library was closed Thursdays, so I could not wait inside. Jamie texted and reported his Jeep had broken down, but his dad was on his way to rescue him. Could I wait? I agreed and wrapped my poncho around me.

As I waited, the sky began clouding over as if to rain. The wind was still swift, and the clouds were moving quickly. Cars at that intersection kept honking at a Chesterhill denizen who was constantly standing out in his front yard talking on the phone. The honking was startling each time. A sense of anxiety crept upon me because I was cold, sitting in a public build-ing doorway with a few people staring, and I felt guilty that Jamie's car had died on his way to get me.

Then, no kidding, a riderless horse clip-clopped right through the middle of town and past the library. It was the strangest sight. It felt like that scene in the play *Julius Caesar* right before the conspirators murder Caesar when there are all kinds of portents afoot: a storm brews, a lioness whelps in the street, an owl is out in the daytime. A man has his hand on fire, only to find the flesh unsinged. Shortly into my *Caesar* reverie, an Amish boy went by, leading the horse home. Jamie said they were on the way. I didn't see Ches-terhill citizens gang up on poor Cinna the Poet, so I knew it was all going to work out, but this was the first time since I have been out here that I did feel just a touch of that homeless/drifter feeling, waiting there by the library. Again, no one's fault. It was just one part of an overall good day.

Jamie and his father arrived in his mom's SUV, loaded me up, and I was saved from a night of camping in the cold. Dinner was a hot and gigantic bowl of chicken noodle soup, I slept like the dead in a small Shasta trailer next to their cabin on a sleeping mat that rivals my Tempurpedic bed, and once again all is right as rain. More help in amazing ways today.

Amie

Friday, April 24, 2015

Destination: Tecumsey Lake, Buckeye Trail, Ohio
Today's Miles: 10
Start Location: Chesterhill, OH
Trip Miles: 593.97

One grocery item I picked up in Belpre the other day was a loaf of Ezekiel 4:9 bread. It is one of the few breads I eat, when I am not walking 8 hours a day, anyway. If you look up this verse in the Bible, it does talk about gathering the different types of grains that go into a wholesome grain-based food. Anyway, I have not had my Ezekiel bread for a while. I found some at Kroger, and I finished the loaf today. Jonesing satiated.

This morning Jamie and I had coffee while I did a small load of laundry. The plan was to have his father pick us up, at which time they would drive me back to my Chesterhill map spot, and they would commence either fixing Jamie's Jeep or arranging to meet AAA and get it towed. It's on point to mention that last night as they drove me to the cabin, I began feeling carsick, even in the front seat. After hikers have been travelling at a walking pace day after day in usually quiet environs, being in a car feels strange. And I sicken easily on curvy roads, so I opened the window last night and was okay.

I don't know what was different about this morning, but about 15 minutes into the car ride, I was so ill. They pulled over, and I sat in the post office parking lot and tried to walk around a bit. I even went behind the PO, because I did not want to puke on their lawn or in the parking lot, thereby putting bad postal service karma out there. I need them for mail drops! I never puked, but I was shaky with weak knees. I got back in the car, and we drove a few more miles. It wasn't 5 minutes before I was obviously in need of exiting the vehicle. This time we were in front of closed-down snack shop and American Legion post. I put my head between my knees while Jamie's dad ran interference with passing traffic. Move along, nothing to see here. Jamie looked at my TBTs and checked them against the Buckeye Trail official maps.

I was nearly down for the count. I again felt so guilty that this great trail angel family was not only taking me somewhere again, but was now babysitting me along the curb in Murray City. I knew all I needed was some Powerade, slow walking, and not being in a smooth car on curvy roads, so I made another judgment call. I found where I was on the map, and said I would just hike from here, no more driving for me. Jamie needed to get his

126

Jeep taken care of, and they have their own trip planned for the weekend anyway. They pinpointed camping spots for the next two nights, I got a can of 7-Up, and I was off, wobbly and slowly. We made plans to meet up again on Sunday. Thank you, guys. I really am not this huge of a pansy 99% of the time.

Today I set foot on the Buckeye Trail, and as the maps say, follow the blue blazes. The portion I did today was challenging for me, not only because I was dangling on the precipice of puking for two hours, but because the trail had many hills, was through a wooded area, had several downed trees over the trail that I had to climb over, and featured a few streams to ford. Luckily the streams were very shallow and I could pick my way around them without getting wet. The trail was very well marked; it was just slow going.

Right next to the lake here is a little town called Sherman. I walked into the town to check for services. There was a couple from England photographing the old abandoned buildings that line the streets. We chatted for a minute before I strolled and picked up a few snacks.

A short day, but I got myself right again. And I know I have skipped over some miles again. I know I have some portions to pick back up if I ever plan to call myself a true ADT hiker. Plus, I need to go slow anyway because I will now arrive in Logan sooner, maybe beating my shoes and my sisters' mail drops. I will go slow again tomorrow.

So here's to not puking in your trail angel's mom's nice SUV, my first can of soda (pop in the Midwest) in months, and to finding one's daily bread in accordance with the scriptures after 40 days and nights wandering in the wilderness.

Cheers!

Amie

Saturday, April 25, 2015

Destination: Buckeye Trail, Ohio
Today's Miles: 10
Start Location: Tecumsey Lake, Buckeye Trail, Ohio
Trip Miles: 603.97

After sleeping a solid 10 hours, I packed up leisurely and was off. Sifting through the booty of last night's grocery run, I chose a bag of original Chex Mix for breakfast, something I would never do unless walking all day. This is the Chex Mix with the little breadsticks, the salty melba toasts, and rice and wheat chex. Wheat Chex, one of Mom and Dad's favorite cereals, always remind me of one morning when I was little. It was breakfast time, and Dad was asking me what I wanted to eat. I think I was pouting because I didn't want to eat or some other silly reason, but Dad opened the kitchen cupboard and ticked off a list of the four cereals that were in there: Wheat Chex, Rice Chex, Honeycombs, and Wheat Bran. I wouldn't pick one, so Dad started stomping his foot and making the cereal names into a jingle or little rap. Here is Dad stomping with one foot, swinging his arms rhythmically in front of him, and chanting, "Wheat Chex, Rice Chex, Honeycomb, Bran. Wheat Chex, Rice Chex, Honeycomb, Bran. . . " over and over until I picked something. I don't remember what I ate that morning. But every time I see Wheat Chex, I think of the Wheat Chex song.

I continued along the BT, and today's trail was good and well marked. I was noticing that rain was going to start falling around 3, so I walked on the dirt roads for the latter portion of the day, rather than take the wooded trails, a couple of which doubled back on each other. I wanted to find a campsite before rain fell.

I forded a couple little streams today. One had a stretch of water that was pretty wide. There was a footbridge over one section. The other section's footbridge was floating out in the water, haha. I only doused one shoe for pretty successful stream crossing. I went through one area in which the color of the trees was a darker green, and there was a black-green pool of water. It reminded me of a forest primeval, or maybe what the Godswood from *A Song of Fire and Ice* books would look like. The black pools of water made me think of the tarn from Poe's "The Fall of the House of Usher."

Rain actually started falling around 1:00. I found the two gallons of water that Jamie, trail name Caboose, left for me up here at campsite two, and so I quit early for the day. I am not sure if I am stealth camping, or if this site is kosher. Regardless, I have Judas Priest and "Breakin' the Law" in my head right now. Rain is plopping on the tent. The rain is supposed to stop to-night, giving me a dry day tomorrow to walk into Logan. I may have to take a zero Monday and wait on my three mail pieces to arrive. We'll see, though.

Every day brings something unexpected, and unless that something is motion sickness, it's usually good.

Amie

Sunday, April 26, 2015

Destination: Near Logan, Ohio
Today's Miles: 13
Start Location: Buckeye Trail, Ohio
Trip Miles: 616.97

The rain cleared out, and I was packing up the tent when a gentleman in full hunting gear approached. He knew who I was, and he approved of my camping spot after the fact. I had pulled my fleece neck gaiter over my head as a beanie and to keep my hair out of my face, so I probably looked like a deranged nun. I loaded up and proceeded on.

The trail today was a nice mix of pavement and dirt road, not much traffic. The sun came out, and I eventually was in shorts and enjoying the warmth.

At one point early afternoon, a man in a maroon truck drove by and then turned around and slowed down next to me. He rolled down the window and took off his sunglasses, then said, "This might sound strange, but I have a question." At this point I am thinking of sloooooowly reaching for the pepper spray . . . But he asked, "Are you the lady who called the post office in Logan a few days ago and asked about mail holds?" I said yes, and it turns out that he was the guy I had spoken with at the post office the other day to tell them about my general delivery. What a coincidence! He said that one of my packages had already arrived, and to call the post office on Monday to ask about the rest. Just ask for Dana. Man, I am doubly glad I didn't puke on the post office lawn.

I rounded out my day, another shortie, and the afternoon consisted of dinner, resupply, and contemplation of the next day's plans. The wild card will be getting my mail drop.

All is well.

Amie

Monday, April 27, 2015

Destination: Lake Logan State Park, Ohio
Today's Miles: 13.50
Start Location: Near Logan, Ohio
Trip Miles: 630.47

When I was 7 or 8 and Andrea was about 5, we lived in Newton, KS, in the house just south of HWY 50. My Uncle Doug and cousin Gyla came to visit us. Gyla is just a bit older than I am, and over the course of their visit, Gyla and I became fast friends and left Andrea out. One night Gyla and I were laughing and carrying on. Andrea was lying next to us whimpering a bit, and Andrea whined, "You guys are laughing and having all the fun. And I'm not having one single fun!" Of course her grammar faux pas made us laugh even harder. To this day, when any of us have had a bad day or something doesn't go our way, in our family we invoke Andrea by proclaiming that we didn't have one single fun. She laughs about it now.

Andrea and the phrase "one single fun" came to mind today because today was a really good day. Today was a mail drop day, one package being from Andrea. The trail was mostly road walking with a couple of miles through a wooded area. I am slow in wooded areas because I try to watch my footing. I don't know what is under the leaves. I don't want to roll my ankle or trip. While road walking, I learned about two plant species of which I was previously unaware: a may apple and a jack in the pulpit. I saw a swan on her nest, but sadly no baby underneath. The weather was warm to start the day, but it cooled off a little as the afternoon progressed.

It was a nice walking day, and I stopped walking a bit early in the day because I wanted to make sure I made the post office prior to 4:30 closing time. My new shoes were waiting for me, and both my sisters had sent me some goodies. I was so excited to find out what they had sent. I was concerned that one of my packages had not arrived, and I might have to forward it to the next post office a few days west of here. All three were there, and I exited the post office victorious.

In addition to my shoes, I received some wonderful snack mix, some energy gel packets, laundry soap, toothbrush, and razor from Andrea and the boys. One or both of my nephews drew an excellent picture featuring a doggie peeking in from the side of the picture. Thank you!

From Ashley and the kids, I received two gift cards. Dain also included two small cards with inspirational messages on them. Thank you, Dain. I am honored! What a treat. I am well provisioned.

I have not made as many miles the last few days, but I figure, to borrow Andrea's expression, I have had about 19 funs.

Perhaps along with my daily mileage count, I will also begin totaling up each day's funs.

Amie

Tuesday, April 28, 2015

Destination: Near Ash Cave, Ohio
Today's Miles: 19
Start Location: Lake Logan State Park, Ohio
Trip Miles: 649.47

Today was a magical and wonderful day of pristine views and more hash marks on my ADT hike's cumulative tally of funs. My host family loaded me up and transported me to the region of the Buckeye Trail about which I have heard rave reviews: the Old Man's Cave and Grandma Gatewood sections. And the stars aligned so that Jamie had a couple spare days to lead me through this section. My trusty trail guide gave me lessons in the history of the area, their family's vast and heartfelt contributions to the BT, and more nomenclature lessons in the flowers that paint the landscape, probably so that I would stop referring to jack-in-the-pulpit as preacher-in-the-pulpit. Hey, my misnomer makes sense though, right? Plus, being led around for a day or two was nice in that I could put the directions and map away for a bit and just breathe and look around. 'Twas lovely not being in charge or feeling the need to glance at the TBTs to make sure I wasn't wanderin' off toward Kentucky or something. This is the section where the hiker wants to have his nose in a map as little as possible.

I absorbed the views of Cedar Falls, Upper Falls, a Sphinx rock, Old Man's Cave, the clear and inviting waterfalls that cascaded playfully into blue-green pools, and recessed caves, portions of which receive little to no rainfall, they are that far back within themselves. I probably got these sights out of order, but they were lovely nonetheless. I paused at one rock formation that did indeed resemble the profile of the Sphinx head. I could make out the facial features, and I laughed because the Sphinx rock reminded me of teaching the mythology unit in my English II class every year at Pioneer Valley, and talking about the myth of Oedipus and the riddle of the Sphinx. Most of my students had never heard of her riddle, and soon it became somewhat of a class joke that, if a student left class to use the restroom and was "mysteriously" gone from class too long, I would ask the student upon finally returning to class if there was a Sphinx in the quad. Were you required to answer her riddle? Is that why you were out of class so long?

The caves and trail were a wellspring of subdued and awe-inspiring funs, I would say at least 10 funs, and today's walk also included some road walking. I learned some more history from my trail guide while on the county roads, mostly history of where the trail used to go, what plans they had for moving it, as well as memories of their BT Association's many shindigs, work weeks, and stories.

I had another two or three funs listening to a few of these tales orated in Jamie's NASCAR announcer accent. For those uninitiated in twangy redneck accents (whether they're real or, in our case, amplified on purpose but called forth upon request), there is a difference in regional dialects and vowel pronunciation. I can hear the difference. I reported to my trail guide that the accent from my side of the conversation is heavily redolent of Kansas/Oklahoma/Texas, while his is Carolina/Appalachia. I think we spent a few road miles collecting another 8 or 9 funs in vacuous banter. Imagine a deep Oklahoma livestock auction and a NASCAR race debating the merits of Castrol GTX and STP in a Georgia Wal-Mart automotive section. The miles passed quickly.

Back to a decent mile count today, great scenery, a pack full of food from which to cobble together a dinner meal, and I am informed that tomorrow there is more. All is well.

Amie

More Scavenger Hunt Items

Wednesday, April 29, 2015
Destination: Near Eagle Mills, Ohio
Today's Miles: 15
Start Location: Near Ash Cave, Ohio
Trip Miles: 664.47

Today's walk included Ash Cave, Pretty Run, and more views of the greening countryside. At Ash Cave, visitors are able to walk down a set of steps to the bottom of Ash Cave. There is a huge rock called Pulpit Rock, and apparently a preacher can perch at the top of the rock and deliver sermons from it. There were many inscriptions along the walls of this cave too, some going back to the 1800s. I was reminded of my Lewis and Clark trip and the only physical evidence that remains to this day of the Corps of Discovery's journey: Clark's signature on Pompey's Pillar in Montana. It was cool in the cave, and the day warmed pretty quickly. The Ash Cave visit was a nice start to my day.

My trail guide and I stopped for lunch near a small church, and I was able to dry my tent. A wet tent sets me back about one fun, maybe half a fun, but the warm sun dried it fast. I was able to eat some granola while waiting.

Today was my last day with my rides and guides. My host had to leave me at the Pretty Run Area, and I asked that they mark the point of my map I had just passed. It now defaulted back to me to navigate myself. Jamie's dad arrived, they marked my maps, and as we were bidding one another farewell, another childhood story popped into my head.

I don't remember doing this, but one afternoon when I was little Mom had some friends over. I was off playing in my room or something during some of their visit, and apparently after a few hours into their visit, I strolled out of my room, marched into the midst of their conversation and loudly inquired right in front of our guests, "Mom, when are these people gonna leave?" Mom had to cover for me somehow. Sorry, Mom, but I guess I was just tired of having those people around and wanted them to go away.

I wondered if my host family felt similarly. *Man, this chick keeps showing back up. When is she going to leave?* I got teased about my car sickness one more time, I received a few last tips regarding my evening walking and potential camping spots, and my hosts were off. Thank you. You guys have been amazing.

I strolled along a few more miles before sitting down on the front steps of another small church. I ate a small snack and looked at the directions again

135

to get my bearings. Making the mental transition back to guiding myself was a bit tiring, I must admit. There were a few more hours of daylight, there were a few more miles in my legs, so I proceeded on. I found the appointed campsite and set up. I saw several deer and thankfully only one ATV rider along that road. A couple of squirrels checked out what I was doing and apparently approved because they scurried away.

Onward tomorrow.

Amie

Thursday, April 30, 2015

Destination: Just Shy of Londonderry, Ohio
Today's Miles: 5
Start Location: Near Eagle Mills, Ohio
Trip Miles: 669.47

Yes, five measly miles, I know. Here's how it happened. Slept nicely and woke up knowing rain was a possibility. I peeked out the tent door to see clouds, no sprinkles yet, so I had some coffee and took my time putting everything in its place. A few minutes later my pack was outside, and I was brushing my teeth when the droplets said good morning. The tent was still up, so I threw the pack back in and sat there still brushing my teeth waiting for the rain to stop before I moved on. It turned into the longest brushing session ever. Finally I was able to exit the tent, pack up, and head back onto the trail.

I walked back down the dirt road and onto the paved road. The sky brightened for a bit, and I was enjoying looking at the farms and increasingly green trees all around me. There were some new calves in the pasture to my left. I began to see a sliver of blue sky, so I got rid of the poncho, thinking the rain was gone. The trail provided in the form of a mini Snickers bar lying on the side of the road. The candy was not hard, and the packaging looked new. There were no tire marks on it or anything. Yep, that's right. I ate it.

I was fooled for two or three nice miles, and then the sky opened. A stoic response to rain is best. There is really nothing you can do absent an obvious place to duck for cover, so I just let my thoughts drift and hoped I was still on the correct road. Really, the rain and the solid green of the pastures were a pretty view. I trudged through the rain for a couple miles.

The trail provided a second time in the form of Mike, long-time hiker host, who had been driving around trying to find me and finally did. He loaded me up, as he and Connie had been expecting me to be coming along that way. At their house, they led me downstairs to lay everything out and get it a dryin'. Mike and Connie directed me to spread the wet tent out over two pieces of exercise equipment downstairs. I did a double take and asked, "Are you sure you want me to put this soaking tent over your treadmill?" Mike replied, "Oh, that's what that is?" Apparently, like our Nordic Track coat and purse rack, they have two 500-dollar tent dryers that I mistook for a treadmill and inversion table.

I showered and had a wonderful lunch, and then the trail provided a third time in the form of an invite to yoga class with Connie. It was nice to sit and stretch. The trail must have known I am missing my Bikram yoga 90-minute sweat fest. I was just teaching my trail guide the Bikram standing bow pulling pose the other day from atop a picnic table. That sneaky trail.

After a little down time, I was whisked away to dinner at the Cross Keys in Chilicothe.

So grateful to be out of the rain and dry. Today was nearly a zero, but the rest of the week is supposed to be nice.

I laugh because one reason I decided against walking the Camino de Santiago was that I do not speak Spanish, and I was afraid of getting stuck somewhere in Spain unable to communicate and unable to make my needs or wants known due to the language barrier. Pretty funny that I keep getting shanghaied in Ohio. I might be out here a while. And I am just fine with that.

I will walk some more tomorrow. The last two months have been a huge blessing. What did I do to deserve getting repeatedly kidnapped by helpful people?

Amie

Friday, May 01, 2015

Destination: Stoney Creek Road at Caldwell Lake, Ohio
Today's Miles: 16.20
Start Location: Just Shy of Londonderry, Ohio
Trip Miles: 685.67

Even though I was out past my bedtime last night and I actually imbibed in the form of two light beers, today was a good walking day. The sun was out all day, everything is green, and I had the most wonderful time letting myself listen to music today. My phone was fully charged, and Mike and Connie offered to let me stay another night. I knew I would have a cell phone charging opportunity, so I walked along with my iTunes that I have not shuffled through since early March. I have missed my music. I particularly enjoyed "Days Like These" by Jason Aldean. Such a carefree song for a carefree, cloudless day. "Gentle on My Mind" by Glen Campbell was another one I liked today, and the Campbell version is much better than the remake, in my opinion. I also walked to "Run" by George Strait. Such a good song. I miss my music every day while hiking. Music makes the miles fly by. I am careful to be safe about it though. I just listen through the little phone speaker. I am not carrying headphones.

Last night after dinner one of Mike and Connie's friends told the story of how he had put a voodoo hex on a guy who had done some shoddy construction work for him and cheated him out of his money. The friend, of course, did not seriously perform voodoo on the shyster construction worker, but that's what he said he would do if the work was not repaired. Lo and behold, a few weeks later, their friend's daughter had called him to report the consturction guy had died. Hahahaha! I asked for the particular incantation or spell that comprised the voodoo hex so that I could call it forth on all the dogs that bark at me and threaten to run into the road. Maybe just jesting about putting voodoo hexes on loose dogs worked because not as many dogs barked today and disturbed the peace of walking.

Speaking of dogs, as I walked through the town of Richmond Dale, a man was out on his riding mower cutting the grass holding his puppy in his lap. The puppy yipped at me as I passed. Puppies trying out their bark when they are little is so sweet. I laughed and waved. The man smiled, waved, and the puppy continued helping his owner mow. I did not place a voodoo hex on the cute puppy, and maybe since the puppy is exposed to the hikers from the outset, it won't threaten future ones when he is grown.

Somewhere after Richmond Dale, a big, loud, gnarly, ante-O. J. Simpson

139

Bronco slowed beside me, and a man who looked like Grizzly Adams on the way to a Vietnam Veterans' reunion asked if I needed a lift. I laughed and said no thanks. I gave him a thumbs up as he smiled and drove off.

I crossed the Scioto River and continued walking on the bike alternates, which are road miles. I am not sure what yesterday's rain did to the trails, and road walking gives me more mileage for the day. I found a good stopping place and an easily referenced pick-up point for Mike.

The three of us ate dinner, and Mike and Connie took me back into Chillicothe. I spelled it incorrectly yesterday-a thousand pardons! I received a tour of what else the town has to offer. We drove past some neat and beautifully kept older homes. The downtown is cute. It reminds me of downtown San Luis Obispo. I would add Chillicothe to places I would consider living.

I had been forewarned that Mike and Connie might drag me over to WV while hosting me to go square dancing. Square dancing never transpired, but I had laughed and told them I want to take clogging lessons. Clogging lessons are certainly a possibility in these parts, I was informed. Connie said that "Mountain Music" by Alabama was a popular clogging song. I remember Andrea clogging to that song when we were young. Her little cheeks would get red while she clogged in the living room. I didn't clog on the trail today, but if Andrea were here walking with me, we could pull off some roadside clogging. Square dancing on the trail would be fun too. If anyone is up for it on a sunny day like this, and I have ample cell phone battery, put on a backpack and come find me. We'll make it happen.

Back to the road tomorrow, and I really hope to make use of the upcoming nice weather to start reeling in the rest of Ohio and the ADT north/south split. I feel so slow. Maybe if I clogged while hiking, I would pick up the pace.

Amie

Saturday, May 02, 2015

Destination: Nipgen, Ohio
Today's Miles: 17.50
Start Location: Stoney Creek Road at Caldwell Lake, Ohio
Trip Miles: 703.17

I am guessing on today's miles because I took the bike alternate here to Nipgen, and it's challenging to keep track of mileage when taking the bike alternates. So I split the difference between what the original TBTs say and what MapQuest says to do. I know I took a more roundabout way than Map-Quest, so I am somewhere in between.

I slept amazingly well last night. I think I moved maybe once. I went upstairs to find that Connie had remembered my telling her one favorite food I miss is yams. I love yams for breakfast with salt and olive oil or butter. She had one in the microwave and the Keurig machine loaded and ready to go. We sat down to eat, and Mike teased her and told her she nuked my yam too long. I said, "No, it's great. By gosh, I will eat it!" And it was perfect except for one hard corner I could not cut with a knife. We all laughed and Connie made another. I was privileged to have 1.8 yams for breakfast.

We did some last-minute discussing of a piece of Ohio road map I have with me today. I like to have a visual of where towns are and where I am headed, along with the TBTs. When taking a lot of bike alternates, the difficult part is that the alternate directions are sometimes on a completely different sheet of paper. So I am double and sometimes triple-fisting several sheets of paper at once to stay on track. Then my mileage between services and my mental calculations are off. It's like trying to play three-dimensional chess, but with three different chess boards. And pretty soon I am so engrossed in the directions that I am not having one single fun. My legs and mind work better when I have a path pictured in my head and I can just go. I will likely veer from the ADT proper the next few days into Cincinnati.

I know I am not a trail purist in this quest. I look at it as I am walking this great land and seeing as much as I can see the best way you can: on foot. As breakfast progressed, Mike started talking about the area again and what kinds of people lived around my route. Among the many types of people in the area, he said there were still pockets of KKK in Ohio, and that they gathered once just near their house. I was somewhat surprised.

We loaded me up and drove back down Stoney Creek. At the stopping point, I was to pose for pictures. The first one was me with no pack. Then I put it on, and Connie was trying to put my water bottle down in the side pocket, when she noticed the pepper spray. She was trying to reorient the spray, and said she was scared she was going to shoot me with my own gun. I said nah, there's a trigger guard, and then I asked if this was the section where the KKK lived. They said no, this part was pit bulls and marijuana, and I hoped the pepper spray wasn't moved too far out of reach. But one good part of morning walking is usually the hooligans are not up and at 'em that early to bother with me. Freshly photographed, I proceeded on.

One part of Spain's Camino de Santiago that I find cool is that walkers may carry a pilgrim's passport. The pilgrim's passport is stamped every so often indicating the pilgrims have made it so far, and Camino hikers may receive a certificate of completion with a certain number of stamps in the pilgrim's passport. I do not have a pilgrim's passport, but in a small way I do. Mike and Connie gave me their card with contact information, and they wanted me to leave them mine. I am getting quite a collection of names and addresses of those who have helped me and other hikers. They want to know how we do after we move on, and to keep in touch. I have a few cards and small slivers of paper with this information. These are becoming my pilgrim's passport through the states.

A couple of miles into my day, I passed a public park and restroom area, and there was a drinking fountain. I knew it would be warmer today, so I finished off a liter and drank as much as I could from the bottle next to the pepper spray. I refilled them both. Easy and on-trail water supply! I replaced the bottle next to my recently shifted spray, and without shootin' myself and getting hoisted by my own petard. I continued on.

The afternoon walking consisted of rural paved roads, a few hills, nothing too strenuous. Many people were mowing their vast lawns. I love the smell of freshly cut grass on a nice weekend evening when summer is just around the corner. One group of people who were gathered around a few trucks offered me a sandwich. I said no thanks, not really feeling the hunger pangs today. Maybe it was the warmer weather.

As I write I am sitting under a covered picnic area next to a church here in town. I thought it looked like a good place to camp. No one was here, so I was hoping that as I typed, someone would happen by or stop. And someone just did, a parishioner who stopped by to turn on the HVAC for the morning service. I was glad to be able to ask. He said he would alert the people across the street who keep an eye on the little building for them. I gave my "I'm not homeless or anything speech," but the church is less worried about me and more worried about someone stealing their air conditioner unit again for its copper parts. Booooo! They waved to me from across the street, so I made a good choice. I can put up my tent in peace.

A good day.

Amie

Sunday, May 03, 2015

Destination: Just shy of Sinking Spring, Ohio
Today's Miles: 18
Start Location: Nipgen, Ohio
Trip Miles: 721.17

I slept well until about 2:30 this morning when a bird in the tree directly above me decided to chirp its complete oeuvre of songs for about an hour. Perhaps the nearly full moon inspired it. I don't know. I was a captive audience for a bit and then slept until about 6. I packed up and vacated the church grounds before services. I offloaded my trash in the dumpsters next to the mini mart as I headed west out of Nipgen. They were not open yet to get coffee, so I ate my last little pack of vitamin C chews for a boost.

About a mile into the day I was pretty sure I found some of the KKK, as there was a ramshackle trailer with a giant Confederate flag in the window doubling as curtains. I then followed Morgan Fork Road to the intersection of Pike Lake Road. It was at this point that the directions ran a savage burn on my early start and hope for strong miles on the day. The directions said to walk 1.5 miles down Pike Lake. After walking the 1.5, the hiker or cyclist then is told to refer to bike alternate directions if you want to stay on paved roads. I went to chess board two with alternate road routes, where it said to backtrack to the corner of Pike Lake and Morgan Fork, re-walking the stretch I had just done. Three extra miles is not much on a bicycle, but it is walking. I shook my fist at the sky and backtracked.

Not only was the extra distance an issue, but on the way down Pike Lake, a man had stepped out of his trailer to ask if I was walking the trail. Yes. Had I been mushroom huntin'? No. The wild mushrooms are a big deal here and worth money. He was just tellin' his momma back in the house that there was hiker, and did I need anything? No, thank you. "Well," he said, "find some mushrooms for me." I will. He gave me two thumbs up and went inside. I now had to pass back by the mushroom man. I had since taken my jacket off. Maybe he wouldn't recognize me in a different top... He didn't come back out.

Back on track and with an improved attitude, I walked some more paved road. It had warmed considerably, and I was down to my special backpack tank top and a lot of sunscreen on my arms and hands. I had picked up two Gatorades and was well hydrated, but an elderly man out in his yard asked me if I wanted a quick break and bottle of water. He said, "I believe in the man above, so don't worry." I sat on the edge of the porch and had some

143

water.

He asked about the walking and then started talking about his favorite TV preacher and the minutiae of the preacher's message on all sorts of topics. He handed me some religious literature and said I could take it with me. The conversation became random, his citing Ezekiel (not the bread verse), Revelations, 10 years, 7 years, 40 years, the chosen, the Promised Land, Easter, the return of Jesus and how that will really be, why the King James version is apocryphal, and so forth. My Spidey sense was tingling that the discourse was waxing strange. I returned the man his literature, thanked him for the water, and said I needed to keep moving. I am not certain whether he was wrong or right, or whether my own conscience needed a good talkin' to or not, but I go with my gut. I proceeded on.

While I was walking up a long hill via Fire Tower Road, two sweet ladies in a minivan slowed and asked if I had room for a snack. I said sure, and they handed me a bunch of grapes wrapped in Saran Wrap. It was as if they had seen me and prepared the snack ahead of time. The driver said she has wanted to hike the Buckeye Trail, it sounded fun, but she was physically unable. I encouraged her and said she could absolutely do it. I told her to get a bicycle and take the bike routes. Just do a little at a time. I encouraged her again, thanked them for the grapes, and they drove on.

In the afternoon, the trail went down a gravel road and past a series of trailers, each of which looked straight out of an episode of *Hoarders*. Each trailer had many different colored Rubbermaid containers sitting out front, all covered with tarps. There were other piles of junk, and those were covered with tarps. A quarter mile later, another trailer, more containers, more tarps, and each section had dogs penned up in front of it, running around barking. A quarter mile later, I think I saw their trash dump, many trash bags piled up in the forest. I walked faster, listening for banjos, eager to get out of there.

I turned right on Pin Hook Road. It was around 5, still plenty of light, but I had been walking for 10 hours, and it was time for the trail to provide a camping spot. I was uncertain if I could make it to Serpent Mound, where there is a shelter. I was descending a hill when a man on an ATV reached the road, cut the engine, and waited for me to approach. We talked about the trail for a minute, and the man was a dead ringer for my cousin Aaron in Iowa in looks a bit, but mostly in demeanor and speech. Rick said he had been huntin' mushrooms, and he had the boots, the scratched arms, and the spoils to prove it.

I decided to reach out for the first time and ask if he knew anywhere I could camp, or who owned the land surrounding. He said he did, it was fine if I camped in their yard, and come on up and be introduced to his lady, Carrie. I did so, and sat in the kitchen, where she was preparing the mushrooms and a homemade breading for them. They came out of the fryer light, crisp, and ready to eat. We sat to supper. They insisted we were all good country folk, and to dig my hands right in and grab however many mushrooms I wanted. They keep sea salt in their home, a perfect addition to the fried mushrooms, freshly picked. I now see what the fuss over these mushrooms is all about. They were so good. Carrie also made me an excellent sandwich, and along with the mushrooms, it was a perfect meal. And I had been introduced to a new food.

Many evenings when it is nice out, Rick and Carrie make a small bonfire on their property and sit and enjoy the waning light. They invited me to join them. Rick talked about his home, and how he initially lived there with no electricity. He had to heat water, wash clothes, and maintain his existence somewhat as our forefathers did. Carrie came along, and they have been updating the house bit by bit. The floors are redone, electricity and running water are now the norm, Rick's artwork is beautiful and on the walls, they have a neat loft, two woodstoves, a cozy kitchen, and they are happy as can be with no central heat or air. The woodstoves in the basement and in the kitchen provide for their heating needs. They grow a lot of their own food, and they have not a whit of stress or anxiety in their lives. I told them I loved their house, and I was jealous of their lifestyle. You are doing it right, guys. Don't change a thing.

Around the bonfire, the conversation turned to my walk, how I stay healthy, what I carry, basic human needs, etc. We talked about the Bible verse (and I am probably misquoting a bit) "And let thou be satisfied with food and raiment." The last six weeks, I am pretty satisfied with food, water, shelter, and mostly clean clothes. I don't want to live this way forever, but I am content right now.

I then laughed really hard as Rick told a story about an outdoor survival competition where a group of men are sent out into the woods with their clothing of choice, sleeping bag, and a knife and piece of flint. Little else. And they had to survive. He said the main reason most men fail at the competition and want out of the woods is that they miss drinking alcohol too much. I reflected back on my list of reasons for potentially stopping my walk, and I am grateful that the presence or absence of the white man's firewater has nothing to do with my successes or failures at this or anything.

My lawn camping evolved into a shower and a bed at their offer, and I don't even remember if I had to give my "I'm not homeless" speech. Thank you, cousin Aaron. I'd like to think your spirit guided me to these good people. Except for walking for a mile past the complete third season of *Hoarders*, this was nearly a perfect day.

Amie

Monday, May 04, 2015

Destination: Serpent Mound Site, Ohio
Today's Miles: 6
Start Location: Just shy of Sinking Spring, Ohio
Trip Miles: 727.17

Happy Birthday, Dad! I hope you all had a good day yesterday.

I wanted to get an early start this morning also, not that I was planning big miles obviously, but that I needed a motel half day to regroup and make a plan for getting to Cincinnati. The ADT cuts south and east here. I am making another judgment call and veering from the trail. I want to walk west and not circle around. Moreover, I have been warned that the southern section of the trail may not be a good place for me. I have been cautioned against possibly unmaintained trail surfaces, rednecks, and meth. And this is from former section supervisors and people who have lived here a long time, not some snooty outsiders. Thank you again to Ryan C, who told me his route across this section. Ryan has been a scout for me a couple of times, and I even got a tip about a cheap and non-putrid motel coming up in a few weeks.

I sat and had a cup of coffee with Rick and Carrie this morning. They sent me off with three cold apples, a fresh pair of socks, and we exchanged info. I added them to my pilgrim's passport and went on my way. Thanks, guys. I hope to take another bonfire with you someday.

Very short walk today, through Sinking Spring, and along gravel or paved roads. Possibly found some more Klan, this time with a handwritten sign in front of the Confederate flagged trailer: "Video camera's [sic] in use. Don't block driveway. I've got my eye's [sic] on you."

Made it to the Serpent Mound memorial site early. I walked the perimeter of the site, climbed the tower with my pack on, and took some photos. This is a really interesting place, along with another Hopewell Indian site back in Chillicothe that Mike and Connie showed me. There is also a small museum and gift shop, but I am scared to walk around it with my pack on. I might swish some trinkets or merchandise on the floor. Seeing the site and reading the info along it are good enough.

Tonight my chores include making a plan for walking, laundry, converting written contact info to email, cleaning out my pack, eating, and finding the next mail drop.

I am having fun.

Amie

Tuesday, May 05, 2015

Destination: Along Concord Road, Ohio
Today's Miles: 19.60
Start Location: Serpent Mound Site, Ohio
Trip Miles: 746.77

Over the course of the day and with the help of several sources, I lined out a route to Milford, where I will pick the trail back up and get my next mail drop. Thank you, sources. I picked up groceries and felt prepared for today, but I woke up around 3:30 this morning with a little anxiety about being off Buckeye Trail again. Was it the warnings about meth, pit bulls, marijuana, Klan, snakes, ticks, and rednecks? Maybe. But it also had a lot to do with the fact that I did almost nothing yesterday, and I am used to sleeping after walking a lot more miles. I took one ibuprofen tab and slept the rest of the night.

I had picked up two Subway salads last night. I ate most of the first for supper and most of the second for breakfast. The motel breakfast of Frosted Flakes, waffles, and donuts did not appeal to me. Thank you, Donna and Ash, for the gift cards. I am craving veggies and greens, and I have noticed my appetite has dipped lately due to the heat. I am careful to eat quality calories. I drank almost a gallon of water today, and I am sure I will do the same tomorrow. I have noticed that I will definitely be needing a smaller size pair of shorts when I get to the outfitters in Milford. I have lost the weight I call "first-world fluff," that extra fluff that we carry around our middle and around the top of the pelvic bone, right where my hip belt sits. I have leaned somewhat. However, I weighed myself two days ago, and I still weigh 130. I am not sickly at all, just toughened up some. I feel strong, and nothing hurts. So far so good.

My alternate route took me from Serpent Mound bearing northwest along various county roads and state routes. I walked along a road called Peach Orchard. It was a nice route with some farms, some of which I think were Amish. I saw two road signs today that warn drivers of the presence of horse and buggy. I also walked along Oak Ridge Road, also a quiet route, grassy shoulder, not much traffic. Plus this road reminded me of listening to the Oak Ridge Boys when we were little.

Early afternoon I was feeling like a sarsaparilla, so I sat down and mixed some water with one of the greatest recent inventions: liquid concentrated Powerade mix. It is lighter than carrying the powdered mix, and there is less of a mess. I just pop the top of the small bottle and squeeze some in there. Instant blue Powerade! I drank this down quickly. I know at some point I may have to knock on someone's door and ask if I may fill my water from their spigot or hose. I have yet to knock on anyone's door. All water has been offered to me from people in their yards. I hesitate to approach someone's house and ring the bell. What if Charles Manson comes to the door? Then I would have to concoct a story to back out of why I rang the bell and be looking over my shoulder. Water, not food, is my latest focus.

I followed the rural roads until about 5:30 tonight. I saw a church off Concord that was open, and people were in the parking lot. I asked the pastor if I could camp behind the church. He was really apprehensive, and he told me so. He is new to the church and wants to trust me and make the right choice. I don't blame him a bit. He showed me a secluded place around back. I promised I would be out of here early in the morning. I think he found my story AND that I am normal hard to believe. Again, I can see where he is coming from.

I will get an early start in the morning. Good miles today despite being a bit tired. All is well.

Amie

Wednesday, May 06, 2015

Destination: Just Beyond Vera Cruz, Ohio
Today's Miles: 22
Start Location: Along Concord Road, Ohio
Trip Miles: 768.77

Last night at dark and after closing the church, the pastor came out back and let me know there was a vacant house on the property. He had unlocked it and said I could use the shower in the morning if I wanted. I thanked him again and fell back asleep. The only resources I used inside the house this morning were 3 liters of water and just enough to make a little coffee, using my own stove. I charged my phone for a few minutes as I packed up. I wrote a quick note on a paper towel, thanking him for trusting me. I left it on the counter, closed the door behind me, and walked on.

The first few miles I enumerated a list of possible misconceptions people may have about me, misconceptions I would probably have about me if I could step outside my own body and watch myself walk down a county road. I might wonder if I were on the run from something, a bad relationship, bill collectors, repo man, drug dealers, the law? I might think I was some kind of professional slummer or vagrant, hopping around, looking for handouts. I might wonder if I had lost everyone in my life or someone important, and was bumming around to let the dust settle and work it out of my system. I understand people's skepticism about strangers with a backpack. I have driven alone a lot, and I would never pick myself up hitch hiking. I have yet to be offended, although none of those things are true of me. I am just a regular person who is taking some time off during this fortieth year of life to walk a trail. That's all.

I continued generally along Highway 131 all day, taking a few county roads for a better shoulder. I must not have offended the trail gods by veering from the book route because for the majority of the day, there was a wide shoulder, or freshly mowed grass to walk on alongside someone's yard or pasture. Several fields were being tended by large pieces of farm equipment. The drivers waved. I waved back. I was fortunate to have been led down fairly peaceful roads during this time off trail, and tomorrow will be the last day of pathfinder walking. I pick up the book route again tomorrow in Milford. It will be a relief, as people are more accustomed to seeing the hikers on the official roads. Today's photo symbolizes my alternate route.

One book I read before last summer's Missouri River road trip was Dayton Duncan's book *Out West: A Journey along the Lewis and Clark Trail*. He had travelled the route in the early eighties, during the Urban Cowboy era and the savings and loan crisis. It is really a great read, even if you find the history aspect uninteresting. It is an overall entertaining travel book on all things driving from how to choose diners to rules and corollaries on interacting with locals. Anyway, he spent a lot of time in small towns on the Great Plains and one observation he made in his book was that he felt safer in places where there were bullet holes in the road signs. If there was graffiti on the road signs, he felt less safe. I agree. I have seen a few bullet holes in a couple road signs this past week, no tagging. And along with this unadulterated sign indicating the presence of Amish, a few bullet-hole-ridden signs here and there did not feel threatening to me.

One threat I am battling a bit is ticks. Early yesterday I took the gaiters off to let my legs breathe, and I assumed I would not need them because I was embarking on road walking again. I ripped open the velcro fronts to find a tick had just attached itself to my shin. I picked him off, making sure I got all of the rascal. I left the gaiters off to keep an eye out for more ticks and to work on eliminating this strange knee-only tan that is developing.

By the end of the day, I had grass in my shoes, two small pebbles that threatened to derail my stride, and my legs were filthy. This morning I remembered that Rick and Carrie had given me two of those citronella bug-repellent bracelets that are supposed to last a long time and repel ticks too. I slipped one around each ankle, and the gaiters are staying on. My shoes and legs stayed free of debris today, and no ticks attached. I saw one tick exiting the gaiters running for the hills, so maybe the bracelets work. I wish I could place a voodoo hex on all ticks within a five-foot radius.

I felt really strong today overall. My system is adjusting to the warmth and a lower calorie intake. The change reminds me of training for half or full marathons. Once in shape, I could complete a Saturday-morning long run of 16 to 20 miles on nothing more than my morning lattes, and one bottled water and power bar I had stashed in the bushes along my route the night before. Our bodies are really amazing at making adjustments. I will remain vigilant in staying hydrated.

I finally broke the seal this evening on knocking on doors to ask about lawn or field camping. There is a cluster of houses here, nothing isolated, and at the first house I chose, the husband was kind of okay with my camping out back, but the wife said no. I thanked them anyway and tried the neighbor. The second person said yes. I was granted the mowed field on the other side of the garage, and the property owner looks nothing like Charles Manson.

Mail drop day tomorrow, back on the ADT, then plans to navigate Cincinnati.

Amie

Thursday, May 07, 2015

Destination: Milford, Ohio
Today's Miles: 16.40
Start Location: Just Beyond Vera Cruz, Ohio
Trip Miles: 785.17

Today was kind of a rough day. It reminded me of that scene from *O, Brother, Where Art Thou*? when Ulysses Everett McGill and his posse are gathered around the supper table with a young boy and his pa. Pa says as he raises his fork with some meat dangling from it: "I slaughtered this horse last Tuesday. I think she's startin' to turn."

Highway 131 has been good to me since Tuesday. Today she turned on me. The shoulder narrowed along the road today at times so much that a shoulder hardly existed. I spent several slow miles stepping off the side waiting for cars to pass, and then stepping back on. Other times I walked alongside the edges of pastures, then climbed back up the ditch onto the road. I also walked through a lot of people's lawns along 131. Any walking surface was fair game today to stay safe and keep moving, however slowly. A lot of stop and go, a tad rough at times. The temperature warmed quickly, and I was glad I had obtained another 3 liters of water early in the day by asking someone if I could fill from an outside faucet.

At about 8 miles in, there was an elderly couple and their son outside. Their son was landscaping for them. They waved and asked me where I was walking. I told them. They asked if I needed anything, and I said I would take a big swig of water, and if they wanted to top off my water, that would be perfect. The lady went in the house, and the gentleman, who was on oxygen and in a powerchair, began telling me that his wife would like to exercise more, but she just had portions of her lungs removed due to lung cancer. She was on month three of a six-month recovery. His wife returned, and she had also brought me four packs of crackers in a ziploc bag. I thanked them and walked on, silently shaming myself that I had just been annoyed by walking through some cornfield stubble. Clearly, I am not in a Hover-ound, on oxygen, or in cancer post-surgery. I have nothing to complain about. I ate the crackers quickly even though I did not feel hungry due to the warmth.

The too-big shorts were another source of vexation today, and I came up with another strategy to keep them from falling down. I fold the waistband over upon itself, and then I roll up the leg openings a few times to tighten them around my thighs. Then I push the rolled legs high up so it takes a while for the shorts to begin falling down again. This brings the bottoms of the lshorts' openings higher than my current tan line. My shorts today were up pretty high and probably violating some public decency statutes, but they stayed up. The position of my shorts reminded me of that scene in *Wayne's World* where Wayne's girlfriend Cassandra is trying to have a serious phone conversation, and Wayne pulls his underwear clear up his butt and prances around the room to make her laugh. Mine weren't that high.

My goal destination today was the Holiday Inn Express, which is next to the post office where I will be picking up my mail. From there, I will navigate back to ADT TBTs. I could approach my destination by continuing on 131, and then backtracking a bit northeast to the motel. But by early afternoon, I was weary of 131 and decided to take Pleasant Hill Road north a bit, and then come down to the motel on Highway 28. I figured 28 had to be more walkable than 131, better shoulder, maybe a little more quiet, etc.

Wrong, grasshopper! The trail gods at this juncture smote me for going off trail because I learned that 28 was limited access, on ramps, off ramps, no pedestrians allowed, not that I wanted to walk on it now anyway after viewing it. I was less than 2 miles from both goals, but I could not get there on foot.

At an impasse, I reached out by phone to my Ohio lifeline Caboose, who Google Mapped me down an alternate road. He talked me to the very precipice of the Inn's path, a half mile or less, but now I would have to walk across access ramps and stoplights for 28 and the Interstate. I was too scared.

I backtracked a couple blocks to the Sherwin Williams paint store, and I was seriously trying to call a cab to drive me literally half a mile. It was quite comical, and the young paint store clerks were offering me water and a ride if nothing solidified. They were so cute. I needed a car ride of less than a mile! So close, yet so far away. Finally a paint van guy said he would drive me. I think he was disgruntled about his job because he indicated he was in the company van and shouldn't, but would anyway.

I earned these net 16 miles (I don't count backtracking distance) and a motel night. All is well.

Tomorrow morning I will have coffee, pack up, and R-U-N-N-O-F-T.

Amie

Friday, May 08, 2015

Destination: Eden Park, Cincinnati
Today's Miles: 14
Start Location: Milford, Ohio
Trip Miles: 799.17

It was decided that my trail friend and Ohio connection, Caboose, would join me for the weekend and lead me from Milford, through Cincinnati, and then walk with me as close to Indiana as possible, given the chances for stormy weather Saturday through Monday. He also offered to shuttle me around so that I could complete a couple of trail chores. This made me very happy. I wasn't too sure about walking through the city by myself.

We set a goal destination of Milford to Eden Park. I left a lot of gear out of the pack today to make it lighter, and we drove to the TBT pick-up point in Milford to start the day.

First order of business: new shorts. The RRT store in Milford is a great resource for hikers coming through the area, and I found a lightweight, wicking pair of shorts with two zipper pockets. Perfect. They gave me their 10 percent thru-hiker discount. We then proceeded through the cute down-town area and to the Milford Trailhead. At this point, a person can pick up several different trails from this one spot. A rail to trail made up the next few miles, and then we made our way through some very beautiful neigh-borhoods. The styles of the homes all seemed to be different, and many were fairly old. I saw one cute house with a light blue door that could have been Miss Honey's cottage from the movie *Matilda*. I was waiting for Miss Honey to come outside with tea and cookies. There were a few homes that looked like castles.

We then walked through a beautiful shopping area, featuring stores that cater to customers of means. It has been a while since I have seen that many yoga studios, juice bars, clothing stores, and specialty gear shops clustered together. Earlier in the day we had taken a quick break at a United Dairy Farmers. Jamie wanted a chocolate milkshake. I wanted to stop in to the juice and smoothie bar.

The ADT continued to follow the Buckeye Trail through town for a few more miles, passing through several parks, which was nice because I could refill my water on this warm day. We eventually reached the beautiful Eden Park, and it is within this park that the ADT leaves the BT to saunter back off on its own course. There is a lookout point from which you can see the Ohio River and Kentucky. There were many geese and ducks and their lit-

154

tluns milling around the ponds and the banks. So cute!

We decided this was a good stopping point for the day, took a break, then began hatching a plot to get ourselves back to Milford and the car. A few ride connections Jamie had tentatively arranged fell through, and we were informed by a nice local couple that the cab service in Cincinnati was a joke. We contemplated using the Metro bus system, but the buses were either not going to Milford, or they stopped running around 5 or 6. We each made a couple phone calls, decided that 40 bucks was too much for a shuttle service, and then decided to start walking back the way we came, hoping something would fall from the sky, as it usually does.

There was still plenty of daylight, and although we were tired from 14+ miles of sidewalk trekking, we still had 3 or 4 funs. After 5 miles of backtracking, we reached a Cincinnati police station. We'd been informed that one of the best ways to get a cab quickly is to have the cops call one for you, as if to get you out of there. And that is just what we did. We sat out front of the station waiting and looking a bit homeless, and Jamie wagered that the first question our cab driver would ask when snatching us from the cop shop would be, "What did you guys do?" Our ride arrived, and we made it back to Milford. I don't know if I can count that as my first run-in with the law on this walk, but if I do, at least it was of my own volition.

Tomorrow we will proceed from Eden Park and continue on, depending what the weather does. Today was one of those days where the outside world did not seem to matter, and all that mattered was the gorgeous day and the walking.

Amie

Saturday, May 09, 2015

Destination: Devou Park, Cincinnati
Today's Miles: 6
Start Location: Eden Park, Cincinnati
Trip Miles: 805.17

Happy Mother's Day, Mom! Thank you again for taking care of my check-book for me while I am out here wandering around.

A short mileage day, but the trail was handing out some free funs, so we decided to grab them. Today a taxi was necessary to get us back to the trail drop point, Eden Park. The cab driver was really nice, but he took a wrong turn and then wasn't exactly sure how to reach the overlook where we stopped walking yesterday, so he said the ride was free today.

From Eden Park, the trail then began making its way downtown. We walked through the Mt. Adams area, where there were outdoor musicians, shops, a very cool atmosphere. The trail descended lots of steps today too as it made its way to the river walk, and all the walking down steps felt like another freebie. The river walk area is fairly new, and in addition to the walking path, there are water spouts that kids can play in, a carousel, and swings big enough for two people that look out over the river.

We found the ADT marker along the river walk. It listed both the mileage from the east coast as well as how many miles to Point Reyes. I tried not to look at the distance to California. I also kept an eye out for an address or anything with the number 800 on it because at some point downtown, I crossed the 800-mile point. I didn't see any, but soon the path went right by Moerlein Lager House. Hmmmmm. We decided to stop there and drink one beer each to celebrate the 800 miles and look out at the unique Roebling Bridge, which we would walk across to return to the other side of the river. Here the trail handed out another fun, gratis. Our server had messed up an-other table's order, and so she gave us the mess up in the form of free pret-zels and dipping sauce. Excellent!

Leaving the Lager House, we ambled across the bridge. Old bridges es-pecially really are a huge feat of engineering. This bridge is painted a light blue, and the blue is offset by the old stonework, which is light brown. There is a metal webwork over which the cars drive, and the cars make a buzzing sound as they traverse the bridge.

We decided to make it a short hiking day and take advantage of down-town Cincinnati for the evening. There was a trolley service to downtown, and a restaurant called Sotto was amazing. The trail provided in a way here, because supposedly there were no tables until 10 pm, but one of Jamie's hiking friends works there, so we got a table immediately. Sotto is one of those places that is below street level. You walk downstairs to a darkened dining room lit by only candlelight and chandeliers. It reminded me of the Olde Hansa in Tallinn, Estonia. The Olde Hansa used to be a Baltic merchant's house, and they serve foods that would have been on the menu hundreds of years ago. For example, many meals come with a side of barley, and you can order wild boar, but only if they caught one that day. At Sotto, I could not pronounce a single food we ordered, except for a black kale salad.

How am I ever going to return to the trail after these last three days? I cannot get used to this.

Amie

Sunday, May 10, 2015

Destination: Hartford, Indiana
Today's Miles: 18.41
Start Location: Elizabethtown, Ohio
Trip Miles: 823.58

Today's trail pick-up point was not in Cincinnati, and there were a few reasons for that. Jamie also wanted to see the ADT north/south split and a U. S. President's tomb, which is along the trail. And primarily, I did not want to walk through the rest of Cincinnati alone. Jamie had to go home today, so we decided Elizabethtown would be a good place to send me off on my own again. I have some more ADT book route miles to go back and pick up, and that's okay.

I am taking the southern route of the trail, which eventually makes its way along Missouri's Katy Trail and then through Kansas. From the split, I proceeded alone along State Line Road and then soon crossed the Indiana state line. I would have gotten a picture of myself with the Indiana sign, but it would have meant crossing HWY 50 again. I settled back into navigating myself and letting my thoughts go where they pleased. The trail soon picked up a bike path. There was water along the route, and the trail surface was paved, but I walked in the gravel and soft dirt off to the sides.

I soon hit my first snag in my next state. There was orange fencing blocking the trail where it enters the city of Aurora. A bright orange sign indicated a portion of the trail was closed until September due to construction. Huh? I checked the TBTs to find that only a mile or so remained on the bike path until I was back on city streets within Aurora. I went online to find the number for the southern Indiana trail coordinator to ask what to do. Seems there currently is no coordinator. Ryan C took the northern ADT route, so I had no one to call for advice.

I then started thinking. It's Sunday. There is no one out here working. All the construction equipment is still. At this point, I may or may not have gone around the fence to walk the last mile to Aurora anyway. I may not have noticed that the trail surface was fine, or that pipeline was being installed under the ditches. I may or may not have emerged from behind another fence blocking the trail and happily strolled through Aurora with a clear conscience and undaunted my first morning in Indiana.

Along the river through Aurora's outskirts, another bike trail contained facilities and water. I made use of especially the water, and proceeded on to Hartford Pike, the road that would lead five miles to a possible camp spot for the night. Along the way I met a man who had met hiker Mr. Lee last summer passing by his house. We talked for a minute. I wanted to ask to camp in his yard like Lee did, but I wanted to make it to Hartford before dark to get in at least an 18-mile day. And I did.

I have to say that my time in Ohio has been my favorite so far. Many people were very generous to me, and it was here that everything finally greened and the weather warmed. The Buckeye Trail and its bicycle alternates were very well marked and easy to follow. Its roads were labeled, and I did not get off track once, except at my own choosing. A thousand thank yous, Ohio.

And hello, Midwest. It's good to see you again.

Amie

Monday, May 11, 2015

Destination: Friendship, IN
Today's Miles: 17
Start Location: Hartford, Indiana
Trip Miles: 840.58

Last night I had a dream that someone was pulling on my legs, but through the sidewall of the tent where there is no door. I tried to talk, and then eventually yell, but no sound would come out. I don't know if it was before or after this dream that the wind picked up. There was no cell service in Hartford, so I waited at the mercy of whatever was moving through. The wind blew for perhaps 30 minutes, and then all was quiet.

The morning sun promised another warm day, so I was on the lookout for water early again. I eventually walked past an area that appeared to be a small bush or tree nursery. I figured there had to be a water tap there. I strolled over, and there was a State of Indiana vehicle. I asked the man inside if I could top off my water. He said there was no tap, but there was a mini-fridge under the shelter, and I could grab some cold bottled water. Thank you, State of Indiana.

The trail then turned down Laughery Creek Road, and it followed this road for over 7 miles before the next turn. This made me happy. I could pocket the directions for a bit and just think. Here is where I did my first bit of backtracking, and it was pretty much confirmed that southern Indiana seems to have no ADT signage, no blazes, nothing, and some small country roads are not marked. Laughery Creek apparently took a left turn over a bridge. I did not know this and continued straight. A man mowing his lawn a few hundred feet later stopped and asked if I was aware that my road was to dead-end in a creek a few more steps hence. Nope. He told me where to turn to pick up Laughery Creek again. It was a short backtrack, but lesson confirmed that nothing is marked.

Back on course, a black dog soon trotted out of its yard and began following me. He was a cheerful little fella, and despite my efforts to swish him back home, he would not go. He would veer off and sniff around others' lawns, and I hoped he would grow bored with me and go back home, but I would turn around to find him behind me once again.

Cell service was in and out all day, and I saw some dark clouds forming. I stopped under a shade tree next to a cemetery and checked the weather. It showed chances of thunderstorms at 4 and then again at 8. I updated the website and took a short break. A couple drove by and entered the cemetery. The dog followed them. I got back up and went on, hoping the dog would latch on to them and forget me, but there he came.

Around 3:30, I neared Friendship. Cell service at this point seemed to enter a parallel universe or different dimension, and I remembered the storm forecast and saw more clouds. Friendship is one huge campground with a small town in it. I paused again under a large covered flea market pavilion area to wait it out again. By 5 nothing had happened. I went through town, and at the other end there were more campsites and more clouds. But still no cell service. I decided to park it there, even though it was still relatively early. There were shelters under which I could hide if the weather got sideways, and I would not have to look for a place to stealth.

Back at the flea market, the dog had lost interest and was nowhere to be seen. Hopefully the little guy made it back home okay. Aside from not knowing whether the clouds portend a little rain or 3-inch hailstones, all is well.

Amie

Tuesday, May 12, 2015

Destination: China, IN
Today's Miles: 19.83
Start Location: Friendship, IN
Trip Miles: 860.41

There was no storm last night, just some rain off and on for less than an hour. The weather system did bring some cooler air with it, though, and I was glad to wear my lightweight long-sleeved shirt all day. It covers my neck and most of my hands too. I need to expose my arms and shoulders to all-day sun gradually. I had gotten some color the last couple days, and was happy to cover up again.

I can tell I am getting back on my home turf, for there has been an increased presence of the cottonwood tree. I am normally a slack-jawed rube when it comes to identifying flowers, plants, trees, birds, you name it, but I can spot the cottonwoods. They are a comforting sight. In addition, I am beginning to see vast fields of the tall prairie grasses and wheat. The wind blew pretty hard today, and the grass rippled in the wind, creating the illusion of waves. It looks like an ocean of green, and then, as summer and the wheat ripen, a sea of gold. The rippling tallgrasses are a vision I haven't seen for a while. This too is very good. And last night I went into a small grocery store, hoping to pick up a gallon of water. They did not sell gallons of water, so I grabbed two bottled waters and a Powerade. As I was checking out, I asked the lady if she knew any updates on the storm that was predicted to move through around 8. She didn't know anything about the weather, but did I need a sack for my beverages? Why, yes.

The trail continued today along Highway 62. The road was very lightly travelled and mostly flat. There was one hill to climb, and at this hill was a state flag crew on traffic control for some roadwork along the hill's shoulder. It was here that the State of Indiana fulfilled my water needs yet again. The flag guys said to ascend the hill, and there would be another truck with a large cooler of ice water. They must have radioed the guy ahead of time because he invited me to grab water before I said a word beyond hello. I topped off the liter bottle and proceeded on. At the end of the workday, they passed me, honked, and waved. I passed through the tiny town of Canaan during the afternoon. Apparently there is a cute bed and breakfast there, but I was not ready to stop yet. I figured I would camp another night in the cooler weather.

I secured a campsite just outside the town of China. So far my first few days in Indiana have been low-traffic, extremely pleasant, and uneventful. A lot of times in life, especially when walking across the states, "eventful" is what you want to avoid.

Amie

Wednesday, May 13, 2015

Destination: Madison, IN
Today's Miles: 12.56
Start Location: China, IN
Trip Miles: 872.97

This morning it was confirmed that I am in need of a town day: I finished off my pack food except for a couple cracker packs to get me through the morning. And . . . I am out of coffee. I packed up and sneaked out of my campsite, following China-Manville Road. The morning brought another peaceful road and cool temps as I meandered toward Manville and my town destination: Madison. At China-Manville Road and Manville Hill Road, I was to take a right, and as the TBTs indicate, there was no sign marking Manville Hill Road. I turned my phone on to find there was just enough cell service for the map app to identify the correct road. Plus, I immediately began climbing, so I was sure I was proceeding correctly.

I soon turned west on Pleasant Ridge, an aptly named road, and anon a small SUV passed me and turned left into the next driveway. A lady got out and asked if I was doing the ADT. I replied in the affirmative. She said they are trail society members, and did I need anything? Restroom? Water? Snack? Yes x 3! Cherri invited me in, where I was treated to some delicious cake, cold fruit, water, and a to-go bag stuffed with almonds, fruit, and cheese. She and her husband Paul own quite a bit of land along the trail, and they have taken an interest in the trail's development and the hikers. They would very much like to offer their lawn for camping, water spigots, and so forth to the hikers, and we all wished there was some sort of trail database where people like me could find those who would offer a camping spot. I was then laughing about not wanting to knock on doors and bug people. Paul and Cherri said they know others who live along the trail who would like to help too. Maybe someday if the ADT gains nationally recognized status, some sort of database could help hikers to know who is receptive to us along the way. Right now, help is abundant, in my experience, but it's pretty much word of mouth, luck, and the result of Trail Journal followers.

Paul got out Indiana maps, and I got an idea of where the next few days will lead me. I thanked them and continued toward Madison. What a great little mid-day break! I walked about 4 more miles before reaching town.

In Madison, I was hoping for a budget room with basement bottom prices, just enough to shower and do a load of laundry. I decided against walking way off trail to reach the Wal-Mart and the motels that looked cheap, and I hoped to find something low end right on trail. Ask, and ye shall receive. I found a place, and the price tells the story: 44 dollars including tax. Yep. The manager's wife is currently doing my laundry for me, a task against which I strongly cautioned her, but she said guests are not allowed in the laundry area.

There is a lady who lives here who just knocked on my door and gave me a sloppy joe. Her name was Stephanie. She reported that her special sloppy joes had been renamed Sloppy Stephanies. The rest of the evening will be spent studying directions for the next couple days, finishing my Sloppy Stephanie, and ensuring my laundry gets returned in its entirety.

Looking forward to longer miles tomorrow, grocery resupply also on trail, and camping again tomorrow night.

Amie

Thursday, May 14, 2015

Destination: Just Shy of Saluda, IN
Today's Miles: 21.03
Start Location: Madison, IN
Trip Miles: 894

Okay, I have officially paid penance for the expensive Cincinnati weekend. Last night's motel was worse than the Grafton motel. I could feel every
spring in the mattress, people were up all night, and now all of my stuff and
I smell like stale, 100-year-old everything. I gave 44 alms, and hopefully I
am absolved of my spending spree after going that cheap and not sleeping
much at all. Not sure where I found the energy for today's miles. I ain't doin'
that again.

The trail this morning went down Madison's Main Street for a couple
miles, and here is another super-cute downtown area I will have to revisit
someday. Many types of cafes and shops dotted the main route. There were
banners on the lamp posts advertising a folk music festival coming up soon,
and many of the homes and storefronts appeared straight out of an episode
of *This Old House* on PBS. Very fun to walk through, and I was able to pick up
enough groceries and coffee for the day.

Soon the trail entered Clifty Falls State Park. This clean park greeted me
with an easy mile of climbing upon entering, and the five miles through
Clifty were basically under a green canopy. There were overlook areas,
plenty of facilities, really nice. I kicked myself for not just pushing through
to Clifty last night and camping one more time.

After leaving the park, it was back onto rural roads. Several people waved.
One man remembered a couple who walked through last year and offered
their house and facilities. It was still early, so I declined this time and
pressed on. Along River Road I saw a marker on a power pole. It marked
where the Ohio River crested during the flood of 1997. The marker was way
above my head. It was sobering and served as a reminder of nature's power.
Then I knew I was tired this afternoon because I kept forgetting the next
road on my directions without pulling them out of my pocket over and over.
*Ten Cent Road? Ten Sleeps Road? Boonslick Road? Blue Tick Road? Hound Dog
Road? Fitty Cent Road?* Ten Cent Road it was.

It was overcast most of the day, which was good. I wore the sleeved shirt
again. I am seeing that it's supposed to be sunny and 90 tomorrow, and then
I may be dodging storms all weekend. Need to sleep well tonight and hit the
reset button on the past 24 hours. Tomorrow I should be back to my normal

livewire self.

Amie

Friday, May 15, 2015

Destination: Clark State Forest campground, IN
Today's Miles: 21.76
Start Location: Just Shy of Saluda, IN
Trip Miles: 915.76

My first short pause this morning was at a mini-mart in Saluda. The lady working there had braids just like mine. I picked up some wheat crackers and a blue Gatorade for breakfast, and we talked about traveling. She and her husband are taking a motorcycle trip this summer along the old Route 66. I told her that out west, they will probably have much of the road to themselves. She wished me well, and I walked on.

Early afternoon a young woman pulled up next to me and said she had seen me walking a while back. She had an organic strawberry garden, and would I like a handful of strawberries? Yes, please. As luck would have it, she had happened to slow down near a group of boys who had been riding 4-wheelers up and down the road. They overheard our quick conversation, and then asked if I needed anything. I was able to fill my water from their outside taps. A snack and water in one fell swoop.

Not much else of note really occurred today, just another peaceful section of trail until I turned south just for a bit onto Highway 31 to reach Clark State Forest. Traffic is swift, but there is a decent shoulder. I found a good campsite quickly, and there is even water available before I leave. I have been contemplating a reroute for the next day or two. The weather is calling for storms tomorrow, I don't know how severe, and the info board at the park's entry listed some trails that were closed. I need to check the weather again in the morning, and I may be heading straight south on 31 rather than go through the Deam Lake area in case I want a roof over my head tomorrow night.

I don't like it when people worry about me when there is bad weather coming through.

Amie

Saturday, May 16, 2015
Destination: Sellersburg, IN
Today's Miles: 10
Start Location: Clark State Forest campground, IN
Trip Miles: 925.76

I will try to make today's journey not sound completely convoluted. Here's how it went down. It rained last night just a little, and I woke up to nearly clear skies. I loved my camp spot, and I was ready for another good day ahead. I made some java and juggled my options, given that a) the weather calls for rain the next 3 days. b) The park info board listed closed areas, and I realized it's Saturday, which means the park office is closed and there is no one to ask about the route in my TBTs and whether it's even passable via my listed trails to Deam Lake area. c) In the TBTs there is an alternate route listed for the main book route, and the alt route's description is 18 lines long. That's the length of an English sonnet plus four more lines. Sonnets are pretty cool and everything, but I don't feel like deconstructing a Shakespearean sonnet just to get out of Clark State Forest, and the alt route might send me into a currently closed area, which I can't ask about because the park office is closed. d) If I stay on book route and head toward Deam Lake area, I would have no chance of getting a roof over my head until Sunday night, and my friend NOAA.gov indicated a 70% chance of storms, possibly severe, and like I have said here before, I'm just not that hardcore.

Therefore, I opted to pack up and go back out of the forest to HWY 31, which I had just walked last night per the TBTs. No problem. This road would take me more directly south to Sellersburg, where I could a) turn west at St. Joe Road and within a 2-mile jaunt be back on my TBTs and forge on into New Albany, or b) get a roof over my head in Sellersburg tonight if the skies turn on me. I really wanted another 20+ day, so I headed south on 31. I had 8 miles to St. Joe Road, and there I would choose the longer or shorter day, depending on whether I was incurring mother nature's wrath or not.

It did rain off and on for several miles north of St. Joe Road, but it really didn't bother me, and I was quite warm. There were periods of no rain as well, and I was actually pretty content. At St. Joe Road, the skies looked to be brightening. Onward to New Albany! Another good day. I turned west to rejoin HWY 111, which takes the ADT the rest of the way into New Albany. Simple. Are ya still with me?

Less than a mile west, it started pouring like crazy. I could soon feel water sloshing in my shoes, and visibility was getting poorer. This was still moderately all right, as I now just had about 11 miles to go, and I would allow myself a motel night after three good mileage days.

Well, the dang St. Joe Road has to cross HWY 60 to continue west to 111. The TBTs also list St. Joe Road as an option to get to town, so this is not just me blindly hacking out a path. At 60, there was so much traffic going both ways, and I had to jog north a hair to continue on St. Joe Road. It was not a direct cross. There was also a hill from my left, so I couldn't see very far south.

It was still pouring, and to my right was one long line of headlights. I waited for a bit for a break in traffic. There was no lengthy break in the headlights, and what if a car came whizzing along without its lights on? I turned left to catch another road to 111, Poindexter Lane, and I hoped this intersection would have a light, or be at the top of a hill. It was still pouring hard, but I was still all right with slogging through to New Albany. I mean, I could not get more soaked, so why not get some miles in the process? And HWY 60 had a huge shoulder, which I only needed for an eighth of a mile or so before it was back to calmer 111.

So I guess at this point you could say I had my first run-in with the law, if you don't count Jamie and I asking Cincinnati dispatch to call us a cab. A Sellersburg officer pulled over just to ask if I was all right. I don't think I was on 60 long enough for anyone to report me. He rolled down the window, and the car looked so dry and so . . . mobile. Plus, the officer was very cute. I found myself explaining my situation with a smile, and then I heard myself asking if he could give me a ride into Sellersburg to the nearest motel. What? No, this wasn't the plan! Wake up, stupid, wake up! He said yes, and I crammed my stuff into the back seat, and . . . Aaaaaaaaah. Yep, I raised the white flag in the pouring rain.

He asked my name and ran my DOB in the computer on the short jaunt to Sellersburg. I must have checked out, no wants or warrants on me. Good thing I returned my last couple library books back in Santa Maria. I shook his hand and retreated into dryness. Everything is strewn about the room true to form on motel night. I am bummed about the paltry 10 miles, but I am delighted to be dry.

So if I still have any readers left at this point to make today's toast with me, here's to not being forced into backtracking on any confusing Clark Forest trails with sonnet-length descriptions, not being stranded in the rain at Deam Lake, and getting rescued by an extremely handsome Sellersburg cop. I feel protected AND served!

Cheers!

Amie

Sunday, May 17, 2015

Destination: Southwest of Bridgeport, IN
Today's Miles: 22.27
Start Location: Sellersburg, IN
Trip Miles: 948.03

Task one this morning was the 3 miles from Sellersburg back to the ADT. This wasn't really extra miles, just a different road back to the trail. I got an early start, hoping to get in some miles in case another storm blew through. New Albany was within my sights as a safe haven.

Back on 111, or Grants Line Road, I walked south. There I was reminded that it is feast or famine when it comes to grocery and shopping opportunities. For two weeks it's nothing but Cleetus's Gas and Grill, and then we have today. I first had a choice between Walgreen's and CVS, where I picked up more sunscreen and some Clif Bars. A few miles later, Kroger was right on trail. I bought some cashews, and then I ransacked the freezer cases for Ezekiel, but got skunked on my Biblical bread. I then walked a bit more, and there was a Wal Mart. I had to go in because I wanted a small can of bug spray. I also wanted some basic cotton socks. I know that cotton is supposed to be the worst fabric to use when doing something like this, but my fancy, wicking, no-blister socks already deteriorated, and I threw them away a week ago. Plus, the only blisters I have ever gotten were during a stint when I was sporting those socks. My best Smart Wool socks are wearing thin in the heels, and the other back-up pair are too thin to wear all day. I don't really like them except for sleeping socks in cold weather. So I bought a 6-pack of basic Wal-Mart cotton socks, and if a pair gets too wrecked or out of control, I won't feel guilty just tossing it.

I continued on through New Albany, the rain still holding off. I actually applied sunscreen several times today and thought I might miss rain completely. That did not turn out to be the case. It rained hard a couple times for 5 or 10 minutes.

South of New Albany is Bridgeport, which features a large Horseshoe Casino and hotel. I was tempted by the hotel briefly, but I kept moving. The trail finally left HWY 111 this afternoon at Doolittle Hill Road. I got to end my day climbing a long hill. I tapped out after the hill, and I spied a good camp spot right at the top.

It can rain now. I am snuggled in. All is well.

Amie

Monday, May 18, 2015

Destination: Corydon, IN
Today's Miles: 15.26
Start Location: Southwest of Bridgeport, IN
Trip Miles: 963.29

Today was day three in a row of waking up wondering about the rain. I started early again, and the trail continued along country roads, houses and farms here and there. I used the last of my water this morning for a small bit of coffee, so I began the hunt for a nice home, not too far off the road, where I would feel comfortable knocking on the door to ask for water. It was overcast and not hot, so I was not feeling desperate or dehydrated.

A cute house on a curve looked inviting. The lady looked wary of me at first, understandably, as I think I had my MK shirt tied around my neck in a weird way. I smiled, showing that I have all my teeth, and asked if it would be all right if I filled from the outside faucet. She instead took my containers in the house to fill from the sink. When she came out, she warned me of ticks and said that a mixture of half Listerine and half water sprayed on the body repels ticks. Never heard of that one. I would rather smell like Listerine than bug spray.

Just a few sprinkles fell here and there, no serious rain at all today, and I continued on toward Corydon contemplating what to do for the night. There is lodging in Corydon, but I didn't really want to pay for motel again so soon. I needed to do laundry, as I have done no laundry since the uber-terrible motel, and I was out of food. The frugal plan would be to restock food and keep walking past Corydon, and at some point camp.

Let me say up front that I believe in this trail magic concept. I don't go looking for it under every rock, and I don't expect it to occur on a daily basis. The really neat coincidences and a helping hand just at the moment of need are rare, but they make me shake my head and smile big when they come out of nowhere. It's like the universe giving you a boost, affirmation, and a pat on the shoulder.

Such a thing happened this afternoon. Just as I reached Corydon, some magic really fell in my lap. A man in a red truck was at a stop sign when I walked by. He cut the engine and asked how far I was going. I said probably to or past Corydon tonight, and then I explained my overall trip and how long I'd been out here. He was floored, and then he said, "You know, Lewis and Clark came through here. John Shields, one of the Corps of Discovery's enlisted men, was given a land grant near here after the expedition, and not

172

too long ago, I found where I believe his remains to be and put a headstone at his burial site." Wow!I told him I had just driven that trail last summer, and I couldn't believe he had just brought up one of my favorite stories from U. S. history out of the blue. He then said he owned an RV park here in town, the Grand Trails RV Park, and that if I wanted to stay there tonight, to tell the office that Dennis sent me, and it's on him. I felt that little shiver when things from way out in the universe converge. And the RV park is right on trail, too. Bonus. Thank you, Dennis.

I got to take care of all my needs, shower, and charge my devices here at the park, and all as the result of a chance crossing at an intersection with someone who had a common interest. I walked the two blocks to the store and restocked. I indulged in a half gallon of whole milk, and among the normal pack food I buy, I got a small chicken noodle soup for tomorrow night. It's supposed to clear off for the week and cool back down, lows in the mid-40s starting tomorrow night. Perfect.

My laundry is drying, there is a cool breeze, and I find myself in want of nothing.

Amie

Tuesday, May 19, 2015

Destination: Leavenworth, IN
Today's Miles: 15.24
Start Location: Corydon, IN
Trip Miles: 978.53

Today's route required another judgment call. Seven miles into the day I was to turn left and follow the Adventure Hiking Trail. The AHT is a little over 20 miles of wooded paths. According to my map, there are plenty of camping spots, which sounded great, but when I reached the AHT, I had a few issues with stepping off into the woods. First, my TBTs say to use the "yellow AHT trail map and description." I don't have this map, and I know it's my fault for not obtaining it ahead of time. I am just not thinking that far ahead these days, and it's refreshing. I was hoping there would be a big map and info board at the trailhead, but there was not. I walked down the path a bit, and I only saw a green signpost. My directions say to follow the yellow. I looked back at my map, and if I followed the complete AHT, I would ultimately emerge back out onto HWY 462 after 20+ miles, whereas if I took the bike alternate route, I would be at 462 in 1.3 miles. Twenty miles to gain 1.3 miles? And the numero uno reason I took the bicycle alternate and avoided the woods is that the ticks are a nightmare, and I am scared of them. That's right, I said it. Call me a withering violet; I don't care. I have no one with me to check my back and head after two days of roaming the AHT. I do use bug spray, and I think I have every little spot on my legs memorized from checking myself often. It's those tiny ticks you can barely see that creep me out the most. I will be more adventurous and feel up to a little side excursion along the wooded AHT when I have someone with me. I have brushed three off of me today, and that was just from walking in mowed grass.

So the bike alternate was very short, and I was soon kicked back onto Route 62. The trail follows this road 8 or so more miles into the town of Leavenworth, and it makes you work to get there. I climbed and climbed today before finally seeing the Welcome to Leavenworth sign.

Coming into town, I spied a large stone picnic area, and I also saw that it contained power outlets for charging my phone. I may be weary early from the climb into town, and I may or may not be calling the non-street side of the stone structure my home for the night. I can refresh on water and a bit of food on my way through town in the morning. If it is like the last two small towns I have walked through, there may be a cute coffee shop along

Main Street calling my name. I can treat myself with a fancy coffee I will drink with my pinky out because today marked two months of walking.

Amie

Wednesday, May 20, 2015

Destination: Just Shy of Dexter, IN
Today's Miles: 18.92
Start Location: Leavenworth, IN
Trip Miles: 997.45

This morning brought about a double blessing: I got to pack up a completely dry tent, and just inside the town of Leavenworth, there is an excellent general store, replete with groceries and a few small tables where I could sit and have some coffee. I drank from a large foam cup, so I didn't put my pinky out, but the morning's perk and conversation with the general store's owners were a great start to my day.

The trail continued through a couple of tiny map-dot towns, and followed the Ohio River for much of the day. At times the trail left the river's edge and entered forested areas that completely blocked the sun, and at times very few cars passed me. These dark, infrequently driven sections reminded me of a show from several years ago that was on The History Channel, I think, *Life after People*. The program was speculative, but it hypothesized what nature would do if humans suddenly went "poof," and the earth was left alone to do as it wished. Our houses, roads, infrastructure, would soon be destroyed by the elements, our bridges would eventually collapse, rivers would reroute themselves, and within something like a thousand years, few signs would remain that people even existed or tried to tame nature. A few times today, I felt like a lone interloper in the *Life after People* film.

The cooler weather was very nice also. It helped decrease my water demands today, and I was able to keep myself covered. I crossed back into the Central Time Zone too. I found the perfect camp spot, and when I got set up, I checked my phone and realized that it was an hour earlier than it felt. That's okay. I will just get to enjoy the morning an hour earlier tomorrow.

Amie

Thursday, May 21, 2015

Destination: North of Tell City, IN
Today's Miles: 16
Start Location: Just Shy of Dexter, IN
Trip Miles: 1013.45

One thousand miles today. Five hundred was a nice milestone, but it's only now that I actually feel like I've done something. To put it in perspective, I have completed approximately 20% of the ADT book route, and I've walked across about one fourth of the United States, if you choose to walk a more direct route.

I did mentally celebrate a thousand miles, but I've also been experiencing a three-day period of ambivalence about continuing versus putting this on pause for a little while. I was walking through the Hoosier National Forest today, and I couldn't stay out of the ticks. Every time I stopped and looked at my legs, shoes, or socks, two or three of those little, tiny ones would be crawling on me. I brushed them off, but I began having visions of tiny ticks I can barely see getting into my stuff and attaching to my head or back, and I would not know until they infected me with something. I got The Fear.

I proceeded on HWY 70 until I finally reached its junction with 32. There was an Indiana DOT complex at the intersection and a small building that I hid behind and obsessively checked myself with a deer-in-the-headlights look. I may have curled up in a fetal position and sucked my thumb too. I don't remember. I wasn't crying, for I have yet to cry on this trip, but I made some distraught-sounding phone calls during which I made some resolutions that had little to do with walking through any more ticks. A thousand miles seemed like a good pause point today. I was no longer zealously attached to the enterprise, and I was close to bailing.

In addition to plagues of ticks that should be mentioned in the book of Revelation, another contributing factor to my waning fortitude has been my diet. Man cannot live on bread alone, nor can he walk 150 miles on little more than saltines and Frito Lay jalapeño, bacon, peanut butter, and laboratory orange cheese Munchies crackers without placing himself in a fugue state. My nutrition has been terrible, and it caught up with me this week.

I headed south on HWY 37. A few miles south of the DOT complex was a church. I stepped inside and sat on the entryway steps, waiting for someone to come along so that I could ask to camp discreetly behind their facility. I made another phone call and contemplated re-entering real life. It wasn't creepers, storms, rednecks, meth, potheads, no-shoulder highways, Klan, or unleashed pit bulls that were defeating me. Rather, it was something the size of a pinhead.

The pastor arrived to lock up. I explained myself and asked permission to camp out back. Instead, he gave me free reign of the church basement, bathroom with shower, kitchen, microwave and coffee pot, whatever I needed, no questions asked. I felt blessed beyond words, and I wrote down my information to affirm that I was legit. Thank you, Pastor Shelby.

Amie

Friday, May 22, 2015

Destination: Tell City, IN
Today's Miles: 0
Start Location: North of Tell City, IN
Trip Miles: 1013.45

I finished walking into Tell City, but I will not count these miles because they were off trail. I have been talked down from the edge of the cliff. I decided to use this holiday weekend to rest completely.

I will continue the trail on Monday!

Amie

The Four Questions

Academic year 2018-19 found me teaching in an alternative high school. I applied for the position because I wanted to try a nontraditional school setting. The school's curriculum was delivered almost exclusively online except for a few offline pieces in most courses. I was not responsible for as much direct teaching or completing truckloads of grading. I was to facilitate students' journey through the online curriculum delivery system, Acellus, and be, as this brave new world of teacher preparation tells us, a guide on the side, an academic cheerleader, and a social-emotional mentor to help students complete classes toward their 22-credit diploma.

This district had, the year prior, been recognized as a Capturing Kids' Hearts National Showcase District. CKH is a strategy for building a positive school culture. Districts implement CKH to better the students' views of school, teachers, one another, themselves, and their academic pursuits. CKH strategies foster relationship-building among staff and students.

Several foundational strategies govern the operation of every CKH classroom. During the first few weeks of school, for example, every teacher undergoes the process of creating with his or her students what's known as the social contract. Students in each period call out a list of words that describe how administrators, staff, and students are to treat one another. The idea is that teachers refer to that particular hour's social contract to redirect students when they misbehave or indulge in learned helplessness, negative self-talk, and the remaining tactics within the panoply of self-sabotaging schemes. The social contract is to help keep order, positivity, and zen flowing in the classroom.

Teachers are to stand in the hall and greet students by name at the door with a handshake every day as they enter the classroom. This promotes positive touch. And it is affirming for kids to hear their name said aloud. CKH also offers some approaches to keep students on task during class. One bedrock classroom discipline strategy is to ask in CKH parlance what are known as The Four Questions. Here they are in order. Teacher: What are you doing? What are you supposed to be doing? Are you doing it? and What are you going to do about it?

Here is the way the CKH trainers and administrators the world over picture these Four Question, teacher-student interactions taking place when a student is off task. (Insert student's name), *what are you doing*? Drawing dragons. *What are you supposed to be doing*? My *Julius Caesar* Act III questions. *Are you doing it*? No. *What are you going to do about it*? Work on my *Julius Caesar* questions. In the ideal CKH world, the student would immediately redirect. The dragon rendering would cease and desist after a teacher-student high five, and no discipline or consequences would need ensue.

Meanwhile, back in reality, here is how the Four Questions go over with defiant, oppositional students. (Insert student's name), *what are you doing?* What does it look like I'm doing? *Well, nothing, and that's a problem. What are you supposed to be doing?* I don't know. I mean, can't find that outline, and you haven't gave [sic] me another one. And I talked to the counselor anyway, and she said she's gonna put me in a different class cuz [sic] this one's too hard. I'm so far behind I'm not gonna graduate anyway if I stay in this class, so the office is putting me in all easier ones. Can I go to the office and talk to the principal? Cuz I've been waiting for the office to call me out to get me outta this class. *Unfortunately, you used all your allotted hall passes the first two weeks of the semester, so you'll have to wait until the office calls down here for you. In the meantime, you probably should work on your outline just in case the counselor leaves you in this class. I don't want you to waste time and get even further behind.*

*Gives seventeen-year-old student another copy of the color-coded outline replete with pictures and sentence starters.

*Student gets a pencil from the teacher's pencil stash because he never brings one of his own.

*Student begins scribbling in the margins of the new outline.

*He then combs through the multi-page outline not reading instructions, but to find the largest blank space he can find and draws dragons.

*The teacher reapproaches a few minutes later, watches the student who is nearing voting age scribble and draw dragons, and shakes head.

*Teacher can feel blood pressure rise and braces self for another round of The Four Questions and a possible confrontation.

(Insert student's name), what are you doing? The fuck does it look like?

Okay, here is where you have a choice. You can alter your attitude and get busy on what you're supposed to be doing, or you can go down to ISS, which means you're choosing a referral for defiance. I told you I don't know how to do this outline!

There is a very simple solution here. You can read the directions and then ask me for help. Instead, unfortunately you've been drawing dragons and you're off task. I cannot allow you just to sit here and waste time. So what is your choice going to be? Stay in here and work, or go to ISS? Fuck this. I'm going to the quiet room.

Okay, I will call down and let them know you're on the way. Be careful how you leave the room; that will determine what kind of referral I will write.

*Student packs up everything except for copy number two of the outline, slams door behind him.

*Later that day, the student is removed from this teacher's class and placed with a different teacher to finish out the credit.

*All offline paperwork requirements have been waived for this student for the course in question.

*Student receives five discipline points and a twenty-minute detention for abusive language, then buys his way out of detention with Hawg Dollars.

Today's teachers also ask themselves The Four Questions. It goes something like this.

What are you doing? Well, these days I'm not too sure. I am serving in a high school building, but it feels like I am teaching third grade English. I work really hard to create lessons and outlines and projects, but it seems that right after I curate a great assignment, I immediately set upon the task of dumbing it all back down. I don't know what minimum expectations seem to be for a 17-year-old anymore. I spend my entire planning period filling out IEP paperwork, mental health or physician's evaluations for students on meds, scanning my gradebook for evidence that I am indeed not violating any one student's IEP within what feels like a three-dimensional chess match of student accommodations in nearly every hour of every day. I spend my planning period grading modified quizzes and tests that seem as if they would take less time, but actually take twice as long. I spin on a never-ending hamster wheel providing meaningful, challenging work to all of my students.

What are you supposed to be doing? I thought my objective as a teacher was teaching students how to read critically, how to organize and write coherently. I thought my goal was that students leave my class with a new set of hard skills that they didn't possess before taking my class. I thought it was a good idea to make sure they were a little bit better spellers or readers by the end of my class. I am not quite sure what the counselors and administrators truly want me to do. What is my number one task? Be every student's surrogate parent, or teach a quality curriculum and foster some expectations? I cannot do both. I think I am to instill work ethic and responsibility into my students. Skills they will need in the workforce. Or . . . am I to do their thinking and much of their work for them so that they can get their diploma and then let the Real World sort it all out? I went into this loving reading and grammar and preparing students for the writing demands that college composition will require. I am not sure if I even like teaching reading that no one wants to do and grammar for which few possess the foundational knowledge to grasp. Do I just give them their A's so that they can keep their GPA? Or do I maintain high standards so that they are not stuck languishing in a remedial writing course they have to pay for, but for which they receive no college credit? Do I continue to differentiate for our bright students and spend my weekends preparing and grading the different levels of work? It wears me out. I don't know any other way to do my job right. Or should I just dumb it all down for everyone and show a movie once a week? Have students make a poster? I honestly don't know why I am here at school most days of the week.

Are you doing it? Delivering an enriching curriculum? Not really. But after nearly two decades in public classrooms, I kinda have to stick up for myself. I feel like there are fewer people who want me to do a good job, or what I consider a good job according my definition of what quality high school English classes should look like. Parents may say they want their child to be challenged and learn, but really they don't. They want the child not to have to work too hard. Most parents want the status quo: mediocrity, winning sports teams, free daycare and meals nine months out of the year. I have sat in one parent meeting *ever* in which the parents expected more out of me. During most parent meetings, if the subject of expectations arises, I leave feeling like the parent wants me to accept less from the child. Twist myself into pretzels to pass the child anyway. Administrators claim they want their teachers to embrace rigor, raise test scores, and hold students to higher expectations, making them college and career ready, but really they don't. Administration cares about all students graduating, regardless of whether they are literate. The students know they are the protected species. Every other child is now a special pleader and enters my class armed with disorders, phobias, -isms, and special plans that excuse them from having to execute in my class or produce a written product with any gravitas. Most of them quickly become aware that they really don't have to perform in any cognitive arena, and that someone—counselor, principal, special ed staff—will swoop in and rescue them at the last second by forcing the teacher to take missing work long past its due date, or to inflate a writing score. I really have little power over what I teach, no power to uphold standards to which I profess to cleave. I have given the very best of myself to this profession. Many teachers feel that their best is not wanted. I feel cut off at the pass at nearly every ascent.

What are you going to do about it? I don't know. By the time my day ends, and especially by the time my week ends, I am too mentally exhausted to think about researching other career fields that I could step into with my English degree. The modern education system is like a cult. Everyone is kept too tired to question anything. Inquiry, doubt, or dissent of every new fad is discouraged or even punished. Members are expected to devote inordinate amounts of time to the group and group-related activities (i. e. inservice days run amok). The public education cult implies that its supposedly exalted ends justify whatever means it deems necessary. This may result in members participating in behaviors or activities they would have considered reprehensible or unethical before joining the group (e.g., accepting disgracefully poor quality work from students, completely abandoning the teaching of workplace skills and behaviors). The group displays excessively zealous and unquestioning commitment to its leader, and (whether he is alive or dead) regards his belief system, ideology, and practices as the Truth, as law (blindly following every new teaching strategy, curriculum adoption, or classroom management philosophy). I don't have the head-space to search for other careers on my weekends either. My weekends are increasingly devoted to grading essays or having uninterrupted time to give quality feedback to my non-IEP, 504, or MTSS students.

I tell myself every summer that I will pursue something different. But summer is when I am taking more classes at my own expense to recertify for the following school year. Or maybe I am continually working toward advanced degrees I do not want so that I don't top out on the salary sched-ule and effectively make less every school year. Summer is when I have time to reflect and revamp my projects and assignments with any sense of objectivity whatsoever. Summer is when I can actually have friends. And when I do take some time to look at other careers, I realize that most require degrees or experience I do not have. I just finished paying off my student loans. I do not want to assume more debt to get another degree right now. And when do I have spare bandwidth during the school year to take courses in a new field? Even online? I feel stuck. I invested years and money into getting this degree. But teaching is affecting my mental health. It affects my relationships. By Wednesday or Thursday of every week, I have nothing left to give. I struggle to refresh and recover enough even during the sum-mers to recharge for another year. I really don't want to do this anymore.

I saw Flip Flippen speak a few months ago. He is the founder and chairman of Flippen Group, the educator training company that developed Capturing Kids' Hearts. Flip's mission is this: "To build relationships and processes that bring out the best in people." Flip is a wonderful man. Lis-tening to him and reading the CKH materials instills in me a tiny sense of guilt. *What am I doing wrong?* Maybe I am just not as good, patient, kind, forgiving, easygoing, or loving as Flip. He could do my job infinitely better than I can. I try to be the best version of myself every day and draw deeply from a bottomless emotional well, yet it never seems to be enough.

It's this fourth question is the one that haunts me still. *What am I going to do about it?* I still don't know.

Monday, May 25, 2015

Destination: St. Meinrad, IN
Today's Miles: 15.86
Start Location: Tell City, IN
Trip Miles: 1029.31

After a holiday weekend of complete down time, I am feeling much better. Thank you, everyone who emailed through this site, texted, or Facebook
messaged me with encouragement, empathy, and even lectures about eating crackers for breakfast. You are correct! One issue with food is that there
are some two or three-day stretches during which the grocery opportunity
is a convenience store with a few rows of basic household staples, an array
of pop and candy bars, party peanuts of the cheapest variety, some canned
or packaged items with a half life rivaling styrofoam, tube-shaped meats
on metal rollers languishing under a heat lamp, or heavy canned goods. In
some of them, I can sit down and order a sandwich or something, but I have
to consider the next 48 hours. Sometimes there are no good protein bars,
and there isn't much of market in a town of 200 for fresh fruit and other
quality calories. Thus the cracker packets.

I looked at the rest of Indiana, and services look to be a little more frequent. That makes me happy. Plus, I have the remainder of my Ezekiel loaf
from the weekend to tide me over.

I also took the bike alternate that gets me out of Hoosier National Forest
more quickly, and today I did not have tick issues. I also have a second type
of insect repellent.

So I got a late start today, but the walking was good. Today was a lot of
country roads, soft shoulders, gravel roads with no dust due to rain, and it
only sprinkled on me for about ten minutes. Nice. I am glad I have another
pair of shoes on the way because these now have 400 miles on them, and I
can tell they are breaking down. The second pair bites the dust. Everything
else is holding up pretty well, including my mojo after essentially three zero
days and lots of family, friends, and reader contact.

I proceed on.

Amie

Tuesday, May 26, 2015

Destination: Lincoln State Park, IN
Today's Miles: 14.63
Start Location: St. Meinrad, IN
Trip Miles: 1043.94

A most lovely nine hours of sleep last night just within the town of St. Meinrad. My first sight rounding the bend into town was this school of theology in the distance. I thought it made a nice picture. My second sight was the town baseball/softball complex with a set of bleachers right next to a power pole with an electrical outlet. I sat, drank water, and charged my phone. In trying to extend the time between motel stays, one must keep the phone charged using alternate means, if needs by stealth.

I left St. Meinrad to walk a few miles in the sun. I put on sunscreen, hoping the rain would hold off. That didn't turn out to be the case. Just inside the town of Santa Claus, it rained pretty hard for about 45 minutes. There was nowhere for me to take cover on this one, so I stood behind someone's F-250 parked opposite some houses where there was a canopy of tree limbs stretching out to provide a bit of cover. I stood with my head down under the poncho and pushed the front of it out from me so that my shoes were also covered. I stayed pretty dry.

The rain subsided, and I walked on through town to find there is a small amusement park there, the Holiday World and Splashin' Safari. I couldn't help but think that the park's name reflected my current and very recent states: I just had a lovely holiday weekend, and I was splashin' through my Tuesday. Not sure about the safari part, but I kind of giggled at the name.

I have decided that when I am wearing the poncho with shorts, what I look like from the front reminds me of a scene from the wonderful film *To Kill a Mockingbird*. Near the end of the movie, Jem and Scout are leaving the schoolhouse after the Halloween pageant, and Scout is dressed as a ham. She walks out of the school still in her ham costume because she lost her clothes, and she has to walk home in the dark as a ham. She is so cute because all you can see is this brown ham with one hole in front for her eyes, and her little legs walking under the stiff ham shape. With the poncho on, the bottoms of my shorts are not visible from the front. It's like Scout's ham costume, except blue, with legs sticking out walking. Except my blue poncho does not have HAM printed across the front.

A few minutes later, across from the Splashin' Safari park, the sun came out for a little while, and then I really took a cue from the universe. I heard some thunder and looked around. There were dark blue clouds gathering again on all sides. In front of me was someone's barn with a lean-to, under which was some farm equipment. The rain had not restarted, but I high-tailed it through some tall grass to the barn. A storm then blew through, and I hid there for about an hour and a half behind the farm equipment. The rain came down so hard, but I was snug and dry. It really was a super-ior hiding spot, and I began making preliminary plans to camp there if the weather looked as if it were to misbehave through the night.

Finally the storm cleared out. At the theme park, there must have been some timber wolf roller coaster ride because while approaching the park, I kept hearing a timber wolf howling noise. When the wolf noise and theme park rides resumed after the hard pounding, I figured that was also my cue that it was clear for a while.

I got held up again today for another two hours or so, but this time I didn't mind. The trail goes through the site of Abraham Lincoln's boyhood home. The family's reconstructed cabin is there as well as some other struc-tures, a short trail to the visitor's center, and the center itself. I spent most of my time at the cabin, listening to one of the interpreters talk, and then I watched him get out an old spinning wheel and spin wool into thread. I have never seen that done before. It was so cool, and a very relaxing task to watch and engage in, as he said. He was good at it too. The freshly spun thread wound perfectly around the bobbin, with very little variation in the thread's thickness.

I milled around the site and then continued on to the state park, where camping was on the menu. There was a fee to camp, I don't believe I have paid to camp yet, but there is a nice facility with showers, clean running water, and I can charge my phone again on the morrow before I leave. Plus there is a security guard who patrols the sites. I think I am the only one here, and I cannot imagine anyone gettin' crazy at the Abraham Lincoln State Park campsites on a Tuesday night in placid southern Indiana after the long holiday weekend's debauch, but I could be wrong. I guess I feel safer leaving my poncho alone hanging in the restroom and shower facility to dry.

A few people who are not on my regularly scheduled text/Facebook list for maildrops have asked about sending me a care package from as far away as Washington and back in Santa Maria. Thank you so much. I think I will reach my next mail drop Friday or Saturday, so too late this time, but I think next time I will just try to reply to anyone who has asked and a general time frame for my arrival. I am flattered. And food today was cranberries and figs, a little bit of Love Crunch granola, and a few more slices of Zeke.

Not many miles and wet shoes, but a good day.

Amie

Wednesday, May 27, 2015

Destination: Scales Lake Park, Booneville, IN
Today's Miles: 19.27
Start Location: Lincoln State Park, IN
Trip Miles: 1063.21

Last night around dark another family pulled into the grounds to camp. The parents had a small girl and a dog named Cuddles. As the family set up their tent and rustled up something to eat, they kept scolding Cuddles and calling it back to the campsite over and over. Cuddles got in trouble incessantly until they went to bed or I fell asleep, whichever came first I am not sure.

Falling asleep last night to Cuddles running amok, I was reminded of these neighbors we had when we all still lived at home. They were a tad eccentric, and they had a dog they named Peaches. They actually pierced Peaches' ear and gave him an earring, Peaches sported a bandana for a while, and one year for St. Patrick's Day, they painted poor Peaches green. It seemed like every night while we were eating dinner, they would fling open the back door and call the dog by loudly screeching, "Peeeeeeeaaaaaa-aaaachessssssss!"

One day we realized we hadn't seen Peaches for a while, and I think Mom asked the neighbor girl what happened to their dog. The girl gave a rather nebulous account of Peaches' demise by reporting, "Peaches died." I don't think we ever knew what happened to Peaches. We didn't want to know. I silently saluted Peaches, while trying to ignore Cuddles, before drifting off last night.

I woke up to a clear morning, and as I had some coffee, I read an email from Dad that confirmed my resupply box had been sent. He also said not to worry too much about crackers for breakfast. As I mention before, my family lived in Estonia for several years, and among Dad's co-workers during that time were many Russians. We still quote his Russian friends from time to time, and via Dad's email I was tutored this morning on the finer points of a healthy daybreak meal. Russians would say (cue gruff Russian accent), "Good Russian breakfast: kaffe and cigarette." This would be followed by a hearty laugh.

This morning I had (cue accent) Half Russian Breakfast, kaffe only. But if I wake up to find a tick attached to me or crawling in my sleeping bag, I may be tempted to have (cue accent) Full Russian Breakfast.

I finished off the last of my pack food, the Love Crunch granola, as I walked out of the park. I knew a small town was just a couple miles down the road, and while I was thankful for a food opportunity as my map indicated, here were my options, in order and narrated in stream of consciousness, as I entered the mini-mart, the only gig in town and the only food source until Boonville tonight, which was 17 miles away. Here we go: Wide selection of motor oil and anti freeze; cooler shelves with mostly pop, energy drinks, some Gatorade; an aisle of toiletries and remedies for the pantheon of gastric complaints; a few granola bars; some Special K bars, candy necklaces, bubble tape; one flavor of Clif bars, pretty expensive, I will grab two; Slim Jims; some expensive beef jerky; hot Cheetos; more chips; a few bags of pretzels and salted rods; some gum and mints; a Jenga game of Busch Lite 30-packs; some nuts but no large containers, I will grab some almonds and one pack of mixed nuts, it had better not be all those crummy party peanuts; some air fresheners; a newspaper rack; a sign admonishing customers that they may not buy lottery tickets using EBT; and the clerk staring at me like I have 6 heads. Six dollars later, I scrounged up enough decent calories to walk to Boonville.

I followed Lincoln Trail Road much of the morning. A storm blew through again around noon. I hid in a conveniently placed barn again and sat down while it rained and thundered a while. It was a nice 45-minute break, and the sky to the southwest soon cleared. I proceeded on.

The last 7 miles to Boonville were tough. Not much of a shoulder and a steep ditch made for slow walking. I took another little break and checked my legs and shoes for the bane of my existence. There were five or six ticks trying to escape my shoelaces or in their death throes due to all the chemicals sprayed on my shoes the last couple weeks. It was during this last break that my phone rang. It was Pastor Shelby from last week. He was just checking on me, and he wanted to know if it was okay to give my number to some ladies at the church. They wanted to send me something. Absolutely, and what a nice surprise.

I continued on into Boonville with sore feet. I walked maybe a mile off trail to reach this park, where a campsite with electricity and all the water I need is where it's at. It may rain a bit tonight. That's fine. I will worry about it in the morning over kaffe, probably not cigarette. Hearty laugh.

So here's to ornery dogs with sugary sweet names inversely proportional to their behavior that thankfully belong to the neighbors, barns that always seem to be there when I need them, and Good Russian Breakfast.

Cheers!

Amie

Thursday, May 28, 2015

Destination: Just outside Venada, IN
Today's Miles: 12.63
Start Location: Scales Lake Park, Booneville, IN
Trip Miles: 1075.84

I left the lake park and walked through Boonville. Much of this town had a Mayberry feel to it. There was the courthouse square, complete with large lawn on all sides, parking all around, and small offices and stores on the opposite sides of the streets. Some repairs or upkeep to the fine court-house's facade indicated the community cared about their town square and its centerpiece. There was a Tastee Freeze around the corner, a 4-H center, and the leisurely pace of small-town life.

I left Boonville and walked slowly down Pelzer Road and Bethany Church Road. There was a soft shoulder at times, but mostly I kind of crept along because my shoes are fried, and my feet get sore early in the day.

Along these roads I heard a sound I have not heard in a while, the buzzing of locusts. There were many locusts flying through the air and lying along the road. Some of them seemed to have red eyes.

There was another sound deep in the trees, the source of which I could not identify. It was sort of a whirring sound. I don't know what animal or insect makes it, and at first upon leaving Boonville, I thought there may have been some factory or power plant off to my left making the noise.

The constant whirring noise reminded me of the noise that would ac-company an alien spaceship landing in the old fifties and sixties Martian movies. Or the noise in an old sci-fi film that would be made when the alien or mad scientist would make something levitate. I thought of Gore Vidal's play *Visit to a Small Planet* and his funny extra-terrestrial Kreton when I walked for a few hours listening to the whirring noise. My reveries regard-ing the differences between the original play and the bowdlerized version that was in the freshman literature book were interrupted when a lady in a truck with hay in the back slowed to ask how far I was going. I explained what I was doing, and she wished me luck before driving on.

A bit later I walked by some homes, and I heard someone calling to me. It was the same lady, and apparently now I was passing her house. Her name was Robbi, and she asked if she could walk with me for a while. By all means!

She was with me for half a mile or more. She was curious about the same details most folks want to know. How far do I go each day? Where do I sleep?

Has anything bad happened? What am I doing when I am finished? Where does the trail end? Where do I get water? I happily gave solid answers to most of these questions. On a few of the questions, I have yet to formulate a definite decision. And that's okay. Robbi bade me good day again and went home.

A few miles later I myself was wondering where I might soon ask for water when a white Toyota pulled alongside me, and a man who looked a little like Robert Duvall rolled down the window and asked if I was homeless. Ha! I laughed and said no, that I was walking on purpose. He said he was going to ask if I wanted a ride, but since I'd just enlightened him, I'd probably say no. I looked at the steering wheel, and he was driving with an open beer. I said I didn't need a ride, but did he have any water? He offered me the beer, and I laughed again and declined. He said I was approaching a farm in about a half mile. There was a tap near the road. Take all I needed, and if anyone balked at my activities, to tell them McConnel sent me.

I proceeded on toward the farm. Soon McConnel drove back by and handed me a cold bottle of Aqua Fina. He still had the open beer, and he said he'd wait at the corner to point out the water. I filled everything, checked for ticks, declined a ride into Newburgh, and expressed my gratitude as he drove away still toting the open container. He probably owns or has been working on that property for decades, and driving up and down the little county road with an open beer is just part of his day. It was funny.

I called it a day well before dark. I laughed again about old McConnel driving around with his open beer. And it was in a koozie.

Amie

Friday, May 29, 2015

Destination: Evansville, IN
Today's Miles: 17.63
Start Location: Just outside Venada, IN
Trip Miles: 1093.47

Early start today because I knew I would make Evansville, and when I give myself a motel night, I like to arrive early and enjoy its comforts for as many hours as possible. Plus, motel night trail chores take some time, and I don't like feeling rushed during this trip. I am taking a time out from real life and indulging psychologically in the following: living in the present moment only, except for plotting resupply; imposing no time frames on my arrival and departure anywhere or sleep/wake cycle; being totally self-centered, which is not the same as selfish; eschewing vacuous outside influences such as the endlessly quacking media or superficial conversation we are all exposed to on a daily basis; allowing my thoughts to tack in the direction of their choice, no reigning them back, unless I have to study the map or cross a busy intersection, of course; and existing in an orb of contentment with only the basic necessities for life. I highly recommend it, if only for a while.

Half Russian Breakfast this morning, no accent since the kaffe came from Casey's General Store in a foam cup. I drank it while walking down the road between Newburgh and Evansville. I received encouragement, as well as some blank stares, of course, at Casey's, and further down the road a lady pulled her car aside and talked to me about the neatest story.

I told her what I was up to, and she asked if I had heard of the Planet Walker. Planet Walker's real name is Dr. John Francis. He began walking around the U.S. after a large oil spill in the Bay Area, I believe in 1970. He ended up walking for about 22 years, and for much of that time he took a vow of silence. He earned his Ph.D., and somehow taught some classes during his reign of silence. She and some others have been reading up on Dr. Francis and have been retracing his steps.

She wanted to know if she could take my picture and add it to the Facebook page or other photo collection of Planet Walkers. I said sure. What an honor! I have not walked nearly as far or as long as Planet Walker, but the exchange gave me a boost.

I continued on to where the trail headed south. The ADT is supposed to follow the Ohio River and then come up into Evansville at its southwest corner. My approach to Evansville almost went off the rails at this point. Lynn

Road turns southwest and then via a gravel road supposedly connects with Shawnee Drive to bring the trail into Evansville. Since these TBTs were composed, a coal company had apparently bogarted a portion of Lynn Road, Shawnee, and another road along the Ohio banks. I turned south per the TBTs onto a road that was now paved and had signs indicating this was not a thoroughfare, and no trespassing.

I headed south anyway, as this was the only route to Shawnee Drive. Dump trucks and large trucks hauling coal passed me, and I didn't care because I had less than a mile of trespassing before supposedly gaining Shawnee. I found that along the Ohio, my road seemed to end. There was a construction trailer, several large piles of coal, two men driving frontloaders, a conveyor belt, and large circular lots for the trucks to maneuver and refill. No gravel road. I stopped at the trailer and turned around to head back north, thwarted.

At this point, I petitioned the universe. What am I supposed to do now? Send me a sign. Send someone down this road to kick me out so I can request a ride past this last 4 miles into Evansville! Am I supposed to return to Newburgh and ask their police dispatch to call me a cab? What to do?

One of the truck drivers stopped as I now backtracked north and asked if I knew where I was. The clickety-clack of the loud engine prompted me to grab the side mirror and pull myself right up as if I were getting into the cab. I pointed my poles south and asked if the gravel road to Shawnee still existed back there. He radioed someone, and yes it did. I stepped down from the rig and turned back south. Again. Another truck that had passed me walking north passed a second time, and saw me again headed south. I am sure I looked like Beavis when he drank too much cappuccino, pulled his shirt over his head, and declared, "I am the Great Cornholio" while pacing back and forth. This truck too stopped. I climbed up. He confirmed the road was there. It was now behind the coal piles, unused, overgrown, and there was a yellow gate blocking it. Just slip under the gate, and I would be on my way.

I continued south and probably befuddled the front loader driver as I strolled back by him. Finally, my road. Thank you to Poshing and Sons truckers for knowing of this now-defunct connection between roads on my map. Once again in Indiana, men who do tough, dirty jobs and drive big trucks have come to my assistance.

I selected this afternoon a bed and breakfast just 5 blocks off trail for my stay. The owners I think were apprehensive about my dragging my stuff upstairs because they knew I had been camping. They were afraid I would unleash a pestilence of bugs onto into their clean rooms. I don't blame them. I left my tent bag downstairs. The owners asked what I did back in real life, and when I told them, they replied, "Oh, you must be on sabbatical!" I said yes, a planned sanity sabbatical.

Looking forward to breakfast in the morning, I took note of a whole foods store that I will pillage and plunder like the warriors from the Capital

One credit card commercials on my way back to the trail tomorrow, and two more days to new shoes.

Amie

Saturday, May 30, 2015

Destination: Burdette Park, IN
Today's Miles: 6.46
Start Location: Evansville, IN
Trip Miles: 1099.93

A really enjoyable breakfast over which I lingered at the B and B, and then rain this afternoon, didn't allow me to get too far today, but I had a good day.

Breakfast was at 8. The proprietors had classical music playing in the background, and I got to the table right on time along with another couple. The third set of guests, an attorney and his wife, left too early for breakfast, and so 'twas I and two college professors, one or both of whom were entomologists. The husband had written several books and articles, had been interviewed over 700 times, and had appeared in *People* magazine and *The New York Times*. He and his wife were researching the cicada populations in the surrounding area. They were really interesting and entertaining to listen to, and I learned that the buzzing I've heard the past couple days is actually cicadas, not locusts.

Or according to Dad, the strange whirring noise is the sound effect used in nearly every kooky space movie viciously heckled on *Mystery Science Theatre 3000*. I also learned that there are locusts in Kansas, along with cicadas, but here in this part of Indiana I have been confusing the two. I also learned that one reason people used to refer to cicadas as locusts was that the preachers would talk about the plagues of locusts, and those who had seen the clouds of insects descending on their land and crops likened these insects to the biblical plagues. Therefore they used the term locust. Fascinating.

The table talk at times drifted off onto esoteric topics to which I could not contribute, so I just tried to keep my elbows off the table and remember that I was not eating in a tent. At one point my cloth napkin slid off onto the floor, being that I was wearing my slippery rain pants, the only clean items I had, at breakfast. I played it cool picking up my napkin and tried to follow the discussion of Egyptian beetles. I was among brilliant company, and I felt like the dirty-girl-from-the-sticks guest, but I had such a fun breakfast and the bacon, eggs, and fruit were so yummy. I was in no hurry to leave.

My clean laundry was eventually released from captivity, and I finally got on my way around 10. I walked the 5 blocks back to the trail, at which point it joined the Pigeon Creek Parkway, a walking and bike path that follows the

Ohio River for a few miles. I think Evansville was preparing for a race or fundraiser walk or something for heart health. I was seeing signs every half mile or so, and a sound stage and booths were undergoing setup along the parkway.

I was reminded again of the many half marathons and marathons I have run all over the western half of the country, and I silently thanked myself again for quitting volleyball sophomore year of high school and going out for cross country. I took it all in and watched people jog or walk by.

Three young kids were enjoying a morning out with their grandparents, and the little ones started asking me questions about my poles, where was I going, etc. I told them, and the grandparents asked if they could take a picture of me with the three little ones. Sure!

The trail left Evansville through an industrial park, but because it is Saturday, there was not much traffic. Not too far from town, the directions indicated Burdette Park, where camping and lodging were available. It was not my intent to stop for the day, just sit at a picnic table and take a break after 6 miles, apply bug spray now that I was out of town, eat a snack, check my phone, turn over to the last page of Indiana directions, and refill my water. I sat a spell and then noticed dark clouds. I walked deeper into the park looking for a picnic shelter in case of rain, and I realized what a neat park this is. There are cabins for rent, RV parking too, a swimming pool, and trails for biking, walking dogs, whatever. I made it to a shelter and waited out the rain. I walked back further and hid again from another bout of rain.

Finally around 3:30, the universe decided. Thunder rumbled, I found a tent site, and succumbed after 6 miles. But I was glad I did. It rained really hard between 4 and 5. I was delighted not to be wet, not to be looking for a place to stealth while wet, and why be in a hurry? Only 16 miles to my next mail drop town, and I can't pick my packages up until Monday morning anyway.

One more day until I can pitch these shoes before they start attracting hordes of locusts-or cicadas-or worse.

Amie

Sunday, May 31, 2015

Destination: Mt. Vernon, IN
Today's Miles: 18.39
Start Location: Burdette Park, IN
Trip Miles: 1118.32

I have decided that Sundays are my favorite days on the trail. I start early, and on Sunday mornings there are very few people out. Those who are out seem a little extra gracious and give me more room along the roads, and on Sundays most people seem to move a little more leisurely.

Today was one such Sunday. The shoulder was nicely mowed grass for quite some distance. There was a long stretch of pea gravel along another infrequently travelled road. Twelve or thirteen miles passed very quickly, and the morning was peaceful.

My only hang up today was staying on Bluff Road. A few miles from Mt. Vernon, the road came to a T, and I was instructed to turn left on Bluff Road. There was no sign, and my map app showed the road as Gun Club Road, which would meet up with Bluff shortly. I thought Gun Club Road was a pretty cool name for a road, so I took it. It led me to Bluff Road.

Just outside town, however, Bluff Road dead-ended. There was a sign and barricades. MapQuest indeed showed that Bluff Road ceased to exist for a mile maybe, and then picked back up in town. I rerouted north and then back south to Bluff Road through another coal facility. No one was really about, and I made Mt. Vernon, just coming from a different direction.

I found this town, and in the words of Dain, it looked old. In the words of Jill back in West Virginia, grubby. Not a town I would feel comfortable camping in somewhere, so I checked out the inn a mile and a half from my post office. The lady at the front desk was so sweet. She gave me two blueberry muffins as I registered, and she insisted I take some apples from the breakfast area too.

A good walk for my last full day in Indiana, if everything continues to go well.

Amie

Monday, June 01, 2015

Destination: Between Shawneetown and New Haven, Illinois
Today's Miles: 21.54
Start Location: Mt. Vernon, IN
Trip Miles: 1139.86

Mail drop day. Shoes! Nutrition! Thank you, Mom and Dad, Aunt Donna, and Andrea and Gary. Everything arrived just fine except one of the little bags of protein powder had ripped a tiny bit. But to illustrate how much I appreciate the powder and quinoa, I swished the loose powder into a corner, neatly slid it into my hand, and ate it anyway. Yes, that is how weary I have become of gas station fare.

More kudos to the owners of the motel, The Four Seasons. Rodney, one of the owners, offered to give me a ride into town to the post office at 8:30. It saved me extra steps. The only extra steps I took today were to breakfast. I asked permission to give their motel some free advertising. Four Seasons, just outside Mt. Vernon, clean, quiet, friendly staff. Go there!

I do, however, feel a little bit guilty for the grubby town comment from last night. But snap judgments are one necessary arrow in the lone traveller's quiver. Plus, outside of town I had seen two road signs with graffiti, not bullet holes, so I felt less safe. I think I came in on the wrong side of town on the ADT, but I am glad I chose the motel. I have a sneaking suspicion that the owners' kindness snowballed into the rest of my day as well.

I finished out Indiana's last eight miles on peaceful dirt roads for the most part, and then a new state. I crossed into Illinois around noon. Thank you, Indiana. Out of all the states I have walked so far, I would describe Indiana as the most pleasant.

Illinois baptized me by fire as the first 7 miles followed a highway with a decent, soft shoulder, but lots of truck traffic. Yikes! A recipe for white knuckles and Full Russian Breakfast. I have formed a hypothesis this past week that the TBTs were written before the proliferation of the oil and gas industry in this area, and the chosen roads did not have this much heavy truck traffic at press time. I support these industries, but it frays the nerves a bit to share the space with so many trucks.

About 3:30, I received a tip regarding some property owners along New Haven-Shawneetown Road who might allow me to camp on their property tonight. I arrived at the first property around 5:30, knocked on the door, and was granted permission by Ed and Judy. After a few minutes of conversation, the camping allowance ballooned into an invitation to a wonderful dinner of ham and bean soup, bread, beer, dessert, a shower, and guest room offer. Thank you, hosts.

New month, new shoes, new pack food selections that don't render me depleted and catatonic, a new state, and a nice first day in southern Illinois.

Amie

Tuesday, June 02, 2015

Destination: Pounds Hollow Campsite, Shawnee Nat. Forest, IL
Today's Miles: 21.09
Start Location: Between Shawneetown and New Haven, Illinois
Trip Miles: 1160.95

A fun breakfast this morning, I was well fed, and Judy confirmed that the upcoming towns along the River to River Trail do have grocery opportunities. Thank you again to my generous hosts.

I continued following the road down into Shawneetown. When I got there, I saw the carnival was in town. I tried extra hard not to look homeless or risk getting co-opted into the ranks of carnies. I whistled past the carnival to the Dollar General, where I picked up some additional insect repellent and fragrance-free baby wipes. Lookin' like about 97 miles to next lodgingand laundry opportunity. This could get rough. In the DG, I discovered a food that I had no idea the market supported: microwave pork rinds. They were in a folded packet just like microwave popcorn. It's such a shame I am not carrying a microwave and had no use for this snack. Maybe next time.

The walking surface and traffic level were really ideal for most of the day, soft dirt shoulder. I knew I was nearing Shawnee National Forest and campgrounds by late afternoon. I did accept a very short ride to escape the remainder of Highway 1 and truck traffic. Lonnie, my driver who appeared dressed for work and not an ax-murdering spree, works for the coal industry, running a loader. He confirmed that fracking in this area is beginning to really boom. He asked where I wanted dropped, and as we were going a bit fast past the Pounds Hollow Rec Area, I said the Rim Rock site would be just fine. Both were in Shawnee NF, and I was pretty sure I could drop anchor in either.

Apparently within National Forest property, the presence of a parking lot, restroom structures, picnic areas, and level grounds do not a campsite make. There were signs at several spots within Rim Rock blaring No Overnight Camping. I went over to the map and noticed that Pounds Hollow offered camping, 1.3 miles back. I sat for a bit, heard Judas Priest in the background, and considered "Breakin' the Law" and camping at Rim Rock anyway, but I didn't. I went ahead and backtracked the mile to Pounds Hollow. I was glad I did. There was water, electrical boxes for mobile device battery reload, dumpster for morning trash offload, peace of mind knowing I won't "get in trouble" on my first night on the RTR Trail, and music to listen to issuing from my distant-enough neighbors as I unpacked. Not Judas Priest, but Tim McGraw. I miss music.

I counted the mile backwards to PH in my daily total, as it was on trail. I won't count it tomorrow. I did not count the car mile or two.

Figs and kale chips for dinner. Contentment is the highest form of happiness.

Amie

Wednesday, June 03, 2015

Destination: Garden of the Gods, Shawnee National Forest, IL
Today's Miles: 8.90
Start Location: Pounds Hollow Campsite, Shawnee Nat. Forest, IL
Trip Miles: 1169.85

Trying to decide if sharing the next 120 miles of trail with horses is going to be one single fun. Left Pounds Hollow to find another cool morning. I had just a couple miles before the trail left the road and joined the River to River Trail. I found the junction and was happy to see the main route (called the 001 Road or the i Trail) was very wide and easy to follow.

About a half mile in, I hit the first mud pit. I looked for a way around it, but poison ivy was gawking at me on both side, so I plowed through the mud. This trail is shared with horses, and I was not long in discovering that every few hundred feet, there is a patch where trail is torn up, and anywhere from three inches to a foot of watery mud awaits.

At mile 4.3, I came into a clearing to a horse camp called High Knob. I walked my muddy self over to a picnic table and sat to contemplate my shoes and socks, check my phone, and eat something. A girl named Erica walked by and said she was preparing lunch, and I should come over and join them. I did so, and to my delight, I discovered Erica had prepared a roast in the crockpot with all the usual fixins including onions and yams. While we were eating, the camp host, JoJo, told me she had considered riding her horse across the ADT ten years ago when she turned 50. It never happened for her, but she knew of the trail. I went over to the High Knob office, where I was outfitted with a map, half a sub sandwich, and an extra pair of shoes that Erica said she didn't need anymore. Thank you!

I returned to the 001 Road and nothing had magically changed since lunch. Churned up patches every few hundred feet, slow going, mud up to and over the tops of my gaiters. From the calves down at this point I looked like I was wearing brown space boots. Not cool.

After several hours of extremely slow going, I came into Garden of the Gods. I rinsed out everything and hung it up to dry overnight. I looked ahead at the rest of the River to River, hoping that the presence of horse traffic would be confined near the High Knob Camp, but there are horse camps dotting the next 120 miles. This does not excite me.

Amie

Road Trip Day
Thursday, June 04, 2015

Destination: The Katy Trail
Today's Miles: 3
Start Location: Garden of the Gods, Shawnee National Forest, IL
Trip Miles: 1172.85

I got up to find my shoes were still wet, which I can normally deal with, but I had been unable to scrub the mud out of them because the water source at camp required me to operate the pump handle continually with one arm to bring up water. I could not get all the mud out with one hand while holding the shoe near enough to the spigot. There was still mud caked on the insides of the shoes. Some bad words issued forth, and I tied them together and decided to wear the shoes that Erica was such a dear to give me. Keep in mind these shoes are water shoes, the kind that are essentially flip flops with nets on top. I decided to give them a chance, packed up, filled my water, and got walking. Before I even got out of Garden of the Gods area, I could feel my left toes touching the end of the shoe and an epic case of shinsplints in the works. Yeah, I wasn't getting too far in these. The other pair with the caked mud inside were likely to start blisters.

I considered my options, which were as follows:

a) Continue on the RTR Trail as marked, fighting calf-high muck. This would nearly double the time between resources, which are sparse in Shawnee NF anyway, unless you are way more hardcore than I am and can hike a lot more miles per day. I can scrape the mud out of my shoes nightly and hope they are sort of dry by morning, only to be disappointed and say bad words, only to repeat this process every day for the next 120 miles.

b) Take a few or all of the bike alts, and battle oil/gas/fracking/coal trucks flying around the curves for miles at a time. I don't know what the shoulders are like on the bike alt roads. I continue to admit I'm not that hardcore.

c) Put Illinois on hold for now. Forego this section until it is no longer horse season, and skip myself forward to the Katy Trail, which I have been looking forward to for some time.

I opted for C. I do not want to quit, but I also do not wish to do this section right now. I would rather come back to the RTRT before or after horse season, toss the ADT directions, and hike the entire 001 Road when our four-legged friends are not turning it to calf-deep goulash.

I was still walking in the boat shoes past a horse ranch when the owners must have taken pity on my ridiculous, shinsplint-mitigating gait and asked if I wanted to stop for a water break. They had been riding their horses along the RTR and admitted it was in pretty bad shape and could not imagine trying to walk it. This information saved me from having to ask untoward questions such as, "So, do y'all's horses, like, screw up the trail for the entire RTR Trail, or just this part?" I laughed and said I had no problem with things with 4 legs or 18 wheels; I just don't want to share a tiny road with them.

They were getting ready to go into Harrisburg, and would I like a ride? Their F-550 flatbed, contentedly grazing horses in the backdrop, and Randy Hauser on the radio did not seem the paraphernalia of a family of ax murderers. Therefore, by all means. I will save this piece of the ADT for another day.

Luckily the sole rental car agency in Harrisburg was Enterprise, not Hertz. Pretty sure I am still on Hertz's secret assassination list. I secured a car for the drive to St. Charles, Missouri, where the ADT TBTs pick up the Katy Trail. Another Hyundai with no cruise control, but it took me several miles to relearn how to drive a car and adjust to highway speed anyway.

What a fun little break I had today. I am always up for a road trip across middle America at the onset of summer. I listened to music and just had a fun 4 hours getting myself to St. Charles. While driving, I also thought of a few other side issues this will solve. One of which was the looming issue of walking through East St. Louis.

Laundry tonight, for dinner a veggie tray, cheese, and some of the quinoa that Andrea sent. I clogged briefly after eating it. Thank you, Andrea. Executive decision executed, and while out of order, yes, a new section tomorrow awaits.

Amie

Friday, June 05, 2015

Destination: Defiance, MO
Today's Miles: 19.60
Start Location: St. Charles, Missouri
Trip Miles: 1192.45

Returned the car early this morning so that I could save a day's rental charge, and I wanted to get started early. Making only 11 miles in the past two days has left me antsy. My cab driver was very accommodating. There were a couple different entry points to the Katy Trail, but he dropped me near the Trailhead Brewery. It was too early to imbibe, so I pointed myself west and set off.

The Katy Trail (KT) is an old railroad bed, similar to the North Bend Rail Trail and the surface of the Towpath. There were mature trees on both sides of the trail for most of today, and the trees provided good shade. I met a couple who are training themselves for a backpacking trip in the Tetons soon. They gave me some good tips on the little restaurants and trailside services. I also pulled up the Katy map on my phone. There is a legend with distance between services and what each town offers.

Early afternoon I really relaxed and fell into somewhat of a meditative state. The trail was so peaceful that I could hear my breathing, slow, deep breaths. A few joggers and cyclists said hello. One couple and their grand-son couldn't quite believe what I was up to. I could hear them talking about me as they biked away. It was sweet.

For a mile or so later this afternoon, the foliage and leaves to my right would seem to quiver on their own as I passed by. I realized that tens, or at times hundreds, of tiny frogs were leaping from the edge of the trail into the ditch as I approached. The teeny frogs reminded me of the time when I was little and went hunting for small frogs. I put them in a jar, and filled the jar almost to the top. The frogs were squirming all over each other in the jar. Maybe frog collective consciousness knew I had confined many of their comrades to a Mason jar decades ago, and they were jumping away from me, thinking I might be hiking along with equally mischievous intentions.

I sat down on provided benches several times today and took a break. I did so simply because the benches were there, and they felt like such a luxury.

I ended the day in the small town of Defiance. I walked past a restaurant with an outdoor patio where people were enjoying the evening. I had plenty of food; otherwise, I would have strolled up onto the patio too. Maybe tomorrow evening. I hope to make Marthasville and a legitimate campground, as this site is not.

All is well.

Amie

Saturday, June 06, 2015

Destination: Marthasville, MO
Today's Miles: 18.69
Start Location: Defiance, MO
Trip Miles: 1211.14

Woke up this morning feeling unwell, sick to my stomach and a little weak. I am glad I chose a secure camp spot because I convalesced in my tent for two more hours by going back to sleep. In my world, sleep, Gatorade, and ibuprofen will cure anything. I bounced back, made kaffe and 2 liters of Gatorade, and was back on trail by 9. I am sure it was something I ate.

As I was walking the 2 blocks back to the trail, I saw a man working in his garden. I laughed because he had a golf bag on the three-wheeled stand, but he had removed the golf clubs from the bag and put his gardening implements in there instead.

Saturday morning on the Katy Trail. There were many people out and about, mostly bicycling, and definitely visiting more of the restaurants and breweries and wineries that are right on trail. A lot of people asked me how far I am going, or where I started. Several people stopped their bikes and dismounted and wanted to hear more of the story.

Most people biking past me observe trail etiquette of announcing oneself when preparing to pass a walker or another biker by saying, "On your left," or something like that. Most riders used verbal warnings, but a few people use the bells that sound like, *Cling, cling!* over your shoulder right before they pass. The bells can be a little startling, and I always wonder if they mean *Here I am*, or *Get Out of My Way*.

The bikes with bells reminded me of when Mom and Dad took Andrea and me to Amsterdam. A lot of people there ride bikes, whether it be to work or to play. You will see many people biking in work clothes, and they make serious use of the bike bells when pesky tourists clog up the sidewalks.

There was one afternoon it seemed like none of us could finish a sentence without a biker dinging at us to get out of the way. We would be chatting away: "Wow, that video of Otto Frank in the Anne Frank House was really powerf-" *Cling, cling!* Oh, crap, sorry.

"So, should we eat lunch at the Hard Rock Caf-" *Cling, cling!* Wow, we're in a lot of people's way today.

"So, we are thinking about visiting the cheese and wooden shoe facto-" *Cling, cling!* Sheesh, all right.

"So tomorrow, I think we should check out the-" *Cling, cling, cling!*

I think we just gave up one afternoon and walked silently and single file until we sat down to dinner, so many bikers kept *cling, clinging* us.

I wasn't in anyone's way, that I know of, and it was warm and muggy but very pleasant to walk today. One couple even rode by and told me how much further it was until I would have shade again. It is equally nice to know exactly where I will find water and how much farther away it is. I am letting go of that hoarding/rationing/stockpiling feeling regarding water especially. I drank a gallon today easily, including the water I used for morning kaffe. There is a legend on the trail map of what kinds of services are in each town, and they are not very far apart. I am in love with this trail so far. I almost feel like I am being pampered or something.

This afternoon I began craving a restaurant hamburger. I can't remember the last time I had one. I ordered a double hamburger with lettuce, tomato, ketchup, and mayo. I asked for an extra ramekin of mayo and dipped the burger in the mayo, smothering it. And the burgers were priced a la carte. I did not want fries anyway, just a hamburger. I was a satisfied customer. When I paid my waitress, I felt bad because the bills were soaked. I explained that it was not sweat, but condensation from my water bottle dripping down onto my little cash pouch in my pack belt that did it. Sorry. I can imagine what it seemed like, a sweaty hiker paying with wet bills. I tipped well.

After the delicious hamburger, I had just 3.7 more miles to Marthasville, where the trail guide showed legit camping. I entered town, and I asked a couple if they knew where the appropriate camping spot was. They said there was a caboose just an eighth of a mile on west, and there is camping allowed there. Sure enough, there was a little red caboose with a giant sign out front that said CAMPING. I found a spot next to a picnic table. There is also water for in the morning.

A really good day. I am having fun.

Amie

Sunday, June 07, 2015

Destination: Just Past Gore, MO
Today's Miles: 16.30
Start Location: Marthasville, MO
Trip Miles: 1227.44

A warm morning for kaffe and packing up in front of the little caboose. I filled my water and was off. A few miles into my day I stopped at one of the many info depots along the Katy Trail. This one was at Treloar. It was around noon, and this was to be my hottest day yet, over 90. I took off my shoes and socks and sat at the covered depot and listened to the wind blow the trees. There was a bar and grill less than a block from the depot, so I passed the noon to 2 heat and waited until I actually felt hungry before venturing over. I ordered a grilled chicken salad, enjoyed the juke box behind me randomly playing a few tunes to invite customers to do so, and drank water. I ate and people-watched. One other table of folks looked as if they might be Katy users. As I was paying, a man walked in with a T-shirt bearing the slogan, "Anything you can do I can do drunker." Not a lofty goal, but to each his own. I exited the establishment to find a small bus painted up with grapes and a calligraphed title: Wine Wagon. I hoped the driver of the wine tour mini-bus wasn't T-shirt man. I left happy and with 2 more liters of water in my bottle, courtesy of my waitress.

During the afternoon, the trail met back up with the Missouri River to my left. I love the Missouri River. It's a wide river with a constant current that looks slow, but the Missouri carries an almost never-ending trail of debris along with its waters. At one point I sat down again on one of the benches that was facing the river and just watched it. I looked for a keelboat and pirogues, but of course only saw them in my imagination. I thought about the paddleboat era and all the commerce that took place along the Missouri's banks. Writer William Least Heat-Moon once described the Missouri River as having a "grandfather spirit." He said that it is a river with a distinct personality, a source, a life. I wanted to camp right there in that spot, but it was still too early. And you really are not supposed to camp along the trail outside of designated spots, ahem. I proceeded on.

A short time later I heard a train whistle from another railroad that was obviously still operational on the other side of the river. It was distant and faint, and it was a rather eerie sound. To hear a train whistle while walking the bed of a rail line that no longer exists is a bit ghostly.

Soon after that a man came driving along the trail in his small SUV crossover. Driving! I am not sure how he got onto the rail bed with all the wooden gates preventing motorized traffic from gaining the trail. Maybe he off-roaded his car through someone's lawn or cornfield because he was looking quite desperate, asking me if I had seen a wallet. Oh my. I reported I had not, but took Phillip's name and number just in case. He took off on his quest for his wallet.

Not too long after that I saw the little SUV driving down a gravel road parallel to the trail raising a huge cloud of dust. Phillip leaned out the window and yelled to me that someone had found the wallet and left him a message. I raised both arms in the air and yelled, "Woo hoo!" He pumped his fist in the air, threw some gravel, and sped back up to obtain his wallet from the good samaritan.

I probably would have off-roaded my car too and risked breaking some more stuff on it to scour the Katy illicitly if I lost my wallet. I quickly checked my pack for my wallet's normal position and breathed a sigh of relief, for me and for Phillip.

I ended the day later than normal, which I must remember not to do, as the mosquitoes come out in full force around 7.

William Least Heat-Moon also said, "Be careful going in search of adventure-it's ridiculously easy to find."

Amie

Monday, June 08, 2015

Destination: Hermann, MO (Go here!)
Today's Miles: 9
Start Location: Just Past Gore, MO
Trip Miles: 1236.44

Around 1:30 this morning, the thunderstorm rolled through. The rain does not bother me, but it's the lightning and possibly high wind that scares me. I know chances of getting struck by lightning are very low, but I do fear that the storm will blow down a tree limb, which will get me. Needless to say, I was awake for the duration of the storm. It lasted until around 4, when just the pitter-patter of rain was all it had left. Then I woke up around 5:15 to vacate my campsite. I packed and slowly worked my way to the McKittridge depot, where I made one of the best choices of this trip, even in my tired state.

Two miles south of the trail across the Missouri lies the town of Hermann. It is an old German town, and contains just a dash of Solvang, CA, but German instead. And there is a heavy "old Missouri River town" feel to it. There are many bed and breakfasts, wineries, shops, restaurants, and a riverwalk. It is small, but one could keep herself occupied here for a few days and not drink or eat in the same establishment twice.

I jetted down here and was allowed a really early check-in, free reign of their laundry at no extra charge, and an afternoon to dry the tent, hit up the Save a Lot for a resupply, shower off the talcum-esque film of bug spray, sweat, and sunscreen that has been accumulating on me, and just walk around town in my flip flops and reconnoiter for the future visit(s) to Hermann that may transpire. I did count the two miles to Hermann in today's total because Hermann is shown on the Katy Trail maps and info depots. I will not count the two miles going back to the Katy tomorrow.

I did take an hour's nap in the heat of the afternoon, and then woke up to walk the last three or four blocks I did not inspect earlier in the day. I still need to organize and repack the groceries, including a 100 pack of Band-Aids from the Save a Lot. It was the only box they had, so I guess I am stocked up there. As I write, the owners are making a fire in the hotel's outdoor firepit, and there is an open invite to roast marshmallows.

Does a Monday evening in June after a random left turn into a town you have never heard of that you end of falling in love with get any better than this? I think not.

Here's to those little twists of fate that turn into something unexpectedly

211

splendid. I am quite tempted to zero tomorrow, but I shall resist the urge.
Cheers!

Amie

Tuesday, June 09, 2015

Destination: Portland, MO
Today's Miles: 15.22
Start Location: Hermann, MO (Go here!)
Trip Miles: 1251.66

The hotel staff sent me off after taking my picture and preparing me a to-go bag with napkins, apples, two pastries filled with cream, and their wonderful egg creation. They take a muffin pan, line it with cupcake papers, line those with ham slices, crack one egg into each paper, and bake until the egg is done. Brilliant! They sent me with four of these eggs as well. Thank you, Harbor Haus, I will be back.

Not as many people on this section of the trail today. I took a noon break under a picnic shelter, and then filled my water before moving on. Water is definitely a more pressing issue as temps climb.

The only other people I really spoke with today included a guy on a recumbent bike who was doing most of the Katy, and a guy late in my day who I think was using the trail to make a beer run. He had on a dirty camo T-shirt and was carting along a pack of Busch beer. Hey, it is a multi-use trail after all.

I camped at a legit site, and the trail provided this evening when I found a quarter on my picnic table. Cool, another quarter for my laundry fund. I thought about leaving any of my non-quarter change behind as a gift to the next person, but that might be kind of a jerk thing to do to the trail in return. I was reminded of that Shel Silverstein poem where the kid trades his two quarters for three dimes or something like that, because three is more than two. I think at the beginning of the poem, the speaker had a dollar, and by the end he had only five pennies left due to trading on quantity not value.

I prefer fewer quality miles over a longer day that was devoid of funs.

Amie

Wednesday, June 10, 2015

Destination: Tebbets, MO
Today's Miles: 15.30
Start Location: Portland, MO
Trip Miles: 1266.96

A shout out to Stephen, the other person who camped at the site last night. Thanks for paying my fee. I packed up a wet tent due to a very muggy morning, no rain, but later I stopped at what looked like an abandoned bar and grill and hung it over the rail to dry.

Another warm day, and more people out and about. I saw what looked like a group of middle-school boys all biking in a line. They had adults with them riding along. Thank you to these parents for getting those boys outside for some exercise and mental stimulation over their summer! Believe me, their teachers this fall would rather read essays about their exploring the Katy Trail than another paper about their ten hours per day spent playing video games all summer.

My stop today was for groceries in Mokane. I sat for a bit too at the trail depot. The water pump there was out of order. This could have been an issue for me if there had been no convenience store in town.

I have never stayed in a hostel, and I must admit I was wary of this Turner Shelter here that serves the trail. But it is wonderful. Hot showers, a kitchen, there is food left for hikers and bikers. I made microwave popcorn, and it tasted so good. Popcorn has sounded awesome a few times, but usually I had no means for popping any. There is a couple here who met biking a few days ago. A romance may be in the works. And there is a nice mother/daughter pair who are biking together.

Oh, and there is a coffee pot for in the morning.

All is right with the world.

Amie

Thursday, June 11, 2015

Destination: Hartsburg, MO
Today's Miles: 22.40
Start Location: Tebbets, MO
Trip Miles: 1289.36

All patrons of the Turner Shelter rose early to get some miles in before
the mid-day heat. Thank you to whoever donated the small cartons of milk
to the shelter. The milk was a treat this morning. I made about ten or so
miles before it got really hot.

Late morning, a dude named Cory rode up to me and asked if I was "the
lady who had walked here from New Jersey." I said I thought so, and made
a few corrections to the story. Cory was an off-gridder, trying to live off the
land and avoid all things fossil fuels, he said. The rolled-up jeans with sus-
penders and no shirt, and hands stained purple from picking blackberries
inclined me to believe him. He asked me a lot of questions and then went
on his way. Never imagined I would be giving advice to those seeking to live
off grid, although I do joke about living in a cabin in the woods from time to
time. But not in a van down by the river.

My original plan today was to make it to North Jefferson, where the ADT
directions indicated camping and a grocery opportunity. I stopped about a
mile short of N Jeff for a break in the middle of the day. I figured, no hurry.
The info depot showed a recreation area just a mile off trail. I walked down
the N Jeff spur around 3:00, thinking that would be plenty of time to find
a spot. To my frustration, the "rec area" was softball and baseball diamonds,
no overnight camping allowed. Apparently the park I had Googled was actually in Jeff City, about 7 miles off trail. I magically found my second wind,
and the sky clouded over a bit too. I booked it into Hartsburg, with camping
and water right on trail. The gnats and mosquitoes had come out, so I gave
myself a second coat of spray. I had become a speed-walking cloud of DEET
at this point.

Right at dusk I rolled into town and parked it for the night. I think I am
now halfway through the Katy Trail.

Amie

Friday, June 12, 2015

Destination: Just Past Easley, MO
Today's Miles: 10
Start Location: Hartsburg, MO
Trip Miles: 1299.36

For the past two nights, I have felt like I've been in one of those old Indian sweat lodges. Last night there was no breeze, and although I lay down after dark, I sweat for several hours before finally dropping off. Plus, there was a pasture right next to my chosen camp site, and there was some gravel on the cows' side of the fence. When the cows walked on the gravel and crunched it, it sounded like human footsteps walking toward me in the middle of the night.

I didn't sleep much, and today I dragged. Near Wilton I stopped at what the directions indicated as an opportunity for "groceries," which turned out to be a small, one-room hideaway full of mostly Indian pottery, handmade beanies, wallets, and purses, and one small rack of snacks. The Frito Lay Munchies crackers and 12-packs of pop leered at me, once again cornering the calorie market. I was able to salvage a couple Quaker granola bars and a lone Nutri-Grain bar. The cashier didn't know the prices of anything, and when I pointed out the price list taped next to the register in 48-point type, he remained befuddled on whether the Nutri-Grain bar was granola or candy.

He then nearly shorted me ten bucks on my change after I paid with a twenty. He happily handed me the extra ten, but I was glad to get out of there and back on trail. I will have to save the crocheted purse and Indian woman decanter set for another trip on the Katy. As I left, I spied a pile of something on a scale that looked like dried kale, only in smaller bits, haha. Maybe the "kale on the scale" was the source of his confusion over the candy-granola enigma and how to count back change. Apparently they offer camping there too. Maybe next time.

But I am so glad I only made ten miles today and eventually stopped at a place called Cooper's Landing. Cooper's is a small marina, bait, and snack shop. There is also a restaurant. A sound stage may be easily assembled out front, and many nights they host live music. I plopped down at Cooper's mid-afternoon and took a nap. I woke up a few hours later in time to hear the sweet sound of a mandolin. I then heard female voices, harmonizing, intertwined and evocative of Tracy Chapman, the Judds, or Alison Krauss. I shook off what was left of the nap and was drawn to the picnic and sound stage area. They finished and a blues act took over. They played for some time until unfortunately a storm blew through, and everyone scattered. The storm lasted about 45 minutes. After the storm subsided, I could hear the two women harmonizing again as I drifted off.

This is by far the best campground I have used. I will have to remember Cooper's Landing.

Amie

Saturday, June 13, 2015

Destination: Rocheport, MO
Today's Miles: 14.80
Start Location: Just Past Easley, MO
Trip Miles: 1314.16

Saturday morning on the Katy Trail. Despite the weather calling for thunderstorms today, many people were out and about. I saw a few people who had the little carts attached to the backs of bikes and a child was riding along. I had forgotten to mention last weekend that I saw one kid asleep in his cart, and his chubby cheeks were jiggling as his dad passed the bike and cart over a few rough spots. One couple today had their dog in a cart. The doggie was happily riding along, watching everyone pass.

I stopped once along the route today at a trendy place called Katfish Katy's. In contrast to yesterday's somewhat dim establishment, Katfish & Co. sell good snacks, they have a neatly mowed flat spot for camping, and a board out front advertised yoga along the river a couple times a week. I am not too sure I could hold many postures with the mosquitoes getting me, but I smiled at the sign all the same.

I got started early because I knew my day was probably going to end early due to storms. I reached Rocheport around 2, and grabbed a B and B room. There are two tiers of accommodations here, the regular rooms and the dorm rooms meant for groups of bikers. I went with the more economical offering, but the "dorms" are still excellent rooms. The primordial screaming on the part of the washing machine out in the hall as I threw my laundry in barely drowned out the sound of pouring rain and thunder that bore down upon Rocheport as I organized myself and finished settling in. Just in time! The tornado sirens also went off twice within a short time frame. I turned on The Weather Channel, took an epic shower, and studied two items: the Katy map for the remaining 80 miles, and the ADT directions, which part ways with the Katy at Boonville. I will think over some options the remainder of my dry and contented evening.

It can rain some more now. I am snuggled in.

Amie

Pressing Pause

Sunday, June 14, 2015
Destination: New Franklin, MO
Today's Miles: 10
Start Location: Rocheport, MO
Trip Miles: 1324.16

A swift ten miles today, and I rolled into the little New Franklin info depot just after it began raining. I hid in the restroom for a while, no Boy Scout leaders in there this time, to wait out the hardest rainfall. I then went outside to sit at the depot, and an offer of a ride somewhere was extended. I accepted and I retired to a dry motel room.

I have been thinking and looking at the next segments of the trail, and I decided that today I will hit the Pause button on this trip. I am finding that after Boonville, the trail goes back onto paved roads, and the distance between services becomes greater again. I cannot keep up with my water needs back out on the pavement, without as much shade as the Katy Trail provides, what with the climbing temperatures. I had not planned ahead for this moment and the summer season by getting a bike or cart or something ready because, frankly, I did not know if I would even make it this many miles. I would need some vehicle for additional water carries, which I do not have at my disposal this very moment.

So my plan right now is to sojourn here in Kansas for a couple more weeks. I will also job search. If real ife wants me back, I will return to work in the fall and work on the trail bit by bit. If real life is not having me back at this time, I will regroup, retool, return to the ADT, and vagabond maybe on bicycle during the heat. I think it might be fun, and I could carry more.

I ended Round One of my trek on a really positive note. I love the Katy Trail, and I spent my last few nights at a fantastic campsite and a great bed and breakfast. I am really satisfied with what I have done so far.

I feel like I am breaking up with the trail and giving it the "It's not you; it's me" speech. I am looking forward to the next couple of weeks of resting my body, and taking a couple of little trips (by car) and then seeing what comes up during July. I will update here my decision either way.

I will let the universe decide this one.

All is well.

Amie

Back to Real Life for a Bit
July 9, 2015

The universe has spoken, and I will be returning to work in August here in KS. I was off trail about 48 hours before I received a phone call to interview, and the next day I had a verbal offer for an English position. I wanted to wait until the ink was on the paper and the job was official before updating again here. It was funny, I had to borrow some clothes from my sister to wear to the interview and scramble to get a quick haircut. My brain was still in foggy trail mode for several days after returning here, and when everyone asked how the interview went, I had to reply, "Uuuuuum,.. I don't know." I felt like I drank hemlock that night and slept very hard. So thus concludes Round One of my stab at the ADT. The Siren song of once again receiving a paycheck has proven irresistible.

Last week I went through a box of old photos and high school memorabilia that Mom and Dad have kept over the years. I found a story I wrote called "The Incredible Camping Trip." My writing has improved a bit over the years, but the voice in my miniature tome from thirty years ago is pretty much the same.

I have still been walking for a few hours a day, but without the pack, and I have been mixing running back in as well. It feels good. There are portions of this trail that I have been talking about and that I want to do again. There are pieces I did not walk that I want to try. I do know that this path has opened up new places I want to visit and new trails I have never heard of. My exploring and travelling list just got a bit longer. I guess I have to return to work in order to fund my new ideas.

Although I was only out there three months, this was definitely one of the best things I have ever done, truly an incredible camping trip. I don't feel like I failed. I wanted to see how far I could get, and I found out. If I had a water fairy to drop a gallon every fifteen miles or so, I would still be walking. I just don't have a reliable ground man and car support right now..

And trail magic has reached out to me even though I am off trail: Lawrence and Judith who hosted me back in WV called the other day. They happened to be coming through KS on their way to Laramie, WY, and would I like to meet for dinner? By all means! I met them in Newton Monday night. We talked hiking debrief and the importance of travel, pushing yourself to experience new horizons.

So I guess that's all for now. Thank you to everyone who contacted me. I did read every single comment. If I pick this back up at some point, I will post here. Writing this has been the source of at least two or three daily funs. My family and I have been laughing that a few people from all over have found themselves using the phrases "Russian breakfast" and "one single fun."

Good luck to both Ryans, Logan, and anyone else still out there. I am rooting for you!

Amie

Let the Backpacking Recommence

Wednesday, June 01, 2016
Destination:
Today's Miles: 0
Start Location: Denton, Maryland
Trip Miles: 1324.16

Another school year: in the books. Summer: achieved! Behold, I shall spend the next ten weeks continuing to backpack across this glorious country. I say ten weeks because I do plan to return to my job in Kansas in August. But we all know that when man makes elaborate plans, the gods laugh. Plus, I haven't actually signed a contract yet, so I could still be fired, at which point I will shrug my shoulders, grab more data book pages, and keep walking west.

Regardless, I currently sit here in a state of bivouac in Denton, MD, logging back into this site for the first time since last July, and contemplating my plan of attack.

Last spring I hiked this trail from the eastern terminus to around Boonville, MO. However, for various reasons ranging from weather, mud, and a scorching case of car sickness, I skipped a few sections out east. I wish to make up those sections first. The first section I will complete is the western Delaware to Denton piece, beginning tomorrow.

I will then drive to Ohio to walk the Buckeye Trail from Chesterhill to Murray City. Then I have most of southern Illinois to St. Charles, MO. At that time, I will return my car, the same one I have had since miraculously getting it out of CA last year, back to KS and ask a willing pit crew member from my awesome family drive me to Boonville, where I will go back "real time," so to speak, and simply continue west.

I wish to do it this way because I don't like having loose ends and unfinished business dangling over my head. Plus, I almost never pass up an excuse to take a long, solo, cobweb-clearing road trip. It may seem bizarre to drive 1400 miles to walk 30, but I do it all the time with running. It is nothing for me to drive 400 miles to run 13.1 or 26.2. More on that later. But I have anticipated the long drive, meeting new people, seeing great trail people from last time, all with joy and excitement.

Yesterday morning I left home in KS and drove to Louisville. There I met the eminent Logan M., who started the ADT last spring as well. We had a great time. He graciously hosted me for a night, fed me, and was a wealth of info on topics ranging from gear, people in 2 or 3 states he knows, food, biking, and camping in state park restrooms with motion-sensor lighting. I also was fortunate to meet and have dinner with Drew, who was Logan's ground man and friend. Thank you, both of you. I have now met every hiker but one from last spring who was part of my ADT hiker class.

From Louisville this morning, I proceeded east. I plan to leave Denton in the morning and walk east, toward Reese and Serinda Connor. It should take me two or three days to knock out the bit I have here, and I am crossing my fingers that Serinda can join me in walking back toward their house on Friday. I have dinner plans Friday evening with the Connors. Friday's rendezvous will round out my time back in this part of the world.

The drive this time has been wonderful. Beautiful weather, I got to see Kentucky and West Virginia green and verdant this time in all their glory. I got to complete the drive in my own comfortable car and on a more relaxed timetable. Last year I had to push hard in order to get the rental car back on time. Plus, the drive was executed in an ergonomically poor Hyundai with no cruise control, the completion of which left my right leg stove up from trying to maintain a constant speed over WV's hills. Last year's drive left me exhausted my first days on the trail and hiking with a stanky leg until I could walk it out and unkink myself from two days of unnatural commandeering of a Hyundai. In short, the drive out here was fantastic. Being this footloose and fancy free never ceases to exhilarate me.

Through Maryland I felt surreal recognition of road and town names I remembered from last year. I saw Whitehall Road, Kent Island, various C&O Towpath access points off the Interstate. I remembered Queen Anne's Highway, of course the Bay Bridge, Tuckahoe State Park. I thought about all the people who helped me and offered me things. I thought about how last year I was pretty much constantly cold until the first of May. I thought about how this segment will likely find me hot the entire time. Which reminds me of another preparation platform to my scheme once I get into MO.

Driving home, I am going to drive the ADT data book directions from Boonville to the Lenexa area and put out water drops for my walking self in the areas of humid Missouri that are sparse when it comes to towns and resources. I will mark each drop in my TBTs. I will likely drop more water gallons out there than I will need. If I end up not needing the water, if someone bogarts my gallons, or if someone mows over one or two with a brush hog, then I will have lost 75 cents. Oh well. But this time of year, water will be paramount.

Moreover, I have not gone back and read one single (fun?) word of last year's journals. Those were 2015's reflections. As a result, I really don't remember what thoughts I put down in here as they arose, versus what just knocked around in my head as I walked all day. The amorphous nature of last year's journals sort of remind me of that scene in *Fear and Loathing in Las Vegas* when Hunter Thompson, drugged out of his mind, narrates some soliloquy that was either offensive or full of non-sequiturs and asks, "Wait. Did I say that out loud? Was I talking?"

This summer's blog will be a *tabula rasa* of sorts. I hope I don't repeat myself. It feels pretty weird having my car here too. It's nice because I have a massive food and supply stash in my trunk. Conversely, I will have to make arrangements for where to leave it in Illinois and Ohio. I am not stressing this yet, and if I do the footwork, the trail will provide. Plus, this one time a few years ago my best friend drove me to Utah to run a race, and I left my car in a sketchy Bakersfield, California, Wal-Mart parking lot for three days. No one bothered it. Pretty sure it will be fine out here whatever plan I contrive.

More tomorrow, as Backpacking 2.0 begins, however convoluted my plans feel. Are You Sure Hank Done It This Way? No, but I'm going to. It's good to be back.

Amie

Farmers' Markets, Toilet Paper, and RV's
Thursday, June 02, 2016

Destination: Along Blanchard Road, Delaware
Today's Miles: 14.50
Start Location: Denton, MD
Trip Miles: 1338.66

Having trashed the Maryland and Delaware portions of the ADT directions last year, I ventured forth this morning using a hybrid of Serinda's dictated directions via voicemail and her texted directions this morning. Sounds confusing, but they were spot on. I had picked up a few items before stepping forth onto Legion Road in Denton, one of which was a gallon of water that I forced myself to drink in less than two hours. I was still a bit dehydrated from driving, and I figured my body was in for a bit of a shock this morning and would need it.

I have not worn my backpack in almost a year. Two major concerns today were blisters and the shock of carrying 30+ pounds again, stone cold turkey. I have been running 40 to 55 mile weeks right up to Tuesday's launch point, but marathon fit is not the same as trail fit. Therefore, I started off slow, slow, slow, poking along, frequently taking inventory on my feet, my pelvic bones where the hip belt tends to dig, and the muscles fibers that are jolted awake when the center of balance shifts, and new tasks are required of tendons, ligaments, and joints. In a word, I crept.

I took my first break about 6 miles into the day. Didn't feel hungry or thirsty, just sat off road on a floor of pine needles and took off my shoes and socks. No hot spots.

The weather could not have been better. Overcast all day, seventies. No wind. Walked past Willoughby Road soon after. Reminded me of that old *Twilight Zone* episode where the man boards the train, and the conductor collects his ticket, whereupon the train transcends space and time to an idyllic town called Willoughby. The rider visits Willoughby and eventually realizes he prefers mythical Willoughby over his humdrum real life. At the end, the rider exits the train and chooses to stay in Willoughby forever and never go back. I'm sure there is a philosophical connection to thru-hiking in there somewhere.

Around 2:00, I finally started feeling hungry. I happened to walk by a fruit stand. I asked the owner if I could sit a while on her outdoor patio set if I bought some fruit. She agreed, and I picked up 5 delicious plums. I started to undo my pack, at which time she pointed to two cushioned chairs with footstools further up onto her property. She offered those, and I accepted. A random cushy chair, and I could prop my feet up and eat fruit on my first day out. Excellent! I ate all the fruit and proceeded on.

Mid afternoon found me well into Delaware and on Blanchard Road. Several people on a porch waved to me and asked if I needed water. They brought out a large foam cup with ice water, and were curious about my activities. I then experienced a first: the lady asked, with an accent leavened with a hint of Oklahoma, "You need anything else? Some tullet paiper or anythang?" I giggled and said I had all that covered. I love Delaware people. So practical.

By this time, my latest status check had revealed still no blisters, but my calves were starting to ache just a twinge. I checked my distance, and I had gone about 14 miles for the day. A pretty good distance, in my opinion. I walked almost to my next turn and found a place to sit and lurk on Google Maps for a possible site to stealth.

A few minutes later a gentleman rode by on his bicycle and saw me. He slowed and asked if I was doing to the trail. I laughed and replied in the affirmative. I explained my plan, and he said that my explanation made sense, for I looked too fresh to have already come 3000 miles. Compliment or insult?

Turns out, the world is small and timing is everything, for Logan had talked about this very person on Tuesday night. I received an invite to stay at their home in their camper just a mile down the road. Gary came back with his truck and picked up yours truly and her backpack. I am promised strong coffee in the morning.

A perfect day in all regards. Day 2 of 2 in Delaware tomorrow. I don't anticipate feeling wrecked, but if I do, I will have a car day on Saturday to recover.

Amie

Friday, June 03, 2016

Destination: Redden State Forest, Delaware
Today's Miles: 14
Start Location: Along Blanchard Road, Delaware
Trip Miles: 1352.66

Last night prior to my repairing to the camper, Gary and Carla and I had discussed who else they had hosted over the years. Several hikers stood out, but I was happy to learn they had helped Tyler Coulson when he and his dog Mabel came through a few years ago. Tyler wrote two books about his cross-country journey. Both are engrossing reads even if you hate hiking, endurance challenges, and have that 0.0 sticker in your back window as an eyeroll to runners. The one I have read twice, and during which I laughed out loud until my sides hurt and finally had to text people who would "get it" in order to share the humor, is called *How To Walk Across America and Not Be an Asshole.*

After I updated here, I was wiped out and lay down in the camper bed, only to notice the unmistakable chirping of a smoke detector with a low battery. These batteries only fail during the nighttime hours, when there are no 9-volt batteries within a thousand mile radius, or when one is deliciously tired from backpacking all day for the first time in a year.

I turned on my flashlight and found the offending smoke alarm. I gently pulled it down and took out the battery, whereupon I collapsed back onto the excellent mattress and wrapped up in my sleeping bag. Another chirp issued from somewhere. I placed the detector outside on the camper step, stood really still, but still heard the chirping. I thought, "To hell with it; I can probably just sleep through it tonight, I am that tired." But no, I got back up after another chirp. By this time it was dark, and with a guilty conscience I began opening other doors and compartments in the camper to look for a second smoke alarm. From outside the camper, I am sure my behavior looked suspicious, what with a flashlight shining into all regions of their RV that I had no business prying into.

After more chirps, I finally broke bad and began full-on rifling through cabinets. I felt terrible, and I didn't touch anything, but I refused to waste a good night's sleep on that great bed over a chirping alarm. I finally located a second alarm in a cabinet next to the toaster, removed the battery, and crashed. Hard. Clearly, I need a refresher course in how to stay in someone else's camper without being an asshole.

I woke this morning and reassessed my condition. My legs felt a little stiff but tough. My left shoulder and the flesh around my pelvic bones are tender due to pack belt and strap contact, but nothing unbearable. I downed 2 liters of water with Nuun, an electrolyte supplement. I sat and had coffee with Gary and Carla. Gary gave me his business card, which I will add to my Pilgrim's Passport collection at home.

At some point during coffee, I was informed that I sound like I am from Kentucky or southwest Virginia. Never heard that before, and I laughed. I love listening to others' regional dialects, their phrasing and different words for things, etc. I was reinformed that Delaware folks say soda. I did not query as to bag or sack.

I set off around 9, and as the forecast called for rain, I placed my poncho and rain jacket under either side of my hip belt. This gave me a buffer to ward off soreness, and they were ready on the draw should rain start. When I approached T. S. Smith and Sons store, the rain began lightly. I paused under their awning to grab some pistachios and throw on the poncho. I did this without getting in anyone's way or being an asshole.

The rain let up soon, and I stopped for lunch and sock/shoe/foot check. I availed myself of a lady's flatbed trailer only because she knew I was coming and she knew Gary, who had decided he wanted to hike with me during the afternoon segment. The three of us gathered, and then Serinda joined us to say hi to me and check my progress. Still no blisters, and after a fun, hour-long chat, Gary and I got moving. I needed to do about 10 more miles to clear the Delaware portion and return to approximately where Jerome and Gisela picked me up last year.

He and I mostly traversed Redden Road and proceeded toward the State Forest. We passed the field where *Punkin Chunkin* was filmed. I hope I misspelled that correctly. We chatted about various topics, decided that hiking was a desirable change of pace and lifestyle, and took things easy until Gary had to return to real life. Thank you, Gary and Carla, for hosting me.

I continued alone until Serinda met me at the Redden Office. She and I decided that what I trekked from Denton to Redden met the make-up work requirement. We then repaired forthwith to Denton and the 404 Taproom. She drove the backroads to Denton. We both loved a tree-lined road somewhere along the way that I decided to rename the Robert Frost Poem Road because it looks like a scene from his poetry.

And for the record, I did come clean to Gary that I opened cabinets in order to find the chirping smoke alarm. I just wanted them to know. Plus, smoke detectors are important. They will likely want to replace the batteries soon, and I wouldn't want my actions to facilitate the burning down of someone's camper. That would really make me an asshole. Delaware and Maryland: completed. Guilty conscience: assuaged. Asshole status: reversed.

Cheers!

Amie

Two Wal Marts, Two Coasts, Two Maps, Two Byrons, Ohio 2.0
Saturday, June 04, 2016

Destination:
Today's Miles: 0
Start Location: Chesterhill, Ohio
Trip Miles: 1352.66

Today was a car day. I shuttled myself west to Ohio, where I needed to make up the Buckeye Trail/ADT portion from Chesterhill to Murray City. I laughed aloud during my drive because I took note that I have now dumped my car in 2 Wal Mart parking lots on literally both sides of the country, and no one has stolen it yet. The locations of where my car waits for me will remain undisclosed until after I get back to it safely, although revealing it on here is probably less likely to get it jacked than leaving it in a Wal Mart lot, especially in Bakersfield, CA. One for one so far on the car issue.

This past year, I have lived with my sister and brother-in-law. My nephew Keaton likes to lie at the bottom of my stairs and listen to various songs and artists on his iPad. Some of Keaton's catalogue contains naughty rap songs, but Keaton is 9 and innocent and does not understand the lyrics. One of his top ten tunes I get to hear repeatedly is Drake's "Hotline Bling." I may or may not have downloaded that one to my iTunes, but I did "make that hotline bling" this morning when I messaged Buckeye Trail friends Jamie, Byron, and Shannon before I left Denton. That can only mean one thing. I need the BT maps for this portion. They indicated I should head to Burr Oak, to a specified camp ground. I headed that way to get the maps from them.

The route to Burr Oak took me along the infamous HWY 50 for some time. I saw the signs for many trail towns in WV through which I passed last year: Parkersburg, Clarksburg, West Union, Cairo, to name a few. More memories from last spring.

I made it to Burr Oak mid afternoon and popped into the ranger station to grab a map of that park so I could find the guys to get the BT map. A map to get a map, haha. The camp area was fairly far back into the park, and, knowing Jamie and Byron's humor, I speculated they would be sitting around placing bets as to whether I could actually find them. I quickly found the site and met other BT people Andrew and another Byron called Good Byron. Wait. Did that make Byron G. Bad Byron? Regardless, they had the goods.

But before I located them, I had driven through an encampment of nineteenth-century reenact-ors. There were lots of tents pitched, people dressed in period clothing, their wares displayed. I could have forgotten about the ADT and tossed axes, churned butter, donned buckskin clothing, or whittled to my heart's delight all weekend. One family smiled at me as I drove by, so I stopped and requested a photo. So fun! We chatted, then I decided to get my newfangled, citified cell phone and horseless carriage out of their area and stay on track.

Jamie soon arrived with updated versions of the BT maps. Whoever bet against me in my imaginary scenario would have lost because one of Jamie's first questions was, "How the fuck did you find this place? This is, like, the hardest campsite to find." Thank you, Jamie and BT people. It was good to see you again.

I then headed back toward Chesterhill to find a place to stay, as I am launching from there in the morning. I reconnoitered Chesterhill for a place to leave my horseless carriage. I have a few ideas. It then started to thunder and rain, so I chose to get a roof over my head.

En route to my motel, I drove the Ohio backroads, some of which I will walk tomorrow. I listened to Chris Stapleton and listened to the rain. And smelled it. So relaxing. It was raining so hard when I pulled into the motel that I climbed into my own backseat and organized 3 to 4 days' worth of food while waiting for it to subside. It worked out perfectly, and I did not have to drag in the whole food bag.

It is supposed to be warm the next few days. Maybe some rain. So that means I can leave my leatherstockings, coonskin cap, and petticoat in the trunk of my car.

If anyone happens to see a horseless carriage with Kansas plates parked somewhere in Ohio for a few days, leave it alone!

I am having fun.

Amie

Sunday, June 05, 2016

Destination: along Branch Church Road, OH
Today's Miles: 18.20
Start Location: Chesterhill, OH
Trip Miles: 1370.86

Woke to rain. So I took my time, or as Dad used to say when we were little, "farted around," getting my things together for 3 days on the Buckeye. Drove to Chesterhill and deposited car in secret location number two, to be revealed after I retrieve it. Let's just say I'm pretty sure it is in good hands.

The trail today was mostly on roads, and thankfully they were nearly all dirt or gravel roads. The trail passed through farmland, no towns. I maybe saw 15 cars all day. Very nice. Whoever marks this section with the blue blazes was very intuitive. Every time my mind wandered, or I snapped to and questioned if I were indeed on the correct road, yep. There was the blue blaze. Whoever cares for this section, good on ya.

I took my first sit-down break after about 10 miles today. Ate some almonds and finished off my water. Legs feel really strong. No blisters. My body remembers this. Thankfully it only rained for about an hour later in the day, so I could keep my poncho under the hip belt to pad where the straps rub.

Today was a longer day, and I noticed that my things are gradually settling into their old proper places on my person and finding their niche, just like last time. Phone in its case in my left shorts pocket that zips. Directions in plastic in right shorts pocket. Tattered little wallet in pack hipbelt zippie pouch. Sunscreen and bug spray in left pack pocket. Water in right pack pocket. I want the heavier water on the right because the pitch of the roads puts greater pressure on my left leg as it is. I always reach for water with my right hand. When the rain starts, I throw over the poncho, and I intuitively make sure my left side is shielded with the poncho to a greater degree because my phone is there. All my small yet crucial items are gradually settling into place like a fine sediment falling to the bottom of a slow-moving stream.

Around 5, I started really studying the map and thinking of where I might sleep. I happened upon a cabin along State Rte 78 that had a covered porch area with a picnic table. It was a cute place, but there were shutters over all the windows, no cars. I tried the outside spigot, no water. It did not appear lived in, yet it was neatly mowed. The yard dipped down to a flat place in the back, also mowed. It would have been a great site. But it was

231

still early, and I didn't want to take the chance someone would pull up. The cabin appeared somewhere in that ambiguous space between cute and rugged. It looked like a place where a nice couple might invite me in for dinner and coffee in the morning. It also looked like a place where a girl could get a sawed-off poked into her tent in the middle of the night. I proceeded on.

A site in which to stealth revealed itself unto me, and I snagged it. I may or may not report on the nature of this site tomorrow after I am out. There is even water here. I treated it anyway just to be safe.

So, one piece of gear I replaced for Backpacking 2.0 was my tent. The Black Diamond is a great tent, but I had ripped it last time (my fault), and even when it is not raining, there is is so much condensation on the inside that my stuff is constantly soggy. So at the last second before this trip, I bought that Big Agnes Fly Creek Ultralight tent that everyone is raving about. It shaves a few ounces from my base weight, has a rain fly to avoid the condensation problem, and is a more muted color. This will make stealthing easier. Tonight is the first time I have ever set it up. I know, shame on me for waiting until I was out yonder before testing out a piece of crucial gear.

The tent's description on the tip of my tongue reminds me of a student I had this year named Shawna. One day Shawna had recopied some of her notes for a class, and she was very proud of how neat and organized she had made them. She bragged to the class, "Look at my notes. They're so . . . notey."

I really like my new tent. It's so . . . tenty.

Amie

New Record for Course Futility?
Monday, June 06, 2016

Destination: Burr Oak Campground, OH
Today's Miles: 10.70
Start Location: along Branch Church Road, OH
Trip Miles: 1381.56

Today's entry will be like stepping into a confessional.

Transgression one: last night I camped in a cemetery. This was the second time I have done this. I did it once last year but never mentioned it. I know there are some who will find this offensive. Let me explain.

Cemeteries are usually flat, usually mowed, and they are peaceful and safe. They also tend to come along in the middle of nowhere when the solitary traveller can sometimes only guess when another good spot will arise. Plus, if anyone is going to get crazy in the middle of the night and start actin' the fool, it probably won't be in a cemetery. I never, never sleep on top of anyone's grave, and I even take care not to walk on any as I look for a spot. I find a mowed place off to the side and plop down. No, I do not find camping in a cemetery scary.

Both cemeteries in which I have camped have been old. I note the dates of those at rest as I pass. 1852-1918. 1843-1899. I think about the souls who lived during those times. What were they doing in this part of the still-young country? Homesteading? Carving out a life? Fighting a war? Trying to tame nature? Doing something that involves endurance and hardship? This is probably just me projecting, but I'd like to think that if indeed these resting souls are judging my activities in their cemetery from the afterlife, that they might understand. The morning after last year's cemetery camp, I packed up and left the cemetery safely, and as I did I walked past the adjacent gravestones and whispered, "Thank you." That moment still gives me chills to this day. I am not proud of camping in cemeteries. But I want to give an accurate account of a woman walking across the country alone, and sometimes you take what you can get.

Upon leaving the cemetery, I continued down Branch Church a couple of miles to the trailhead of Wildcat Hollow trail. The Buckeye/ADT is supposed to meander south of the Burr Oak Reservoir, eventually reaching Burr Oak Campground. This footpath crosses several water sources. I planned on a 15 to 16-mile day. The footpath takes the hiker along some really nice paths on high ground lined with pine needles. There are some low, muddy spots. There are a few spots badly overgrown, but I didn't encounter any briars and just endured it.

Trail transgression number two: I knew my next water source was Boat Dock 3, and soon the path widened and I saw civilization. The parking lot and cars and restroom facility all looked eerily familiar. Somehow I had gotten turned around on the Wildcat Hollow Trail and gone back the way I had come. I don't know how or when, for it was clearly blazed, but there I was right back where I had started a couple of hours ago.

I sat down and changed socks. I felt a hot spot on one toe. I briefly contemplated being mad, but then I got out the Buckeye Trail map. I simply rerouted myself around the north side of the reservoir on dirt township roads to arrive at Burr Oak. And that's what I did. All in all, I inadvertently hiked an alternate route to my planned destination with a "fun-run" side excursion down some mysterious vortex within Wildcat Hollow.

Not the trail's fault. I blame Kansas. In Kansas, west is west. South is south, by god. The roads are straight and are intersected at every mile. In Kansas, we don't take too kindly to all this circling around. Tell a Kansan to head southwest on a curvy path? Pull out the fainting sofa. Start in with all this business of, "Head in a general southwesterly direction, bearing east at a few points and traversing a series of switchbacks in the opposing direction, checking compass readings frequently . . . " Whoa, whoa, slow down there, Hoss. Iterating trail data directions like that to a Kansan is liable to get a man shot.

So, I stopped early today, grabbed a campsite, set up my cute little tent, took a nap, looked ahead at the Illinois data pages, drank a lot of water, got sniffed and slightly violated by someone's off-leash dogs, and ended about halfway to Murray City here on a nice evening. Not bad mileage for my late-morning trail foul. The BT map shows ten miles to Murray City. I plan to get an early start so that I can coordinate with my shuttle and get back to my car.

The trail straightens out a little tomorrow. More west and south. Them's some directions I can understand.

Amie

Last Day in Ohio
Tuesday, June 07, 2016

Destination: One mile from Murray City, OH
Today's Miles: 19.75
Start Location: Burr Oak Campground, OH
Trip Miles: 1401.31

Today started out lovely, went dark side for a bit, then ended good, good, good. But first the revelation of where I stashed my car for this leg. I had stalked Chesterhill and jotted down three possible places. Sunday morning I went to my first choice, but no one was there, and there was a huge chain across the parking lot entrance.

My plan B was the Chesterhill Fire Department. I pulled up and popped in. Two ladies, one of whom was in Fire Department garb, were making coffee and there was the aroma in the air of bacon frying in the morning, a smell that reminds me instantaneously of my grandparents' old house in Iowa. That smell suggested I might be in a good place.

I didn't have the backpack on and I didn't look the part of a vagrant at that moment, so I didn't deliver my typical preface of "Hi. I'm not homeless or anything . . . " Instead I opened with, "Good morning, my name is Amie. I'm from Kansas. I'm not weird or anything, but I have a question." I explained, she laughed, and assured me it was fine to leave my car in the lot. Just park it next to the Sheriff's cruiser. I had just landed the safest parking lot in Ohio.

Just to be sure, I had prepared a note ahead of time. I placed it on my front windshield next to the car's VIN number. It certainly reads like a classic case of "The lady doth protest too much, methinks," but Chesterhill is a small town. Small towns often beget suspicion. Dented car with out of state plates? Not moved in a few days? What would I think?

Here is what my note said: "My name is Amie. I am hiking a portion of the Buckeye Trail. I have parked here with permission. I am not weird or sketchy, and this vehicle is not being used for any illegal purposes. My phone number is 805-xxx-xxxx." My note said it all. Just wanted to cover all the bases.

So this morning I left Burr Oak with what I believed was a ten-miler ahead of me to Murray City. Starting to think there is a voodoo hex on me and this section. I first walked some gravel roads, then turned off onto what was supposed to be a quick off-road section. The blue blazes were clear on the yellow gate. I picked my way down an overgrown path, seeing the blazes

235

increasingly hidden behind foliage. The last blue blaze I saw was right before a steady climb, then nothing.

I found myself on a rutted Jeep or 4-wheeling path. I had a moment of that panicky feeling. I checked the BT map and saw I must have entered the designated Ohio Wildlife area. There was no way I could get lost in the woods because the Jeep path would have to intersect eventually with one of two township roads to the west or north. I just kept going. Hate to say it, but the Jeep road was easier to follow than the BT in that area. Plus, I knew the Jeep road had to end back in civilization. There was a trail of breadcrumbs leading out of the woods, i. e. 4-wheeler tracks and beer cans. Their Busch Lite cans and tire tracks led me out of there and back on the map.

The Jeep path popped me out onto Johnson Run, even further from Murray City. Another county road that was on the BT map no longer exists and is blocked by an orange gate, so I just started walking to my destination the looooong, roundabout way.

I wasn't hungry or thirsty, and it was a really nice day, so I just sort of put myself on autopilot the way I do on those Saturday morning, three-hour long runs. Thinking, not really in need of anything. I took my first break in Glouster after going 15 miles. Picked up two Powerades and rested on a picnic table behind the library. I contacted a lady named Bobbie, who was my wonderful prearranged driver for the ride back to the Mothership. Told her of my veering off course, and gotta be honest: I kind of blame the trail and not Kansas for this one. Mapquest said 5.1 more miles to Murray City. I started off and told Bobbie she might see me on the road as she headed east to get me. Along the way a man pulled over to ask what I was doing. Then he wanted to shake my hand.

Probably a mile from Murray City, she found me. *Only a mile out- it counts, dangit!* We felt like we already knew each other from keeping in contact over the previous two days regarding my progress. On the drive, we discussed a lot of things, mainly all the side benefits of backpacking. The mental rest, how it changes a person, the things we hold onto that we need to let go. The layers of the onion that are peeled away the longer one just walks, all day, every day. The minimalism, the silence, the energy and stamina you never knew you had. The way it reaches into other areas of life and calms all seas. I told Bobbie I had seen an expression that applies to what long-term backpacking does to you. It is not polite conversation terminology, but it makes you *unfuckwithable*. Not nice, but true.

I encouraged her to get a backpack and just start walking with it. She dropped me at the mothership and tried mine on. A good sign.

I then got to drive a really pretty stretch of the Ohio countryside on a sunny evening. I got to encourage someone to try backpacking. I got to walk into this hotel lobby with dried mud all up and down my right leg, shoes caked in dried mud, gaiters flipped up on my calves inside out, hair windblown, have not looked at my appearance in three days, and have an aura of wildchild about me. Pretty funny. It was a really good day.

To sum up, God bless blue Powerade, Bobbie, the Chesterhill firefighters, sunny cool evenings on backroads, and those Ohio country boys muddin', 4-wheeling, and drinkin' beer.

Amie

Scouting and Water Caching 1.0
Wednesday, June 08, 2016

Destination: Marion, IL
Today's Miles: 0
Start Location: One mile from Murray City, OH
Trip Miles: 1401.31

Made solid use of a motel night, which means staying as late as possible, wiping down all muddy gear with motel towels, and hanging one's rain fly over the shower bar to let it dry. And maybe eating breakfast twice.

Today was a car day. Onward to Illinois. Last year I skipped most of this state due to heroic levels of nearly knee-deep mud on the River to River Trail and long stretches without towns or water, particularly on the bike alternate route.

I have three arrangements to make in Illinois prior to walking. First, where to park the mothership, for two weeks at least. That was arranged this morning. Second, checking out the route that is the bike alt. What is the shoulder like? What services are actually in the small towns? Where can I possibly stealth camp? Third, I decided while hiking the past few days that I will place water drops out ahead of myself for Illinois as well. I am already drinking a gallon a day easily, and that was in relatively cool Ohio. I swigged a gallon today just while driving. There just aren't enough reliable water sources close enough together. Sure, I can knock on doors and ask for water. But it takes time and extra steps off trail. And if Jeffrey Dahmer comes to the door, I have to contrive a way to back out of it. Not that a Jeffrey Dahmer is running any of these beautiful, pristine farms down here, but I just prefer to be self-sufficient as much as I can.

I dropped down off the Interstate in western Indiana, and I actually ended up driving the ADT book route for some time before getting to Shawneetown, which will be my launch spot on Saturday morning. I saw more familiar towns and roads. At Shawneetown, I took out the Illinois data pages, and here was my thinking. In the service-barren stretches, I hid a gallon of water about every 8 to 12 miles. I pulled the car over at an intersection or waypoint, and jotted down in my data book where I hid the water. "Next to light pole and electrical service box." "First dirt road after bridge across from junky old house." "At two green gates right after the river crossing."

I also wrote down possible stealth camping sites: "Derelict school across from mini-mart." And so forth. How cool to be able to drive the route right before one hikes it. Doing this scouting plus the caching is a lot of work, but it is actually really enjoyable. It's like playing a game with yourself, or setting your future self up for success-and the anticipation of seeing if all the water drops are still there. I listened to music the whole afternoon, studying, riding point. I realized that I had reentered the Central Time Zone, and that I had an extra hour to drive and drop. Perfect. I put out drops up to around Goreville, with the rest to be dropped tomorrow.

The only drawback to this practice is that I will take two days off from hiking just as I am getting my 20-mile legs back. However, time lost to searching for water, dragging too much water along with me, steps off trail to hit up that mini-mart all add up. I hypothesize that this method will allow for a few miles more each day, so in the end, for me it will be a wash, or to some in this part of the country, KS included, a "worsh." The results will speak for themselves as I see how quickly I can make it across Illinois and Missouri after caching for my future self.

As I closed my trunk lid over 18 remaining gallons of water this evening, I was reminded of my current favorite Netflix documentary, *The Barkley Marathons*. It is a docu about the hardest trail race in the world that takes place every year near Brushy Mountain, Tennessee, in the tough mountainous area that was the site of the James Earl Ray escape. Basically, the event coordinator, Laz, has a twisted sense of humor and constantly undertakes to make the race as hard as possible and taunt the runners in any way possible. Laz makes the race hard to enter. You have to write an essay and pass a test in order to get in. He never tells the runners when the event will begin. Everyone just has to show up and camp, and be ready at any hour day or night for the race to start.

The race checkpoints are various books that Laz hides in the woods, books with comical and subtle titles such as *Lost in the Woods, The Last Mile,* or *The Idiot*. Runners have to tear the page out that corresponds with their bib number, which changes every loop. No GPS is allowed. When a runner quits, which is almost everyone, Laz requires that TAPS be played, as the runner has tapped out. There are no aid or support stations for the event; runners have to carry everything they need for a 12-hour foray into the Tennessee woods on their backs. With one exception: Laz does put out one water drop somewhere along the course, which is also unmarked. One water drop for a 26-mile loop. The water drop is a cluster of gallon jugs. And one of the jugs is filled with moonshine instead of water. Nobody knows which jug it is.

A glance into my trunk and at all the water made me think of this docu that I love so much. Perhaps I will fill one of my jugs with moonshine, then drive crazily and mix them all up in the back so I am ignorant as to the magic jug. I will surprise my future self with some fire water. Nah, better not do that. I'd be in a bad way.

Reminds me of that line from Shakespeare's *Macbeth* regarding overconsumption of alcohol: "It provokes the desire but taketh away the performance." Shakespeare's porter wasn't alluding to a ruined hiking perform-ance, but that's what moonshine on a hot day would do to me: taketh away my performance.

Tomorrow will be another day of scouting and caching. Pretty sure there are some people staying at this motel who know where I can get some moonshine. I'll think it over. If I change my mind, maybe I can hit them up in the morning at one of my two breakfasts.

Amie

Thursday, June 09, 2016

Destination: Marion, IL
Today's Miles: 0
Start Location: Marion, IL
Trip Miles: 1401.31

This past year I had an English III student named Brandon. Brandon is one of those perceptive kids who lack a filter for their thought-to-speech superhighway. This past spring we were reading Miller's *The Crucible*, and we got to that scene where Reverend Hale asks John Proctor to recite his Ten Commandments. Not that I was attempting to indoctrinate public school students on the Good Book (cue collective inhale of moral outrage), but I asked the kids if they knew any of the Ten Commandments.

They got the basic two, "Thou shalt not kill or steal," then crickets. Brandon raised his hand and asked, "Isn't there one about, like, not being a douche to your neighbor or something?" After I collected myself and took a sip of water, I confirmed his incisive grasp on the importance of not being a douche to thy neighbor, and then worded that Commandment in verbiage more consistent with the King James Version than the Urban Dictionary.

Point being, today was another water drop day, and I tried to cache water without encroaching on anyone's property. I dropped the jugs at the bases of light poles or in the untrimmed grass at the base of a highway sign. In one tiny town's park, there was some tall grass behind the restroom facility. I hid a gallon in there. All in all, I cached today without being a douche to my neighbor. The only "douchey" thing I did while caching was drive too slow at times, searching for the next turn off listed in the TBT data book.

One upcoming section is the 14-mile stretch of levee following the Mississippi River. This one was tricky because there are no road signs along the levee to serve as markers. So my data book notes reflect descriptions of what lies down in the floodplain, or what the farmhouse looks like, to the right or left of where I dumped the gallon. The levee section was also mowed, but only on one side. I put one water on the unmowed side with two auxiliary forces on the mowed side a bit further down. Hope no one mows for a week or so until I get there.

I repacked everything, knowing I won't have access to the goods in my trunk for two weeks or more. I also decided I will leave the trekking poles in the trunk this segment and try hiking without them. I am bringing along my Chrome Dome umbrella starting tomorrow, and I will also need a hand to tote along a water jug as I drink it. Things flatten out a lot here too. In

241

fact, when I was on the Katy, I found myself just carrying the poles a lot.

I found myself also entering that grey area between planning too much and just letting the trail provide. I finally stopped caching at Chester and headed back here. I have seen what lies before me for the next ten or so days, and I believe I will be fine. My primary concern is all the coal truck traffic around Chester.

I am hoping for a 20-plus mile day tomorrow to the very excellent, non-douchey Pounds Hollow campsite.

And I didn't put out any moonshine.

Amie

Doctor Tom 2.0, Biker Fest, and Riding Drag
Friday, June 10, 2016

Destination: Pounds Hollow, Shawnee NF, IL
Today's Miles: 22.70
Start Location: Outside Shawneetown, IL
Trip Miles: 1424.01

Dropped car at its third rendezvous point this morning. This one will remain anonymous forever because the couple who are generously letting me leave the mothership at their place have good hearts, but don't want their property to be known on the Internet as "that one house." It will be safe. Thank you. I am blessed.

I quickly walked the 12 or so miles into Shawneetown without taking a break. There were 2 differences this morning. One, no trekking poles. Benefit: a more natural arm swing and feeling like I am walking faster. Drawback: nothing to prop me up and keep me out of the ditch when a big truck blows by.

Second difference was the chrome dome umbrella. Benefits: shade, a lifesaver! It is very lightweight and has a reflective treatment on the top. Keeps arms, shoulders, and, if held correctly, even parts of the legs out of the sun. Benefit two is that when one needs to make a quick technical stop 30 or 40 feet off of a busy road, the umbrella provides a shield behind which one can complete the technical stop in case a rogue car happens by.

Third, when vehicles come along, you can drop the front of the umbrella just a bit, shielding one's appearance from the car, avoiding eye contact. Drawback: when a huge truck comes along, you must either retract the umbrella in time, or grab its top center to keep it from being blown inside out from the truck's wash. Notice that both drawbacks today are the result of sharing the trail at times with 18-wheelers. *Res ipsa loquitur.*

Took my first break in Shawneetown in a shaded area and ate a small snack. I had been warned this morning that there is a biker rally going on in the area this weekend. There might be a lot of biker traffic along Route 1. I began to see the bikers in Shawneetown. Man, last time I was here there was a carnival in town, this time the biker jam. I fit right in here. Both times! And that is not a slam on Shawneetown.

Yes, this is my second trip down this same 23-mile stretch. Why? Last year, I had a hiking buddy through Cincinnati proper until Eden Park. I did not walk the 24-mile stretch through west Cinci to Elizabethtown, where the trail splits north/south. I choose not to walk through west Cinci alone, and I have no clear ideas on a car stash in this area, so I am rewalking this portion to atone for those missed miles. Plus, I love Pounds Hollow. Camping there last year was one of my happiest nights. And most of them have been happy.

Also in Shawneetown, a man in an SUV slowed and asked if I had come all the way from Delaware. This time I could say yes with no caveats, and I recognized him as Dr. Tom, the small town physician who had stopped and talked with me last year. He remembered me. I told him just what in the heck I was doing back here, and that I was hiking the bike alt around the slow, muddy horse trail, and that I had just cached water along the route. He approved of all of this. We bid farewell, and I proceeded on to the Dollar General for 3 Powerades of varying colors.

The trail winds around Ringgold Road, and there I located my first water drop. One for one. Success. I drank half of it, filled my bottle, and proceeded the last few miles to Pounds Hollow, mostly uphill, both ways.

I believe I camped in the exact spot as last year, close to the entrance and water. Set up my tent, ate some more. A local man walking his dog said he had seen me along the road and was glad I was camping here. I received my second warning about the Hog Rock, I think it is called.

A solid 20-plus day. If my activities are nice-local-man AND career-physician approved, I am pretty sure I am on the right path.

Amie

Saturday, June 11, 2016

Destination: Rudement, IL
Today's Miles: 19
Start Location: Pounds Hollow, Shawnee NF, IL
Trip Miles: 1443.01

So last night was the first night I have used this tent without the rainfly. The top two-thirds of it is simply a net, which helps make it so light. But the rest of the campsite will definitely be privy to one's tent goings-on until well after dark. There is no privacy without the rainfly. Fine by me. Ya can't backpack and wear the demure, ladylike mantle. Reminds me of a mini-mart I shopped in back in Indiana. The two cashier ladies were asking me what I was doing. I told them, and one lady said, "I think I could do that." The other one looked at her and replied in a sassy drawl, "Oh, ya could not. You wouldn't be able to carry enough hairspray."

Packed up and continued down Pounds Hollow Rd, which became Karber's Ridge, and stayed on it until the T in the road and my second water drop. I took my first break at 8 miles. I sat at a picnic table and examined my feet. Cue primordial scream: blisters. I was rather certain this would happen with the hot weather. I nursed them and covered them with Band-Aids, and let my socks dry. I ate a small snack and actually offloaded some food today. I left a bag of sunflower seeds on the picnic table. I am coming up on the Mitchellsville mini-mart sooner than I thought, and I have too much food. Hopefully someone in need will find it. The sunflower seeds don't even sound good to me right now except for the salt. I gifted them to the universe. I was rewarded later in the day because I found 5 bucks in the ditch. When the sun had moved and ruined my shade, and when my socks were stiff, I knew it was time to get moving.

For all the warnings, these Hog Rockin' bikers are truly a benign presence while walking. They are easy to share the road with. Only a couple honked at me. One offered a ride. I continued riding drag behind water cache two, and when I got to the T intersection, I was pleased to find it intact as well. I took it up some steps to a small shaded building and sat for an hour, drank water, watched the bikes ride by, and waited out the noon heat. I saw several trucks with horse trailers headed up Karber's, probably toward High Knob Horse Camp. I would rather share a path with the Hog Rockers and the occasional semi than the horses in this circumstance. The truck traffic is way down this year. I was told that the coal mines around here are, in too many cases, either played out or are subject to so much regulation that some have shut down.

I downed as much water as I could and when my socks were stiff again, I proceeded on down Route 34. I have found that about a third of the gallon is easy to carry. Like the backpack most of the time, I really don't notice its presence. I carried water today because at either of my planned camp spots, I do not know if there is water.

During my third break of the day, I saw my first scary snake. I had sat on a gravel area behind some tall grass along the road. I was hidden from the road, and not in the grass to avoid bugs. I leaned back against my pack under the umbrella and sort of closed my eyes. I reposed so for a couple of minutes.

Then I heard a crinkling noise in the grass. I looked over, and a snake was slithering out of the tall grass. It stopped about 6 feet away. I slowly got to my feet. The gravel was so hot that I slowly, slowly stepped onto the stuff sack that holds the poncho. The snake did not coil up, but it sort of pulled its head back into itself. I froze and just stared at it. My plan was that if it struck, I would lower the umbrella, as I was still holding it, very quickly and hope it struck the umbrella instead of me. It turned around and slithered away. I don't know what kind it was.

I got about 5 more offers for a ride on the way into Rudement. One was a dad teaching his son how to drive their Kawasaki Gator utility cart thing. Very cute. I had spied out a covered picnic area here with tables, and I walked over to it and succumbed to the table and shade. Before drinking the rest of my carried water, I looked around for another available water source in the morning. I took off my shoes and socks, walked behind this small pic-nic area, and two wonderful things happened.

First, it was like that scene in *The Lion, the Witch, and The Wardrobe* where the children step through the wardrobe into the secret world beyond it. Behind my area was, like, an entire town park complete with freshly mowed baseball fields, more covered areas, a garden hose on a water tap, and hidden flat areas abounded on which to plop down. I walked over to the garden hose and sprayed off my dirty legs. I may wash my hair in it in the morning. Thank you, trail.

Second, the cool grass felt so good on my sore feet. I almost wanted to cry, and I don't remember the last time that happened. Walking in the grass was like childhood summers, and I felt zero blister pain. So amazing. Earth, heal my feet.

Sometimes I think each of our five senses has certain memories buried deep within them. The smells here, the view, and the soothing touch of grass on feet is a thousand good memories. I looked over at the open field, the sun descending upon it, this perfect park, the southern Illinois expanse of farmland behind it. There really is no place I can think of that I would rather be tonight. Yeah, my feet kind of hurt, and the snake scared me a lit-tle. But would I rather be not hiking and teaching summer school or some-thing? No way. Teaching summer school would turn me into a clock tower sniper.

Supposed to hotter tomorrow. Not sure what my mileage will look like. But right now all is well. No, it's perfect.

Amie

Sunday, June 12, 2016

Destination: JCT Route 145 and 147, IL
Today's Miles: 19.30
Start Location: Rudement, IL
Trip Miles: 1462.31

Last night I had a dream that I could reach my arm through the side walls of my tent, like magic. In my dream, I was reaching through the wall to a side seam, trying to pull the tent around me like a blanket. Then I had the distinct sensation of a hand on my right shoulder. I flinched in my sleep and woke up briefly. Nothing. No one was there, of course. The dream was probably the brainchild of residual fear over the snake encounter and discussing the netted tent wall. I slept well the rest of the night.

The first stop of the morning was the Mitchellsville Stop and Shop. I picked up 4 Clif bars, 4 Powerades, and as they did not sell Band-Aids, the nice lady behind the counter gave me several from her personal stash. I headed straight south on Route 145, which was what the trail consisted of all day, and I immediately set to drinking. Powerade, that is.

I mentioned earlier that I got back into running while off trail this year. Running felt really good again and came easy. To get me through the winter, I trained myself for my first ultramarathon in Fort Worth, TX. I ran the baby ultra, the 50k, which is about 31 miles. I read a lot about how to train for these longer-than-marathon distances, and while doing so, I read a great quote by athlete Sunny Blende: "Ultramarathons are eating and drinking contests with a little exercise and scenery thrown in." The same can be said of backpacking. The trick to staying hydrated and fueled is doing one's best to stay out ahead of it. Don't let yourself feel thirsty. By then it may be too late, and you might bonk.

Applying this principle, I finished off one bottle immediately and started the next one. Powerade instead of plain water because in the mornings I can never down water as quickly. I can inhale the Powerade or Gatorade like a champ, though.

Took my first break at another roadside picnic area. I had gotten in 7 miles before that 10 a.m. heat starts radiating. I sat for quite some time and watched the cars go by. Saw more trucks and horse trailers headed north on 145. Some beautiful horses gazed out their trailer windows as they passed. In my imagination, I saw them bob their noses at me, and I heard them taunt, "Heyyyyy, gurl. We're gonna wreck that River to River Trail." I squinted my eyes back at them as they passed and drank another Powerade. Carrion birds squawked and circled above.

I proceeded on for a few more miles and took a few more breaks. It was a really uneventful day, not too much traffic. Luckily I have been able to stay off the pavement most of the time because there is a gravel or grassy shoulder. Didn't make it to water cache 3 because this stretch didn't need one. There was another minimart at Eddyville. Plus, I only received one offer for a ride today, and although I declined, I did accept a water. I will reach my next gallon in the morning.

As I neared the Rte 145/147 split, I began thinking about where to sleep. I started really early this morning, and was ready to quit early as well. Blisters were not bothering me, but my feet were overall getting tired. I didn't want to push it. I saw a highway sign for a campground and lodging, one mile off trail, and I took it. Hated to go a mile extra both ways, but a shower and possibly laundry would be worth it. I did not count the mile to camp in today's total.

I approached the camp and saw that it is also a horse camp. I squinted my eyes again but then saw the place was virtually empty. I entered the office and chatted a bit with Linda, the owner. She said the lodge was just vacated and had not been cleaned, but I could have it all to myself. Hot shower? Laundry? Many of the beds went unused anyway? I'll take it. She only does cash, and I had 26 bucks. I told her I doubt I will turn on the AC because I am used to going without. Deal.

I took a long, scalding, ecologically unaware shower. Still need to revisit the office for laundry.

Handling this pile of my laundry on a Sunday will certainly violate one of the Commandments.

Amie

Monday, June 13, 2016

Destination: Tunnel Hill, IL
Today's Miles: 17.30
Start Location: JCT Route 145 and 147, IL
Trip Miles: 1479.61

Thanks to Linda at the Bay Creek Ranch, I received front-door delivery of clean laundry this morning. While I waited on it to be finished, I made coffee at the lodge and read the news for the first time in several days. I took a 20-minute glimpse into the outside world. Yep, I am content to retreat back into this world for a little bit longer. I've seen enough.

Headed straight west on IL 147 to start the morning. Fewer cars on this route, but a very still and muggy morning. I reached water drop 3 early. This one was just after the first bridge the trail crosses on 147, down the first gravel drive after the bridge, and across from the falling-down house at the base of the light pole. It was just as I left it, and I drank over half of it quickly.

My first sit-down of the day was at 5 miles. I got a little later start and missed those cooler morning hours. I felt a bit hungry but mostly was craving the salt in the pistachios and almonds I ate.

The first turn today in the data book said County Road 4, but I had made an error while scouting the route and missed it because the road sign only calls it Gilead Church Road. I remembered my error and turned down Gilead Church. It was then that I noticed the Bike Route signs that were posted along the way, and that they are certainly marking the bike alternate. The next few intersections in conjunction with these signs confirmed I had made the correct turn.

My feet today seemed to have joined the rest of me and toughened up. They felt better, just itchy, like things are healing and they are developing that additional layer that takes a few weeks to shed after going off trail. Had to walk on pavement a little more today, which tires me faster for sure. Overall, feeling good, nothing hurts, and the tired at the end of the day is that deliciously tired feeling that means one has done something challenging, but not crossed the line.

It clouded up for a little while this afternoon. I knew there was a slight chance of storms. I looked ahead for a place to duck and cover if called for. There was one house that had a man-shed or man-room-looking outbuilding. I hearkened to an excellent Oldies Country station playing loudly from within. Man, a song I haven't heard in a long time serenaded me as I passed, the one about you're "just a Coca-Cola cowboy." I smiled. In this era of silly bro country and hip-hop country, it was a refreshing song to hear.

I was ready for another break when I reached a campground at mile 10 or so. I set my pack down on the front bench and stepped in. No one was in there. Had hoped to buy a couple Gatorades, so I sat on the bench out front in the shade and waited. A couple on horseback came riding up. They thought I worked there, and we laughed because I had hoped the same of them. They had ridden their horses all the way from Grand Tower. I confirmed I was walking in the direction of Grand Tower. They wished me good luck.

I waited a bit more. Finally two guys in a lifted Ford diesel came driving up. I asked if they worked there. One replied no, but his family owned the place and he came by to check it out. He said there was water, Kool-Aid, and whatever else in the cooler in the truck bed. And to take whatever I needed. I took one water, smiled, and thanked the universe for sending more guys in big trucks to my rescue.

The afternoon waned. My scouted data notes reminded me I had spied a place to stealth right at water drop 4. Drop 4 was thankfully waiting at attention for me. I sat and drank some while, as typical at a possible stealth spot, I judged traffic levels, sight lines, general likelihood of being seen, who in the vicinity might be put out by a little tent going up for a night, sources of noise, and so on.

As I type, I hear the report of gunfire in the distance. The kind that means good country folk at target practice. I feel pretty safe.

Amie

Bike Route Concurrent with . . . Wine Trail?
Tuesday, June 14, 2016

Destination: Outside Lick Creek, IL
Today's Miles: 15.70
Start Location: Tunnel Hill, IL
Trip Miles: 1495.31

Last night the coyotes started yipping. Given that my campsite was up on a hill, the yipping almost sounded like it came from all around me. Coyotes in stereophonic. Seems that coyotes yipping is never something you can be totally prepared for. Every time it is startling, chilling, captivating, and wild.

Now for some early morning backpacking humor. I heat water for coffee every morning unless I have camped somewhere totally illicit and am trying to get outta Dodge. I never like to set the cookpot down directly on the tent floor or sleeping pad because the bottom of the pot is hot and sometimes dirty. Setting it down outside the tent gets it dirtier if I am on grass. This morning the only item I had at my disposal for a hot pad was yesterday's underwear. Always good to make your basic items do double duty when possible.

Not too much into my morning, I began seeing cyclists who are on the bike route and Trans-America Trail through this portion. One guy stopped and talked with me. His group is on their way to Oregon. A bit later a lady cyclist approved of my Chrome Dome in what I think was a lovely Australian accent: "Oh, that's smart. You got your umbrella there, eh?" I waved and smiled.

Walked through Goreville and bought a few things at the Dollar General. I sat in the shade in the park to reorganize, shed outer packaging for the groceries and Bandaids, take a little break, and sneak a phone charge. A grandfather-grandson pair and another gentleman were at the park briefly. They asked about my backpacking, and of course bid me be careful. I said thank you and that I try to be careful. Then the man stated, as we often hear when visiting a small town, "Yeah, people around here are nice. Don't gotta worry too much around here. Just be careful out there. Other places, ya just don't know."

Most of us have probably heard some variation of this statement. I take it sincerely every time, but it's interesting how it's usually "those other guys" or "out there" or some other abstract place or population that is to be tip-toed around cautiously. Wouldn't it be nice if terrible events never occurred to "us guys" or "right here and now." I promised to look out for myself "out there."

I crossed two Interstates today, both on overpasses, and I wondered how long it takes for us to feel that walking is the normal speed, and car travel is just way too fast and the weird pace. I wonder if it has happened to me again yet.

Okay, too serious. Another immature underwear story? You got it! These Outdoor Research shorts I bought last spring in Milford, OH, I'm afraid, will also prove to be too big soon. At some point yesterday, after executing a technical stop, I was ambling along with a foreign sensation in my right hip area. I looked down and right to see that my undergarment band was outside my shorts on that side in glaringly obvious fashion. Seriously twisted up, down and around and at rest on top of my shorts, near the right pocket. Not sure how that happened or how many cars saw, but oh well. May have to switch out shorts when I return the mothership to KS.

Wow, did the trail provide in the form of water today! Thank you, people of southern Illinois. I swear, half the population down here kindly offered me a ride, Gatorade, water, asked if I were broken down or stranded. One guy slowed and just handed a cold bottle out the window. A couple who have a lawnmower repair service went in the house and came out with a to-go cup with icewater. Even the UPS guy asked if I needed any. I found an unopened minibottle on the side of the road and drank it. I even stopped at a bed and breakfast out here, and upon my deciding it was a bit pricey, was thanked anyway and sent out the door with water. I am blessed.

In this area the road names in the TBTs continue to differ from the sign names. Again today, I made a guess as to what road I should be taking based on direction and distance travelled. This afternoon I surmised that the bike route follows a wine trail that goes through here. Following the wine route is what I shall do; surely this can't be wrong. *In vino veritas.*

Camping tonight. Except for muggy clothes, sleeping bag, food, directions, hair . . . underwear . . . all is well.

Amie

Wednesday, June 15, 2016

Destination: Anna, IL
Today's Miles: 9.40
Start Location: Outside Lick Creek, IL
Trip Miles: 1504.71

Slept really hard last night but not before a 30-minute downpour came through. I had my rainfly cocked and ready. Everything stayed mostly dry, as dry as can be expected in 99.9% humidity. The only exception was the umbrella and poncho, which I left outside as a ground cloth.

Walked very quiet backroads to begin the day. The tent and accoutrements were all wet, which made everything feel so heavy. I was slow this morning, but shortly the trail provided another picnic area where I could set everything down and let the soaked pieces hang to dry. The rafters even had little nails and staples every few feet, on which I hung the items. Thanks, trail. I sat for a long time waiting for things to dry out. Still humid and not much breeze.

I had planned on doing a motel night soon, and my next map town was to be Cobden, IL. There is one bed and breakfast there, but upon calling, I was politely (glad the owner didn't see my appearance, heh heh) informed that she was not taking guests this week due to some construction. She did, however, suggest a place in Anna. I thought it over and asked the trail to show me what to do, as I was also out of food. I veered off the data book just a bit today. Anna, south of Cobden, had a cheaper Super 8. I decided not to spend energy hunting down the bed and breakfast. Anna also has more options for groceries and resupply.

I am so glad I wandered off course. Another hard downpour hit when I was a couple of miles from Anna. Poncho and umbrella combo kept everything dry, but of course my shoes got drenched. This would not help my feet situation, what with blisters healing and feeling swampy anyway due to humidity. I took the last couple miles carefully, feeling like I was doing a Frankenstein walk to avoid the hard, pushing-off movement that would make my feet slide around in wet shoes. Eeeeh.

I hit a Subway right when I entered town and got my protein and greens fix. This afternoon's clear objectives were to dry my shoes, stay off my feet, drink water, do laundry, and make use of my mobile cellular device for finding a route to get back on the TBTs quickly. I don't like veering off course too often, and I cannot circumvent my water drops. Yes, people have graciously stopped and lavished me with water, but it is both lazy and dangerous to make others' kindness your only plan. It is 14 miles from here to Wolf Lake, which is on course, has a water cache marked near it, and has my scribbled notes indicating a place to stealth. Yesssssss.

Feeling like this was a pretty boring entry about a basically utilitarian day, so while I wait for my laundry to dry, I will talk more about this very real but precarious notion of the trail providing. One must do the footwork and make solid plans for the necessities, like water. For example, yesterday it would have been foolish for me to ignore water sources and think, *Yeah, the UPS guy will probably come along and offer me something. Totally not worried.* It is our job to prepare as best we can for the known knowns and the known unknowns. The route itself and good people take care of the unknown unknowns. That is trail magic.

So one morning this past winter I was out for a long run. On long runs I prep for known knowns by taking a Power Bar or a little serving of almond butter with me to eat about halfway through. At about 15 miles, it appeared that a sack of someone's groceries had blown out of the back of their truck, and items were lying out on the dirt road for the taking. One item was a massive bag of peanut M&M's, and I'm talking the family-size bag. Colored candies peppered the brown and grey landscape. I jogged over to the exploded bag with fingers crossed. That's right, I ate the two handfuls that were still in the torn packaging. And they were amazing, just what I needed for a tiny boost. I will absolutely eat food off the ground.

I laughed that winter morning that the trail had provided.

Amie

Thursday, June 16, 2016

Destination: Wolf Lake, IL
Today's Miles: 15.10
Start Location: Anna, IL
Trip Miles: 1519.81

Tried to start as early as possible again this morning, about 6:15. I stopped at the Kroger, which was on route, for a resupply and a gallon of water to get me back on the grid. I took my sacks outside to organize everything. There was a cute patio set right outside the double sliding doors to the store. Perfect. I sat my pack down to put everything in its place, and while I was organizing, my movements kept making the auto sliding doors open and close. Open a different pack pocket? Doors open. Then close. Reach behind me to throw that excess packaging away? Doors open! Close. Open. Close. I started giggling every time it happened. And I know my nephews Dain and Kaden would have found it hilarious.

So after I wore out the automatic doors at Kroger and set off, I found myself in downtown Anna. Quaint, peaceful. A man named Randy stepped out of a coffee shop and asked if he could buy me coffee. I declined the coffee, but we chatted briefly. He said he had seen me walking into Anna yesterday. He asked if I had read any Peter Jenkins books. Yes! Conversations like these are one of the most fun parts of doing this, meeting random people who have read the same authors, and who share this interest.

First break was at 8:30. I had downed half the gallon of water. I wanted to see how much longer I would be on route 127 before I turned off onto the State Forest Road. The grain and coal truck traffic wasn't too terrible, but I wanted a heads up on how much longer before peace reigned again. I had 1.9 miles. Okay, girl, you can do this. The remainder of the day was on the Trail of Tears State Forest Road, huge shoulder, freshly mowed, and I was back on the map.

Today was supposed to be the hottest day of the week: 97. I did not have cell service much of the day, and I considered ignorance bliss in this regard. I just kept drinking and then found a shaded picnic area at a horse camp that was blocked off and out of use for some reason. *Haha.* I slept away the 11 to 3 heat, the worst part of the day. Back on the forest road at 3:30, and there was water at the forest visitor center. Refill for sure.

The last few miles into Wolf Lake, I felt good. I experimented with carrying a nearly full gallon jug. I swung it from my right hand. Then my left hand. I carried it like a football. I put it up on each shoulder for a while. I even stuck it up behind my head and balanced it between my neck and the pack frame for a while. Water gallon perched behind my neck on the pack frame is my favorite. Hands free.

Stealthing tonight. Only supposed to be 91 tomorrow. Should hit my next water drop in the morning.

All is well.

Amie

Friday, June 17, 2016

Destination: Gorham, IL
Today's Miles: 16.90
Start Location: Wolf Lake, IL
Trip Miles: 1536.71
Island Road, aptly named

Set off this morning with a dry tent, dry shoes and socks, dry air, and a projected high of only 89. What a difference a few degrees and low humidity make. As I walked in the cooler morning, I started thinking that this Illinois piece is quickly becoming one my favorites. Everyone has been helpful, almost no one has honked at me. In fact, a couple of times, including this morning, I have received an extended left arm giving a thumbs up out a passing car's driver's side window. Almost zero unrestrained dogs have accosted me following by snaggled, haggard-looking owners whom the dogs ignore. And roadside shade and camping spots have been abundant.

The morning was mostly a short state-route stint, followed by several miles on Island Road leading into Grand Tower. Island Road was a shorter preview to the 14-mile stretch on the levee tomorrow. With less than a mile to go before Grand Tower, I saw some people camped down on the land side of the levee. There was a camper, a huge tent, about 6 coolers, a campfire, and two puppies. Jessie and Bob invited me down for a water break, and I sat there in the shade talking for a few minutes. This is what I learned: Jessie's uncle owns the land on which they were camping. Jessie and Bob and their families come out here to camp in the summers. They mow a swath for their campsite, but the rest of it is the state of Missouri's problem. Missouri? Yes. For a time this morning, apparently I was in MO because the Mississippi has rerouted itself such that the levee extends into MO for a bit. During the flood of '93, this portion of the levee did not fail. However, Jessie had come out here to get his aunt and uncle out of their place and to safety because the Mississippi was about even with the levee. He said his aunt left, but his uncle refused. Jessie said that walking on the ground on this side of the levee was like walking on a sponge. It was the weirdest sensation. He had to leave his uncle because the old timer would not budge. Their things survived, but the feeling of the earth under his feet was a strange memory.

I drank two bottles of water and proceeded on to town. I needed to get two days' food to get me to Chester. I picked up beef jerky and the non-junkiest carbs I could find. Plus a jar of peanut butter and blue Powerade.

Continued on Route 3 for a while. There was actually wind today as well.

Very nice. Along Route 3, I saw two little girls in their yard out by the road. One of them had a sign on a stick, and the other had a spiral notebook. Both were being waved around at passing traffic. I figured the girls were running a car wash or lemonade and cookie stand or something. I asked them if they were selling lemonade or anything. They replied, "No, we're just waving at the cars as they go by." It was something my sisters and I would have done.

I realized another benefit to the umbrella today. I can go without a hat. This keeps my head cooler, especially when there is a breeze. And I must restate how much I like being able to hide behind this umbrella when cars pass. But the reflective top calls attention to my presence simultaneously. It's a rather comical paradox: "You can't see me. But haha, made you look!" Reminds me of that Geico "oldest trick in the book" commercial with the Medieval monk and his scribe. The monk says to the scribe, "Lookest over there." The scribe does, and the punchline is "Madest thou look." Funny. That's the awesome part of this attention-grabbing umbrella in the face of oncoming cars. Thou cans't not see me, but madest thou look.

I walked on into Gorham. I had cached water here, and had noted a place to camp. I walked the couple blocks into town to the community center I had checked out last week. There is a huge lawn, little fire department adjacent, and no houses or roads to the south and east. I sat and performed recon as always. No one in the town seems nosy. No one really took note of the backpack girl sitting in the center doorway. Plus, my water gallon had been hiding in plain sight for over a week and was fine. As I waited, an Aaron's truck pulled up to the house across the street. When it left, the Aaron's delivery guy gave me bottled water.

I finally decided on the lawn area closer to the fire department. There is a picnic table sitting out here. If there is a picnic table, that just screams camping. This appears to be city property. Plus, both times now the fire department has looked unmanned, and if I get caught in the morning, at least I can probably go in and have coffee with them while I explain my activities.

A good day. A sunny, quiet evening in a tiny town. To echo *Car Talk*, you just wasted another perfectly good three minutes reading this journal.

Madest thou read!

Amie

Hoary, Gnarled Questions
Saturday, June 18, 2016

Destination: Rockwood, IL
Today's Miles: 18.40
Start Location: Gorham, IL
Trip Miles: 1555.11

Success on last night's camping spot. It can't really be called a stealth since I was out in the open, but I and my few things I left sitting on the picnic table were undisturbed.

The path today started alongside Route 9. There were 2 miles to cover before heading up onto the levee. The rumble strips outside the white line-you know, the ones that alert the wayward driver they're fixin' to drive off into the ditch-provided the perfect surface, if you have to walk on pavement, that is. I placed the arch of my foot on the apex of the bump and pushed off each step with my arch as opposed to the ball of the foot, which takes the worst beating when walking. I next ascended the gravel road to the levee, and I had to ask myself the hoary, gnarled question, "What happens if my three water drops are gone or annihilated by mowers?" Plan B would consist of descending one of the entry/exit roads along the levee and inquiring at one of the farms for water. I doubted the BTK Killer was out on the tractor this morning managing one of the neat rows of crops.

My first several miles up on the levee went very quickly. I came to my first water cache. Success! I sat down, ate a snack, and drank about 3/4 of the gallon on the spot. I didn't want to carry the rest, so I must report that I littered and left the remainder of the water to the universe. I am sure I will be punished for this offense by abiding more loud trains all night just as I have the past two nights.

The rest of the day on the levee found me with two good problems to experience: there was a wind that was whipping my umbrella around but keeping me cool at the same time. And I literally had too much water on my hands. I skipped levee cache two, and picked up the third gallon just as I had left it. I drank nearly all of that gallon as well, then worked my way into the town of Cora, with only two miles to go until Rockwood, my planned camp spot and yet another water drop.

In Rockwood, I sat down at a picnic table to get off my feet and check things out. A man named Schmitty, longtime Rockwood resident, stopped by to chat. He has seen many walkers and bicyclists go through here over the years. He commented, "Y'all got some hair on yer butt goin up and down this road." I briefly pondered if that was the same as having a set, and then I told him I had already scouted this area. I was well aware of all the coal truck traffic near Chester. And that I just stepped off into the ditch and didn't fight the trucks for a piece of the road.

Schmitty also commented on the flood of '93. He was also the third person to lament the shutting down of the coal mines and third to say, "People just don't know what they're gonna do."

He left, and I thought I had a spot secured when a different guy came riding up to the lawn next to the park on a mower and started mowing. That raised the hoary, gnarled question, "Crap. How late is this dude gonna mow?" I continued to sit. Finally I walked over to retrieve my water that I had literally hidden in the tall grass behind the park restroom building here. As I was bent over getting my jug, I am sure the hoary, gnarled question in the minds of passers-by was, "Now just what in the heck is that gal doin' foolin' around behind that outhouse?"

Drank some water. Still waiting on the lawn mower man to cease and desist for the night. Only 8 or so miles into Chester in the morning. At which point I will grapple with the hoary, gnarled question of going off the data book and connecting the dots up to St. Charles as opposed to sticking to the TBTs and peregrinating through St. Louis.

Aside from this marathon lawn session that is holding up my dropping anchor for the night, all is well.

Amie

A Quasi-Zero Day
Sunday, June 19, 2016

Destination: Chester, IL
Today's Miles: 8
Start Location: Rockwood, IL
Trip Miles: 1563.11

Slept very well last night tucked among the little Rockwood post office building, its propane tank, and its steps. There was playground equipment to my northwest also to obscure the view. Again, no one seemed to notice a tent in their park, or if they did they paid me no mind. It was noticeably cooler last night. A few nights ago, I didn't want to touch my sleeping bag. Last night I got in it and snuggled. This morning while packing up, I put on long sleeves.

When one is out here and has detoxed from life's routines, the ebb and flow of time becomes strange. You often have no idea what day of the week it is. *Amie, what's today's date?* Dunno. *Amie, what time is it?* I haven't the slightest; I will check the time when it feels like a couple hours before dark so that I can look for a place to camp. *Amie, how long has it been since you went back on trail?* I don't know. I think about two weeks. Maybe more.

Point being, I am so grateful that today happened to be Sunday. I didn't think about it until last night. The truck traffic I was thinking about, and that Schmitty said required of us ample bum hair, was nonexistent. The coal barge loading area along Rt 3 was at a standstill. The traffic was light. Again, timing is everything and some problems solve themselves.

And in addition to entering a time warp when doing this, I also at times enter a geography bubble. I know the names of the towns coming up and what services I may expect, but sometimes I lose track of exactly where I am positioned in a particular state. Last year in Indiana, I for some reason pictured myself walking in the middle of the state, when I was hugging the southern rim the whole time.

To my point, I have noticed a heavy accent here, and I am startled when I hear it because I think of Illinois as Midwest, and as having a similar neutral dialect with maybe a slight twang like Kansas. Most people here, such as Schmitty last night, sound rather Kentucky or Tennessee, to which this part of Illinois has been closer than I realized. The coffee company owner from a few days ago had that northern Illinois, Great Lakes flavor to his speech. Interesting. I have been farther "south" than I knew.

Upon entering the town of Chester, I passed through a mile or so of cute, modest houses. Made it to State Street and decided to do a motel/shower/laundry/charging/clean-up night. State Street is also home to the Wal-Mart, somewhere I never do cartwheels when thinking about patronizing until I am out here.

In addition to the usual trail chores and absolving sinful laundry, I needed to rebag my instant coffee and powdered milk. It has been so muggy out that my coffee has started to make itself inside the bag. Reminds me of the dueling banjos over coffee at home with Andrea and Gary. I like strong coffee; Andrea and Gary, not so much. We can all partake of the same pot, and those two will have to be peeled off the ceiling after a cup, while I down two cups and remark to them, "Man, sorry this coffee's kinda weak this morning." Andrea, you would love my camping coffee. And I'm just messing with you guys. I'm the one with the coffee problem.

So the main point of this afternoon was to make a plan for connecting the dots to St. Charles, MO. I am going to cross the Mississippi in the morning here at Chester and go off the data book to get to perhaps Defiance or Augusta, MO. Either of those towns, or others just east or west, will then put me back on the Katy. And then I plan to take the Katy backwards until I reach St. Charles. Two reasons for this plan. One, I have a huge trail crush on the Katy, and all the best towns and services are in the eastern portion of it anyway. I'll take any opportunity to get me some more Katy time.

Reason two. Okay, seriously, even in the ADT directions there is a note typed by whoever created these directions at one of the waypoints coming into East St. Louis that reads, "It is not safe to camp here." I have looked at waypoints line by line for nearly half the country now, and I have *never* seen that comment anywhere but around the STL area. I have laughed about that comment numerous times. Funny. Until I'm there.

So I am going rogue the next week and working my way around St. Louis from the west side, using my phone as a primary guide. We'll see how this goes. It is supposed to be 99 on Tuesday and Wednesday. And MapQuest had better not be wrong. It was wrong once last week.

Picked up a little bit of food, some more sunscreen SPF Nuclear Option, and a Missouri road map with the northeast corner cut out as a secondary source. Took a long, environmentally disastrous shower. Will repack everything in the morning, have some Andrea-and-Gary-style coffee at the free breakfast in the morning, and prepare to cross the mighty Mississippi if the universe allows. To cross, or not to cross. That is the question.

I think crossing this river means I will officially be in the West.

Amie

Bob Dylan, Radio Tradio, and That Slow Burn
Monday, June 20, 2016

Destination: Just shy of Ste. Genevieve, MO
Today's Miles: 20.30
Start Location: Chester, IL
Trip Miles: 1583.41

Mississippi: crossed. In white-knuckled fashion, I might add. The long bridge over the river leading into Missouri indeed had a raised pedestrian walkway, but it was maybe two feet wide. At times the concrete was crumbled away, exposing rebar. There was one small section where the concrete was completely gone, rebar only, and I could look right through down to the water. Whenever a semi came toward me, I turned sideways as if I were gazing out at the river. *Ewwwww, lawd.* It was the kind of sustained, scary bridge crossing that could make a girl wanna celebrate reaching the other side with a full Russian breakfast. Regardless, Illinois: done! Thank you, southern Illinois. You, as has been every other state, were very good to me.

I did a cell-phone recon of water sources and route for today. Once I crossed the river and pried my fingers from the umbrella handle, I headed down Missouri HWY H and then onto HWY 61. Along H, I discovered I was once again following the Trans-America Bike Trail. I took this to be a favorable sign. Two cyclists stopped me. They wanted my picture. Turns out, they are both teachers as well. As they pedaled away, one called out, "You make us look like wimps."

Took my first break at ten miles. I sat in the shade just inside someone's barn. I drank the rest of my water, as the next watering' hole was just a couple miles away. I had my "Sorry to trespass; I'm not homeless or weird" speech all ready to deliver in case I was discovered sitting on the tongue hitch of someone's farm equipment.

I sat and ate some of the only food that appeals to me lately, almond butter. It is really all that sounds good. Except for greens and red meat, of course. But for a walking food, it is all I want. I wondered why. I knew it had a lot of vitamin E, but I studied the label and saw that almond butter has lots of magnesium too. Magnesium is good for that slow burn. That sustained energy. I would bet that's why I want this food right now. The body usually tells us what it needs. I'm listening. Grocery store in the morning. I will buy more.

I left the barn and proceeded on. As the day progressed, my shorts

264

once again became sweaty, expanded a little, and started sagging. I started laughing because I thought I needed to trade them off for something a wee bit smaller in the waist. Laughing because it reminded me of Radio Tradio. I hope I get this story right.

There is this radio station down near Grove, Oklahoma, that has a call-in session periodically called Radio Tradio. Apparently you call in if you have something you want to trade off, sell, barter, or flat rid yourself of. According to Andrea and Gary, and it's funnier when they tell it, people will call in to trade ANYTHING.

Cue my sister affecting an Oklahoma accent imitating a Radio Tradio caller: "Yeah, I got this parakeet cage I'd like to trayde. Holds two parakeets. Now the door is a little rusty, and she squeaks a tad when ya open it, but it'll do real nice if ya wanna come take a look at it and if ya got some parakeets need housin.'"

I laughed so hard today thinking I need to call Radio Tradio about these shorts: "Yeah, hello. My name's Amie. I got this pair a shorts, they's gettin' a little big. I'm gettin ta be right worried that mu rear might be showin' when I'm tryna walk down the road in 'em. They don't stank or nuthin. They gotta bout 800 miles on 'em. They's a little worn in the butt, but they'll do real nice. 'Dlike a smaller set that I don't hafta hitch up awl the time. If ya wanna trayde, y'all'll hafta come find me, now. I'll just be walkin' down the road. Yeah, I know it's hot out. Brang me some water and I'll getcha a little better deal. Bye now." I entertained myself thinking about Radio Tradio.

Break 2 came just outside my next water stop. Sat on the steps of the Masonic Lodge near the minimart. I saw an outside tap, but no water came out. I guess their water is a big secret as well. Went just a quarter mile off route to pick up 4 Powerades and a gallon of water. Drank about half of it quickly to lose the weight. I then continued straight up HWY 61. Not too bad of a shoulder. I will "revisit" this highway again tomorrow. There's a Bob Dylan album title in there somewhere.

Ran across this place to stealth just outside of town. It is marked as Missouri State Park property. It is freshly mowed, so I can't imagine anyone coming back here and throwing me out. It's possible, of course.

Tomorrow's route is planned. Food and watering holes identified.

God bless almond butter, friends I can contact who've walked this route before, the rainless forecast, and my family's voices in my head imitating Radio Tradio to make me laugh on this nice evening.

Cheers!

Amie

Gear Fail, Mmmmmm, Hmmmm
Tuesday, June 21, 2016

Destination: Ste. Genevieve, MO
Today's Miles: 3
Start Location: Just shy of Ste. Genevieve, MO
Trip Miles: 1586.41

Last night brought about my first major gear fail that, as the Bard might say, didst sucketh mightily. As I updated on here, I was lying on my sleeping pad. By the time I was finished, I wondered why both arms were falling asleep and my spine was digging into the ground. The sleep pad had totally deflated. This happened once last year. I had thought it was punctured, but it had been my moronic error in not closing the valve all the way. This time it truly has a rip in it. I inflated it four more times just to make sure. I could hear the air leaking out from a side seam rip. The rip extends to the underside too. By this time, it was too late to repack everything and make it into town by dark. In a comic act of desperation, I got out my biggest, stickiest Band-Aid and tried to repair the rip just for one more night. Maybe it would work. Nope.

With no choice but to deal with it, I tried wadding up my sleeping bag and putting it under my pelvic bones for extra cushioning, and achieved a state resembling sleep, sleep in fits and starts until daybreak. Needless to say, I felt like death warmed over this morning. I ain't been this stove up since I drove 1300 miles in a Hyundai with no cruise control.

I knew this would happen eventually. I am surprised the sleep pad has lasted this long, to be honest, as much as I drag it around and slam it down on stuff. Plus, gotta be honest, it smells horrible. I wouldn't even try to hawk this thing on the Tradio. It is tapped out. So I whipped up some horrifically strong coffee to make the couple miles into town and to shock my mental faculties into forming a plan.

What I preferred to do was continue on to Festus and do a motel night there, make a reservation, and have a new pad shipped to Festus to wait for me. But it was 32 miles to Festus from my camp site. I cannot go 32 miles in one day, especially after sleeping on the ground. And I obviously did not want to camp again somewhere south of Festus and on the ground.

So I walked into a Ste. Genevieve motel and, after clarifying my status as not homeless or weird, asked if I could have a package shipped there overnight. And if I could please check in at 8 in the morning. They were very accommodating. And I needed to get the pad ordered ASAP so that it could ship this morning.

In a word, I speedily placed the order, checked in early enough to get breakfast. I was kind of a hit at breakfast among a few older people who had all kinds of questions about my trek. It was really sweet. Nevertheless, I hate taking a zero when I don't need to and nothing hurts. And I really hope that the pad arrives in time for checkout in the morning so I don't have to zero another day, or have to mess with having something bounced ahead if I am no longer here to receive it.

However, one positive about staying here is that I encountered my first grocery store that actually had a produce section. I bought some more almond butter for the road. I also bought a giant bag of greens and a pound of lean ground turkey breast. I cooked the turkey in my room using my camp stove. With the window open of course.

I also used this down time to survey carefully the next few days' watering holes, resupply opportunities, and backroads. I took meticulous notes.

Random observation for the day: the hallway in this motel looks like the hallway in Kubrick's version of *The Shining* where Danny is riding his bigwheel and encounters the dead Grady twins. I really want back on the road tomorrow. It's like this hallway is crooning, "Come play with us, Amie. Forever. And ever. And ever." Noooooooo, I want outside!

So in honor of my Uncle David who made me laugh this evening with a hilarious YouTube video about a man who trolls his family Slingblade style, I will deliver an overview of my day in the style of Slingblade: "Last night I was tinkerin' with my gear and whatnot. That there sleep pad is goin' in the trash soon enough. The world'll be shut of ya. Mmmm, hmmmm. Ordered me a new one, shaped like a bananer. Mmmm, hmmm. Had to stay in town today for a great long while. Mmmm, hmmm. This here motel gal offered me a square deal on a room. I reckon I oughtta thank ye fer it. Mmmmm, hmmmm. I asked to get in here pert early. I said 'Whatever you take a notion to; don't mean to put ya out none.' Alright tyen. Went over there to that market for a great long while. You got any biscuits for sale in there? Reckon I studied on them waterin' spots. Mmmmm, hmmmm. Studied on it quite a bit. Alright tyen, if ya see that UPS feller, tell 'im to hurry on up over here. Got me some walkin' to do."

Amie

Wednesday, June 22, 2016

Destination: Bloomsdale, MO
Today's Miles: 11.40
Start Location: Ste. Genevieve, MO
Trip Miles: 1597.81

Noon was the bewitching hour today. At 11:46 the front desk called to say the box had arrived. I packed up fast, checked to see that my sleep pad was correct, and made noon checkout.

I revisited HWY 61 to get in a decent half-day's hike.

No pavement walking today, yippee! The shoulder was gravel or someone's mowed lawn the whole way. Just before town, I sat at an abandoned loading dock for a short break. I ate a little, thought on what to do about camping for the night, and enjoyed the breeze, the rest of my water, and had one of those complete moments of contentment, not needing anything.

Lawn camping tonight in town behind a place of business. With permission too. It was offered, along with water, as I passed by.

Nothing funny or odd to report, just a nice, uneventful half day. Wow, I am going to need that full day tomorrow to churn up some fodder for tomorrow's entry because this entry is way too short. This simply won't do.

Back in the saddle, and back in business as far as a sleep pad.

All is well.

Amie

Katy Trail Creeping and No AC
Thursday, June 23, 2016

Destination: Festus, MO
Today's Miles: 19.40
Start Location: Bloomsdale, MO
Trip Miles: 1617.21

Wow, so I used the new sleep pad last night. I thought it had been me or the backpack also heavily contributing to the symphony of smells when tenting at night. It was that old pad the whole time. Good riddance!

Thank you to David for letting me anchor behind his shop last night. And thank you for coffee this morning. I packed up and was on the road by 6:30. Today was my last day on HWY 61, and it bid me adieu in fine fashion. Very wide shoulder, grass or gravel to walk on. No showdowns with dump trucks or semis. In fact, I felt so comfortable on 61, and I knew I would get a town night tonight in Festus, that I allowed myself to listen to music for most of the day. I think this is the fourth day in 1600 miles that I have allowed myself to do that. It was really nice.

I drank a full gallon of water by noon. Stopped around 2:30 and picked up a chocolate milk, two Powerades, and a couple Clif bars. It was overcast most of the morning, not feeling that hot. But I have adjusted to the heat. I actually started making myself acclimate to heat before I even left home. I didn't run my AC at home. Driving out here I barely used the AC. I am to the point where I find AC kind of obnoxious, really. I never turn it on in motel rooms. I just run the fan. It was 95 around 3 pm, the last time I checked today. I prefer the heat to rain.

I really don't notice the heat too much as long as I keep moving, which creates the breeze effect. I stay in the shade when possible, including my Chrome Dome shade. In this heat and humidity, I drink close to two gallons of fluid per day, which includes water for coffee in the morning and 2 to 4 Powerades a day. The body will adjust to no AC. The only time the heat totally su-huuuuuucks is at night in the tent when it is muggy and still, and you just lie there and sweat. I have experienced a few nights like that, and last night was one. Otherwise, things have been cooling down okay at night.

This heat and no AC reminds me of spending time in August at my grandparents' house in Iowa. Southeast Iowa is just as muggy and still as it is here in MO. Grandma and Grandpa did not have AC in the house. We all just dealt with the heat. We also roamed free all over the little town and out in the cow pastures all day, no shoes most of the time and no sunscreen. In addition to eschewing the need for AC, Grandma was a rebel and bought untaxed, unregulated, non-USDA approved eggs from the Amish. These eggs we ate heartily after sweating half the night in the upstairs bedrooms usually devoid of a breeze unless we took a fan up there.

We also dug around in the upstairs closets and played with old toys that probably contained lead, or would today be on some sort of recall list. In today's sideways world, I am sure there are some do-gooders out there who would call up and inform on Grandma for child abuse, what with us suffering so under those conditions. Those no-AC summers were the furthest thing from child abuse. Really, lack of AC is a minuscule blip on the human body's radar most of the time once we have acclimated. I try tol listen to the body's signals and drink a ton.

I started early and ended early, rolled into Festus mid-afternoon. A trail connection and friend from last year graciously donated a hotel rewards points complimentary night to me, and so I took the opportunity tonight. A thousand thank-yous! I am blessed.

One aspect of this hiking project that ceaselessly astounds me is how much the people of this country take care of me. Even in the littlest things, like sticking a bottle of water out the car window. I am almost halfway across, and America has been good to me. No, I am not getting complacent as far as being careful and watching my back.

Once I checked in to the hotel, I took a long, scalding, ecologically apocalyptic bath and shower, scrubbing the road grime and sunscreen off.

Tomorrow I head west on HWY A for a time. Then I will turn northwest tomorrow afternoon, gradually approaching the Katy again. The Katy Trail should probably get a restraining order against me. That's how much I have been thinking about walking it again for a couple days.

I remembered this past winter when I met up with trail friend Cynthia, and we talked about how we wished the Katy went all the way across the country. And I noticed that another ADT hiker called the Katy Never-Never Land. Others like it too. See, I am not the only Katy stalker.

Amie

Like Manna from Heaven
Friday, June 24, 2016

Destination: House Spring, MO
Today's Miles: 24.30
Start Location: Festus, MO
Trip Miles: 1641.51

On the road by 6:30 this morning, leaving Festus on HWY A. I had been walking for about 30 minutes when a woman came walking up from behind, a little out of breath. She said she had seen me, and figured she had enough time to pull into the Phillips 66 and buy me a water. She handed me a Propel water and went back to her car. I said thank you and drank it immediately. I was also carrying a liter to tide me over to the next minimart 5 miles away.

The morning brought 4 more mini-blessings. The first was that I did not have to carry any food today. I ate breakfast, and there was a place to buy food every few miles. This helped me go faster. Second, the high today was only supposed to be 91. Third, thank you, state of Missouri, for making your roads with wide shoulders. Fourth, thanks to the person who let that 20-spot blow out of your car window. I found it on the grass and picked it up.

Around 11, something else occurred. I reached a highway junction, where there was a Circle K. I always laugh about Circle K because it reminds me of *Bill and Ted's Excellent Adventure*.

I was standing on the concrete island waiting to cross to get a snack at the Circle K because I knew it was going to be mid-afternoon before I would run across food again. I was waiting on the light, and another woman slowed down, rolled down her window, and said she wanted to give me her lunch. I didn't quite understand at first. She said she had a packed lunch with her, but she felt that God was calling her to fast that day, and she had seen me and felt she needed to make sure I was provisioned instead. She retrieved from the passenger seat a sturdy little basket full of food. I said, "But what about your basket?" She said that was the least of her worries. She wanted me to have it, and God bless.

I took it and was rendered totally speechless for several minutes. It took a while for all that to sink in. It was another of those moments out here that kind of gave me chills. In a good way. Something miraculous was afoot at the Circle K. I turned the corner to my next road, and found a place to sit and eat. The basket contained milk, a flavored tea, chips, yogurt, and sandwich fixings including bread, meat, mayo, lettuce, celery, and another dressing or dip, probably for the celery. I drank the milk and ate the yogurt and chips immediately. I knew the sandwich items would be fine for a couple hours, so when I finally recovered myself, I proceeded on.

I walked most of the afternoon on Hillboro-House Springs Road, a calm road passing by nice houses on large lots. The only drawback was having to walk on more pavement today. I stopped again a couple hours later to spell my feet and to eat the sandwich. It was so good. I finished off the rest of the tea as well, and then I looked at the basket and petitioned the universe for something constructive to do with the basket. I was currently sitting on the lawn of a small chapel, under a shade tree. I wanted to leave the basket at the front door, but there was nowhere to dispose of the trash, and I was not about to leave a basket of trash at the chapel door.

I carried it a bit further after I packed up and went on. I finally threw the trash away in someone's dumpster out by the road. There was soon another roadside chapel, and I placed the now empty basket at its front door. I hope they make use of it somehow. It reminded me of a Little Red Riding Hood basket. I wanted it to have a good home.

Continued on toward House Spring, stopping a couple more times. Here are some random funny umbrella facts since my last Chrome Dome report. Twice now in the jet wash of passing trucks, the umbrella has gotten blown inside out. It has felt like a scene from a Roadrunner cartoon both times it has happened. Also this morning, when two vehicles passed me at the same time but going in opposite directions, the umbrella couldn't decide what to do in the confusing air pockets from both, so it just slapped me in the face. I'm sure I did something to deserve that.

I really made it this far today only due to others' generosity. I didn't have to carry food because I ate breakfast this morning at the gifted hotel stay. I only had to stop once for fluids because people kept giving me stuff. Thank you. There are resupply stops on the way out of town in the morning. Lawn camping tonight via invite. Humble Christian charity is real. Trail magic is real. Except for sore feet due to pavement, kind of a storybook day.

Amie

A Comical or Tragic Day? Both!
Saturday, June 25, 2016

Destination: Pacific, MO
Today's Miles: 16
Start Location: House Spring, MO
Trip Miles: 1657.51

Okay, so if yesterday was a fairytale day, today was a comedy of errors. Note to sensitive readers: all ye who enter today, beware. I am going to discuss underwear again in some detail and at length, not to be gratuitously inappropriate, but this is just what happened.

I slept well and vacated the man's lawn very early as promised, giving me another top-o-the morning head start on the heat. Hit the Price Chopper on the way west for a gallon of water, a Powerade, some nut mix, and as they did not carry almond butter, I dragged my standards through the gutter and settled on some Jif peanut butter bars. I headed toward Pacific, MO, on a backroad.

My first major road combination ironically set the tone for what happened around noon. According to Google Maps, I was to take HWY F, then FF. Wait, or was it FF then F? I had to keep checking to make sure it was FF then F. I was immature and laughed. It reminded me of the Nicholas Cage movie *Honeymoon in Vegas* and that scene where Nicolas Cage is trying to understand directions given over the phone by a Hawaiian operator. Cage asks, perplexed, "Is it Kapa'a, or is it Kapa'aa? Kapa'a or Kapa'aa? Is it two A's or three?!"

Once I settled the F FF versus FF F issue, I realized I had a lot of climbing to do. This was fine. Going up is easier than coming down hills with a backpack. It is the downhills, especially paved ones, that can wreck the achilles, the hamstrings, and the feet. Climbing actually feels pretty good. Today it was hot early, and there was no breeze. I had downed most of the gallon by noon, and I finally found a little turnout where I could sit in the shade and finish the gallon off before treading lightly downhill. I was sweating a lot.

Let me pause here for a sec and provide context for what happened next. I know that cotton is a huge no-no when trailing, I get it. However, I have tried really hard to like Smartwool socks, for example, and I just don't. The only time I got blisters last year was when I wore Smartwool. I like cotton socks. I run in them. My feet are used to them. It is what I have worn every day out here. However, the predilection for cotton doesn't really cross the threshold to underwear, though, when on trail. Most of the time. I have two pairs of wicking Exofficio underwear. But I do have one pair of cotton underwear with me. I don't know why. And for some moronic reason, I put the cotton underwear on today.

I sweat so much on the few miles uphill that I experienced chafing that transcends the space-time continuum. The chafing had manifested itself at the very tops of my inside thighs where the undies touch the legs. This is likely the same area where guys get jock itch, but as I have no experience in this field, I can only speculate. I plodded downhill trying to ignore the chafing at first. I mean, my feet healed up fast. I'm pretty tough, right? *Ignore this self-inflicted pain and keep moving. It's hot out. There's no shoulder at all to stop and tend this beast. You've done this to yourself. Just keep walking!*

Five minutes later, I wilted. I had taken out my mini jar of Vaseline with cocoa butter. There was seriously nowhere to stop, no privacy, cars were wending their way up and down the winding hill, and I was sticking my hand either down my shorts or up through the leg holes swabbing the chafed spots with half-melted Vaseline. All while walking downhill, trying to stay out of traffic.

I got the sore spots covered, but then the sweat-soaked underwear would touch them again and shoot fire into every step. I tried pulling my underwear so far up in order to avoid touching the raw spots. So far up that they were lodged in every crevice as well as up really high on my abdomen, under my shirt. They looked like Borat's neon green mankini that Sacha Baron Cohen wore with his brown dress shoes on the *Borat* show and in the movie. This didn't work either. The underwear just kept slipping back down.

Finally I found a small turnout. I got into my pack strap pouch and procured my Swiss Army knife. I cut the underwear waistbands on both sides, yanked them off through my shorts' front waistband without removing my shorts, and hurled my underwear into the woods. My throwing technique could be likened to an NFL quarterback throwing a long, hail-mary pass deep into the endzone.

I resumed walking, now with a bowlegged, modified cowboy walk. The objective was to keep my shorts from touching the chafing. I think I whimpered a few times. My shorts are loose and airy anyway, but I now tried on purpose to wear them really low, yet simultaneously remaining mindful that I was full commando, and was doomed to be so for at least four more miles. I could not wear them too low.

Upon entering Pacifica, I stopped at a lumber yard and home improvement center. It was closed, thank God. There was a gazebo display with a picnic table for show. I threw my pack down and just sat in the shade, contemplating the destructive nature of moisture, as well as what to do next. I decided a 16-mile day was all right and I would stay in town here. I walked another mile or so, desperately needing to reswab the raw spots with Vaseline. But it is Saturday, people were out and about, and the neighborhood had several of those "We report suspicious activity" yard signs warning me not to instigate any bodily contact under the clothing for a few more blocks.

All I needed now was to be sticking my hand down or up my shorts again and be reported for lewd acts in public.

Pretty sure I will reach the Katy tomorrow, barring terrible weather or more underwear misadventures. Wonder how tomorrow will be characterized? Hopefully not as a Greek tragedy. Today's tragic flaw was thinking it was all right to walk in cotton skivvies on a hot, no-breeze day. This was not a terrible day by any means, and I am laughing really hard as I write this. Hiking commando: a first!

Here's to two pairs of Exofficio wicking underwear, reporting for duty in the a.m.

Cheers!

Amie

Donning the JCPenney Bathroom

In the effort to keep my thinking straight during the school year, I often run, hike, or ruck after work while listening to podcasts. My favorite podcast creators are accomplished, athletic, brilliant people who speak to human wellness, intentional ultra-endurance training, as well as mindful, intentional living. I am not superwoman. I need this type of content infused into my essence to maintain my own healthy, deliberate mindset and spiritual vibrance as public education runs increasingly counterproductive to sane psychological practice. One podcast interviewee whose philosophies I have mined for nuggets over and over is South African doctor Frank Lipman. Dr. Lipman has fused Western medicine with traditional Eastern medical practice to treat thousands of patients, many alarmingly young, who come to him with all varieties of auto-immune disorders and low-grade bodily maladies that will not subside. Dr. Lipman's functional medicine approaches help his patients who come to him reporting that, among other vague symptoms, they are tired and can't poop.

Dr. Lipman is at his most professional when he discusses patients who can't poop. It is a systemic problem in our culture of poor diet, lack of exercise, and unabating stress. There is little amusement in one's true inability to perform this normal animal function. Teachers know that public education and its actors and playwrights create an environment in which students and staff alike languish in poor nourishment for body and intellect, a sedentary culture despite physical education, and tensions that manifest in a host of corporeal ailments.

To be blunt, I also write from a place of professional honesty when I say that the school week takes its toll because classroom teachers can almost never pee, poop, or fart. Those who are not teachers and who have never experienced the average school schedule and climate may find this ode on the porcelain urn ridiculous. *What? What's the big deal about peeing, pooping, or farting? Just go to the bathroom.* It's not that simple. As teachers know, eliminating becomes a complex tactical operation. Every. Single. School day.

Let's start with peeing, the least taboo of the three. During the typical day, teachers have between three to seven passing periods, varying in length from five to ten minutes, depending on the size of the campus and the level of trust administrators place upon students not to smoke pot in the stairwells or act upon notions that ten unstructured minutes generate. The teacher's first challenge is making it through class without leaving upwards of forty students alone to go pee. Particularly challenging are

Mondays following consumption of any alcohol, as the body is now shedding the extra liquid. In my case, when I am training for a marathon, I have consumed massive amounts of water to recover from weekend long runs of twenty miles or more. Combined with the gratifying exhaustion of my long run, I have also by Sunday finally "come down" from the school week enough to sleep Sunday nights really deeply. I may sleep for nine or ten hours on Sunday nights, which leaves me slightly dehydrated Monday morning. I then play catch-up on drinking water to prepare for the upcoming week's training block. And Mondays follow Sundays, relatively relaxing days of peeing, pooping, and farting on a schedule nearer to our bodies' natural rhythms rather than eliminating in lockstep with a bell schedule. First and second hours often find me jiggling my knees, randomly circling the room to "monitor student work," or doing Kegel exercises not for reasons proposed in *Cosmopolitan* magazine, but to lock and load the urine in my bladder until I can gnaw my arm off at the end of class rush to the loo in a tunnel-visioned haze.

The next trial presents itself during passing period: finding an open staff bathroom. At the large California school where I taught, my classroom was on an outer corner of campus next to the FFA garden. The nearest staff bathroom was in the next building over. Most passing periods, teachers from our wing on the periphery of the campus would begin jockeying for position to the humanities building, where the first floor featured a mere two staff toilets in each hallway. Within smaller campuses, the teacher-to-bathroom ratio may be even lower.

At a different school, an additional staff restroom was located in the library. The library was closed two or three days per week, so if you were a lower-strata teacher without a library key, you were relegated to one of the two hallway teacher restrooms. Teachers there quickly learned the golden calves in the building who had a library key, and stalked them during passing period to make a mad dash into the secret recesses of the closed bathroom bibliotheca. No student traffic disturbed the pastoral peace of the closed library john. However, I still waited in line for this toilet because it would have been a massive social faux-pas to cut the line in front of the teacher who had the key in the first place to let me in. The sweet sound of the occupant washing his or hands pealed forth. The door opened as the waiting teachers began losing consciousness. I then slammed and locked the bathroom, whereupon I tore down my clothing as my ureic jet stream splashed the seat, perhaps mixing with liquid of dubious source already on the toilet seat. Someone else's pee, or errant water droplets from the prior user's handwashing? A secondary concern at this point.

Achieving an open toilet is but the first skirmish in the battle to go pee. The teacher can never get too comfortable in the closed-eye, relaxed-thigh bliss. The line to the restroom comprised of those slower, less savvy toilet-locating chumps will form outside. In fact, now while the teacher is peeing, the sound of the bathroom door handle jiggling will send shots of adrenaline up the spinal cord and into locked the door behind me, I jolt every time the handle jiggles.

Did I really lock the door? Fears of the door flying open to reveal a once-hallowed professional with trou around ankles activate the limbic the psyche, which is attempting to relax and enjoy peeing. Regardless of how deeply I am certain that I locked the door, the line outside does not allow me to relax enough to let all the pee out. And if the doorknob-jiggler gives up and retreats to another restroom or heads back to class, another potential user may grab the handle anon, desperate to find the campus's holy of holies unoccupied despite a closed door.

Plus, unless I locked my classroom, I am wondering while I pee what the students are doing in there unattended. Knowing that precious passing period minutes are ticking away, I capitulate, pinch it off, pull up, and return to class having typically failed to pee all the way. This only starts the cycle over again second hour. The teacher now holds round two of coffee or beverage consumption plus last hour's unexpelled pee. And if the school is on block schedule, the period can be 90 minutes or more, 90 minutes of holding it atop what is still in the bladder. The teacher has forced the pee to crawl back up inside the bladder to avert walking into class tardy. Teachers also seek to effect classroom re-entry without finding something of theirs stolen, hidden, or sabotaged, or to interrupt *in medias res* yet another session of grab-ass or sack-tapping, horseplay in which freshmen boys especially are wont to engage.

Pooping at school tics up a notch from the Busch League of teacher problems. I rarely poop at school, and during the week I often stop pooping altogether. When school starts in August, teachers have had the summer weeks for their bodies to return to stasis and relearn to pee, poop, and fart with their natural physiological rhythms rather than when an artificial bell schedule allows them. Going back into the classroom and the associated angst we feel before students even arrive throws off the system. Attending to matters that plague the first week of school produce in me so much anxiety that the body's systems slow down. Being in front of one, perhaps even two hundred new students I may not know, anticipating every possible contingency from curriculum, technology glitches, making a decent first impression while coming across neither as a boring hardass nor a doormat, I have left school the first week realizing that all day my body has been rigid, my neck tight on one side. I realize at the end of the day I've been flitting around like a ferret, plunged back into a world where most of one's audience has the attention span of a housefly. I have entered new school years feeling ever-increasing pressure to perform as if on a stage, emptily promising the Snapchat generation edutainment. Standing all day wound like a piano string, I have stared into the next ten months knowing that I cannot begin to compete with students' cell phones, Chromebooks, handheld video games smuggled into class in backpacks and hoodie pockets, or their other shiny baubles. The need to remain in a constantly wired, constantly "on" state short circuits the mind-body superhighway that allows teachers to depart from fight or flight to the more natural state of rest and digest.

As the school year progresses, the strain rarely abates; it just shapeshifts in accordance with public education's unpredictable barrage of stressors. And the bowels slow accordingly. I remember a few weeks into my first year at a midsized district in Kansas, my lower abdomen had become painfully distended. My body fat was quite low, as I had just been backpacking for three months, yet my stomach jutted out over my jeans, distended to the point that my lower back muscles ached. One weekend, starting on Saturday morning during my long run, I pooped seven times within 36 hours. Seven elimination sessions resulting in immense movements. My body had been harboring all of that as the result of massive anxiety. And it wasn't the only time. Now that I reflect over two decades, most weeks of my teaching career have found my GI tract a victim of decision fatigue and a mind running at elevated emotional RPM's with little respite. I have spent most of my professional career mentally tired and unable to poop.

When my nephew Dain was about six years old, he had gone to the bathroom one morning and produced a rather large bowel movement. Instead of flushing, he went and grabbed my sister's iPad and proceeded to film a short video reflecting on his leavings. It went something like this. "This is Dain. Yep, that's a huge poop. A really big poop." Silence for reflection. "And I pooped it out." Another pause, then the flush, at which point the viewer was blessed with watching it twirl and disappear.

Numerous Saturday mornings, especially during my August-to-May long runs, have found me staring aghast at my own flagship spoor left in the grass behind a tree out along the dirt roads, fighting the temptation to take a picture. And in the punch-drunk mentality of mile 16 of these endurance efforts, sending the pic to a fellow runner, to anyone, who would get it, with the accompanying text, Where did this come from. How has my body held onto this for five days? Praise God for long runs and weekends. Otherwise, I would never come down off the week and go poop.

The teachers who do poop at school poop at their own risk. Pooping at school cuts into one's passing period even further because wiping now becomes an Olympic event. Scores tally for cleanliness, not getting any on the dominant wiping arm's sleeve cuff, or, heaven forbid, being the one who clogs one of the few teacher restroom johns. Pooping at school is to be done as fast as possible because those outside the door will probably jiggle the handle, and they're certainly now on to which restroom task you're performing because it's taking forever and there are no restroom noises issuing forth. In my case, when I actually do poop at school and I know there are others in the queue outside the teacher bathroom door, I perch my undercarriage on the precipice of the toilet seat so that when I poop, I do not generate the tell-tale plopping sound into the toilet water, which would belie my bathroom activity. I would then have to exit the bathroom post-poop and walk the gauntlet of knowing eyes before absconding back to class. Therefore, I deploy the strategic flush, whereby one turns to depress the flush knob at the precise moment the poop falls into the water, disguising the sound.

It's not merely bathroom noises that make pooping at school not for the squeamish. I have crossed the threshold into teacher bathrooms, the prior occupant having rendered the atmosphere of the restroom a hazmat sector. No amount of potpourri spray, hand soap residue, or match-lighting can camouflage what had been performed just moments before.

When my sister worked at Helzberg Diamonds at a large shopping mall in southern Kansas, she bemoaned the fact that the one unisex Helzberg bathroom was directly adjacent to the sales area. She noted that the entire sales staff were privy to any restroom exploits. As a result, Andrea began walking the few hundred feet to the adjacent JCPenney store to poop so that she would avoid fouling the sales floor. She joked that she established a rather predictable JCPenney pooping timetable in their rear customer restroom; likely JCPenney's loss-prevention staff were on to what she was doing. Andrea was sure that her cloak-and-dagger pooping attempts were captured on security footage and commented upon by staff: "It's 11 o'clock, and yep, here comes the Helzberg Diamond Pooper. Barreling down the men's sock and brief aisle toward the rear restroom, right on time. "

Certain teachers and paras leave a stench in staff bathrooms as one leaves a calling card. One semester, I headed toward our corridor's one teacher restroom—during my planning period—only to meet our psychology instructor and football coach, first name Don, face to face as he exited the loo. Clearly the architect of what even he believed to be a no-go zone, he came clean, "Uh, yeah, you don't want to go in there right now." I pivoted and made my retreat to the library restroom or just waited until later. I don't remember. From that day forward, my significant other and I have sometimes alluded to pooping with the euphemistic, Hey, I'm gonna go 'Don the JCPenney bathroom.'

Once a month or so during the school year, I have raised the white flag when it comes to pooping according to my body's own volition. By Friday morning when I have not pooped for several days and my stomach is bloated and tight, I succumb to breaking out a $.99 Kroger saline solution enema to make myself go before heading off to school. Desperate, I have been willing to abandon my dignity at 6:30 on a school morning. However, a hurried morning enema-assisted poop is not always the perfect solution. The entire contents of the bowels does not always issue forth immediately following an enema. In my experience, aftershocks of the salt water dose in the form of leakage of varying viscosity may surprise the user up to an hour or two after administering the enema.

One school morning found me driving to work post-enema only to experience a sensation somewhere in that grey zone between farting and pooping. I got to school and entered the restroom—before contract time and early enough to have privacy, I might add—to realize that my underwear was a bit messed as a result. I was then presented with the option of removing my undergarments and free-balling the rest of the school day or cleaning my underwear with single-ply toilet paper and soldiering on through my Friday. I elected not to finish out the day commando.

I remember one summer at basketball camp in Oklahoma, my friends and I were sitting in a semi-circle on the gym floor listening to one of the camp's coaches giving his closing remarks. We noticed a wet spot in the anal area of his bright yellow Bike coaching shorts. We giggled and discreetly pointed at the time. I feel guilty for having laughed. Now I get it. The poor man probably did not poop the entire week of dealing with a couple hundred middle-school girls with court skills ranging from promising all-conference athletes to how a colleague described a particularly poor showing from the local college women's team during one home game: "They looked like Teletubbies floundering around on the court."

Perhaps a week of teaching left-handed layups and rebounding drills left him with irritable bowel syndrome in the same way that clarifying for sophomores the difference between quotation marks and parentheses for the fiftieth time in a week has left me with epic gas and constipation by Thursday.

Farting at school is also treading a minefield. Farting audibly in front of students with nothing handy on which to ascribe the source of the noise can be a career ender, or at the least would prompt me to contemplate switching schools. I know I have farted audibly in students' presence. However, each time I successfully played the sound off as my old Doc Marten shoe squeaking on a tiled floor, or I acted as if I were straightening my classroom rows of desks if passing gas became inevitable. Like a mockingbird mimicking notes, I dragged a desk loudly across the floor to produce a farting sound.

In poetry, there is a device called the slant rhyme. Slant rhymes are words that don't actually rhyme, such as parse and curse, but these words rhyme closely enough to achieve the desired effect at the ends of poetry lines that are intended to rhyme. By midweek, my midsection is at times so bloated from not pooping that I have to fart to relieve pressure. I have retreated to my file cabinets to pantomime retrieving a fake file just to produce noise while emitting air, supplicating the gods that if I do make noise farting, that a slant fart will be produced by the filing cabinet drawers squeaking. It's school, so I can't blame it on the dog.

The restroom is not a safe zone for farting at school either. Particularly if the teacher has abandoned ranks in the fight for a teacher bathroom and bolted for one of the nearer student restrooms. At the alternative school, the student restroom was few quick steps from my classroom. Nonetheless, I seldom experienced a full pee, poop, or fart session without a student entering the restroom or another pair of shoes signaling that listening ears already staked out a claim in a nearby stall.

Even performing the innocuous task of peeing is fraught with perils in the student restroom. Anxious about returning to an occupied class quickly, I would try to push out my pee as fast as possible. But I could not push too hard or I might fart. Then I would have to wonder if the student, in a moment of crude jocularity, would tell her friends, "Oh my God, our English teacher just blew some major ass in the bathroom last hour!"

Another maneuver teachers employ is to finish peeing, having held in the fart, and then flush. Many schools' toilets flushes are quite powerful and exert James Dyson-worthy suction even as the flush culminates, which makes the flushing very loud. Therefore one may cleverly emit the fart during the flush's apex of decibels to disguise it from neighboring ears. This is a strategy not without its pitfalls. The danger here is that the fart will outlast the duration of the flush. My timing has been off before, and my pent-up fart has crept past the end of the flushing vortex's sound and fury.

A weak approach to disguising a student-bathroom fart is to anticipate the start of the fart while peeing and loudly unroll one's toilet paper while farting to cover the noise. This can work, but if the fart draws out, then the teacher must keep hammering out more and more length of bathroom tissue. That much toilet paper use to neighboring ears may draw suspicion; plus, the teacher now has to decide what to do with the surplus toilet paper she's unraveled that is now probably cascading onto the student bathroom floor and folding over onto itself. Waste precious school resources and flush the whole wad? Or reverse-reel the excess back up onto the roll, letting the next user partake of tissue that has touched the floor?

To complicate farting even further, it is less than plausible to go on a fart walk during school. Certainly one may fart walk down the hallways during passing periods, crop dusting students and fellow staff. The risk remains, however, of someone hearing the gas pass. Plus, it feels so unprofessional to blast hapless students or staff members whom I respect. If a hallway fart becomes that pressing a need, find a group of male students near whom to deposit the fart, and walk away laughing at their circular firing squad of blame.

I have retreated to the confines of my car at the end of school day so bloated after eight hours of not farting—and probably days of having not pooped—that I have emitted farts that mimic the high-pitched keening sound as when one pulls taut the opening of an inflated balloon. Once at the end of another fartless school day, I texted my sister (the JCPenney pooper) that I had performed what I dubbed a bull-riding fart. I emitted a fart that lasted eight seconds at least.

One of the few redeeming qualities of teacher inservice days is that I know I will be able to drink as much water as I want and have unfettered access to a restroom. While that administrator is pontificating about the district's newest initiative, acronym, or intervention strategy designed to increase achievement in the most apathetic of chronic nonattenders; while that guest speaker is holding forth about the latest educational fad and the additional inservices needed to bring the staff into full compliance, the teacher can steal away from the commons or auditorium at one's leisure to pee, poop if we're lucky, and probably fart.

And so lies one of the many hidden intrinsic qualities of summer. Teachers, admit it. We can pee whenever we want. We are eating slowly and absorbing our food rather than inhaling everything during a bell-to-bell 25-minute lunch while trying to grade and make last-minute copies; therefore, we don't need to fart. We are not tired, and we can poop.

Dr. Lipman would be proud.

Sunday, June 26, 2016

Destination: Dutzow, MO (and the Katy)
Today's Miles: 21.10
Start Location: Pacific, MO
Trip Miles: 1678.61

I love walking on Sunday mornings. Few people are out. My objective today was to make Dutzow at least so that I would reach the Katy. I left the town of Pacific on Osage Street, which paralleled I-44 for some time. From there I took HWY 100. There were many quickie-marts all morning, so I could get away with carrying only a liter of water or one Powerade at a time. I got started around 7, and since it was overcast, I could tuck the umbrella between a side pack strap and my body, giving me some hands-free walking. I passed a couple of signs early in the morning that said I was on the old Route 66 Byway.

The weather report indicated today was to be another warm, humid one, but that a break was coming for next week. That was nice to hear, and it meant if I could drink and power through today, some relief would grace my last couple days before the break to get my car.

Along HWY 100, the trail magic was keepin' it 100 when I found an unopened bottle of water in the grass. I picked it up. Hmmmmm, a gift of water. Was this yesterday trying to make amends? What early water so sweet saluteth me? I drank the water, squinting my eyes, still unsure if I forgave the trail from yesterday.

There was also a breeze this morning. I had to keep the umbrella under control due to some wind, but that's okay. I'd rather tangle with a surly umbrella than be constantly begging for a breeze.

Made it to the town of Washington, where I had scoped out a place to cross the Missouri River. Washington was a decent-sized town. I saw my first Target since leaving home, and swooped down on it to pick up some more almond butter and Powerade. This was the hottest part of the day, and I regrouped to check the miles to Dutzow and to pep-talk my feet into more pavement walking. Just a few more miles, and then the soft railbed of the Katy.

I turned north on HWY 47. From this point on, the off-book route was gonna make me earn my way back onto the map. HWY 47 was more heavily trafficked, loud, and when I reached the Missouri River bridge, I knew something ill was probably going to befall me. It had even less of a shoulder than the bridge at Chester, believe it or not. I still have yet to stick my thumb out for a lift, and keeping this tradition alive, I just started walking across.

Eeehhh, mistake. I turned toward the water several times to make myself as small as possible as cars went by, several annoyed with me and rightfully so. I was a little over halfway across when a police officer pulled over and told me it was illegal to walk on the bridge. I asked if he could give me a ride the rest of the way. He sounded annoyed as well but said yes. I opened the back door and heaved my stuff and myself inside quickly. I told him I wasn't homeless or anything, and that I really had no clue the bridge was like that. He said judging from my gear, he didn't think I was homeless. I said my destination was Dutzow, just a few more miles. He asked where I had started. When I said Delaware, he muttered, "Holy shit." He dropped me at the first turnout past the bridge. I smiled as I opened the door and said, "Sorry to be a pain in the butt. Thanks!"

He was fairly cute, but not as handsome as the officer who rescued me from the rain back in Indiana. Nothing like feeling protected and served in another of our great states!

Passed a small runway, a tree farm, and finally got off HWY 47 to the serenity of the Katy. I sat at Dutzow's little info depot for an hour or so, looking at the historical markings on the depot wall, studying the trail map's guide to water and services. I remembered how content I felt last year in Augusta, Rocheport, and at Cooper's Landing campsite.

I reached into my right pocket and retrieved the corner of the Missouri state map that I cut out and have been carrying with me. I could now throw it and my handwritten directions away. I am camping on the grass here behind the info depot. I don't think you are supposed to, but I guess if someone wants to come out here in the soft rain and throw me out, so be it.

Amie

Stealth Us This Day Our Daily Bread
Monday, June 27, 2016

Destination: Defiance, MO
Today's Miles: 16
Start Location: Dutzow, MO (and the Katy)
Trip Miles: 1694.61

I lingered longer than usual at the Dutzow trailhead. Felt luxurious to have the simple necessities for, in the parlance of a Victorian novel, one's morning toilet. There was a drinking fountain, a trash can, a picnic table on which to set my things and keep them off the ground when packing up, and a proper toilet that flushed and everything. I brushed my teeth extra long because I had plenty of water on site. I drank two liters of water mixed with G2 packets I had picked up at Target yesterday.

I took three Katy brochures and tucked them into the flat pocket of my backpack. I run across people every now and then in real life who insist they could never walk a long way, but they have always thought about trying a bicycle trip. I also encounter those people sometimes who have that faraway look when I talk about taking adventures like this. Maybe I can get these informative and persuasive trail brochures into some of those hands at the appointed hour. There is no greater panacea than walking all day on a quiet, shaded bike path with the infrequent soft swish of bike tires as basically the only external stimuli.

During the early morning, I snapped a few pics of the info depot, the trail bed, and whatnot. I texted them to Bobbie back in Ohio. I told her I would be pestering her about going on a backpacking trip. I delivered on that promise with a few snaps of the early morning quietude.

Late morning, I came to the next trailhead. I needed water but not food. I hated walking off trail into town just for water. I sat at the info depot and looked around. It's Monday. The trail towns are pretty dead after the weekend's biking and convivial libations; in fact, some of the little bars and shops are not open on Mondays, or they open later. All I needed was some *aqua vitae*. There was a cute bike shop just across the parking lot, not open yet. Outdoor tables and chairs were set up. There was quite a bit of landscaping and flowers about the patio area. Where there is high-maintenance landscaping there is usually water . . .

I walked around behind the bike shop to indeed find a garden hose neatly rolled up in one of those hose storage boxes with a multi-function spray tool attached to the end. I turned on the water. I did not pull the handle on the spray tool quite yet, as it took a few seconds to get both my water bottles out, the lids off, and poised for some stealthed bike shop water.

When I engaged the spray nozzle, I was immediately punished for my misdeed of sneaking the water. Pressure had been building up in the hose. Pretty sure the sprayer was clicked onto the most fast and furious water pressure setting because water shot out of there apace, knocking over a water bottle, ricocheting out of the rear corner of the building, and spraying me all over my face, arms, and front. The water felt good, but I looked around to see if anyone had witnessed my folly before I took my glasses off to wipe them. I clicked the spray tool over to a more gentle setting and proceeded to fill the bottles. The water had stale garden hose undertones, so I used the last of my G2 packets to make it more palatable. It was enough water to get me to Defiance.

I later took a second sit-down break with my poncho spread out as a groundcloth. A kid probably in his early twenties, and also hiking with a backpack, rounded the corner to the little off-trail shaded area I had found. He asked to sit with me a sec. I said sure, and I learned a few things. His name was Alex. Today was his third day hiking. He wanted to hike the Katy and then keep heading west, maybe hitchhike up the west coast. He was on a pretty low budget. He had camped somewhere just outside St. Charles two nights ago and then behind someone's business with permission last night. He was concerned about the scarcity of water on the Katy.

It seemed as if Alex just wasn't too sure quite yet what he wanted to do with his life, a feeling we all have known, I think. I gave a short synopsis of what I have been up to. Then I told him to pay close attention to the trail guide. And I also explained where I had just found water behind the bike shop a couple hours prior so he could load up there. Sorry, bike shop. Probably sent another water stealther your way. I forgot to warn him about the extremely high-pressured nozzle.

I then gave him a second piece of advice, as he had never been to California. I told him that HWY 101 is a popular hitchhiking and professional bumming corridor, and that he would probably have luck getting a ride and meeting others on that road.

Reminds me of an article I read in the *Sacramento Bee* several years ago. The northern California town of Arcata, in Humboldt County I believe, finally had to outlaw the banging of bongo drums in public. Apparently an influx of professional slummers and transients were forming too many bongo-drum circles in town, becoming a total public nuisance. Hilarious. Because I don't live there. Sorry, California. I may have just sent you another hitchhiker. Alex and I shook hands, and I wished him luck.

Made it into Defiance with just enough of everything. My daily bread expended. I have been making arrangements for rides and so forth for the next few days. It is time to get my car, so I will be on pause for a few days. Will definitely update as prep, caching, and resuming of walking transpires.

All is well.

Amie

A Few Zeros to Prep for Next Leg
Wednesday, June 29, 2016

Destination:
Today's Miles: 0
Start Location:
Trip Miles: 1694.61

Yesterday and today I performed some trail "homework" by checking out New Franklin, MO, on west in the data book. I noted areas that looked sparse as far as water availability. In addition, I was privileged to have dinner with an old high school classmate. He lives in St. Louis, and we graced Ethyl's Smokehouse with our presence. I got my red meat and greens. Furthermore, I lapsed into tent manners by eating some of Matthew's grilled nachos after I had obliterated my meal. Fun night! We talked about how weird time gets when backpacking. I was searching for another word for how time feels to me right now. Matthew said, "Time feels elastic?" I said absolutely and received permission to quote him for that very apt description.

I also had a wonderful hour drive from Evansville to eastern Illinois to retrieve my car. Sondra, whom I met in Evansville last year, agreed to pick me up after I dropped the rental car. We had a great conversation. She had been reinspired to work on the ADT some more, and it was my pleasure to connect again with yet another person from last spring.

I didn't think I would make it all the way back to KS with my car tonight, so I rewarded myself for connecting the trail dots. I drove to the Katy Trail campground Cooper's Landing for a rewind stint there. I got to watch the sunset over the Missouri River again. I got to hear some more impromptu music. I got to sign the camping agreement and chuckle over the clause prohibiting public nudity at Cooper's Landing, a clause I did not remember from last year. The camp host said they'd had issues with nudity. Funny, but not surprising considering this is one of those places where you might find a bongo drum circle. I set up my spot without encountering any nudity or bongo drums.

It was great but odd to have my car again. It threw off my normal evening tent routine. I had driven all day, so I did not need to peel off any Band-Aids from my feet. I didn't spend 10 minutes itching my feet or letting them dry. I didn't have to take my braids out. I wasn't doing the stiff-legged I Just Took My Pack Off walk. I didn't have four layers of dirt and road filth to wipe off below the knees.

Plus, I had all this extra weird stuff in my tent. My car keys. My headphones. An extra full gallon of water from the trunk. Some strange, heavy foods I would not carry.

These incongruities were small and amusing. It was odd, similar to when two completely separate parts of your life converge in one place or unit of time. It was weird in the same way it caught me off guard when my best friend from CA was in the same room with my KS friends one evening last month.

Camping with my car also reminded me of how I felt in Olathe, KS, a couple months ago. There is a lady known as Gypsy Runner who travels all over the country and sells neat running gear at the marathon race expos. In San Luis Obispo, CA, four years ago, I bought a shirt from her. The shirt featured a white chalk outline of a dead body lying on the ground, but looking as if it had been murdered mid-stride. The caption read, "I run so I don't kill people." When I saw her at a race expo in Olathe. I thought, "Wait. What are you doing here? This is KS."

Similarly, what are those car keys doing in the corner of my backpacking tent? There was nearly a rent in the space-time continuum.

Sondra and I had discussed the difference between having one's car-and maybe even another person-as a support vehicle versus being totally on your own. Getting back to the car support is akin to being able to call time out in a child's game of tag.

Once the supports are back home, you're It.

Amie

Course Record for Caching Futility?
July 1, 2016

Destination:Just shy of DeSoto, KS
Start Location:Olathe, KS
Today's Miles:11.60
Trip Miles:1706.21

Well, I've done it again. After scouting the New Franklin, Missouri, to Kansas state line section and caching approximately eight gallons of water, I have skipped a section again and picked up elsewhere. Here is how it happened.

I got home yesterday early evening. Talked with my sister about weekend plans, who could or would want to drive yours truly to New Franklin. Turns out, Mom and Andrea had a wedding to attend tonight in Olathe, KS, about two hours west of New Franklin.

Everyone had odds and ends to attend to all weekend, so my choices boiled down to the following:

a) ride up to Olathe with Andrea now, just find an intersection in the ADT TBTs and get moving again today, or

b) wait until Tuesday and ride back to New Franklin with high school friend Matthew, who was travelling back home to see his folks for the Fourth anyway and then returning to St. Louis. A ride with Matt would have been a riot, and I would have emerged from such a car trip much smarter, as he is a nuclear engineer.

However, I did not want to sit around at home until Tuesday. I am either all in or all out of this life, and at this moment I am still all in. I opted to skip ahead and go now from Olathe. Missouri (Missoura in the right circles) ain't goin' nowhere. I didn't lose anything except the dropped water and one package of powdered Gatorade. My sincere hope is that the Missouri county or state mowing crews will find the water on a hot day. Just another small tithe to the universe.

My sixteen hours at home last night reminded me again of the The Barkley Marathons, a race almost no one finishes. The race is essentially five marathons run back to back, and runners have only 60 hours to complete it. One key factor in finishing this race is not to rest between course loops too long or let oneself get too comfortable in camp. Go into your basecamp after each lap, change your shoes, eat, tend to blisters, sleep if you think you have time, and then get back out. Don't linger and begin to tarry.

Likewise, last night I was clearly not ready to be done walking. I barely took anything out of my pack. Just laundry. I dipped into my resupply closet upstairs for a few things. But don't get used to that salon shampoo. Don't turn on the AC upstairs, fan only. Don't get used to that Tempurpedic bed again; don't even get under the comforter. Just snuggle with the sleeping bag. Don't get used to how good it feels on your scalp to brush your hair with a real brush rather than a small comb. Don't enjoy that coffee pot java with real milk. Don't linger in camp too long. Get back out.

I did spend a few minutes last night switching out a couple items. I left the neon yellow Kansas Half Marathon shirt at home. It says Kansas really huge in blue letters. I giggled the several times that I had approached a new person from another state in that shirt, and the person deadpanned, "You must be from Kansas." Figure that since I am now in KS, I don't need to represent.

I brought my light blue ADT logo tee in its place. I was going to wear my Fort Worth Ultramarathon race shirt to count how many people this time around would quip, "You must be from Texas." I would claim Texas too. Public bongo drumming is likely frowned upon in most of Texas. I also left the blue Columbia long-sleeved shirt at home. I grabbed one more pair of socks and an extra bandana. Pink this time.

It was a really nice ride up to Olathe with Mom and Andrea. We went out to lunch, and Andrea sent me off with a two-for from Panera. Thanks! And today was the first time that Mom has ever witnessed the drop-off. The departure. The exodus into the relative unknown. My walking off onto a road or into a strange town with nothing but this pack. We were eating lunch, and Mom said she felt bad just... dumping me off somewhere. I said that this has been happening for 1700 miles. She knew, of course, but never had to watch.

We found an intersection on the map and pulled off. Andrea's sense of humor runs parallel to mine in most aspects: Andrea put the car in park and said, "Okay! Get out!" Haha. Mom gave an audible sigh or two as I stood behind the car and arranged everything and put the pack on. And there I went, north on Ridgeview Road, toward the old Santa Fe Trail.

It felt so good to walk again. I went just a mile or so before turning off onto the Mill Creek Trail, and boy, does that trail have a thousand names. The TBTs calls it the Mill Creek. Google Maps calls it the Santa Fe. Mapquest does not show it, and several of the mile markers along the way called it the Gary Haller Trail, in addition to something else I can't remember. I found my way though, and it is an excellent trail. A trail by any other name would hike as sweet. Mowed shoulders on both sides. Shaded. Benches. Top notch.

A goodly little half day's jaunt. Stealthing tonight in the perfect spot. Huge baseball diamond complex with a massive, freshly mowed field behind it well off the road, and with a Kansas Department of Transportation canopy next to it filled with sand and salt road mix.

So unless we get a freak July ice storm tonight, I am probably safe here.

Amie

Saturday, July 02, 2016

Destination: Eudora, KS
Today's Miles: 19.10
Start Location: Just shy of DeSoto, KS
Trip Miles: 1725.31

Camping behind the baseball field and the DOT facility was a success. That was one of the more superior non-campsites that I have ever found.

Woke to rain. Knew it was coming. Packed up quickly, not overthinking things, just preparing myself for a full day of wet shoes. It rained softly most of the day with a break here and there.

I made it onto Eudora early afternoon and found a sports complex. I wanted to stop early for two reasons. One, I needed to give the tent pieces time to dry before another night of use, and there was a breeze and break in the rain to do just that. Plus, the covered dugouts were a great place from which to hang the pieces and let them flop in the wind without worrying about them snagging on anything.

Two, I needed to let my feet dry and harden again before tomorrow. Don't want to start the blister process over again.

Pretty much a day to put my head down and go. I must deal with one more day of wet shoes tomorrow. It is about 14 miles to Lawrence, the way the data book flies, where I will dry my things out again. Nothing else to report today.

In the words of Jeffrey Lebowski, the Dude abides.

Amie

Sunday, July 03, 2016

Destination: Lawrence, KS (Go here!)
Today's Miles: 16.50
Start Location: Eudora, KS
Trip Miles: 1741.81

The rain paused again right before dark last night, and dusk began weaving a tapestry of hilarity. The first funny thing that happened, not like "haha" funny, but surprising and darkly comic, was that my new tent began swamping. The water was not entering from the top, as the rainfly was staked out securely. It had to be coming in from a hole or tiny rip in the bottom. Nothing had gotten wet yet except my sleep pad bottom and one side of my pack. Time was of the essence. I had noticed in the school building close to the sports field that there were several recessed doorways under which one could take cover if necessary. My top priorities for remaining dry were my cell phone and sleeping bag, so I quickly jammed my phone and the bag into my one Sea to Summit sack, grabbed my pack and sleep pad, slipped into my flip flops, got out of the compromised tent, and ran over to the school building. Ran is the wrong word: I did that awkward tiptoed, high-kneed, trying-to-run in flip flops twinkletoes jog, with my orange sack and still-inflated sleep pad flying behind me, all while carrying the umbrella in case it started raining again while I was trying to get to the school. It reminded me of the movie *Sideways* when Miles and Jack are arguing and chasing each other down a steep hill somewhere in Santa Ynez Valley wine country while one is carrying an open wine bottle and trying not to spill it.

I left the tent and my shoes under the dugout. The covered door area was about 20' x 20', and it was clear from the rain's highwater mark on the pavement that if I slept close to the doors, I would stay dry for sure. And that's what I did. It ended up working out because if I had set up there initially, I would have been caught. Earlier in the evening I had heard the distant sounds of a family playing on the playground equipment right by my entryway. There was a live electrical outlet there as well. The only issue was that the light above the door kept periodically brightening and dimming all night, probably a security feature. It was cool enough out that I covered my face with the sleeping bag to ignore it. I slept all right, better than the night my old pad deflated.

Woke this morning to no rain, cool and overcast, so much so that I put on my jacket and rain pants over my clothes. The absolute last thing I did was put the soaked shoes back on. What I really wanted for my last act of the morning was to walk over to the tent on my way out, kick it, and leave it there, but I packed it up anyway. The Big Agnes Ultralight now seemed to weigh fifty pounds.

The putting on of wet shoes was actually the only crummy part about today. It did not rain any more, and the majority of the route was on gravel roads. Thank you, trail. I was on Alexander Road for several miles, and except for the hills, it felt like walking the dirt roads around Derby. Except I didn't get powdered by the Derby school bus flying down the road like it does every day after school. And it was probably too early on a Sunday, but I also didn't receive the two-fingered steering wheel wave from any drivers of trucks with EAT BEEF front license plates. I didn't see anyone driving Priuses featuring social or ecological lectures on bumper stickers either. By their bumper stickers ye shall know them.

Along one of the dirt roads, I came as close as I have ever been to one of the huge, center-pivot irrigation sprinklers for farmland use. I kind of wished it had been running. I have wanted to brush my teeth or wash my hair under the spray of one of those ever since I saw Alexander Supertramp do it in the movie *Into the Wild*. And that is not the Reese Witherspoon hiking movie.

Just east of Lawrence, the trail turns down Lyon Road. And I had the eerie feeling that I was walking right through someone's farm. It felt as if I were trespassing, and the ADT could have used an update here. Sure enough, upon turning off of Lyon, there was a sign declaring it private property.

The last mile into Lawrence was also on excellent terrain: the gravel levee trail road. I walked into town having crossed the same levee and bridge as I did last November at the half marathon I completed here. The ADT did well to take the trail through downtown Lawrence. This is definitely a town in which one would find public bongo drum sessions. Lawrency has great restaurants, shopping, and swanky little beer joints. Overall, an attractive place.

Another of the many good things about Sundays in the backpacking world is that motels are usually available and cheap. I claimed my room and immediately set my toxic shoes to drying. I took the entire tent bag and all its contents into the shower with me the way a parent just showers with a small, filthy child because it's just easier. After I rinsed out the tent, the shower looked like a crime scene, but with dirt instead of blood. I hung the pieces up to dry well before heading down Mass Street to the Casbah burger joint. I boldly ordered two meals for myself, a burger and chicken Caesar salad. I studied the maps from Lawrence west.

To recap my day, here are ways I have found much irony and mirth in the last 24 hours.

a) The ever brightening and dimming light reminded me of Logan M's story of his trying to sleep one night on trail in a restroom with a motion-detecting light.

b) If for some reason I ever interview for a teaching job in Eudora, KS,

I will sit there feeling guilty, wondering if they ever checked their security cameras from July of 2016 and saw me sleeping in their school doorway. I can redeem myself by knowing the cameras caught me throwing away all my trash, however.

c) I immediately turned on the heat in my motel room. In July. In Kansas.

d) I can now officially say I have slept in a doorway.

I will deal with the leaky tent later. I am not zeroing again to tinker with the tent now too. It is not supposed to rain next week.

Onward tomorrow!

Amie

Happy Independence Day
Monday, July 04, 2016

Destination: Just North of Ottawa, KS
Today's Miles: 25.40
Start Location: Lawrence, KS (Go here!)
Trip Miles: 1767.21

I think this is my longest hiking day ever. Almost walked a marathon. I think today's distance was the product of synergy resulting from a few factors. Great breakfast this morning of blueberries and walnuts with milk. I headed south on Mass St. where I had scoped out a Dillon's to pick up a few groceries. The ADT then heads over to Iowa St., which is also HWY 59. The directions have us leaving Lawrence and walking 21 miles on HWY 59, all the way to Ottawa. I was skeptical of this, but the shoulder was wide, and overall it was pretty placid walking.

A Douglas County sheriff's officer pulled over a few miles into HWY 59. He was really nice and told me he was called out to do a welfare check on me and on a bicyclist who had also been called in, also on 59. He said in Douglas County, everyone looks out for everyone. He suggested Old HWY 59, which I had seen on Google Maps, as a viable alternative all the way into Ottawa. I showed him the ADT directions taking us down this way, chatted with him a bit, bid farewell, and then climbed the hill to the access road to Old 59. Seriously, I am going to have to start taking selfies with these cute officers because this is now four for four. By now my reporting on this matter probably sounds suspect.

It was overcast most of the day, which also set the stage for good mileage. The gravel shoulder to Old 59 was soft from the recent rain. My shoes were dry, my spirit light and jaunty. The miles passed quickly. I knew it would be really pushing it to make it into Ottawa, and my Google maps showed a church camp facility along a dirt road also heading south into Ottawa. I decided to check that out and arrived on the property to find no one. I looked around for someone to ask.

While I sat and waited, I decided to finally type a list of reasons I like doing this and what I get out of it. A lot of people ask me why I am out here. Do I have a cause? Am I trying to find something? Am I raising money or awareness for something? Am I on a spiritual quest? My list of reasons will likely sound more boring than these questions, the answer to all of which is no. So here is what I came up with as I was waiting for someone to come along here at the camp.

WHY I DO THIS, IN NO CERTAIN ORDER:
1. Daily, all-day hiking hardens the body but softens the spirit.
2. I just wanted to see if I could do it.
3. It's a mental detox from artificial timeframes, societal norms, vanity, superficial concerns, and cloistered indoor settings.
4. Backpacking strips everything down to the basics.
5. I like to see the country slowly sometimes too; walking it is like a slow pano shot seared into the brain one scene at a time.
6. Seize the day and try things.
7. We all can do more than we think.
8. Something is not truly a challenge if it's easy. It has to be hard to be a challenge.
9. Puts you in a parallel universe of contentment with the smallest things.
10. I am an endurance activity habitué.
11. I am a frequent and zealous victim of the wanderlust.
12. I like passing on an Everyman inspiration or small nudge to people. If I can do this, so can you.
13. Daily exercise in humility and gratitude.

I am sure I will think of more. Soon a couple and another lady walked over to the front porch of one of the camp buildings. I asked if they were in charge of the camp. They were not, but their son was. They directed me back to his house, where I explained myself and asked to sleep at the camp, no bunk needed, just a piece of ground, and I'd be gone in the morning.

The camp director reminded me of the new pastor of a church back in Indiana who seemed skeptical and really wanted to check me out before saying yes. This is completely understandable. After viewing my things and a few minutes' conversation, permission granted.

A really strong day. God bless an 85 degree day in July, my KS people who called the sheriff to check on my status, my family and pit crew who have been texting me July Fourth party pics here at press time, lemon-lime Gatorade, the Lawrence Dillon's for selling kale chips, this camping facility, and the freedom to answer the call of wanderlust.

I guess I am celebrating Independence Day by being independent.

Amie

Westbound and Down
Tuesday, July 05, 2016

Destination: Pomona, KS
Today's Miles: 27.40
Start Location: Just North of Ottawa, KS
Trip Miles: 1794.61

Up and out early, and 'twas several miles more before entering Ottawa. The route goes through the cute Ottawa downtown. Then it turns west on 7th Street. Then you continue west on 7th Street for 9.98 miles to Pomona. The TBTs tell a lie of omission here, as they leave out the part about 7th Street morphing into KS HWY 68, a no-shoulder, steep-ditched corridor of hiker purgatory, replete with bridge crossings featuring a two-foot high barrier between you and a precipitous drop into the muddy rivulet below and no exiting side road for at least three miles, forcing you to suffer patiently the passing of semis, all the while mentally preparing your last will and testament as well as an excuse-laden speech to deliver to the law enforcement personnel called out by rightly concerned motorists regarding the latest imbecile trekking along this ten-mile segment with a backpack.

And that's my nice description HWY 68. I befriended Google Maps yet again and turned what should have been a 17-mile day into a 27-mile day by walking extra on the backroads so that I could be certain none of the above actually occurred.

I had loaded up on water in Ottawa. I moved fast again today. I had already gone 20 miles before I availed myself of the Greenwood Community Center picnic shelter and water. I sat for about an hour, letting my socks and feet dry out from sweat and wet grass this morning. It was really hot today, but the thing about Kansas is that there is almost always a wind or at least a breeze blowing, so the heat does not feel as bad.

I kept myself on gravel or backroads all the way into Pomona. Stopped into the Dollar General for a few things, and scoped out a place to camp here in town.

Here are some random thoughts from today. I always feel like a wide load in Dollar General. Their aisles are narrow, and I feel like I am going to swish merchandise onto the floor. The last two days have been my longest. I have walked the equivalent of two marathons two days in a row. This is a first. Tomorrow calls for four more miles on 68 and then 268 into Osage City. Trying not to contemplate whether that shall sucketh mightily and if to circumvent 68 again.

I thought of another reason I like doing this.

REASON 14: Hard things such as this are stepping-stone activities. Think to yourself, "If I can do A, then surely I can do B." Another confidence builder, perhaps.

Amie

Wednesday, July 06, 2016

Destination: Lyndon, KS
Today's Miles: 17.80
Start Location: Pomona, KS
Trip Miles: 1812.41

Woke this morning around 4:30 to a delightfully cool wind blowing through my tent, which I had parked right behind the Pomona city park picnic shelter. I basked in the lovely breeze, then thought, *Wait a sec. In Kansas, that breeze can only mean one thing: a weather event is upon us.* There were a few flashes of lightning off in the distance. I got up and moved my backpack to a picnic table in the shelter, and then picked up the tent with everything else still inside it, and moved it under there as well, still fully set up. It started to rain about ten minutes later. I went back to sleep listening to the rain hit the metal roof of the shelter. It was wonderful. I slept until 7:30.

I drank coffee and packed to the unmistakable sound of air brakes. Cattle trucks coming into town from HWY 68. This sound reaffirmed my decision to again parallel 68 and 268 into at least Lyndon today. I brushed my teeth and filled my gallon jug from the park water spigot, and I set off. I was able to stay off the highway all day except for a couple of miles on 268. I mostly took the gravel road 245th.

Today's inferno was of course the temperature. High 90's I think, but the breeze takes the edge off. The almost constant breeze reminds me of the Ken Burns film *The Dust Bowl.* That film features several people who lived through the Dust Bowl, most of them from the Oklahoma panhandle area, a few from Morton County, KS. One of the ladies interviewed talks about the ever-present wind in this area. She said that a lot of the time it is very noticeable, other times not as much, but it's always there, maybe just touching your cheek. I thanked the breeze today and its cooling effects.

Today's purgatorio was the couple miles on 268. I have been on Google Maps a lot, and I have noticed the Flinthills Nature Trail runs parallel to our route as well. It appears to be a rails-to-trails project. Pretty sure it goes all the way into Council Grove. I am going to hop on it tomorrow as I leave here. It will get me to Osage City, and I can see what it is like. This could be another viable option. Just concerned about water.

Paradiso is taking off shoes and socks at the end of the day, and that feeling of being deliciously tired.

REASON 15: Your body learns to draw on its own resources. Hikers, ultrarunners, etc. eat a lot, but at the same time, the body learns to use its stored energy. The appetite is regulated to signal hunger when physical hunger is actually the stimulus.

The mind learns to draw on its own thoughts and resources as well. Thinking is its own entertainment. I laugh out loud probably several times every day just thinking and remembering things. Sometimes I jot these thoughts down as notes in my phone. Sometimes I forget. Every now and then I will fume about something for a minute or two. Sometimes I think about serious things or future plans or some books I want to read. Sometimes I think about nothing. The need to check the phone every five minutes falls away. The need for some external stimuli or external source of entertainment fades too. Sometimes I wish I had someone with me to talk to, but most of the time I can happily fritter away the hours with my own mental acrobats and private reveries.

Goals for tomorrow include staying off of highways and seeing what the Flinthills Nature Trail has to offer. Oh, and trying to ignore how gross my clothes are becoming.

Amie

Paralleling the ADT via the FNT
Thursday, July 07, 2016

Destination: Miller, KS
Today's Miles: 23.40
Start Location: Lyndon, KS
Trip Miles: 1835.81

Received another 5:00 am wake-up call from Mother Nature. I had set up my tent in the narrow space between two school buildings. This little nook looked good because it was covered, and you really had to look to see me because there was also a stairway rail in that corner that followed some steps down to the cellar of one of the buildings. This stairway was also covered. The wind picked up severely about five, so I quickly packed up sloppily and sat in the covered stairway, hugging my pack as it sat on the step in front of me. I covered myself, pack, and my shoes with the poncho and waited it out for 20 or 30 minutes. The storm passed, everything stayed dry, and I walked over to the covered gazebo on the corner to repack in a more organized manner. The only casualty of the fierce but quickly departing storm was that one sock blew away.

I had been checking Google Maps regarding this Flinthills Nature Trail, another old rail bed. It looked to parallel HWY 56 and the ADT for the most part all the way into Council Grove. I decided I would check it out today, and if was horrible and overgrown, or a bunch of spots were washed out, just generally unsafe, I could always jump back onto a gravel road, a road also closely following the ADT. Towns and watering holes continue to be a concern as I approach the wide-open space of the Kansas Flinthills.

I headed north out of Lyndon up HWY 75. I grabbed a jumbo coffee and a snack at Casey's on the way north. I knew I only had to abide 75 for a couple of miles before it hooked up with the FNT. It began raining again, nothing severe, but I did throw on the poncho. I could see a decorated, narrow overpass above 75 on the horizon. Then as I came closer, it sure enough was the trail, but there was no entry or access road to it. It simply passed over the highway. I sat under the overpass for a few minutes, knowing my only option here was to climb the hill. I saw HWY 31, the data book route, just a tenth of a mile south of the FNT, and there was no shoulder. Ain't doin' that, so I waited out the rain again and climbed up. This is the second time I have done this. The first time I climbed an overpass hill was along 59 just outside Lawrence at the suggestion of the officer in order to gain Old 59.

The few minutes I sat under the overpass in the rain, I am sure I appeared homeless and down-and-out. One person pulled over and asked if I needed a ride. It was one of the very few but interesting contrast moments I have had out here when I am pretty sure my appearance was at complete odds with how I felt. I know I appeared to be a dirty drifter with wet shoes sitting under a bridge with a poncho on, gazing down, trying to go unnoticed. In reality, I was completely fine, just having finished a hot coffee with real half and half, drinking my Powerade, looking at the ground to check the rain-drop frequency, contentedly taking a little break before climbing the hill to a secluded trail. It was definitely a moment that probably elicited sym-pathy from drivers, spying the "hitchhiker" lady between windshield wiper swipes.

The rain continued a bit longer as I got a feel for the FNT. Definitely rougher and less maintained than the Katy. No info depots, no restroom or water facilities, no handsome brochures, historical explanations, benches, or bike repair stands every 15 miles, but I'll take her. Some tall grass here and there to wade through, some low tree limbs, but overall satisfactory and much easier on the feet and the psyche. I walked as the rain lifted, thinking that with some TLC, some dumptruck loads of gravel, and some repairs to the old railroad bridges here and there, this could be the Katy's western cousin through cattle-grazing country. The sun came out late morning, and there were actually many shaded spots along the FNT, a neat little surprise.

I made it into Osage City around noon. A Thriftway grocery was a few steps off trail. After I picked up a few things, I sat on an outside bench re-packing and sneaking a quick phone charge from the same outside outlet that powered the coin-operated children's horse ride.

As I sat, a lady named Jann stopped to talk to me. She was curious about my trek, and I asked her about her Hoka running shoes. We connected on many levels: running, being teachers and both having coached running sports and all. She was thinking of the tiny towns the trail passed through coming up. She wanted to make suggestions on where I could get water and camp. She said Admire had a community center, covered picnic area, and water. I said that would be pushing it for me to get to Admire.

Jann then suggested Miller and a little white church there. She knew many of the ladies who attend there, and said she might make a few calls to check if the church was unlocked. Jann had also completed the Bike Across Kansas event, and was very familiar with the idea of camping wherever, such as school gym floors, churches, people's homes or lawns, etc. Jann gave me her number and said to call if I needed any supplies or anything. I thanked her for the heads up and proceeded on.

I continued on the trail toward Miller, which became my goal. I had plenty of water and calories, but Admire would be too far for me today. I approached a gate across the trail, climbed it, and then took the 330 Road into Miller.

Just like Jann said, there was the church, unlocked. I don't know if she had called anyone about me, but I went to the fellowship hall area, where there was a couch, some other miscellaneous furniture, a restroom. I immediately brushed my teeth, combed my hair out, laid my stuff on the floor neatly next to the couch, drank some water, took out my sleeping bag, and curled up on the couch. I don't know what time I went out like a light, but it was before dark. I was not bothered all night.

To anyone out there who prays for my safety and guidance, I want you to know that I believe this awesome lady was sent.

Amie

Jann 2.0 and Cowboy Humor: This Ain't
a First Rodeo for Any of Us
Friday, July 08, 2016

Destination: Council Grove, KS
Today's Miles: 20.10
Start Location: Allen, KS
Trip Miles: 1855.91

Sent, I tell ye.

I pretty much died on the church couch and came back to life around 6:30 this morning. I had mostly packed up and was halfway through my coffee when the door to the fellowship hall popped open. It was a sunny, smiling, relieved Jann, relieved that I had found the church and was all right.

As many people do when they encounter hikers out on the roads or in towns, they later think of questions they want to ask, or think of things they could have offered to help. Or sometimes, as in the case of Jann, they really have something tugging at their mind to check that the person is all right and had found a place to sleep.

We chatted some more as I finished packing. She had dispatched another friend she knew to look for me at the community center in Admire. When I was reported not there, she figured I'd be here in Miller.

She offered to take me to a little cafe, which was nearby in driving-distance standards, or to her house for food or supplies, but I assured her I really did have enough to get to Council Grove, and that topping off my gallon jug would round out my preparedness for the day. I did say, however, that I would accept a ride that would bump me a few miles closer to Council Grove, as it was about 28 miles down the FNT, doable, but barely. Plus, I considered a bump forward extremely fair and not cheating because I walked 6 extra miles just on Wednesday to avoid HWY 68. A 6-mile compensation westward is squared in my conscience.

On the drive to the town of Allen, I learned the following: Jann had placed a sign on one of nature trail gates. I didn't see it last night either because I took Road 330 into town, or I had not gotten that far west. The sign contained words of encouragement and an offer for a ride. I learned Jann had also been to Hermann, MO. And that she knew one of the administrators who was at Flinthills School District for a few years I was there. I saw HWY 56, which the ADT follows for many miles through this area. There is no shoulder, and Jann commented that she doesn't really like to ride her bike

307

on it. Drivers don't seem to be as courteous as they used to.

We pulled over in Allen, which was still a fair piece from CG and would give me a full day's walk, but not a psycho distance to cover. We took a few pictures so that her husband and friends would know I really do exist, and she sent me on my way with a couple Gatorades and granola bars and an inspirational bracelet. A wonderful start to my morning.

The FNT improved today as I neared CG, and I actually saw someone biking it. The landscape definitely changed today. Almost no corn fields to the right and left. Fewer trees, mostly cattle grazing country, the precipice of the Flinthills. I walked along, thinking, looking at the vast openness, checking my distance from CG periodically, and searching for some motel that was supposed to be on the western edge of town. The Old Trail Inn? The Trail's End Lodge? Google Maps called it the Prairie Lodge.

I rounded the corner up Old 56 to find the lodge and lots of trucks in the little circular drive out front. I walked up and stood outside the office behind four nice-looking cowboys, who had just gotten out of their F350 pulling a long trailer.

One of them asked, "So, are you on a pretty good lick?" I replied, "Oh, about 1800 miles." It got real quiet for a few seconds. They just sort of stared.

I sat down on a chair and asked, smiling, "You're asking how far I've gone, right?" He replied in the affirmative, and I repeated my answer with some elaboration and back story. They were really funny and had all kinds of questions, one of which was, "Dang, you wanna beer?" I laughed and said sure, and he offered, "Or how 'bout a Gatorade?" I took the Gatorade instead.

They continued unloading their truck, and the guy who originally inquired as to my "pretty good lick" commented, "Man, I'm tired just from the drive up here."

His quiet friend upstaged him with, "Hell, you wadn't even the one drivin'."

Apparently the little Prairie Lodge had no more room at the inn due to the rodeo in town. But the lady in the office said she also worked for a bed and breakfast here in CG, and she'd definitely find a spot for me. The cowboys had informed her in the office that I might need a room more than they did.

She was helpful and kind, and she drove me into town to a beautiful bed and breakfast, very reasonably priced.

I never would have thought that a 20-mile day in the no-shade July heat after a 5-day lick with no shower could yield one of my favorite hiking days.

Amie

Saturday, July 09, 2016

Destination: Wilsey, KS
Today's Miles: 11.30
Start Location: Council Grove, KS (Go here!)
Trip Miles: 1867.21

Today's mileage reflects a half day of walking because Mom and Dad drove up to meet me and eat brunch at the famous Hays House restaurant. Our table was laden with farm-fresh eggs, bacon, biscuits, fresh salad bar fare, and general yumminess all around. They also brought me a few resupply items from my upstairs closet stash and a new pair of shoes that have been lying in wait since January. Thank you, thank you, Mom and Dad.

We walked and drove around Council Grove for a bit after eating, and they dropped me at an intersection with the Flinthills Nature Trail.

Overall, Council Grove as an ADT town is a very excellent gem out on the prairie. That stretch between Lawrence and here is a dry one, and Council Grove has a lot to offer: full grocery store, lower-priced motel, two B and B establishments, a couple of parks in which one could likely stealth, lots of pioneer history, and the Hays House to boot.

Upon being dumped out-err, I mean dropped off-I walked a half mile or so on the FNT, and then the trail really deteriorated. The only trees I encountered today were growing straight up and out of the middle of the trail. That is exaggeration, of course, but not by much. But it was impassable today. No Katy any time soon on this section. No worries though; I paralleled the trail with a couple gravel roads and made my planned destination of Wilsey by a secondary route.

I performed recon of the city park for a camp spot, but I walked around town a bit and settled on a spot behind an "official" Wilsey city building that is also hidden by a row of bushes.

Nothing else interesting for today. Just a pleasant, quiet, relatively slow day to break in the new shoes and get a few more miles west.

Amie

Sunday, July 10, 2016

Destination: Herington, KS
Today's Miles: 19.90
Start Location: Wilsey, KS
Trip Miles: 1887.11

This was the first tent morning in a while when I have not had a storm nipping at my heels. I leisurely packed and then set about to continue Road V on west. After a few miles, I jumped north a mile to Road U. This road went all the way to Herington. Gravel roads both U and V, run along just south of HWY 56. Forsooth, I have become reacquainted with my alphabet on this, my Hike 2.0, in the year of our lord 2016. FF, F, U and V. What next?

I really noticed the wind today. It was much stronger, and made a low, moaning sound, a wind tunnel-like noise as it whipped over the ground and over the corn fields, through the telephone wires and around the poles. Unless I passed by a shelterbelt of trees, the wind was a constant presence today. It kept me cooled off and reduced my water needs. But at the same time, the low, wind tunnel sound it created was eerie. I can see why some early settlers and homesteaders to this area went crazy, or packed it up and went back east. Especially during the Dirty Thirties. Without modern TV noise and our screens and distractions, some days really are nothing but the wind.

Almost no cars passed me today. This was nice. Similar to my dirt road running routes at home, I pretty much had the roads to myself. A guy and his daughter who were driving around on a utility cart vehicle stopped to chat. The man remembered another bicyclist or two who had come through Herington a while back. I assured him I had plenty of water to get to town, and he and his daughter proceeded down the dirt road in a cloud of dust.

I am feeling ambivalent about my replacement shoes. They are the brand Montrail, what I have always worn out here, but a slightly different model. Again today, they were fine the first few miles but then began feeling too inflexible as the hours passed. It's like they're too sturdy of a shoe or some-thing. Most of my shoes the past few years have been rather minimalist, and I am not used to such stiff footwear.

So I decided to try something. I took off my shoes and socks and put my Reef flip-flops on. I carry them as a camp shoe. I took some tentative steps. It felt pretty good on the dirt roads. On pavement the flip-flops were not pleas-ant, but I did my last 6 miles today in them.

I have been intrigued by the barefoot philosophy, and I really think there is a lot to it. I think tomorrow I will start out in the stiff shoes again and then be open to walking in flip-flops once the trail goes back on a dirt road. I would just go barefoot, but there are many rocks that are too large.

I am back on the official route tomorrow. The ADT returns to dirt roads, county roads, and generally quieter paths to McPherson.

Amie

This Wind
Monday, July 11, 2016

Destination: Tampa, KS
Today's Miles: 23.20
Start Location: Herington, KS
Trip Miles: 1910.31

So having returned to Kansas about a year ago, I have been wondering where all the crazy KS wind has been. This year was a glorious late summer and fall season, sunny nearly every afternoon and evening, almost no rainy fall days. Light winds. Even this past winter was a mild one. The insane north wind I had been dreading materialized with a fury only a few times. The KS wind was kind to us this year, and at times the north wind was even magnanimous to me. For example, one evening in February or March, I was running west out on one of the dirt roads around Derby, and some kid in a crummy little car drove by me and purposely tried to spin his tires and throw gravel up at me as he passed. The strong north wind that afternoon blew all the dust and debris to the south side of the road before I could even reach his wash. Haha, missed me. Thank you, Kansas wind.

The wind reintroduced itself to me today for sure, in case I forgot it existed or didn't appreciate it enough yesterday. Today's southerly wind was even stronger than yesterday's. Another day to put your head down and go. Literally. Leaving Herington on a county road, the path was a mix of paved backroads and dirt roads through the town of Ramona to Tampa. I stopped in Ramona to sit out the noon heat and wind for an hour or so. I sat on the front steps of the small city hall building.

A lady named Jeannie was mowing the lawns of the few city properties, and she came over to talk for couple minutes. She was not familiar with the ADT, but she did know the Bike Across Kansas event. She said she had just popped a Powerade in her fridge prior to mowing, and she offered it to me. I said sure, and after she finished mowing, she went home with my water gallon jug and filled it, returning with it and the Powerade. She had also put a few ice cubes in my jug. Thanks!

I have not given the Chrome Dome report in a while, and sadly I must report that the wind today was almost the *coup de grace* of my umbrella. Two of the supports had snapped by the end of the day, one has ripped the reflective fabric and poked through, and now one side hangs limp. Dang. It really was quite comical wondering what I looked like as I tucked the umbrella handle under my chest pack strap and held onto the sides of the umbrella with both hands. Sort of wish I had some video footage of me today trying to stay shaded with the umbrella flapping really hard.

And now that it has ripped, the wind turns it inside out quite easily. I fear that if it's windy again tomorrow, it will be reduced to an umbrella skeleton. In fact, I became a bit peeved about the wind late this morning, but then my friend Amanda texted me a picture from her summer school class. Meh. I would much rather walk headlong into 40 mph wind gusts than teach summer school. Onward!

The unrelenting wind also reminded me of a scene from the book *Dead Man's Walk* by Larry McMurtry. When the main characters reach the end of the Jornada del Muerto, a long, dry, dusty, windy trail, they are eating their first refined meal in a long time, hosted by a wealthy English lady who is not used to the winds of the desert southwest. When the Englishwoman comments on the terrible winds, the normally chatty Billy, rendered briefly taciturn by his meal, affirms her disdain for the wind with his laconic retort between bites: "It blows, don't it."

It blew today. Called it a day under a picnic shelter in Tampa. There is a small chance of storms tonight, so I set up my tent here under cover. There is a 100% chance of having electricity and water in the morning because I checked out both before settling on this site to park myself this evening. A camp spot with clean water and a phone charge is a thing to behold.

The new shoes are still less than satisfactory. I reserve the right to walk unshod again tomorrow.

It really is a beautiful evening right now at dusk. The KS wind has died down. A family who lives near this park just now brought me a cold bottle of water.

I am content in all things.

Amie

Nice Try, Kansas Weather
Tuesday, July 12, 2016

Destination: Hillsboro, KS
Today's Miles: 17.40
Start Location: Tampa, KS
Trip Miles: 1927.71

All right, so I gotta hand it to you, KS weather, last night was one of your best efforts I have seen in a while.

I woke up around 12:30 a.m. to the sound of distant thunder and flashes of lightning off in the distance. I had set up the tent under the Tampa town sports complex picnic shelter, right in the middle, and as I was on concrete, the rain fly was not staked out. This worked for a while.

The rain fell hard on the metal roof, and I snuggled up again and just listened. A few tiny droplets blew in, dotting my face. It felt cool and nice. Then about 2:00 this morning, the wind increased violently and picked up to the extent that it was blowing ride sideways. Water blew into the shelter area. The rain pelted everything, and at this point there was no stopping it from getting in the tent, no time to pack necessities in dry sacks. Everything, sleeping bag, pad, pack, all of it got soaked. All I could do was wrap my cell phone in my rain jacket and wrap myself in the wet sleeping bag, hug my knees in a sitting position, and ride it out. It rained and blew sideways for about 20 minutes.

The storm stopped about 4:00, and there was nothing I could do until daylight. I tried to curl up and sleep until light, at which point I took off my wet clothes and changed into my rain jacket and rain pants, with my poncho on too as an extra layer for warmth.

I made coffee, and studied on my next move. Camping tonight would be out of the question with the bag soaked. It was cloudy and cool all day as well, giving me no sun to dry anything. I headed south into Hillsboro instead of taking the right turn toward Canton. This path would not consist of extra miles, but heading south earlier. Tomorrow will be due west all day into McPherson.

My things are hanging all over the motel room. They do not have guest laundry here. This means that my clothes have been washed in the sink, but, you know, they're not truly clean.

So, Kansas, you have to try a little bit harder than that. With the exception of one of your tornadoes, I am not so easily sent home by my own state until I am ready.

Amie

Lesser of Two Evils and Handsome Cop 5.0
Wednesday, July 13, 2016

Destination: McPherson, KS
Today's Miles: 21.10
Start Location: Hillsboro, KS
Trip Miles: 1948.81

Eleven and a half hours of the sleep of death. Went down to breakfast and coffee around 6. Struck up a conversation with the table of four men next to me. They asked me if "that was my bicycle outside," and I replied no, I am on foot. Of course that retort got the ball rolling. They asked all the usual questions, except whether I am carrying. No one in Kansas has asked me that question yet. This is odd, now that it is easier to carry in KS. Maybe KS is now like West Virginia, where I was told by a local that, in WV, everyone assumes everyone else is carrying.

They guys next to me wished me safe travels and left. The front desk lady had overheard our conversation, and she offered the motel dryer for my sleeping bag. The only thing that hadn't dried overnight. I brought it down and asked for maybe just a 30-minute stint in the dryer on a low heat setting. She even brought it up to my room when it was done. It was dry, and the loft had returned to it as well.

After I had my fill of coffee, I then had to decide between two things that suck: waiting around until later in the morning to start walking, or risking wet shoes. A storm front had come in from the northwest, and we had all been watching it from the breakfast room window. The weather reports showed it moving out of Hillsboro around ten, so I decided that waiting sucked less than wet shoes. I waited it out. I hate sitting and waiting, so I passed the time by looking at Google Maps and forming a Plan B and Plan C in case McPherson was not doable for me today. I opened the room's window and listened to the rain and thunder.

At ten, the sky cleared, the sunshine was imminent, and I was out the door. McPherson was a straight shot west along HWY 56. What I had seen of 56 the past few days lacked a shoulder, but like most highways, I will start out on it with an alt route in mind if available, and think to myself, "Welllll, this is the quickest way; let's see if it sucks." The shoulder was huge, but I have been teased like that before, so a couple miles west of Hillsboro, I struck out north onto a gravel road to get off 56 and parallel it instead.

Here is where I had to choose once again between two things that sucketh greatly: highway walking or epic amounts of mud. The gravel road turned to pure dirt road about a tenth of a mile north. The dirt was wet underneath from the rain, and the silty dirt on top was that dirt that is loose enough to stick to the shoes. And then a few steps in, you have twenty pounds of mud built up on each shoe, extra surface area on the bottoms to pick up more mud, and mud weight compounding exponentially with each additional step. I turned around quickly and headed back toward 56, collecting more mud while backtracking. I decided highway walking sucked less than high-stepping through 20 miles of dirt road mud. The highway it is for me today.

I scraped the mud off my shoes in the wet grass and pointed myself west, which is easy to discern in KS, by god.

The trail provided today because HWY 56 actually had about an 8-foot shoulder the whole way. Plus, there was some road construction, and that slowed traffic down for several miles. The large shoulder was soft, rained-on gravel most of the way too.

I was about 14 miles into my day when a state trooper vehicle pulled off onto the shoulder, headed toward me. An officer got out, and once again, wait for it . . . That's right, he was blonde, very cute, and nice. I said hello and asked if someone had reported me for vagrancy. He said no one called me in, that he had just seen me and pulled off to see if I needed anything. He saw my water gallon and gear and knew I was probably all right, just checking. He didn't ask for my name or my ID or anything. Just a quick hello.

I started laughing a bit and was quite tempted to ask for a selfie. I almost did. But I just couldn't bring myself to ask, what with all the crap our police officers have been getting lately in light of recent events, police under scrutiny in the news media, and so forth. I did not want him to think I had any low-rent ulterior motives for wanting a picture with him. So I let pass yet another photo op. I said thanks for checking on me and proceeded on.

A few miles later, a Kansas Gas Company truck pulled over, and a guy hopped out and gave me water. Later on, a truck with a flatbed trailer went by honking conspicuously. Some arms waved from the windows. Pretty sure it was the guys from breakfast, as the truck logo looked like ones I remembered from the motel parking lot. That was lively honking and waving at someone you don't know. I laughed as the truck disappeared around the bend.

I took my first break at 19 miles in the small town of Galva, just outside McPherson. Looked at maps, checked food options for first thing in the morning on trail in McPherson. Looks like I will need two days' food to Lyons. After that, I will be getting close to two thousand miles.

Once I got moving and settled on a dang route, a terrific day.

Amie

Friday, July 15, 2016

Destination: East of Lyons, KS
Today's Miles: 21.90
Start Location: McPherson, KS
Trip Miles: 1970.71

Zeroed yesterday in McPherson due to rain, more rain, and predictions for overnight storms. Figured that with a leaky tent, I would stay off my feet for a day, eat a massive box of salad, listen to an audiobook, and make a new running playlist on Spotify. The skies were clear by 3 in the afternoon, but oh well. The audiobook was hilarious, and I can cross one off my ever-ballooning list of things to read.

Started early and ended early today. I basically took Frontier Road. This road is on the ADT books, but then it parallels the paved road official route. I took Frontier Road as far west as I could get. It was a really nice day. Highs in the 80s, some wind, a little cloud cover. Due to all the rain, the mosquitoes are out. But as long as I kept moving, they weren't too much of a bother.

Around 4:30 I found a roadside "Oak Tree Study" area or something. I stopped here to sit down for a sec. Then I noticed a fire pit, tables, and mowed grass that screamed camping. So today was one of those days I could have gone farther, but I found a good spot, so I dropped anchor. Plus, there is nothing between here and Lyons. Just fields.

Amie

Last Installment in the Chrome Dome Chronicles
Saturday, July 16, 2016

Destination: Chase, KS
Today's Miles: 23.40
Start Location: East of Lyons, KS
Trip Miles: 1994.11

Camping off road at the Masonic Roadside Oak Tree Viewing, Study, and Contemplation Park Thingie with Tables, Firepit, and Primitive Outhouse-Style Privy was a success. It didn't even rain last night. The wind died down around nine, and I slept well.

So I knew stopping early last night would be a double-edged sword. It meant a long, no-shade slog into Lyons this morning. About a 14-mile trek with only a couple of albacore tuna packets left and a half gallon of water. I had to make myself not eat the albacore last night. Dusk is about the only time of day when I feel ravenous and can eat like a beast.

Made it into Lyons around 12:30, and headed toward the Foodliner. As I walked through the nice residential area on my way to the store, a lady came walking down her front lawn toward me with a cold water bottle. She wanted to know how far I had come, all about my gear and where I sleep at night, and the common questions folks have. We talked for a minute. She offered to pop back into her house to grab me some cookies, but I told her she didn't need to; I was on my way to the Foodliner to get some food anyway. I thanked her for the water and went the couple blocks to the store.

It is always funny to watch people's reactions when I enter a grocery store. Some people stop their shopping carts dead in their tracks and just stare. Some people give me knowing smiles. Some try not to look, but then I can see them staring from my peripheral vision. Makes me giggle. A lot of times when I enter a full-on grocery store, I have not looked at myself in a mirror for a few days. I don't know what I look like, but I can probably guess. Today I received a mix of all reactions as I picked up some more bug spray. The mosquitoes are everywhere, even in the day. I bought some steel-cut oats, a small bag of baby carrots, and more water of course.

I sat out on the front bench in the shade to eat my carrots and rest a few. A bit later LouAnn, who gave me the water in front of her house, came around the corner. She was glad I was still there because she had run up to the thrift store really quickly and purchased me a new umbrella.

For the final Chrome Dome report, allow me to explain what a sad affair my poor sun shade had become as a result of KS wind. Three of the spokes were now broken. There were two holes ripped in the top from the broken-off pieces of the supports poking at the top. One whole side now sagged against my face, pack, or shoulder when open. Every time I opened or closed it, the broken pieces would catch on something, threatening to rip the top even further. And I had to keep breaking off the busted spokes as close to the base as possible because they kept dangling from the top and stabbing me in the head as I walked. The Chrome Dome survived 600 miles until I made it to Kansas's plains. Then it was no match for the wind. I was just tryin' to suck as much life out of it as possible. But LouAnn thought I needed a new one. It was sweet, hilarious, and generous all at the same time. I thanked her and promptly deposited the poor, wind-battered Gossamer Gear Chrome Dome in the Foodliner trash can.

Small world alert: LouAnn has relatives in Derby, KS.

I sat for a while longer, knowing I had around 9 more miles to my destination for the evening. I engaged in some Facebook banter with another ADT hiker just ahead of me, laughed, and drank about a half gallon of water before proceeding on.

I got back on the dirt roads toward Chase around 3. The wind had really picked up again, and there was no windbreak all the way into town. Home tonight is the city park covered area. Today was a mentally tough day, lots of open, barren straightaways and just plain ol' visible ground to cover staring you in the face.

But today was also a fun and really good day, feeling lean and tough. Nothing hurts. Got some healthy, non-crappy gas station food from a real store. Cool evening here in the park, wind subsiding, no calls for rain. Aura of an innocent Midwestern small town all around me. I feel like the luckiest person alive on evenings like this.

Amie

Sunday, July 17, 2016

Destination: West of Chase, KS
Today's Miles: 7.70
Start Location: Chase, KS
Trip Miles: 2001.81

Turned 2000 miles this morning, thus ending Backpacking 2.0 for this stint.

Last weekend I had decided to pause when I reached 2000 miles. I like nice round numbers and loose ends being tied up neatly. So basically this morning I walked a few miles west, paralleling HWY 56 on a dirt road, until the rendezvous point with my ride home. I spent the afternoon cleaning and organizing gear and putting everything away for this year.

I've hoofed it about halfway across the country now, and I wanted to provide a quick debrief and analysis as a reflection. Some of these points are answers to common questions. Other points are just thoughts I have on the experience so far.

First, STUFF THAT HAS NEVER HAPPENED

1. I have never stuck my thumb out to hitch a ride.

2. I have never been messed with at night while camping, legally or stealthily.

3. I have never been threatened or physically harmed in any way.

4. I have never been "run out of town" or escorted to the county line with an implicit "and stay out!"

5. I have never been denied service anywhere due to my appearance or smell or general transient aura.

6. I have never gotten lost. Off course a few times, backtracked yes, but never utterly, devastatingly lost.

7. I have never gotten dangerously hungry or dehydrated.

8. I have never gotten sick. Queasy for a few hours once.

9. I have never seen a bear.

10. I have never been a motel breakfast bandit.

11. I have never been full-on busted executing a technical stop alongside a road. Very close a few times...

12. I have never dropped or lost or left behind anything vital. A few small things, pack towel, water bottle, but never anything huge like my wallet or phone.

BIGGEST THREAT SO FAR
By far, hands down, people's unrestrained dogs.

HOW I FEEL MOST OF THE TIME
In addition to my "reasons why I do this" list, I think a good way to describe my status as a cross-country hiker is that I have been treated like America's surrogate kid. So many, many people want to help, give me something, offer a water, a place to sleep, concern for my safety. With a few minor exceptions, I have felt protected and supported by my fellow country men and women. I have felt like everyone's kid.

WHAT NOW?
1. Spend a couple weeks shocking my psyche back into compliance with societal norms and schedules. Re-entry is hard. I could elaborate on the trials of re-entry for pages. Also spending time with family and my friends. I have missed them.

2. Begin training for a fall marathon, then explore the possibility of doing another ultra.

3. Go back to work.

4. Remain thankful I have the freedom, mettle, health, and support to have put this past seven weeks under my belt.

This again has been wonderful, tough, and really fun. Fun in a way that is hard to explain. Thanks again to everyone who sent an email or little note. I read them all. Good luck to Brett, Stephen, YoYo, and anyone else out there on the ADT.

Until next time!

Amie

A Master's for Thee, but Not for Me

This summer I began submitting my writing to a few small literary journals. In doing so, I have been prompted for the first time in my life to create my own short, third-person author bio. In fifty words or less, my professional and personal snapshot melded thus:

Amie Adamson holds a Bachelor's degree in English. She has taught secondary English for nearly two decades. When not teaching, she enjoys spending time with her boyfriend riding on the back of his Harley and basking in the serenity of paddle boarding at Beaver Lake. Amie also hikes, rucks, trains for marathons, and travels, all while vehemently refusing to earn a Master's degree.

I wrote it quickly, without overthinking, and with tongue firmly in cheek. I read it aloud to my boyfriend. I wanted to hear how the boiled-down ethos that I was willing to show strangers rolled off the tongue. For a minute, I contemplated omitting the part about refusing to earn a Master's. It sounded curmudgeonly, angry even, not an image I want to present to the world. My boyfriend laughed and insisted it stay. For it is a running joke within our circle of close friends, all of whom are or were teachers, that two of us refuse to get a Master's. Just the other afternoon at our community pool, a local fourth grade teacher and I high-fived over her lone parchment hanging on her proverbial wall. It's almost as if we who eschew so-called advanced education degrees are a secret society. I am not even close to earning a Master's. In fact, I have made it a personal aspiration to complete my career in teaching without ever having obtained one. I have dug in my heels. Here is why.

The primary reason I never got a Master's is rooted in money and how I have chosen to spend mine. I am from a middle-class family. When I went through college, I had to pay for nearly everything on my own. I have two younger sisters, both of whom relied on my parents' financial support to finish out their respective high school careers and begin their own journeys into post-secondary pursuits. As in most families of modest means, this meant that my sisters and I had to take out student loans.

Teacher prep programs further encumber their graduates by requiring student teachers to pay full tuition for a semester while they work. For the uninitiated, student teachers pay to work full time for five months. And student teaching is so exhausting that one does not have time to side-gig elsewhere. In fact, teacher education programs discourage work outside the student teaching assignment. Unless burgeoning teachers have a benefactor footing the tuition bill or taking care of basic living expenses, the loans rack up that final semester.

By the time I graduated with my Bachelor's, I was tired of signing the student loan promissory notes. I had become inured to using student loans to pay rent for what was a subsistence in a cold cement block apartment infested with cockroaches that crawled into my bedding while I slept. Immediately embarking upon graduate school would have meant taking out more loans. Living a decent life was one impetus behind finishing a degree in the first place. I was ready to look for a job and start earning. Aside from needing to escape the tiny, extremely dated, roach-infested apartment that smelled like old grease from an Asian restaurant, I needed to be able to purchase a basic shirt or a new pair of shoes without calculating its devastating impact on the month's finances. And most of all, I needed a car.

There is no more storied vehicle within our family lore than the 1984 Buick Regal we once owned. We bought the used Buick from a nice couple my senior year of high school. I drove it without ado for a year or two. But by the time sophomore year of college arrived and the Buick was a decade old, things began to go wrong.

One weekend after my college classes had ended, I was preparing to drive home for a couple of days, and I noticed the Buick's tailpipe had come unattached from its exhaust system. It was nearly dragging the ground. I tied the tailpipe in place by attaching it to the car's undercarriage with an old shoelace to make the trip. I do not recall how long I drove the Buick with this fix worthy of Sanford and Son.

The Buick's horn broke next. At the time, I was working on our college campus in the theatre, where I was on a crew that set up lighting and sound systems for travelling performances brought in by the local arts council and the university theatre. Our crew operated lights and sound for concerts, plays, and dance troupes including New York's Alvin Ailey Dance Company.

Even Mummenschanz came to our university's theatre. Once crisp fall afternoon, my coworkers and I were for several hours subjected to the condescending Francois, Mummenschanz's stage manager. Francois assailed us with French-English hybrid demands for exactly how to fix a stage light intended for cunning Mummenschanz puppets that would not be seen by anyone in the theatre's furthest balcony seats, as Mummenschanz failed to pack the house.

We were putting the finishing touches on the gels and lighting cues when, from inside the theatre, I heard the sound of a steady, uninterrupted car horn honking. I shook my head, unsure whether I would rather hear more of Francois' barking unintelligible commands in French at us hayseed theatre workers, or listen to the car horn operator shatter Mummenschanz's sustained pretentiousness. I went outside to see who was honking so obnoxiously and why. It was the Buick.

Mortified, I ran over, unlocked its eighty-pound driver's side door, and threw it open. I tapped on the horn, I beat on it. It would not stop honking into the autumn air. I did not know what to do. A co-worker came outside shortly after and bade me pop the Buick's hood. He disconnected the horn and silenced the Buick at last.

The following year, the Buick began running poorly. It chugged and shuddered when I pressed the gas. The engine finally quit one day, and our mechanic delivered the disheartening prognosis: blown motor. I was on a steady college diet of Top Ramen and had signed my existence to student loan overlords several times over by that year. I had no money to fix the Buick at that point in my life. I had made a few of its payments, but I really had no choice but to give it back to my parents. It belonged to them. Mom and Dad paid for a rebuilt engine and then kept it for my youngest sister's use, as she was commuting to a high school twenty minutes away from home and was also in need of a car.

Even with the rebuilt motor, the Buick never really ran the same after that. In the dead of winter, Dad would venture out in subfreezing windchills to start his, Mom's, and my two sisters' cars to let them warm up, the Buick included. This was primarily out of kindness for them as to not make them get into a freezing vehicle for the morning drive. But his gesture was also partially out of necessity. All of their cars were old behemoths. Their cars were of—what our extended family called—the "chizzler" variety: built in the '80s, had bodies by Fischer that were actually made of metal, and which had doors of a weight and girth that required a MLB pitcher's windup in order to gather enough force to shut them securely. Their aging innards had to warm before one stepped on the gas. That is, if the drivers wanted any power, velocity, or confidence prior to edging these bruisers out onto the two-lane highway from the driveway, where they could sputter and die in path of an oncoming semi.

The Buick also had broken hydraulic lifts that held up its hood. I cannot recall if the lifts failed after we purchased it, or if they had always been broken. Family Buick lore becomes fuzzy on this point. Regardless, we had to place a 2 by 4 of just the right length under the hood and set the piece of lumber precariously on the inside corner of the engine compartment. If it wasn't wedged just right, the 2 by 4 risked slipping, and down came the heavy Buick hood onto the head of the poor soul bent over rubbing his temple, confounded by the Buick's latest shenanigans.

One particularly cold morning, Dad was struggling to get the Buick started and keep its rebuilt innards firing in the frigid air that swept unprotected across the Kansas plains and battered the Buick's lean-to carport a few hundred feet from the house. The Buick kept starting then dying, starting and dying. And while Dad attempted to locate the source of the motor's misbehavior, he could not keep the hood raised. The Buick's appointed 2 by 4 must have been misplaced. Or perhaps thrown in a fit of rage across the backyard's expanse similar to when Dad threw a wild cat across our rural Iowa rear lawn after it climbed the back screen sliding door and clawed apart the screen for the hundredth time. The cat had reportedly landed on all fours and walked away unscathed. The same cannot be reported of the Buick. One of my sisters walked out to the lean-to prepped for school only to find Dad wielding clinched fists at the unresponsive Buick's front end with gritted teeth, vociferously challenging it with, "Do you want a piece of me? Huh? Ya wanna piece of me?"

Fast forward a year or two later. My parents and youngest sister moved overseas, nearly a half a world away. And I inherited the Buick back. Like a bad game of hot potato, the Buick returned to me with a couple of new quirks which became, in my fifth and final year of college, my problem. Dad took the job overseas for many reasons, the most significant of which were the wonderful opportunities it afforded his career and their ability to travel and see the world. But I have sometimes wondered secretly if one of the reasons they picked up and moved to northern Europe was to get away from the Buick.

Nonetheless, I abided the Buick for one more year. Its driver's side manual window roller had by this time broken off. If I wanted to raise or lower the window, I had to pick the bar up off the driver's side floor, attach it to the piece that barely stuck out from the door's interior and that resembled an allen wrench, make the connection, and then twirl the left arm quickly to get the window up before the small roller arm detached from the hexagonal inner piece, and the roller went crashing to the floor in my shower of epithets elevated in word choice and intensity from "Ya wanna piece of me?"

That final semester of college in the spring of 1998, as mentioned, I forked over another few thousand of borrowed tuition money to carry out my full-time student teaching assignment in an eastern Kansas town perched on the edge of the Flinthills. This region was a green, bucolic grassland for part of the year. The remainder of the year it was a brown and grey windswept flatland. The public middle school in which I completed my student teaching was on the outskirts of town, the January winds blocked by a few twigs and some playground equipment. I beseeched the gods to grant the Buick five more months of life.

February and March dragged on. I continued, in the vein of Hank Williams, Jr., the "family tradition" by starting the Buick each morning to let it warm. I would listen at our apartment front door to its chugging motor. When I heard the engine sound as if it were going to die, I would run out into the wind, yank open its door, and pump the gas pedal to rev it back up. I continued this pattern for a few more weeks. It limped to and from our cockroach palace to my student teaching assignment. The Buick soon went belly up again. I had towed it off to a repair shop and borrowed a car from my then in-laws to finish student teaching.

Needless to say, by the time May rolled around, I needed to spend some remaining student loan money to fix the Buick. I did not even walk at my college graduation because I could not part with the sixty bucks for a cap and gown. Graduate school tuition? Perish the thought. I wanted to halt the student loan snowball that was rolling downhill and gaining momentum every new undergraduate term. And I needed a new car.

Aside from my very meager finances when I finally earned a Bachelor's, there would have been an opportunity cost to hours spent toiling on a Master's. Right after I graduated, my parents generously flew me to Europe as a graduation gift and as an opportunity to share this new place in the world where they lived and were thriving. Let me see, spend summer completing Into to Graduate Studies and Critical Approaches to Literature, earn five dollars an hour setting up and striking another run or two of Mummenschanz . . . or go to Europe for three weeks? The choice was clear. I was fortunate enough to travel abroad twice more. I have not once regretted spending time and money on those excursions. I learned more visiting the Anne Frank Museum, the remains of the Roman Forum, the Eiffel Tower, the excavated ruins of Pompeii, the Vatican, Shakespeare's reconstructed Globe Theatre, or Peter the Great's summer palace in the Baltics than I would have by taking a survey course on any of these fantastic places and their rich history.

In 2009 I moved to California. I lived in northern Santa Barbara County for five years. In my view, this hidden wonder of central California's wine country is one of the most beautiful places on earth, California's best-kept secret. While there, I had to take a few online courses to secure my out-of-state credential, and those courses could move me over on the salary schedule, sure. But nearly every hour I was not at work, I was outdoors exploring all that California's central coast has to offer. I learned so much during my time in this fantastic place. I visited the Winchester Mansion, the Hearst Castle, and several Missions up and down the El Camino Real. I took every advantage of the outdoor opportunities, the backroads wine trails, the scenic drives, and the hiking trails, namely Johnson Ranch, Orcutt Trails, and the famous Cuesta Ridge, which afford amazing views of San Luis Obispo, the ocean, Morro Bay, and the relatively unspoiled live oak-dotted landscape of the coastal hills. Moving to California set my life onto a whole new trajectory. It is one of the greatest choices I ever made, moving there. Like the speaker of Wordworth's poem "I Wander Lonely As a Cloud," I reach out to the central coast in my mind's eye, often in the dark and bleak winter months. I think about the deep blue of California's clear skies, deeper blue than any sky I have experienced in the Midwest. I re-experience the bus trips up the mountainside to visit "La Cuesta Encantada," steeped in the Golden Age of Hollywood. I can whenever I want conjure up a heady and distinct combination of smells: red oak barbecue combined with the smell of pinot noirs, grenache, and syrahs soaked into the wood and very fabric of the Santa Ynez Valley. In my memory, I stroll through San Luis Obispo's wine country establishments, I sample the Santa Maria style barbecue epicurean delights for which the region is famous. My years there were a delicate yet time-curated balance of smells, tastes, vistas, and vibe that I have experienced nowhere else.

In 2013, I began reading about United States History, particularly westward expansion, manifest destiny, and the Corps of Discovery Journey of 1804-06. That summer, rather than sitting at home writing papers on mental health issues plaguing today's students or learning basic Spanish, I took off on a 6300-mile road trip up the Missouri River, following the Corps of Discovery's journey as closely as our modern highway system allows. I gazed in awe at Sitting Bull's grave and the trinkets of homage that other visitors had placed around its base. I walked over the mounds that to this day mark the loci of the Mandan and Hidatsa villages. I watched firsthand the Great Falls pour over the rocks to cascade down and create the water visuals that Meriwether Lewis so eloquently described in his journals.

I took a boat tour up the Missouri into the Gates of the Rocky Mountains and watched the towers and battlements formed out of the Montana mountainside open and close as one ventures slowly upstream. The illusion enraptures. My mind and soul took more from this journey than an online history course haphazardly rushed through for recertification or addition of a social studies teaching endorsement.

It is one thing to study moments and places in American history. It is quite another to see them and let the stories soak up through the soles of my feet into my psyche. My soul longed to visit those map coordinates. What does it profit a man to be information rich but experience poor? Information can be had at a whim by swiping and tapping our devices. Experience takes effort, a measure of discomfort, but the view at the top of the mountain is so much greater.

It was during my time in California that I discovered backpacking. I bought a backpack and peregrinated further nooks and crannies of San Luis Obispo County that basic road running had not revealed. In 2015, after vigorous hoarding of money and dispatching all personal debt, I embarked on a coast-to-coast hiking trip during a period of strategic unemployment. Walking east to west, I hiked through Delaware, our first state. I walked across Maryland and learned about the old C & O Towpath. I ascended the mountains of West Virginia where one afternoon I was surprised to learn that I had surmounted the Eastern Continental Divide. I traversed Ohio, where I learned about the amazing Grandma Gatewood, who hiked the Appalachian Trail twice in Keds and carrying a shower curtain as her knapsack. I tested my mettle in Indiana, where I crossed the remote Hoosier National Forest and visited President Lincoln's boyhood home. I walked southern Illinois, the western end of which I stood atop the engineering feat known as the Mississippi River levee. Missouri showed me the wonderful Katy Trail, a divine railroad gravel bed that crosses the length of the state, an enchanted land for cyclists and hikers, a peaceful Narnia that lulls its users into thought and reflection with the meditative crunch of content footsteps and steady bicycle tires, a hiker's nirvana that caters to their needs via its tiny towns along the way. I walked across my home state of Kansas nearly to Kinsley, which marks the geographic center of this great nation, and the halfway mark of hoofing it cross country. A Master's degree cannot supplant the 2200 miles of seeing this beautiful country on foot.

Backpacking eastern portions of our great nation far outweighs the five months I could have devoted to advanced degrees in education that seem to have little application to real life or even the realities of teaching a quality English curriculum. The grit, determination, self-confidence, stamina, and inner peace derived from doing hard things such as thru hiking, exerting my independence, and the rewilding of oneself transfers to all other aspects of my life, including my job. Far greater than paying $300 for a 500-level summer class on "methods for teaching grit in the modern classroom."

Investing in advanced degrees also encroaches heavily on a teacher's limited free time. Especially teachers with heavy grading and paperwork loads and teachers who coach all year to make a decent living. I was accepted into an MA program at Wichita State University in the summer of 2007. I began working on this degree a course or two at a time, primarily during the summer months. However, I took a 900-level American literature course during one fall semester. I loved it. I discovered Charles Brockden Brown and his dense Gothic prose. I relearned a love for American authors that I never appreciated my junior year of high school. But the heavy reading demand took its toll. I had 80 of my own students' essays and other work to grade. I was training for a half marathon. I adopted quite a hermetic existence just to keep up with my students, whose grades I considered my first responsibility. I finished approximately half of my Masters, then gazed down the path of even heavier literary coursework that increasingly was not offered during the summer. I chose my profession, my students, and my own need for self-care and physical vitality through hours of running.

I had also run out of spare cash to pay WSU's graduate tuition. I shunned the idea of even more student debt. *The borrower is slave to the lender.* Further indentured servitude to my student loan overseers was an unpalatable and Sisyphean option. I have always felt as if the money spent on tuition was not worth the jump across the salary scales when it meant more debt. When I began the MA program, I was still paying off my undergrad education. I never finished the Master's.

And what of the knowledge imparted within these education Master's degrees and their fellow travelers, the continuing education courses for teacher recertification? Jim Fay conferences, constructivism, whole language, no-zero policies, PBIS, differentiation, all pure bilge. Another year or a new administrator leaves the once-vaunted strategy or intervention discarded along the roadside. Teachers become enervated within a semantic fog, unclear on what faddish strategies will fill the evaluating administrator's checklist. A lesson plan that follows Madeline Hunter must now be fleshed out with a K-W-L chart, a Kagan structure, assessments that comport with at least four of Gardner's Multiple Intelligences, and use of a Chromebook app somewhere in the milieu. We've overcomplicated education into an instructional strategy Mad Libs game. I've grown weary of sacrificing my dollars on the altar of teaching fads that soon vanish into the ether.

What's more, the byzantine nature of recertification is straight from behind the Iron Curtain. The graduate course content that might have interested me since I exited college and commenced my own self-appointed curriculum of curiosity would not have been approved by my school district, my local professional development committee, or whatever other peripheral agencies have been set up to approve or deny teachers' forays into additional education on our own dimes. After three trips to the Baltics and neighboring nations, I became interested in taking courses in pre and post-Soviet Europe. My local PDC council and the State of Kansas would not have blessed those types of courses, as they did not directly pertain to methods of teaching English or furthering whatever district improvement objectives were set in place at the moment. Advanced courses that hold my interest and warrant my dollar are those which feature instructors much smarter than I, the sages on the stages. I want to come away from thousand-dollar courses with a new hard skill. A new level of understanding of English grammar, linguistics, or literature. Instead, continuing teacher education courses are all things nebulous, hazy, and soft around the edges. Teacher education workshops have never met a standard they could not lower, a hard academic skill they could not obfuscate.

I sparred a few years ago with a Kansas Department of Education credential renewal czar over a three-hour course I had taken while living in (cue collective inhale of outrage) California, and therefore was unable to have the class knighted by my local PDC committee. The Department of Education czarista told a humorous yet telling anecdote. Back in the "old days" of teacher recertification, a high school instructor could take just about any college course in any area and receive salary schedule credit. A teacher from those halcyon days had taken Mortuary Science toward recertification for middle-school math, or some other unrelated field. Talk about a hard, recession-proof skill applicable to the real world. Maybe that math teacher had the foresight to begin exploring a new career outside education, while simultaneously earning himself a paltry bump on the salary scale.

An increasing number of teacher education courses have their content rooted in reaching out to our society's latest contrived or poorly cobbled together victim group. I was made to care about the plight of young girls in the '90s. Students with exceptionalities took the forefront for a bit during that same decade.

English Learners were all the subject of much hand-wringing for a while; in many parts of the country they still wring many a hand. Boys were falling behind for a spell, and they continue to. We have a boy crisis on our hands, yet education has been content to medicate them, collude in keeping our boys illiterate, and move on to the next victim pool to fill more inservice minutes. Students in poverty then became all the rage. Now students with trauma and abuse require a fresh slate of summer courses and hundreds out of teachers' pocketbooks.

Who is next? I cannot stay afloat in this roiling sea of damaged, underserved, or unprepared constituencies. I do not deny that many students have psychological problems. Severe ones. But most teachers are not equipped to provide psychiatric services as well as educate. I know I'm not. I went into English, not therapy. Callous? Maybe. I do not surmise that any worried parent who takes her child to an hour-long therapy appointment would expect that the psychiatrist would also teach grade-level math—as well as remediate all the missing math knowledge due to chronic psychological issues—alongside restoring the child to mental health. I am not a miracle worker, and I have no interest in paying an educational institution or school guest speaker to guilt me into accepting a role for which I am highly unqualified.

I remain unconvinced that, when I look back on my life, I would have swapped travel, backpacking, and personally driven exploration for more time on my duff in university lecture halls or drab classrooms. I am but a simple English teacher.

More letters after my name have never seemed like a square trade for life experience. Perhaps it will at some point work to my detriment, but I have never much cared about building my professional resume.

In the words of entrepreneur and ultra-endurance athlete Jesse Itzler, I have opted to spend my prized free time and conscientiously amassed dollars building my life resume.

Saturday, June 02, 2018

Destination: West of Boonville, MO
Today's Miles: 6.20
Start Location: New Franklin, MO
Trip Miles: 2008.01

After two school years, a few days of packing and prep, and an eleventh-hour car repair delay, here I am.

I had meant to begin picking up this section I skipped two years ago, the section between New Franklin, MO and Olathe, KS, on Wednesday and resume updates here right after school let out, but my car broke down. I am still driving the '02 Infiniti. I found myself with a couple extra days on my hands waiting on it. So I took advantage of the extra time to do the packing of my personal effects at home to prep for storage.

I was antsy and ready to come up here to New Franklin Wednesday, and I sort of felt like Mountain Man from the TV show *Duck Dynasty* when I realized I would be delayed getting to the Katy: Welllllll, not too sure what's wrong with my car... Might be the alternator... Could be the distributor... Guess I better get my camp stove out and make sure it works... Reckon I could repack my backpack like I remember... Sure could use some more storage containers from down at the Wal Mart... Hope my Thermarest still hold air real good...

Regardless, I am thankful that it's the Katy that will be easing me back into the ADT the next several days. The soft, forgiving railbed, the quiet surroundings, and its map of services are really great. Plus, the new Rock Island Spur is now open from Windsor. This means more off-road miles to connect the dots to Olathe. Another reason I am thankful for Katy Bootcamp is that not only is the nice railbed soft-I am soft. I am not in shape. I have been trying to work in ToFwBP (Time on Feet with Backpack) in the last three months. I have been hiking around parks and a great bike path in Wichita, carrying about 26 to 28 lbs. No 20-mile days this week for me though.

I officially put shoes on the ground around 2:30 this afternoon. At the New Franklin info depot, I remembered vividly approaching the town three years ago. It was storming, I had a ripped tent, and I knew I needed to do some gear repair and retooling before proceeding on. I remembered the grain elevators, the road leading to town. The lady who took me into Boonville that day.

This afternoon I filled up my water, arranged things in my backpack, pointed the tiny compass attached to my hip belt west, and put one foot in front of the other. Slow, easy, gentle on myself.

The railbed quickly gave way to pavement for a bit as the KATY crossed the Missouri River into Boonville. I stepped off onto the grass as soon as possible, near a pretty POW-MIA memorial in town. The path wound around to a beautiful depot and a market, went by a green and yellow caboose. The Katy was brick for a few hundred feet. People were setting up a little farmer's market, it appeared. The Katy then went back to gravel. A couple miles later, I found a good spot to drop anchor. I have to relearn my system of unpacking everything, in what order, and where I like it in my tent at night.

Less than a half day of walking, short mileage. What I needed to ease me back in.

Amie

Sunday, June 03, 2018

Destination: Clifton City, MO
Today's Miles: 19.10
Start Location: West of Boonville, MO
Trip Miles: 2027.11

A shortie tonight. I had a long entry typed out, and apparently this new journal site deletes everything you type when it times you out due to "inactivity." Soooo, I will try to pick up tomorrow what I had said tonight.

This morning I made it into Pilot Grove after a nice, cool 8 miles in the Katy's shade. There was more bicycle traffic this morning. I talked to a couple who had been on Kansas's Flinthills Nature Trail. They wished me luck and warned me that there was no water at Clifton City. I giggled and said I was aware and had just cached a gallon of water at CC the day before.

Made it to the depot and found my water gallon unbothered. Another little gift from my past self to my current self. Or wait, was it a gift from my current self to my future self?

All is well. And apparently I was just kidding on the "no 20-mile days for me yet" comment last night. Hope I don't pay for it in the morning.

Amie

The Things I Carry
Monday, June 04, 2018

Destination: Sedalia, MO
Today's Miles: 16
Start Location: Clifton City, MO
Trip Miles: 2043.11

After my *War and Peace*-length post was deleted last night and I hastily reposted the abridged version, the camping follies continued. First, the spot I chose was hidden from both the bike path and the gravel road, but it was on a slight downhill, so I experienced the fun-house effect all night.

Second, there was a fly in my tent. It was one of those flies that won't land long enough for you to smack it or, in my case, point the bug spray at it long enough to spray it into oblivion. I turned my phone back on to use the flashlight, but the stinkin' fly was flitting around too quickly for me to spray it. After 20 minutes or so of seek and destroy, the fly finally landed within the folds of the plastic bag in which I keep my shoes for the night. I doused the plastic, hoping I got it. I heard no further buzzing, and turned my flashlight off and curled up. A minute or so later I heard the buzzing of the fly in its death throes. I did not even put my glasses back on or turn my phone's flashlight back on. I just blindly shot more sprays at the plastic bag. The fly gave no further trouble, yet if I mysteriously begin growing a third arm, it will likely be the result of my inhalation of excessive Cutter insect repellent fumes throughout last night from trying to kill one fly.

Like the previous night, I slept pretty well given the abrupt change in sleeping surfaces. I woke a few times both nights to a hand about to fall asleep or my neck in a bizarre position. Most times upon waking, I was pulled from a vivid dream, the contents of which are now hazy and jumbled. And that's okay because I heard one time that if you are dreaming, you're recovering.

Of course I started both mornings with a half Russian breakfast, kaffe being my one vice I refuse to leave at home. It has been cool in the mornings and most of the day, so I zipped another panel on my Sahara pant. This gives me capris pants. Capris reduce the sunscreen demand. They, along with my Tilly hat, probably make me look like I am on a safari.

I packed up at the depot's picnic table, downed about a third of the cached water gallon, and set off. Yesterday's 19 miles left me what I call "good sore" this morning. All athletes know this sore. It's the soreness of muscles that have been asked to do something new. The body has been pushed just past its high-water fitness mark or pulled out of the entropy of sedentary life. I had felt a hot spot on one left toe last evening, but no blister. I put a band-aid on it anyway for the day. I spent the first few miles again enjoying the soft surface and going slowly, being good to myself.

The Katy leaving Clifton City is a long, gradual uphill. There was more traffic this morning than yesterday. I met a long line of boys and their adult supervisors, Scouts maybe. Several families were out today and many older people. More people today looked like they were on perhaps a longer trek rather than just a day's ride. It was overcast much of the day, less wind. Really nice.

I crossed one the Katy's many wooden bridges, and there was a group of cyclists stopped, chatting and watching the river. I walked past and one said, "Just want you to know as inspiration that I have walked the entire width of the Appalachian Trail." I totally missed the joke. When his friends started laughing, I finally got it and said, "Aaah, so about 10 feet?" He said, "Yeah, if that." They wished me a good day and headed east.

A few miles later I sat down and took my shoes and socks off. I finally ate the Mountain House dried meal I had in my pack. It was the turkey and dressing casserole. It was really tasty. I had never tried any MRE-type foods because they are kind of expensive, but I would be willing to try some more MH meals. Note to self for rounding out my resupply boxes. Lightweight and yummo.

I sat a bit, changed socks and shoes, and thought about, in addition to food, the things I carry. Here are the gear pieces that are the same. Sleeping bag, sleep pad, stove, tiny cookpot that I mostly use as a mug, two pairs of shorts, socks, Dirty Girl gaiters, Sierra Designs tank top, and backpack. I still use my Flash 52 pack, which now has over 3500 miles of ToFwBP, including training walks in CA and KS and actual hike miles. It is getting a little shabby and has a couple rips, but it still works. I know all its pouches and know instinctively where everything goes; it quickly becomes a part of me and most of the time, after the tops of my pelvic bones get used to its presence again, I don't really notice it's there.

Something else the same but resurrected is my Black Diamond tent. I used the Big Agnes tent last time but grew tired of all its set-up steps and the gamble on whether to use the rainfly. I prefer the quicker set up of this tent.

I had called Black Diamond in March and told them I had ripped the tent, and asked a price for having them repair it. They said they'd fix it for free, just send it on in. Thank you, Black Diamond. I set it up the other day, closed it all up, and doused it with the garden hose from outside it to see if it is indeed watertight again. I got in and felt around. It was dry. But there's only one way to find out if the fix is solid. It hasn't rained yet.

Things I left at home and don't carry this time include my GPS and headlamp. My phone and Power Practical charger both can perform those functions.

Now for items I carry that are new. I picked up on sale a Patagonia super lightweight long sleeve top with zip collar. I wanted this to keep the sun off of me and further reduce the sunscreen and bug spray demands. Due to Kansas's infamous wind, my Gossamer Gear Chrome Dome was ripped beyond recognition two summers ago, so I ordered another one, this one collapsing even smaller. I also picked up a Gossamer Gear hip belt zip bag. This just gives extra backpack storage. My phone charger accessories in a ziplock bag fits perfectly there, and I now have easier access to it.

My bandana of choice this year is my American flag bandana. I picked this one because this is a great country, and I remain grateful that I continue to be able to satisfy my wanderlust by traveling freely among its diverse states, both on four wheels and on foot. I also picked up a new stuff sack for my tent. I am now using an Osprey 30L for all tent items. The old one was ripping.

My goal destination today was Sedalia. There was a brief detour on pavement to the Sedalia depot. The Sedalia depot has a bike shop right next to it. At the bike shop I got intel on camping spots, notably the Missouri fairgrounds campsite 2.8 miles further west. I also tried my first almond and hazelnut Snickers bars. I went the 2.8 additional miles down the Katy here to the fairgrounds. I was able to set up for 9 bucks. The no-hookup fee is supposed to be 12 bucks, but 9 in cash is all I had. The Missouri Parks guy said he would get the other 3 bucks for me. He only had 2, so I guess we were both complicit in scamming Missouri Fairgrounds a dollar. Either that, or he just pocketed my 9 bucks, in which case scamming Missouri Fairgrounds ain't danglin' over my conscience. I know I am safe here, and there is water 2 feet away for in the morning. The final destination of my 9 bucks is inconsequential.

An elderly couple came out of their RV this evening and took a little walk around the grounds. I noticed from afar their unique walking sticks. The man and woman each had a stick that looked to be decorated. They came over to say hello, and each showed the detail on these creations. They had carved their own sticks and then put small souvenir plaques all over the sticks, plaques representing all the places they had been. Many national parks, many states represented. They told me I must visit Mesa Verde. I saw a plaque or two from my beloved Montana. It was a really neat idea. I set up my tent and let last night's condensation dry out. Totally keeping an eye out for any more flies. Overall a very good day. I am deliciously tired, sore but not wrecked.

So random humor for the day. Another reason the Katy is pretty amazing is that every few miles there are benches where one can sit and rest. The area around the benches is usually nicely mowed, and the somewhat hidden areas behind these structures create a discreet place for the female cyclist or walker to make a quick technical stop. Even now on my third time along the Katy, my *modus operandi* is to place my hands on top of the bench and allow it to hold my body weight as I lean down and back, then upon conclusion of the technical stop, pull myself up and save the feet and legs from bearing the stress of standing up with the pack on. These benches are mounted pretty solidly into the rail bed, but the Katy is somewhat elevated above the surrounding fields through which it passes.

Yesterday while making a technical stop, I had a vision of myself hanging onto the top of the bench, and upon bringing the technical stop to fruition, the bench suddenly pulling up out of the ground, sending me, my pack, two trekking poles, and a gallon of water crashing backward through the trees and flying into someone's pasture. As my grandma and grandpa Adamson used to say, "Whyyyy, that would sure be a fright."

Amie

The Things I Carry Part II
Tuesday, June 05, 2018

Destination: Windsor, MO
Today's Miles: 16.30
Start Location: Sedalia, MO
Trip Miles: 2059.41

Slept really hard last night. The fairgrounds constituted a nice camping spot. I used 9 dollars' worth of fairgrounds water to prep a half Russian breakfast, brush my teeth, and top off my gallon. I popped 3 Nuun tabs in it and forced down half of it. The remainder in the flat-bottom gallon jug rested easily behind my neck on the pack frame. A mere half a mile back to the Katy.

I started the day again feeling delightfully sore but not trashed. There were fewer people out today, and I retreated into my own head. Not much noise except the birds and my personal pattern of crunch, crunch, crunch, click-click: three footsteps for every two trekking pole clicks was the steady rhythm I fell into this morning. You soon find that open-eyed meditative state, where the face relaxes, the miles pass swiftly, and the body kind of goes on auto pilot. It is a state that's a kissing cousin to runner's high: the mind takes over and usurps the body's efforts sometimes during a good long run. Somewhere along a gravel road or at an intersection you snap out of your reverie and think, "Oh, six miles have gone by. When did that happen? Cool."

It's a feeling that your body can almost effortlessly maintain; push a little more and it responds. Sleep. Recover. Hydrate. Then push again the next day and find out that you can do more. Unbroken focus. My friend Matthew C. two summers ago called it achieving a state of *fiero.*

I had 9 miles to Green Ridge, the next water and snack source. Given that I am not in shape, my state of *fiero* was elusive this morning and only lasted about 6 or 7 miles. I sat down around 11:30 and checked the distance to Green Ridge. A mile to go. At Green Ridge I sat under a picnic shelter just a couple hundred feet away from the Katy to get my bearings and contemplate the Casey's next door. Picked up a chocolate Muscle Milk, an almond Snickers, and an assortment of Clif bars. I decided to push ahead to Windsor, where I could do a motel night, shower and laundry, and plan my attack of the Rock Island Spur headed back northwest toward Olathe.

Most of the section into Windsor had no shade, so I put my stuff down on a bench (mounted very firmly into ground, mind you) at the Katy high point and got out the new Chrome Dome. No shade? I created my own and took my hat off to enjoy the nice breeze. I decided that I now probably looked like a deranged Mary Poppins on a safari. It's a little cumbersome to hold both the sunshade and my trekking poles, so I tried mounting the shade's handle under my pack's chest strap. The breeze was just a bit strong and whipped it around a little too much. So I just hung onto it. Can't have my Chrome Dome 2.0 tore up on the first day. Besides, we still got half a' Kansas to go.

All day at the Katy's highway crossings, I kept seeing signs that forbade horse-drawn vehicles from using the trail, and I wondered if the Windsor area was Amish country. After I turned south into town I saw two ladies driving a horse and buggy. They were in the pastel and black dresses and bonnets. I feel pretty safe in Amish territory.

Made it to the motel in Windsor and snagged a Rock Island guide at the front desk. After showering then sequestering abhorrent laundry items from the rest of my pack, I finally threw away my Katy guide that I have had since 2015. When I went through my data book pieces a couple weeks ago, I realized I still had my OG Katy map I had picked up in St. Charles 3 years ago. I had cut the map way down to show only the info I needed, and I had continued trimming pieces from it the further west I walked. It was creased and faded, but I wanted to carry it and not a new map to finish out this short section to Windsor. I finally laid it to rest tonight.

I thought some more today about the other things I carry. I am still carrying Grandpa Adamson's little green army bag. In it, I keep small emergency items I hope never to need, but I know the bag and Grandpa are with me.

Also doing something different with shoes this time. I brought two pairs of my best running shoes, Brooks Pure Flow. They are minimalist and very lightweight. I remember my high school cross country coach telling us never to try anything new on race day. Wear the same shoes or racing flats, same socks, eat the same breakfast, don't bust out any new dietary experiments or clothing on a morning you have to perform. The blowback could ruin your race. I put this philosophy to use and decided to walk in what my feet and body already know, the Brooks. The weight issue is probably a wash since I ditched the flip flops ("thongs" if you grew up in the '70s and '80s) as camp shoes.

Drawback is that the Brooks are not water resistant. Hence the two pairs. If one gets soaked I carry a dry pair. Again, it has not rained so I've not had a chance to test this theory. So far only hot spots on my next-to-pinky toes, and I don't think about my feet.

I also carry a light heart and unburdened soul. I carry a desire to live in the moment, to live in this day only, just for a while, concerned for the future only in terms of water, calories, and sleep. And most of all, I try my best to carry faith. Faith that whatever is supposed to come after this will fall into place, as it always does.

Amie

Digressio
Wednesday, June 06, 2018

Destination: Leeton, MO
Today's Miles: 10.50
Start Location: Windsor, MO
Trip Miles: 2069.91

This past school year in my Honors English II class, I taught the eight part Greek classical essay. It is a basic persuasive essay with a few extra parts, including countering opposing viewpoints and writing a paragraph known as the Digressio.

In the Digressio, the student is to tell a personal story that illustrates his or her thesis. One student named Racquel wrote her essay about how today's technology may actually be harming young people's emotions, social skills, and intellectual development. Racquel decided to write her Digressio over how technology was a negative influence on her spiritual growth at church camp one summer.

In her paragraph, Racquel described how all church campers were to avoid cell phones at camp, especially during quiet time. Quiet time was supposed to be a personal time of prayer and reflection, a spiritual connection with the Lord in which one's mobile device has no place. However, Racquel had decided during one quiet time session to stealth some cell phone use by sneaking off, walking up a hill, and pointing her device at the sky, desperately seeking out one tiny bar of service to commune, presumably, with her social media notifications rather than the Lord. In helping her conclude her Digressio paragraph, I asked Racquel specifically how technology had harmed her that day. She said she guessed that technology ruined her relationship with Jesus and destroyed her communion with the Lord.

Last night in Windsor I could not access the wi-fi and there was zero service in my motel room. If I sat outside my room or circled the motel parking lot with my arm pointed to the sky just right, I had service for a few seconds, and then nothing. As I did laps around the lot and pointed my phone in all four directions, I felt like Racquel during church camp quiet time. The lack of wi-fi technology was ruining my relationship with letting my loved ones know I was okay. Ruining my relationship with plotting out my next water and food sources. I succumbed to the universe and finally gave up and went to bed, giggling about Racquel's Digressio and how, hundreds of miles away and months later, I could totally relate. I needed my phone.

This morning after a laundromat visit, I got a late start. I started at the Katy/Rock Island crossroads, where instead of making a deal with the devil for more cell service, I headed off onto the new spur back toward Kansas City. The spur was lightly travelled, mostly shaded, and I saw ample evidence of someone's having recently ridden it on horseback. I went slowly today. Took a break every couple miles. Got up to 90 today, and I could tell the difference. I made it to the Leeton depot mid-afternoon. I ambled leisurely over to the Casey's for a couple nights' food. I spent an hour under the Leeton park picnic shelter, finishing off my Powerades, reconnoitering the town traffic level, looking at my new map and thinking over water for the two days into Pleasant Hill.

Here is some info for the imminent Rock Island traveller. The info depots are brand new, as are the restroom structures and picnic tables. Community services are not outlined at the depots quite yet. The RI paper and online maps say there is no water at Leeton, but there is a new drinking fountain here at the trailhead. It works, and I am making use of it. Leeton is overall a decent stop, given how new the RI is.

Random humor for the day. I bought a small bag of almonds and a bag of cashews this morning, and I had stuffed them in the top pouch of my pack, the zipper of which is right behind my head as I walk. I finally felt hungry early afternoon, and I decided to try to be smooth and unzip the pack pocket, blindly feel around, and extract whatever bag of nuts I grabbed first. I grabbed the corner of a bag, pulled, and the partially opened zipper ripped open my bag of almonds, sending most of them to the gravel path. I salvaged the rest in my hand. But did I five-second-rule the ones on the ground and eat them anyway? That's right, I ate them. I figured the Rock Island Spur is so new, the floors have gotta be clean.

But I digress!

Amie

Thursday, June 07, 2018

Destination: Medford, MO
Today's Miles: 17.40
Start Location: Leeton, MO
Trip Miles: 2087.31

Slept poorly due to a house a block from my camp spot. A guy was up much of the night banging around and burning stuff. Trash? Who knows. The banging would subside for a few hours, and then he would be at it again. Randomly banging his junk. I suspect illicit drugs were somewhere in that equation. I was walking this morning by 6:30.

The 7 miles into Chilhowee went very fast, and here are some random observances I made during those miles.

First, I have noticed that whatever method I begin the day with, trekking poles with sunshade packed away or sunshade deployed and trekking poles together in the other hand, tends to set the precedent for the day's pace. If I start off with the poles, I tend to go faster. I wear the long sleeves and hat and don't really consider getting the chrome dome out. If I start out the other way and carry the dome in one hand, it's not long before I start thinking, *Sheesh, why did I bring these crummy trekking poles along? What a nuisance.* Today is a pole and no sunshade day.

Second random observation, no matter what pace I maintain, I can hear my breathing. Walking with weight makes you breath out a lot. It's as if you exhale more air than you inhale. I know that doesn't make sense. But it seems that in real life I find myself doing so much breathing in. Planning, thinking, overthinking, eating too fast so that I can get on with my day makes me breathe in too much. That's probably why in yoga or crisis response training, the teachers keep reminding the pupils over and over to focus on breathing. Of course, breathing in is very important! But I like breathing out.

Third, there were some sections here where the railroad ties had been taken out and simply tossed to the side. I wondered what happens to all the removed rails and ties.

At Chilhowee, I stopped for a break. RI Walking Report: the Chilhowee Trailhead has almost no shade, no water, and no depot yet. However, it does have a porta potty and a huge parking area. I walked a block into town and found a place to sit. I had been prepared for two days to have to scrounge for water at Chilhowee. I had put my thinking on hoarding and rationing mode. I checked Google maps again, as I was prepared to ask for water at the little post office. My Plan B was to ask at the church.

I headed toward the USPS first and as I turned into the main drag, I spied a tiny brick corner building that said Chilhowee Bank. I decided to ask there first, but when I opened the door, I was pleasantly surprised to find it not a bank but a corner market. Two ladies greeted me, filled up my water for free, said I "looked clean compared to some of the bikers that come through there," and reported that they had been open about a year. I picked up some oatmeal packets, a banana, a cup of mini Nutter Butters, a Gatorade, and a Snickers. What a great place! The town also has a park with another small covered picnic area. I repacked my purchases and proceeded on. Chilhowee is another great little resupply spot; don't be put off by the lack of an info depot just yet. This spur is a work in progress.

With 10-ish miles to Medford, I took frequent afternoon breaks. By one o'clock, I had seen a few cyclists and one walker, a lady out for a morning stroll. I felt very fast and tough through the early afternoon. At 2, my hair was wet. At 4, I was officially tired. I dragged the last mile and a half to the Medford Trailhead. The depot is in progress here also.

I am looking forward to a peaceful night's sleep with no one banging around all night. Walking all day and staying tough is also a work in progress.

All is well.

Amie

When's Our Next Marathon?
Friday, June 08, 2018

Destination: Pleasant Hill, MO
Today's Miles: 17.20
Start Location: Medford, MO
Trip Miles: 2104.51

Skipped the kaffe this morning because I needed to ration my water. Wasn't sure I would be equal to the task of walking into Pleasant Hill with no kaffe. I am not equal to many tasks without kaffe.

Started about 6:15 to get the majority of walking in before it warmed up. Walked quickly, 10 miles by noon to the Rock Island parking area just a few miles from Pleasant Hill. There in the shaded area, I took off my shoes and socks and sipped water. I watched a few cyclists go by. I wanted the sun not to be straight overhead before continuing on the RI. When the sun is on one side of the trees lining the trail, there is shade on one side of the path or the other. I waited until the sun moved, then got moving. The last few miles were a rough push. I sipped on my last half liter of water, which was loaded with electrolyte powder to push me through.

So the verdict is that the entire Rock Island Spur is walkable. However, caching a gallon of water per person at Medford is advisable, two gallons if it is hot, or be prepared to carry. I carried and arrived in Pleasant Hill pretty parched. I advise caching, not carrying.

At Pleasant Hill, I sat in the shade on a bench in front of a small business and waited on my friend, boyfriend, and best person Chad to pick me up. He arrived just in time, late afternoon. I was visibly pretty shot, and it reminded me of the time this past December when Chad went with me down to Dallas to support me in the BMW Dallas Marathon.

As the runners come through the finisher's area after running 26.2 miles, they receive a box of recovery snacks. On the snack box there is a notice to trashed runners that says, "Ready for more? 2019 Dallas Marathon entry opens tomorrow!" Talk about being immediately taunted while stumbling through the finishers' chute.

And not only that, on the way home, Chad, who had never been to a huge road running event such as the Dallas Marathon, said, "That was really fun. When's our next marathon?" We joke about that question a lot. *When's our next marathon?* I read one time that you should never run another marathon until you forget your previous marathon. The recovery takes a lot of time.

Yesterday as Chad was driving me from Pleasant Hill, my depleted status must have suggested my post-Dallas condition because he looked over and me and quipped, "So when's our next marathon?"

I will zero tomorrow in the area and make a threefold plan: drinking water, looking at the route walking into Olathe, and hopefully hooking up with family members in the Kansas City area. We ain't gonna be runnin' no marathons.

In whatever ways we push ourselves, here's to knowing when it's the season to be good to ourselves. And being equal to the task.

Amie

Sunday, June 10, 2018

Destination: Greenwood, MO
Today's Miles: 7.10
Start Location: Pleasant Hill, MO
Trip Miles: 2111.61

Started around noon today at the Pleasant Hill depot. The rail bed meandered out of Pleasant Hill for another few miles before ending at Smart Road, a gravel road that wound its way toward Greenwood and passed by some pretty homes with nicely manicured lawns. I hugged the sides of the gravel road to stay in the shade.

A couple miles along Route 150 brought me into Greenwood. The first three or four establishments I passed were a row of antique stores. Greenwood must be a mecca for antiquers. I found a small gazebo and sat in the shade, where I waited on my cousin Gyla to "kidnap" me for a day or two. Nothing really of note happened today, just an uneventful 7 miles, so I will pick up where I left off last time on my list of reasons why I like to do this. I started this list a couple years ago. I hope I don't repeat myself. If I do repeat a reason, then I guess I believe it enough to say it again. Here are a few more reasons, in no certain order.

16. It whets the mettle.
17. The body is in perpetual motion while the mind is in stillness.
18. It kind of gives you an extra layer, physically and emotionally.
19. You should be lonely, but you're not.
20. "There's a big difference between empty fatigue and gratifying exhaustion. Invest in meaningful activities that move you." I saw this quote a few weeks ago, and I saved it because I think it is so true. I have tried to make it a point in life to invest my time and money in things that are joy giving, not joy depleting. Things that leave me gratifyingly tired but quickly and easily recharged. I know this cannot always be achieved. I like things that are new and interesting and challenging, but hard in a gratifying way, not in a way that leaves me an empty shell.

I have read a lot about hiking, including the Camino de Santiago. Many people, once they have completed their camino, go back and do camino after camino. Maybe the Camino Frances over and over again. Maybe the Camino del Norte next time. Most of the time The Way is gratifying exhaustion. That good tired.

Buen Camino!

Amie

Letter to a Parent

The following is an email reply I sent a parent. This particular student's mother had emailed me three times over the course of two months. None of her messages opened with any sort of salutation. No greeting, no introduction. Each hit the ground running asking why her daughter was doing poorly. The first two emails I replied with the truth in professional but matter-of-fact tones: her daughter needed to study a little more and complete her work on time. And she needed to put her cell phone away. The third email from this parent arrived at some point in January. Her daughter's grade was still hovering in the low D range, status quo for my English class and a few of her other courses. Again, no acknowledgment from the parent, simply opening with, "This is my third email to you." The rest of the email was by that time a tersely cobbled together Gregorian chant of potshots and blanket statements, all of which I quote and address in this reply. At this point in the year, I knew I was not returning to this district. I no longer cared. I was emotionally wrung out. I spent a Friday evening pounding these words out on my keyboard, all day Saturday stewing over this reply and adding to it, and finally sending it Sunday afternoon. I said what I meant, and meant what I said. Before pressing Enter, I asked my own mother and two close friends, both teachers, to read this reply. They said, "Hit send, as long as you're sure." I was.

I copied a colleague in our math department when sending. The colleague also had this student in class. The mother had emailed my colleague as well, but Mom did not wield the accusatory, passive-aggressive tone to the other teacher. I copied my colleague in sending this partially to cover my own behind, in case this mother tried further to build a case against me by manipulating the original contents or tone of my email in any way. A second reason I copied my colleague was that I viewed this is a platform from which I could voice how I, as well as other English teachers in that district—and everywhere—feel. I wanted other teachers to read it. I secretly wanted the administration and counselors to read it. This was an Everyman email, any other teacher's letter, really. In what follows, only the student's name has been changed and the name of the school district omitted. Everything else is verbatim.

Good afternoon.

I apologize for the delayed response to your email. Let me start by saying that I was a bit taken aback by the blanket statements that I am "all over the place," "nothing is ever the same," they are "all confused" "all the time" and the vague statements "a lot of your students," "parents would agree," and "something needs to change." As a result, I have given these unclear statements a lot of thought. I will respond to them. But first, I will address the specific items you mentioned.

SEATING CHART   The seating chart did change on January 3. Julie sits on the opposite side of the room now from where she sat first semester. Last semester she was not allowed to sit next to her best friend, as I knew coming in that there was a potential for socializing. This semester I put students in completely different places in the classroom, again away from others who may be a distraction. Sure, I can move her for a third time, but I don't believe another revamped seating arrangement would address some of the issues I will talk about later.

CELL PHONE   Students know per the course syllabus, per my requests, per asking specific students (including Julie) to put phones away, that phones are not allowed during class. The only exception is the last five or so minutes when we have "stopped" for the day and their work is complete. I fought the cell phone battle with struggling students pretty hard my first year at this district. I quickly learned it is futile to do so. It is highly unfortunate that our school allows phones to be carried in class. It approaches insanity to fight the veritable tidal wave of students' cell phone notifications, the volley of Snapchats in classes and passing periods, and the addiction (yes, addiction) to these shiny baubles. As it is "up to the teachers" to establish a classroom phone policy, I have done so and continue to issue occasional reminders. During test and quiz situations, I am really strict about putting phones away. During class time, however, when I am teaching or when students are working individually, I choose not to destroy my serenity, interrupt everyone else, and create classroom scenes any more than I already do by feeling like little more than a patrol officer babysitting 97 cell phones every day. Choosing to wage a constant cell phone battle wastes massive amounts of class time. Cell phone Whack-a-Mole is emotionally exhausting. The cell phone battle keeps me disengaged from the class and the material. Moreover, daily asking for individual students' phones has resulted in accusations of my "singling kids out," my being "unfair," etc. And it is the struggling students especially who seem to be emotionally tethered to cell phones. It is the struggling students unfortunately who pull off task and disengage, with the phone as emotional anodyne. The very students who need to practice unbroken focus are the same ones who most frequently imbibe the disease as the cure, leaving reading comprehension in the wake of another covert, under-the-desk, ten-second nip at the glass flask. Managing to wrest students' cell phones out of their possession/onto my desk for even a few class periods has proven to be a Pyrrhic victory at best.

I have a few times asked Julie individually to put her phone away, whereupon it may go away, or she then may use it behind her textbook. We are reading *Romeo and Juliet* at this time, and I have seen her on her phone a couple of times while other students are reading aloud. She had it on top of the textbook, obscuring the print on one of the pages. At the end of the day, if parents are going to reach the family decision to buy $1000 devices and allow the child to have a data plan that is accessible during school hours, then ultimately the student must take the responsibility to stop playing on it in class. Or when the phones become a damper on grades, the parents need to yank it or turn the thing off. I put comments regarding inappropriate cell phone use in the Skyward gradebook precisely so that the parents may see that phone use may have been a contributing factor to an incomplete assignment, lack of understanding, or poor test. I suppose this may make me sound lazy or uncaring; I can assure you I am neither. I am willing to be the bad guy when it is called for. But cell phones in class are simply no longer a hill I'm willing to die on.

VOCABULARY QUIZZES   I hand out a vocab lesson nearly every Monday. There is a quiz nearly every Friday. The lessons themselves are very thorough, and they contain a variety of activities that teach the words. We complete approximately 80% of the lessons every week together in class. I may assign one or two short activities a week to complete as homework. During class when we work on vocab, I often give students time to think over a section and try it on their own, and then I will check it with them. The theory is that we work a little bit on all the words every day, all week, mostly together. I have never, ever just given students a list of words for the week and said, "Here ya go! Learn these! Quiz Friday! Good luck!" If Julie just views that five or ten minutes I give them as time to sit and wait for the answers instead of trying, then she has given up an opportunity to study. Sometimes I see her looking through the lesson and filling some words in. Other times, she may just sit. As far as studying outside of class, here is the website: www.vocabularyworkshop.com. Simply navigate to the page with the book covers, and click on the picture of her book. The 9th graders are in the Level D book. I have had the website written up on my front whiteboard—along with what vocab level corresponds with what grade level—since August. The website is also printed on the vocab lesson every week, appearing at least twice on different pages. There is also a QR code on every single lesson that the student can scan, and it takes the student directly to this website. In fact, the second week of school I pulled the vocabulary workshop site up on my whiteboard during class to show everyone all the puzzles and games the site offers to help students learn the words. There is even an iWords activity that speaks aloud, pronounces the word over and over, and gives definitions and sample sentences that differ slightly from what is in the lesson to give a broader context. Using this website a little every night and completing a different game can help Julie learn the words. But the students have to be active and self-disciplined in using the site. Just staring at the printed lesson, or hurriedly completing the vocab homework and inadvertently filling in a bunch of incorrect answers at the last second will not help. Vocab quizzes are doable, but they take work.

Now I wish to address items in your email I found ambiguous or all-too encompassing. I apologize that this is getting long, but unfortunately I can only speculate due to lack of details. And I will only talk about English I given that English I is Julie's class.

I AM "ALL OVER THE PLACE"   I don't know what this means. Here is a brief format of how my class operates. I usually start off class with the DOL (Daily Oral Language), which is a proofreading activity of two sentences per day. Like vocab, I give students a couple minutes to look for the corrections. Then I literally give them the answers. Then I will reread the sentence. Giving them the answers again. This is the easiest way to earn points in my class. There is never a reason to miss anything on the DOL unless the student chooses not to try and—again—sit and wait for the answers and scrawl the sentences out at the last second. We then will shift gears and spend a few minutes on vocab on a typical day. We do DOL and vocab almost every day of every week. Then we may spend the remainder of the class on the reading or some classwork. Julie's class has written one essay. Is this what is meant by "all over the place?" Doing a few different activities every day?

Maybe the complaint of "all over the place" is because I differentiate and operate my class using two different levels of vocabulary. There are a few students in my Eng I who have volunteered to work on some harder vocabulary lessons. I do not leave them to their own devices, and I check their lessons during Julie's class too. It is not confusing if students are mentally participating in class. I always announce which vocab level I am checking, and sometimes I have the students choose which vocab group goes first. Is this what "all over the place" means?

Maybe "all over the place" refers to the fact there are many facets to English. I am responsible for teaching literature, writing, grammar, vocabulary, spelling . . . that's a lot! I try to touch on a little of everything. Many of our freshmen students will be electing to take the PSAT early their sophomore year, perhaps including Julie. The PSAT is heavy in reading and complex sentence structure. This test is about seven short months away, and I feel partially responsible for relaying some of the PSAT topics to my freshmen. Maybe mini-lessons in sentence structure on the DOL feel random. Is this the genesis of "you are all over the place"?

"NOTHING IS EVER THE SAME"   I am struggling with what this means as well. To my previous point, my weekly class pattern for the most part . . . is the same. Vocab and DOL have procedures that rarely change. The little grammar rules we discuss in the DOL every week are rather repetitive in hopes that the rules will stick with the kids over the course of a year. I do throw in a new grammar rule or concept every now and then, absolutely. But we work out the DOL sentences together. I don't give tests and quizzes that are a mystery or have nothing to do with the course content. Regarding the literature, nope, the textbooks this year are not the same. They are new and a bit more challenging. The questions over the literature require students to dig a little deeper and find text evidence. Students have to reread. They are not used to this and probably balk at having to go back into the literature. Is this what is meant by "nothing is ever the same"? I want my procedures to be basically consistent or "the same," and they are. Conversely, I would never want the reading level or content to remain "the same." I want students to be challenged and move up. What is it exactly that students want to be "the same"? Do they want easy work that they already know and a class that does not require them to think, read harder literature, expand themselves, and try? I won't do that. Yep, that's a hill I'm willing to die on.

"THEY ARE ALL CONFUSED" "ALL THE TIME"   All of my students? All the time? All hour from beginning to end? All semester? Certainly if everyone were confused all the time, I would have had a roster bursting at the seams with F's for semester one. This was not the case. In fact, not a single one of my 97 English students failed semester one. Zero F's. There were many A's and B's. And that was with no extra credit. If "all were confused" "all the time," why did almost no English I students take the initiative to come in during Advisory to ask questions? I am at school around 6:45 every morning. Why have these droves of "confused all the time" students not been there? Further, anyone who has ever even popped into my classroom knows that every day I write the complete agenda for the day on my white boards. I write the day's class agenda in blue as well as any homework or upcoming tests in red. I have done this every school day for seventeen years. All any confused student would have to do is write down in their (free) agenda book (that the school provided) any homework that is due soon. It is all in plain sight what every class is working on. Every day. If Julie lost her agenda or chooses not to make use of it, she (or anyone) can simply take a picture with her phone before class or on her way out after the bell if she needs a reminder of what is coming up. This would be appropriate and helpful use of her phone since she is allowed the privilege of having one.

"A LOT OF YOUR STUDENTS" and "PARENTS WOULD AGREE"   Please do not name any specific names beyond Julie's. But I would ask you to consider students with whom you are speaking. Momentarily aggrieved students love to build a case against a teacher, and they love to do this when they think they may have the ear of a parent.   Likewise, I do not want you to divulge names of which "parents would agree." If a parent has an issue or questions he or she would like to discuss with me, those parents can contact me directly if their grievances are as strong as yours, and I will respond in kind as I am doing now. I am still unclear on specifics of these complaints about my class except vocabulary. Yes, my class is kind of hard in some regards, but it is conquerable. No, the students cannot goof off, and they have to complete all the work if they want to do well without relying on extra credit to save them at the eleventh hour. It is human nature that teenagers want to gripe when a class is hard. They love to commiserate about a teacher when a class is challenging. I overhear students sit in my classes every now and then ripping other teachers because something didn't go their way. For example, I have overheard an Advisory student or two sit and trash a teacher, and when I politely ask the student if he or she wishes to go ask the teacher in question about the misunderstanding or poor score, the answer is usually no; they would rather retreat into their cell phone or continue complaining to their captive peer audience. I can only surmise that this propensity to group-complain is the case until these individual parents of "a lot of my students" contact me directly and broach specifics.

"NEEDS THINGS TAUGHT A DIFFERENT WAY"   In my class, I explain directly or read aloud a lot of content. I will sometimes let students read aloud (as we are doing with *Romeo and Juliet*). Sometimes students can read with a partner to each other. Students have the option of completing written work with partners sometimes as well—or alone. We take notes every now and then. I create outlines and give students a lot of past student examples when we write essays. I give students proofreading checklists for essays. We did a mythology project. We play BINGO or Jeopardy once in a great while to review for a test. We have watched movies over harder literature such as Homer's *Odyssey*. I have given all freshmen students their individual passwords to their Collections textbooks online, where they can access the book online, play the read-aloud audio, and look at tutorials. This site is my.hrw.com. I have brought brownies as a vocab-quiz reward at least once a month for two years. I reward a lot with candy, stickers. If you have any other specific ideas for me to implement in the classroom, or ideas for extrinsic motivation, pray tell. But whatever the method or motivation may be, the students have to avail themselves of it.

"HELP ME HELP YOU"   Julie can go to the my.hrw.com website from home and reread parts of *Romeo and Juliet* and play the screencasts that explain passages. Plus the vocabularyworkshop.com site. She can have you quiz her over the vocab words for fifteen minutes or so every evening. You can have her give you a one or two-minute summary of what we read in *Romeo and Juliet* that day. There are many ways she can learn the material in and out of class. I hope these suggestions help. Feel free to come to my class with Julie. Shadow her for a full day at school in all her classes. Do the work right beside her. My door is open. Let me know if you want to do this, and I will have extra copies for you.

"SOMETHING NEEDS TO CHANGE" One day last semester, I had reminded Julie not to forget to come in my room and take care of a missing assignment or something of that nature. I saw her later that day outside my room while I was standing in the hall. My classroom is in the junior hallway, and she was standing about four feet away from me next to a junior boy. I again reminded her to come in and take care of English business. She did not even acknowledge me. No reply, just ignored me and walked off with the boy. Julie never came in to make up whatever it was I was reminding her about. Another day last semester, the students had been allowed to choose a group with whom to complete an assignment. The next morning, one of her partners talked to me privately and was upset that Julie had promised she would take a portion of the assignment home to complete it, but Julie did not. It was an assignment over the *Odyssey*. The group's grade suffered due to Julie on that one as well. Another day last semester, she called me by my first name in class. Attention-seeking behavior. Not acceptable.

I am not trying to get her in trouble all over again for situations where she fell short before Christmas. But maybe . . . just maybe . . . the onus is primarily on Julie to change here in this situation rather than the nebulous complaints swirling about English. Some more follow through on her part would help. A little bit more effort and engagement. Fewer passive or attention-seeking behaviors. Just a thought. Gotta admit, it has seemed like you and I have cared more about her English grade than she has.

No, I do not think I am perfect. I am not Teacher of the Year. No, I am not of the opinion that things are never my fault. But I know I work damn hard for my students, top to bottom. I expect the students to step up and take initiative as well. They don't have to be perfect to get good grades for me, but exemplary grades will not just fall into anyone's lap in my classes, top to bottom.

"NOT GROW TO HATE GOING TO YOUR CLASS" A valid concern, and one I share. If Julie feels she truly cannot make any of the previous specific changes to her level of output, if Julie honestly feels as if she is giving her 100% effort in my class, if Julie knows deep down that she and I have irreconcilable personality conflicts, and if Julie's personal learning style is not being adequately served in my room, then perhaps a change of teacher would offer her a new environment? There are two other teachers who also teach English I, and they're both really great. We are all on *Romeo and Juliet* right now. I have always supported school choice, class choice, and teacher choice, whether that means a student wants in my class—or is clamoring to get out of my class. I believe in teacher preference, and I have told our counselors as much. I like Julie, and I am not trying to get rid of her. She has a fun personality when she chooses to participate in class. But it will not hurt my feelings if you and she sincerely feel that a different English environment is the best course. Just a suggestion. Take it or leave it as you see fit. I'd like her to stay.

To sum up, if you would like to let me know specific complaints Julie has about English I, respond and I will definitely reply. Most of what I have written here pertains to all of my classes, not just Eng I. Nothing in this email is a secret. Apologies again for the length; just wanted to cover all the bases. Indeed, the depth and breadth of your concerns bore fruits of self-reflection that cut a wide swath.

Oh, and I gave Julie the vocab lesson 12 early. Lesson 12 is for next week. I usually have these lessons ready to go a week early, so that students can have them a few days earlier if they so desire. As a result, and to end with some good news, Julie has had a couple extra days to study Lesson 12 for Friday's quiz.

Thank you for reading, and have a great rest of your Sunday.

Sincerely,

Amie Adamson

On the following Friday's vocabulary quiz, Julie earned a 100%. And the minute I began class, she put her phone upside down on top of her desk, where it remained until I allowed students to pack up for the day. The mother never emailed me again.

Tuesday, June 12, 2018

Destination: Belton, MO
Today's Miles: 10.10
Start Location: Greenwood, MO
Trip Miles: 2121.71

Gyla returned me this morning to my pick-up point in Greenwood. Picked up a gallon of water, a Clif bar, and set off. I had again Google mapped a direct route toward Olathe, and I ended up being happy with my selected route. I walked on mowed grass the majority of the day, sweeping lawns of residential areas and mowed shoulders primarily. I had to endure some sidewalk coming into Belton-*ouch!* But really another fairly quiet, uneventful 10 miles. It was overcast and in the 80s. In fact, I had grabbed a gallon of water from the Casey's cooler, and when I set the cold, flat-bottomed gallon behind my head on my pack frame after swigging as much as I could, I was a bit chilly with it pressed against my neck.

Indeed I have been off the ADT data book and have been forging my own route the past couple weeks, possibly with the exception of the Rock Island spur. I thought I had read somewhere that the ADT was looking into running concurrent with the RI, but I don't know if the Missouri state route has officially changed or if that was ever really the plan. Maybe someone can correct me. Perhaps my mind manufactured this rumor during hours of running or walking.

I am off the official course in another sense too. I am also falling off the approved route of life for just a bit. Life's data book calls for industry and work and the hamster wheel of productivity and saving, and maybe-just maybe-one day when we retire we can disembark from the assigned route of life and take some time to do all the things we want.

I am off the official course of life for just a little while because it is nice to reconnect. Literally speaking, of course, it's desirable on my part to re-connect my hiking route's single, unbroken pencil line across these United States in the most direct and safe way I can. Figuratively, it is also nice to connect with relatives we rarely see because the official route of life consumes us, consumes our time and emotional wellspring. It is good to step off the data book route and just be. Just walk. Just ride. Just read. Just think. Just chat. Just look. Just listen. I would be remiss in not thanking Gyla and John for the entirety of this list.

Tomorrow my renegade route crosses back into Kansas for more connecting. In both senses.

Amie

Wednesday, June 13, 2018

Destination: Olathe, KS
Today's Miles: 20.90
Start Location: Belton, MO
Trip Miles: 2142.61

Got started around 6:15 this morning as the humidity, according to my weather app, was 100%. The sky remained fairly overcast, however, and there was a little breeze, so along with a gallon of lemon-lime Gatorade and mowed grass for a walking surface all day, conditions were .

I veered north a bit coming out of Belton, then west along Blue Ridge Blvd to cross the Kansas state line. Not knowing the nature of the areas through which I would pass, I messaged my cousins in Lenexa that if my planned route was going to walk me through the Hood, pray tell, and I would pick another way. Aside from a couple blocks of vape shops and Boost mobile storefronts clustered together, my route ended up being quite the opposite. Grand homes, trendy eateries and strip malls. In fact, I sat down for an hour just before noon in Gezer Park in Leawood. The picnic table cover was an expansive pergola. There were several fountains and a pond in the park, and what appeared to be a 5 or 6 row vineyard right there in the park also. I fully expected to be reported for vagrancy in such a genteel park. I finished off my gallon of Gatorade with my pinky out and proceeded on.

I dropped down a block and chose to walk my way into Olathe on 135th. I passed REI. I did not go in, for I could not think of a single thing I needed.

Walked by St. Thomas Aquinas High School. Realized I was crossing ground zero for private schools-the only schools-that beat us in high school cross country. Bishop Miege High School was probably skulking around a nearby corner as well. I gave Aquinas and Miege some major side eye and proceeded down 135th.

Around 5 miles from my cousins' house in Lenexa, I made contact with my aunt Donna and cousin Dillon. They came strolling down a residential block carrying water and cookies. They walked the rest of the way with me north right up to Jessica and Dillon's front door. Thank you, thank you, thank you to Jess, Dillon, and Donna for a wonderful dinner and evening.

Missouri . . . done!

Third time's a charm.

Amie

The Interim Report
Thursday, June 21, 2018

Destination:
Today's Miles: 0
Start Location:
Trip Miles: 2142.61

Have taken a few days off back home for personal business, but a couple things have happened that merit reporting because these events are part of my prep work and overall saga.

First, the interim report must include the drop point for the mothership, the location of which I will now reveal because my car is no longer there. Given that I mostly shuttle myself around to trail pick-up locations, I again needed somewhere to leave my car while I hiked the 140-mile point-to-point section. I had chosen the New Franklin, MO, Katy Trailhead this time as my car stash spot. Furthermore, a week prior to leaving, I had also called the number on the Katy brochure and map for making official arrangements with Missouri Parks for long-term parking at the trailheads. Several days' parking is fairly common, as people may park at one end of the state, bike the Katy, and then shuttle back to their vehicles. The Parks lady with whom I spoke had taken my information, including how long my car would be sitting there, added a couple extra days for good measure, and assured me that all appropriate law-enforcement would be notified.

Beleaguered is probably too strong a word, but apparently within a week after I resumed walking, the New Franklin Police were assailed with reports of a vehicle at the trailhead that hadn't moved in several days. The police ran my tag and made contact with the Derby, KS, police, whereupon I was informed that my car was reported for possible abandonment. I called the New Franklin police, and the chief seemed to know who I was before I could get my entire first and last names out. The police chief was very nice, we unraveled the situation, I apologized for the drama, and then shook my fist at MO Parks for not "contacting all appropriate law enforcement."

In the aftermath, my cousin Gyla and I
a) Decided my car is the most frequently non-abandoned vehicle across America,
b) Hoped that the mysterious white car did not cause a huge to-do in New Franklin, and
c) Speculated on various sensational and paradoxical New Franklin

newspaper headlines including "Non-Missing Kansas Woman Found!" or "Abandoned Kansas Vehicle Now Allegedly Stolen!"

On a serious note, I do appreciate the NF citizens' concerns, the NF police phone call, and their patrol of the Katy. I don't want to make complete light of the situation. But all in all, the grand takeaway is that I should have left another car note, similar to the one I left on my front dashboard back in Chester Hill, Ohio.

Second item on the interim report is that I am currently spending a few days doing route recon and caching water out ahead of myself, primarily in western Kansas. Today I cached a few gallons in locations from Chase to Kinsley. The way I figure it, spending a few days taking route notes, campground amenity notes, and stashing water will save me steps, peace of mind, and phone battery life later. And not to be a purveyor of the obvious, but I can go faster carrying less water. In the end, it's a wash. Or in southern KS, a worsh.

I will devote a couple more days to this task and then pick up walking from Chase in about a week. I will update when I actually have miles to report. All is well, and to invoke the movie *Office Space*, if it could, like, stay 82 degrees through western KS as it is right now for the remainder of the summer, that'd be grrrrrreeeeeaaaat.

Amie

Friday, June 29, 2018

Destination: Ellinwood, KS
Today's Miles: 9.90
Start Location: West of Chase, KS
Trip Miles: 2152.51

I can always tell how far off the grid I am by the size of my keychain. Typically for ten months out of the year, I have a car key, house key, classroom keys, work badge, safe key, storage lock key, and a lanyard. During the summers I may put away my badge and classroom keys, but my keychain would retain some of its real-life heft. As of yesterday, when I turned in my apartment key, my keychain got a little smaller so that I can walk a bit more.

Thank you, Mom, for dropping me off at my 2016 stopping place, somewhere west of Chase, KS. I had planned for a short day so that I could reach Ellinwood tonight. Thus is the launch point for my strategic rendezvous with the ADT's western KS towns and my water drops out here. I want to hit them kind of just right.

I paralleled HWY 56 along L Road all the way into Ellinwood. I think it was 98 this afternoon, but the wind was pretty strong, so it was all right. It took me 3 or 4 miles to find my rhythm after 2 weeks off. Step, step, step, click-click. Around the time I got my walking mojo back, I encountered one of the center-pivot irrigation structures that was actually on, and the wind was blowing its water nearly out to the dirt road. I walked a little closer and let my clothes and head get misted. Who knew the perfect prairie mister would grace this section of the ADT?

The data book shows for Ellinwood's services that there is camping in the park. When I arrived into town, google maps showed 3 different parks, one with RV hookups. I walked over to it, and on the way saw the Ellinwood police station. I popped in and introduced myself and my hiking project. I asked for a safe and legal place to camp, and indeed the RV park was just fine. No ID or fee was requested. I must have sounded halfway legit.

Which reminds me, I have been mentally editing and revising my introductory overture for those few times when I am introducing myself to city officials or requesting camping. I think it might go something like this: "Hi, my name is Amie, and I'm from Kansas. I'm not homeless or anything. I'm working on a coast-to-coast hiking project in increments" OR "I am hiking across (insert state here if party seems skeptical) and I am needing a safe and legal place to camp tonight. I will be gone by daybreak, I don't start fires, and I don't smoke *anything*."

The not smoking anything part is not my trying to win the morality decathlon, but I figure the closer I get to the Colorado border, I oughta throw in that last part. I may tweak it and adjust my rhetoric according to my audience.

Amie

Saturday, June 30, 2018

Destination: Cheyenne Bottoms Wildlife Area, KS
Today's Miles: 13.30
Start Location: Ellinwood, KS
Trip Miles: 2165.81

The ideal morning pack-up consists of a perfectly dry tent, including no inside condensation. Check. All the water I need for kaffe, brushing teeth, and hydrating early. Check. Power for charging phone whilst packing. Check. A port-o-john as the *pièce de resistánce* of a dignified morning routine. Check!

Headed up 100th going north out of Ellinwood. I soon reached my first water cache. It was just as I left it, buried pretty deep in the grasses around a telephone pole. I used my trekking pole to extract it from hiding.

The book does not go straight west into Great Bend, but rather veers north to feature Kansas's Cheyenne Bottoms Wildlife Area. I entered the wildlife area, which heads north toward the lake. Took a break at the shaded info station and contemplated my next move. The TBT's say that the official route goes all the way around the lake, but they also say you may take a shortcut to the left, which is 60th road. I took the shortcut. Besides, I had already driven around the lake on Water Cache Tour 2018, so I did not feel the need to walk the 6 extra miles only to net 2 westward miles.

The lake was to my right for a bit, and I felt like Chevy Chase in the movie *Vacation* as he bobbed his head a couple times at the Grand Canyon, then jetted out of there. I bobbed my head at the lake a few times and kept walking.

The route then follows another stretch of wetland canal for several miles, then continues adjacent to farmland along 60th. Hidden behind some trees along the dirt road is the Cheyenne Bottoms campground. This is where I retrieved water cache two, also undisturbed. Chance for overnight storms may not leave me undisturbed. But as long as no other campers show up and no flies stealth into my tent, my chances of going undisturbed increase exponentially.

Amie

Sunday, July 01, 2018

Destination: Great Bend, KS
Today's Miles: 9.10
Start Location: Cheyenne Bottoms Wildlife Area, KS
Trip Miles: 2174.91

I went undisturbed until midnight, when a storm passed through. At which point I was disturbed for about an hour. The tell-tale increase in the wind pulled me to the surface from a really hard sleep. A few things occur when the wind picks up like that and I know it's a harbinger of something wicked this way coming. First, I turn my phone back on and check for warnings and watches, not that I could really do much about tennis-ball sized hail bearing down upon me. But like Odysseus facing the terrible straits of Scylla and Charybdis, at least I know what's coming.

The next thing I do if the wind is strong is sit up and place my back against the side of the tent that bears the brunt of the wind. At the same time, I begin organizing my belongings into two piles. One pile is items that must remain dry, will go with me in case I need to bail, or that get a waterproof stuff sack. These items include my phone, jacket, shoes, my tiny wallet, poncho, and sleeping bag. These items I gather and begin stuffing in my backpack.

The other pile isn't really a pile, but things I categorize as "Just Let 'er Go" in case of tent failure: sleep pad, stove, cookpot, dirty clothes. Last night, however, the wind blew for just a few minutes, and it rained a little. Soon the wind died and it just sprinkled some. I relaxed, got my sleeping bag back out, and fell asleep listening to sprinkles. Sprinkles are pretty relaxing. Here is a shameless plug for Black Diamond: I gotta hand it to this tent; in over a thousand miles with me, it has proven that it can weather some weather.

It's always funny the songs we get stuck in our heads sometimes. I distinctly remember back in Maryland on the Towpath getting Toby Keith's famous song line, "I Ain't As Good As I Once Was, but I'm As Good Once As I Ever Was" revolving nonstop in my brain for two days. Last night when I was awake for about an hour, I was hearing "Shoot Me Straight" lyrics by the Brothers Osborne incessantly. I was listening to the wind and singing in my mind about lettin' a hard rain "burn the whole way down." And "layin' my six-foot, four-inch ass out on the ground." The storm was pouring it on like a shot o' whiskey, and the wind was shooting my tent straight. I know my tent is not 6 foot 4 inches long, but I don't want its ass laid out on the ground either.

Slept really hard until about 6:30. I indulged myself at first in a slow pack-up partly because it was so cool this morning that I snuggled deep in my bag extra long. And partly because I really just wanted to make Great Bend today, which wasn't far at all. While I was snuggling, I heard an owl very near me hooting loudly. It sounded so cool but also somewhat ominous.

I read once that according to Indian lore, (white?) owls signify death. I didn't peek out to try to find the owl and discern its color. But to heed any possible portents tossed in my direction, I figured I had better get moving. I drank about half my unopened gallon of water, let my almost-dry tent billow in the wind like a kite or like the parachute game in elementary school PE class, packed up, and hustled my 5' 4" ass into Great Bend.

Town night on the westernmost end of town, shower, groceries, laundry. Planning for a longer day tomorrow. Checking maps and water drop mileage so it won't burn the whole way down heading toward Pawnee Rock, and I can shoot it straight.

Amie

Monday, July 02, 2018

Destination: Larned, KS
Today's Miles: 19.40
Start Location: Great Bend, KS
Trip Miles: 2194.31

Making one's way out of Great Bend is like walking giant, one-dimen-
sional stair steps down gravel roads along HWY 56, which cut southwest
today. One mile west, one mile south, two miles west, another mile south. I
could always hear the hiss of HWY 56 traffic and see it to my left or in front
of me this morning as I cut right, left, repeat. Sometimes close up, sometimes from about a mile away. Seven miles went by in this zig-zag fashion
very quickly. I hit my next water drop at the corner of 100th and 40th. On
my directions I had written, "Water at base of shorter pole." Three for three
on water drops, undisturbed. Thank you, past self.
   Felt really strong today. I did not take any breaks until mile 15. This
would have been about stair-step 12, at the Pawnee Rock Landmark along
the Santa Fe Trail. There is a circle drive, a picnic area, and shade. It is up on
a hill and overlooks the plains, the tiny town of Pawnee Rock, and miles of
farmland. It really is a neat place just to take a breather and amidst the open
space all around and contemplate that you're nearly at the geographical
center of the country. And from its vista, one can acknowledge that even in
our tech-centered world, always building, always upgrading, always subdu-
ing and developing the open space, that there are still a few portions of land
that, since the days of the Pawnee, haven't much changed.
   I drank down more of gallon two for the day and thought on my options
for the afternoon. I had spied out a camping option in Pawnee Rock, but I
was not ready to quit walking yet. Larned was still 11 miles away via the
book route, 8 if I wanted to walk on 56. I think that only major arterial
bleeding would prompt me to walk on 56.
   Additionally, sleep options near Larned included two motels of questionable existence and quality as well as Camp Pawnee, which was even further
west and south of Larned. I did not want a motel again. I preferred to camp.
Town was the closest sleep option making for a full marathon on the day's
mileage. Wasn't sure if I had completely forgotten Dallas yet, and the campground would be even further. So I handed it over to the universe and just
kept trekking on the backroads toward Larned.
   The day remained cooler again, overcast mostly, and there was the ever-

present Kansas wind to keep me comfortable. I carried about a fourth of the gallon resting on my pack frame with really no compulsion to drink it. I knew I had water drop four heading south down into Larned, and puzzled over the irony of again having possibly too much water on my hands in central KS in July.

My water supply versus demand ironies remind me of that fine line between preparing and over preparing. Between being prudent and beating it to death. Between not being a dingbat about stark western landscapes and just letting the universe take care of me. This fine line is one I have butted up against both times when out caching. I have ensured there is a water source about every 10 miles, be it cache, roadside park or camp facility, the trail passing through a town, or Cleetus's Gas and Grill where the blacktops meet. But after so many miles of prep work and driving 6 mph down dirt roads looking for places to hide a gallon of water, I say, "That's enough. I am now flogging it to death. If I even make it this far, the universe will come through on water."

Today the universe took over in the form of the Schmitzes, a sweet elderly couple who pulled over around mile 19 and asked if I wanted a ride. I folded and let them drive me the off-trail miles down to Camp Pawnee. I introduced myself and they said, "We're Schmitz. Yeah it sounds funny-we're that too!" They were so sweet, finishing each other's sentences regarding directions, which street will get me back north out of the camp area, who used to live where around Larned, what friends have died around here and whom they can't keep track of, hushing their small dog in the backseat with me, and their Lottery numbers, which they have been playing for years. The Lottery was actually the sole reason they were driving into Larned. Picking me up was just a side hustle and a few minutes' conversation with the strange girl from another part of Kansas. They dropped me at the camp, I wished them luck on the Lottery, and I enjoyed a really nice evening with a warm southerly breeze and lots of shade.

Thank you, universe. I never made it far enough south on 110th to need water drop four on the day. It is officially tithed to the firmament. So if you happen to be out dirt-road cruising 110th just north of Larned and need a sarsaparilla, there is a gallon of water at the base of a large roadside yellow rain gauge.

Amie

Tuesday, July 03, 2018

Destination: Larned, KS
Today's Miles: 6.30
Start Location: Larned, KS
Trip Miles: 2200.61

Walked back up to Larned this morning to complete the remaining mileage into town. Larned, of course, is home to the state's mental health correctional facility. No one questioned my activities, so perhaps I fit right in.
My friends are kidnapping me for the fourth of July extended weekend!

Amie

◆ ◆ ◆

And that was the end of my hiking project. I have received a few messages from Trail Journal followers as to why I stopped, why I never gave closure on my blog or even reported what I was doing next, why I just let it go dark and marked my hiker status as inactive.

Although I have never gone back and given a retrospective on any of my blog entries, I will do so for the day I hiked through Cheyenne Bottoms. It will partially explain why I stopped hiking.

Thru hiking requires one to be free from emotional entanglements back home. It is nearly impossible to devote the energy to making daily mileage with energy left over to nurture a relationship with someone who is not hiking with you. It just doesn't work. Man cannot serve two masters. I could not give Chad, my significant other, much of my attention at any time of day. I had tried the months leading up to my resuming my walk to explain some realities of thru-hiking. I tried to explain that radio silence on my part had nothing to do with not loving people back home. Backpacking is all-consuming in a wonderful way, but in a way that requires all of one's energy systems consumed in exertion and self-preservation. At the end of my hiking days the summer of 2018, I found myself explaining and re-explaining my whereabouts, my encounters that day, and when I would be coming home. The closer I got to Colorado, the more dejected Chad became, and the more selfish I felt.

I could hear the hurt in his voice and fear of losing me. Hurt gave way to anger the day I hiked the Cheyenne Bottoms. A series of text messages between Chad and me revealed a hurt in his heart that I had never detected before. I cried that evening after I set up camp. I had never cried before while hiking. This was the blubbering, wiping tears and snot from my chin, keening type of crying from my depths. I could not justify continuing my hike. I began feeling like a colossal jerk in risking my relationship with a good, kind, caring, strong man. I just refused to continue and put my adventure above my relationship.

Moreover, I had seen something my mother posted on Facebook about my hike. She had replied to someone's comment on my trail journal entry that she shared on her Facebook page. Mom replied to the effect that she just prayed and handed me over to the Lord every day, and that was all she could do. Seeing this comment made me feel even worse.

When I had begun planning my hike and talking about it with my parents, it was 2012 into 2013. Mom and Dad had seemed a little less vulnerable then. They seemed sturdier, in a way, and had become inured to my backpacking plans. Acceptance had even given way to a little excitement after I had explained the nature of the American Discovery Trail and the fact that I would not be out in the woods completely away from civilization, brush cutting with a machete and killing my own food to eat. But in 2018, something within me could not worry my parents anymore. My hike began to pivot from a fun adventure into something I was doing that was bordering on cruel to those who loved me the most.

Precisely how to walk the West also became a barrier. The logistics of continuing west on foot past central Kansas also must change for any hiker. I had cached water into western Kansas. However, studying the route and other hikers' journals--plus using common sense--made it clear that past the Rockies, I would not be able to continue with just my backpack. I would need to get a cart to carry increased volumes of food and water. Or I would need a car-support person to drop water gallons in those desolate areas of Colorado on west. Let me explain why, in 2018, I eschewed both the cart and car support options.

Most hikers who cross the West and finish the ADT push a cart hundreds of miles. A sturdy cart of some sort would curtail my freedom as a solo, female walker. In particular, pushing a wheeled vehicle would inhibit my freedom to hide myself and to walk on unpaved paths should I desire. It was important for me to be able to stealth camp, to traverse softer surfaces when available to save my feet and legs, or to hide quickly for whatever reason. I feared a cart would be a hindrance to those objectives.

In 2016, I had a couple of offers to provide car support. Both car support offers came from individuals about whom a stench of irresponisiblity hovered. In order for me to have a support person, I would have felt obligated to offer my own car for use. And my support would have free use of my vehicle for strings of days. I was still driving the same 2002 Infiniti, which had turned over 200,000 miles by that point. I needed it to last, and I did not trust anyone to be careful with it. Additionally, I of course would pay for my car support person's gas, food, lodging, and other needs since he or she happened to be out there because of me. That would mean more expenses.

And what exactly would they be doing all day *in* and *with* my car while I was walking? Would they respond to my calls for help in a timely manner? It may be snobbish to think, but the reasons most potential car support drivers were not working for six months were likely much different from the reason I was able to go six months without working. I envisioned both car support candidates spiraling into a huge headache and a liability for me on several fronts. I need all of my mental energy when hiking 20-mile days. I can't worry about things beyond my body's needs for the next 24 to 48 hours. Babysitting a car support individual wasn't worth it.

In June of 2015, after my first walking stint, Mom and Dad had talked with some excitement about helping me cross the desert at some point by their serving as my car support. We discussed their taking an extended vacation through the western states. They could put out water and supplies for me, go visit a place for a few days, come back and pick me up. Resupply me, go visit another great place in our amazing American West. But Dad was not retired yet in 2015. It was not something they could do at the time. Even in 2018, they had other obligations and household projects they wanted to complete. Both parents experiences a few health issues later into my hiking project as well. Living out of a car, motels, or a fifth wheel for several weeks was not feasible for them.

Another obstacle that I and my ADT contemporaries must contend with is that the directions are aging. The names of some roads in several states have changed over the years. Some roads have been rebuilt and rerouted. Speed limits and traffic volume have changed. This is not the fault of the ADT Society or the state coordinators. The 6800 miles of directions and trail data are an incredibly laudable feat! But staying on top of the hundreds of miles of turn by turns in each state is a volunteer yeoman's effort. I stopped several times on my own journey to discern whether I was turning down the correct road due to the roads' names or numbers no longer matching those in the directions. The very reason I chose to use the paper directions was to avoid the need for cell service and phone or GPS battery life. I found myself wasting valuable daylight and cell battery figuring out several updated road names and where to go. And this was in the eastern part of the country where services and water are closer together.

The prospect of taking a wrong road in the sparse west, getting stalled out, backtracking, and finding myself too far away from my next water opportunity in the Colorado mountains or the desert is a fearful possibility. Certainly one can walk Highway 50 all the way to Sacramento and ditch the intricate directions. But part of the allure of backpacking is getting away from the noise, the bustle. Road walking with traffic flying by at 80 mph is unsafe, not to mention antithetical to a meditative, restorative experience. Another aspect of the directions that had challenged me was the services listings for services that no longer existed. In many smaller towns, the listings for water availability, food, camping, or dining were woefully incorrect. Again, not the ADT's fault. It would be a herculean effort for all of the volunteer state coordinators to drive or bicycle their route every year to ensure that Cleetus's Gas and Grill out on county highway FF is still in business; or that that water fountain at a remote roadside scenic turnout still gives forth potable water. Inaccurate service listings were a mere annoyance in the east. But in the sparse west, the danger quotient multiplies if the hiker has not curated a formidable back-up plan for water. After 2200 miles, my complete trust in the ADT turn-by-turns was waning enough to concern me.

So I have the Great American West yet to conquer. Despite my concerns about the West, I still want to walk across the rest of the country. I don't know when I will be able to finish. It's a known unknown whether the factors that would facilitate my success will ever congeal to allow me to complete my walk, e.g., trustworthy car support, trustworthy directions, not alienating everyone who loves me.

On a not unrelated note, I've often said that I have three best things I have ever done. One was opting not to play volleyball sophomore year of high school and going out for cross country instead. Our wonderful high school coach, Ron Koppenhaver, was a good man and opened up to his athletes the gift of distance running. Running has given me so many opportunities: the travel, the fun and inspiring race atmospheres, and most of all running has gifted me a connection to myself. Running gives me clear and sober thoughts, answers to problems. The road unravels many knots, no matter if we're running or ambling along at 2.9 mph.

The second greatest thing I have ever done is moving to California. My time on the beautiful central coast is a gift as well. I think about it often. California opened up to me the idea of backpacking and provided verdant training grounds for me to prep for a trans-continental hike attempt.

But by far, the greatest thing I have ever done is walking out. To reject for a time what society says is normal. Walking out across eight states is a peace and mindset that I can access at any time. Walking out was an act of fortitude that has been surpassed by nothing I have done before or since. Walking out was a platform of quiet confidence from which I can launch new and unknown endeavors, knowing that, since I have done A, I can also succeed at B, given the correct focus and effort.

Walking out is something I encourage everyone, of any age or skill level, to try. And it doesn't have to be a cross-country hike that you walk out into. Walk out of that toxic or abusive relationship. Plan and execute an exit strategy from that suck-ass job that drains your soul and would replace you in a week if you dropped dead. Walk out of not caring for yourself nutritionally. Walk out into the type of life that gives you peace, the life from which you do not need a vacation.

Walk out of situations that are joy-killing. Gravitate toward new things in your life that are joy-giving. If I can, anyone can. I am nothing special. I am not gifted beyond anyone else intellectually or athletically. My message to the many wonderful people I met while walking is that if I can plan and execute an extended hike, you can too.

When life feels inside out, when the world has gone crazy and down feels like up, I can retreat inside myself and reach for the way walking out made me feel. I can access that part of me, if even just for a couple of hours on a long run. I can put on my backpack, weighted down with a gallon of water or two, shabby with its side pocket elastic stretched and useless, grab my trekking poles, and just walk for a bit. Breathe out. Find the peace of the trail even just for a few miles around home before going back to real life once again.

Buen camino!

Amie

Made in the USA
Las Vegas, NV
30 November 2021